W9-CNS-890

Language ESSENTIALS

Grammar and Writing

THE EMC MASTERPIECE SERIES • CEDAR LEVEL

Credits

Editorial

Laurie Skiba
Managing Editor

Brenda Owens
Editor

Becky Palmer
Associate Editor

Nichola Torbett
Associate Editor

Jennifer Joline Anderson
Assistant Editor

Valerie Murphy
Editorial Assistant

Lori Ann Coleman
Editorial Consultant

Lisa S. Torrey
Educational Writer

Paul Spencer
Art and Photo Researcher

Senior Editorial Consultant

Dr. Edmund J. Farrell
Emeritus Professor of English Education
University of Texas at Austin
Austin, Texas

Design and Production

Shelley Clubb
Production Manager

Jennifer Wreisner
Text and Cover Designer

Matthias Frasch
Production Specialist

Sharon O'Donnell
Proofreader

Terry Casey
Indexer

Julie Delton
Cover Artist

ISBN 0-8219-2520-2
© 2003 EMC Corporation

All rights reserved. No part of this publication may be adapted, reproduced, stored in a retrieval system, or transmitted in any form or by any means, electronic, mechanical, photocopying, recording, or otherwise without permission from the publisher.

Published by EMC/Paradigm Publishing
875 Montreal Way
St. Paul, Minnesota 55102
www.emcp.com
E-mail: educate@emcp.com

Printed in the United States of America
10 9 8 7 6 5 4 3 2 1 XXX 10 09 08 07 06 05 04 03

Language ESSENTIALS

Grammar and Writing

REDWOOD LEVEL

BIRCH LEVEL

CEDAR LEVEL

WILLOW LEVEL

OAK LEVEL

PINE LEVEL

MAPLE LEVEL

CONTENTS IN BRIEF

CONTENTS

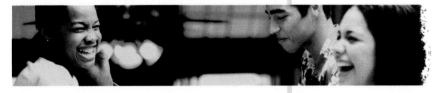

UNIT *16* CAPITALIZATION

UNIT *17* SPELLING

UNIT 18 ELECTRONIC COMMUNICATIONS: ETIQUETTE AND STYLE

PART IV WRITING

UNIT 19 WRITER'S WORKSHOP: BUILDING EFFECTIVE SENTENCES

UNIT 20 WRITER'S WORKSHOP: BUILDING EFFECTIVE PARAGRAPHS

UNIT 21 THE WRITING PROCESS

UNIT 22 MODES AND PURPOSES OF WRITING

Literature Models

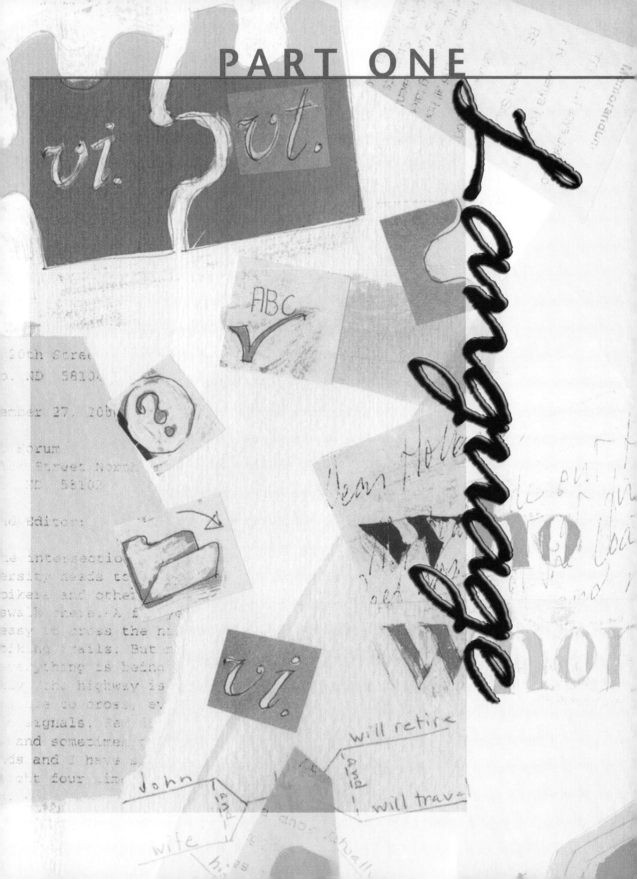

PART ONE

Language

UNIT **/** THE ENGLISH LANGUAGE

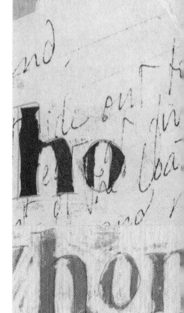

UNIT OVERVIEW

THE ENGLISH LANGUAGE

THE DEVELOPMENT OF THE ENGLISH LANGUAGE

The chances are that you know some words that are unfamiliar to people older than you. In every generation, the language changes. Over time, these changes accumulate until an entirely new language emerges. Over the centuries, the development of the English language has been divided into three stages: Old English, Middle English, and Modern English.

Old English

When the Anglo-Saxons invaded England in the fifth century, they brought with them the West Germanic dialects (spoken languages), which are known today as **Old English.** The English language, descended from Old English, is related to modern Danish, German, Norwegian, Icelandic, and Dutch. Old English was spoken in Britain from roughly AD 450 to AD 1100. Look at the following examples of Old English.

MODEL

Hwaet we Gar-Dena
Yes, we of the Gar-Danes

in gear-dagum,
in days of old,

þeod-cyninga,
The great kings'

þrym gefrunon:
renown have heard of,

Hu ða æþelingas
How those princes

ellen fremendon.
bravery displayed.

from *Beowulf*
Anonymous

A thousand years ago, that's what the English language looked like. Today, because of the changes in the language over time, it is impossible to read Old English without special training.

However, it is still possible to make out many words. Compare the following words:

MODERN ENGLISH	OLD ENGLISH
come	cuman
fiend	feond
folk	folc
heaven	heofon
holy	halig
king	cyning
love	lufu
mind	mynd
see	seon
sit	sittan
work	weorc
what	hwæt

As you see, there are many Old English words that you can still recognize. A thousand years from now, speakers of English or of a language descended from it will probably be able to recognize a few words from the language that you speak today.

Middle English

Middle English, which developed from 1100 to 1500, was strongly influenced by the Norman French language spoken by the ruling class after the Norman Conquest in Britain in 1066. As a result of the borrowings from French that began in the Medieval Period, today it is almost impossible to write an English paragraph without using many words of French origin.

EXAMPLES
French words

| assembly | council | customer | empire | error |
| government | mercy | property | receipt | restaurant |

Modern English

The version of English that we use today, known as **Modern English**, emerged in the two-hundred-year period from roughly 1400 to 1600. Of great importance to the development of the language we use today was the introduction by scholars during the early Modern period of thousands of new words from Latin and Greek.

EXAMPLES
Latin words

| corp | creed | donate | flex | form |
| move | script | sign | void | |

Greek words

adapt	arena	benefit	circus	crisis
democracy	energy	exist	genius	idea
theory				

In addition to borrowing from Latin and Greek, early Modern English borrowed heavily from other European languages, especially from French, Spanish, and Italian.

USAGE tip

Etymology is the study of the origins of words and how they evolved. When you look up a word in the dictionary the etymology of the word is given in brackets:
pasta [It (Italian), fr. (from) LL (Late Latin)].

EXAMPLES
French words

| battery | comrade | entrance | essay | mustache |
| pioneer | trophy | vogue | | |

Spanish words

| apricot | bravado | cavalier | embargo | guitar |
| tornado | | | | |

Italian words

| artichoke | balcony | bankrupt | cameo | fresco |
| pastel | piazza | porcelain | traffic | |

American English

Beginning around 1600, the English colonization of North America brought the subsequent creation of a distinct American dialect. The English language we speak today in the United States has developed and changed as we have adopted new pronunciations and spellings of words and borrowed words from the languages of other peoples of our country, such as American Indians, African Americans, Asian Americans, and immigrants from around the world, to form our own unique **American English** language.

EXAMPLES
African words

banana	cola	marimba	safari	samba
yam	zombie			

American Indian words

barbeque	canoe	hickory	raccoon	savanna
tomato				

Arabic words

admiral	alcohol	algebra	coffee	cotton
magazine	sofa	zero		

Chinese words

china	chow	soy	tea	tofu
typhoon				

East Indian words

bungalow	cashmere	cheetah	curry	jungle
khaki	pajamas	shampoo		

Japanese words

bonsai	honcho	judo	karate	origami
sayonara	tycoon			

FORMAL AND INFORMAL ENGLISH

To write or speak effectively, you must choose your language according to your audience, purpose, and the occasion or situation. **Formal English** contains carefully constructed, complete sentences; avoids contractions; follows standard English usage and grammar; uses a serious tone; and uses sophisticated vocabulary. **Informal English** contains everyday speech and popular expressions, uses contractions, and may include sentence fragments. Formal English is appropriate for school essays, oral or written reports, interviews, and debates. Informal English is appropriate for conversations with friends, personal letters or notes, and journal entries.

> EXAMPLES
> **formal English**   Mary's frustration turned to anger.
> **informal English**   Mary sure lost her cool!

Standard English is the variety of the English language taught in English-language school systems and is characterized by universally accepted and understood words, phrases, and pronunciations. Standard English enables all speakers of English to communicate and understand the spoken and written word in a common language.

Dialects

There are many different varieties of informal English, developed from the use of dialects, including slang, colloquialisms, and idioms. A **dialect** is a kind of English spoken by a particular group of people in a particular area or place. Dialects are characterized by differences in pronunciation, word choice, grammar, and accent. They are usually based on regional or social differences. In the United States, the major regional dialects are northern, southern, midland, and western. Everyone speaks with some type of dialect.

Differences in dialect show up especially in the terms people use to describe or refer to things. For example, depending in which region of the United States you live, you may say the word *soda*, *pop*, *coke*, or *tonic* when referring to a carbonated beverage.

EXAMPLES
regional dialect   Randy lives down the road a ways.
standard English   Randy lives a short distance from here.

Writers sometimes use dialects in dialoque to make their characters' voices sound realistic. In the following novel excerpt, the writer uses dialect to recreate the different voices of people living in an old fishing village on the Essex coast in southeastern England between the late 1930s and 1940.

Literature
M O D E L

Rhayader looked and marveled, and said: "Child, where did you find it?"

"In t' marsh, sir, where fowlers had been. What—what is it, sir?"

"It's a snow goose from Canada. But how in all heaven came it here?"

The name seemed to mean nothing to the little girl. Her deep violet eyes, shining out of the dirt on her thin face, were fixed with concern on the injured bird.

She said: "Can 'ee heal it, sir?"

"Yes, yes," said Rhayader. "We will try. Come, you shall help me."

from *The Snow Goose*
Paul Gallico

Slang is a form of speech made up of invented words or existing words that are given a new meaning.

EXAMPLES
"Hey, bro'!"
Man, I bombed that audition.

USAGE tip

Keep in mind that slang is inappropriate language except for the most informal forms of writing or speaking, such as a personal note or an informal discussion.

A **colloquialism** is a word or phrase used in everyday conversation. An **idiom** is a common expression that has come to have a meaning that is different than what the individual words within the expression literally mean.

> EXAMPLES
> **colloqualisms**
> What are **you guys up to?**
> **How's it goin'?**
>
> **idioms**
> Betsy always gets **butterflies in her stomach** on the first day of school.
>
> Marcus will be **green with envy** when he sees your new mountain bike.

Try It Yourself

EXERCISE 1
Identifying Formal and Informal English
Identify each of the following sentences as an example of formal or informal English.

1. The scam to fleece the consumers backfired on the telemarketing firm.
2. Did you notice that Eric seems kind of down today?
3. The new discount store is inexpensive, but the employees are unhelpful.
4. As soon as they heard the hurricane warning, people sought shelter.
5. After running in the 10K race, I was really whipped.
6. The poetry reading at the library was pretty far-out.
7. Sandra played down her championship, claiming it was no big deal.
8. Before work Ms. Bishop ate a healthy breakfast and read the newspaper.
9. Jonah lost his head during the emergency.
10. Within a year, Mason had saved enough money for a week at camp.

EXERCISE 2
Understanding Formal and Informal English
Revise the sentences in Exercise 1 that are written in informal English to formal English.

EXERCISE 3
Using Formal and Informal English in Your Writing

Imagine that you've been granted a trip in a time-travel machine. What time and place would you choose to visit? Write a description for your friends back home of what you see and hear during your time-travel trip. In your description, include quotations of dialects, idioms, and slang that illustrate how people speak, what words they use to describe specific things—such as items of clothing, food, or their activities. Be sure to translate for your peer audience what the language describes. Before beginning the exercise, conduct research on the Internet to find out more about the dialects of a specific place and time. For example, a search for "Civil War-era slang" will help you find language such as "snug as a bug," which is an idiom that means *cozy and comfortable*, and "sawbones," which is a slang term for *doctor*.

APPROPRIATE USES OF ENGLISH

Language is a powerful and complex tool. What you say, and how you choose to say it, matters. Think about the great number and variety of messages you communicate in one day to friends, family members, classmates, teachers, and many others. Language helps you to communicate the meaning of your message—whether in a chatty phone conversation with your best friend or in a persuasive editorial for your school newspaper. To communicate your messages effectively, however, you need to think about who your audience is and make choices, such as whether to use formal or informal language. You also need to consider whether other elements— such as sarcasm or slang—are appropriate and they might affect your message.

Consider the following examples. Which do you think would be appropriate to communicate to a group of friends, and which would be appropriate for an article in the school newspaper?

EXAMPLES

Ya know, Washington, DC, is the coolest place. We eyeballed everything from the Smithsonian to the National Gallery. The White House is a beaut of a building, but they're really hyper about security and can make you paranoid. I could really have hung out there, gaping at all the historical paintings and furniture. My main man, Senator Lieberman, gave us an awesome tour of the Senate chamber and office building. We weren't even close to ready to pack it in at the end of the weekend. If you didn't go on the trip, you should really eat your heart out!

Washington, DC, is a wonderful place to visit. We saw everything from the Smithsonian to the National Gallery. The White House is an amazing building, although the guards are obviously very alert to any breaches in security. I would have liked to have stayed there longer, admiring all the historical paintings and furniture. However, I didn't want to miss the tour of the Senate chamber and office building led by our very own Senator Lieberman. None of us were ready to leave at the end of the weekend. If you didn't go on the trip, you missed a memorable three days.

As the examples illustrate, the audience and your purpose for writing will shape the language you use to communicate your message. Before writing or talking about your topic, ask yourself these questions:

• What is my purpose for communicating? (to inform? to entertain? to persuade?)
• Who is my audience?
• What are the audience members' ages, backgrounds, and interests?
• What does the audience already know about the topic?
• What do they need to know about the topic?

EXERCISE 4

Understanding Appropriate Language

Consider each example of communication listed below. Then in your own words, describe for each the kind of language you would consider appropriate to the audience and purpose.

EXAMPLE

a young adult's book teaching the importance of personal hygiene
(informative; direct vocabulary; some characteristics of informal language such as contractions to make the message appealing and accessible to the audience; conversational tone with touches of humor to help readers identify with the subject)

1. an e-mail telling team members about a change in practice time
2. a letter to the editor urging people to boycott a local store
3. a thank-you note to your grandparents for a birthday gift
4. a list of school supplies you need to purchase at the mall
5. a fan letter to your favorite author
6. a eulogy at a funeral service
7. an Internet home page for your school
8. the minutes of the Student Council meeting
9. a summary of a social studies chapter for review
10. a travel brochure for a family vacation package

EXERCISE 5

Using Appropriate Language in Your Writing

Write two separate paragraphs reviewing a film you've recently seen. In the first paragraph, use language appropriate for a letter to a friend who shares your taste in movies. In the second paragraph, use language appropriate for a newspaper entertainment column and for an audience of newspaper subscribers who have a variety of tastes in films. In both cases, review the strengths and weaknesses of the film, and try to persuade your audience to see or not to see the film.

FIGURATIVE LANGUAGE

Language that suggests a meaning beyond or different from the literal meanings of the words is called **figurative language**. A **figure of speech** is meant to be understood imaginatively instead of literally. Many writers, especially poets, use figures of speech to create vivid, memorable images and to help readers see and understand things in new ways. Think about the difference in meaning in the following two examples.

> **EXAMPLES**
> **literal meaning**   A petite ballerina danced across the stage.
> **figurative meaning**   The fiery flames danced across the campfire logs.

In the first sentence, the verb *danced* conveys its literal meaning "to move rhythmically to music." In the second sentence, the verb is used figuratively to create a striking image of the flames' movement.

Three common figures of speech are **simile, metaphor,** and **personification.**

A **simile** compares one thing with another using the word *like* or *as*. What two things are being compared in each of the following similes?

> **EXAMPLES**
> The happy man whistled **like** a cardinal on a bright spring morning.
>
> His teeth are **as** yellow as old ivory piano keys.

USAGE tip

Some similes are overused and become clichés, such as "He is as sly as a fox." Avoid using clichés in your writing.

A **metaphor** compares one thing to another without using the word *like* or *as*. In a metaphor, one thing is spoken or written about as if it were another. Metaphors can be especially helpful when describing difficult or abstract ideas, such as love, joy, sorrow, truth, and so forth.

EXAMPLES
The clouds were giant marshmallows floating in the sky.
Her moods roller-coastered through life.

Personification is a figure of speech in which something not human—an animal, object, place, or idea—is given human qualities and characteristics.

EXAMPLES
The sound of the sea sang me to sleep.
Good fortune forgot to knock at our door.

Try It Yourself

EXERCISE 6
Identifying Figurative Language in Literature
Identify five figures of speech in the following excerpt as simile, metaphor, or personification. Then tell what two things are being compared in the simile or in the metaphor. Also tell what is being personified and what human characteristics or features have been given to nonhumans.

Literature
MODEL

Like horses with their swerved necks,
I concentrate on grass.
Earthworms insert themselves into the earth
like glossy, pink pins!

Against the green, a yellow shrub
furiously sprouts
in a trance of burning stars.

Branches are suns
that glimmer from within
taking life
here, under the apple tree,
where a crowd of petals close their eyes,

CONTINUED

where scraggly layers of trunk
seem to slowly come apart.

excerpt from "Under the Apple Tree"
Diana Rivera

EXERCISE 7
Identifying Figurative Language in Literature
Tell what figure of speech is used in each of the following
excerpts: simile, metaphor, or personification.

1. We sit for a long time in that sand white as a bridal gown.
   —*from "Searching for January" by W. P. Kinsella*
2. "We are jumble sailors on the rough sea of life," her
   mother would say. —*from "QWERTYUIOP" by Vivien
   Alcock*
3. Into the jaws of Death, / Into the mouth of Hell / Rode
   the six hundred. —*from "The Charge of the Light Brigade"
   by Alfred, Lord Tennyson*
4. Once I smiled in secret at the gossip of the starlings —
   from "Forgotten Language" by Shel Silverstein
5. the sky was candy —*from "the sky was" by E. E. Cummings*
6. And the snow which had fallen during the night glistened
   like a million diamonds piled together. —*from "A Secret
   for Two" by Quentin Reynolds*
7. Wrinkles formed intricate spidery webs in the skin below
   his gray eyes. —*from "Zebra" by Chaim Potok*
8. Hope lies to mortals / And most believe her —*from "I to
   My Perils" by A. E. Housman*
9. Unlike Dad's, her blood must circulate like a racing
   stream, what with all that rushing around. —*from "Be-ers
   and Doers" by Budge Wilson*
10. I have seen machines eating houses / And stairways walk
    all by themselves —*from "The City Is So Big" by Richard
    Garcia*

EXERCISE 8
Understanding Simile and Metaphor
To help you understand how to compare dissimilar objects and ideas, fill out a chart like this one. After you have brainstormed a list of characteristics, think about what else shares them and then make your comparison. The first two items are completed for you.

Person, Place, Thing, or Idea	Characteristics	Comparison
river	flowing, rise and fall of tide, spring floods, swollen riverbanks, branches out, provides water and nutrients	river = vein
helicopter	whirring sound, shimmering wings, hovers above	helicopter = dragonfly
hope		
rain		
bread		
fog		
rumor		
snake		
desert		
friend		

EXERCISE 9
Understanding Personification
Give each of the following words qualities of living things by listing a series of images and characteristics. Then utilize your ideas by personifying the word into a sentence.

EXAMPLE
stars (bright, in the sky above, twinkly, looking down on us; *The stars winked at me from the heavens.*)

1. old house
2. city

3. sunset
4. fear
5. pine tree
6. window
7. telephone
8. candle
9. money
10. book

EXERCISE 10

Using Figurative Language in Your Writing
Complete the following sentences by using similes, metaphors, and personification. You may add a word, a phrase, a clause, or another sentence.

1. Her eyes were as brown as _____.
2. Suddenly, his courage deflated like _____.
3. The willow tree's long green branches _____.
4. The classroom was as empty as a/an _____.
5. His success was a/an _____.
6. Hope _____ in her heart like a _____.
7. The early morning fog _____.
8. His voice sounds as _____ as _____.
9. Waiting in its web, the spider _____.
10. The moon is the _____ of the _____.

THE IMPORTANCE OF GRAMMAR AND SYNTAX

Grammar is something you know, even if you have never studied it. Inside the head of every person is a sophisticated part of the brain that learns, all by itself, how to assemble words and phrases grammatically. Read this sentence:

Fox the ran road quick the across.

Does it make sense to you? The sentence doesn't make any sense because it doesn't follow the rules of English grammar and syntax. You probably already know more about grammar and syntax than you think you do; otherwise you wouldn't be able to communicate and make your meaning clear. You have already learned, unconsciously, many thousands of rules governing how words can be put together and how they can't.

When you study grammar, what you are really learning is not the grammar of the language—for the most part, that's something you already know. What you are learning is terminology for describing what you know so that you can understand the patterns of the language that you use to communicate more effectively.

Grammar refers to the rules and conventions for organizing words into meaningful sentences. **Syntax** refers to the order of the words in the sentences, or *word order*. When the words in the nonsensical sentence are reorganized according to the rules of grammar and syntax, then the sentence conveys a clear meaning.

> EXAMPLE
> Red a wore shoes sister pair Jacqueline's of.
> Jacqueline's sister wore a pair of red shoes.

Different languages have different rules about word order. In the English language, most sentences follow the word order of subject-verb-object. In contrast, other languages such as German and Japanese place the verb at the end of a sentence.

> EXAMPLES
> **Brian** (subject) **practiced** (verb) his **trumpet** (object) after dinner.
> **He** (subject) **polishes** (verb) **it** (object) every week.

As you can see, grammar and syntax make the meaning of a sentence clear. Word order in a sentence can affect or change meaning, too. Consider how the different word order in the following two sentences affects meaning.

> EXAMPLES
> The dog on the beach chased the squawking seagulls.
> The squawking seagulls chased the dog on the beach.

The use of modifiers is also ruled by grammar and syntax. In the English language, adjectives usually come before the noun or pronoun they modify.

> **EXAMPLES**
> **Loud** thunder shook the **glass** windowpanes.
> The **mischievous** chimpanzee stole the **zookeeper's** lunch.

Try It Yourself

EXERCISE 11

Understanding the Importance of Grammar and Syntax
Reorganize the word order in the following sentences so that each makes sense.

> EXAMPLE
> First of on daffodils spring the day bloomed.
> *(Daffodils bloomed on the first day of spring.)*

1. Windows the stew the steamed simmering.
2. Bee a near ear Courtney's bumble buzzed.
3. January both in were a brothers born snowstorm during.
4. Crashes least week each computer at my once.
5. Serve our player team's star tennis the aced.
6. Of the maze group lost became children the in.
7. Behind door from erupted the closed laughter.
8. To dive wants how Lucy learn to scuba.
9. Everyone sudden in a class startled explosion the science.
10. Hung web old a drape like lace the spider of.

EXERCISE 12

Using Grammar and Syntax Correctly in Your Writing
Write at least three sentences using only the following words. Then discuss how different word order in each sentence affects meaning.

carefully   watched   the lion   the hunter   solitary

UNIT / REVIEW

TEST YOUR KNOWLEDGE

EXERCISE 1
Identifying Formal and Informal English
Identify each of the following sentences as an example of either formal or informal English. (10 points)

EXAMPLE
My, aren't you pretty as a picture! (informal)

1. You're not turning weird on me, are you?
2. The snide remark was inappropriate and rude.
3. Kevin gets all wound up over the littlest things.
4. My kid brother was bouncing off the walls with energy.
5. Beatrice packed her bags, pulled on her boots, and ran for the taxi.
6. Every time Dad tries a new recipe, we pretend not to like it.
7. The address you're looking for is down the road a stretch.
8. We keep in touch once in a blue moon.
9. The politician's campaign strategy dragged his opponent through the mud.
10. Grandmother Higgins frowned and shook her head in disapproval.

EXERCISE 2
Identifying Figurative Language
Tell whether each of the following sentences contains an example of simile, metaphor, or personification. (10 points)

EXAMPLE
The eye of the tornado had us in its focus. (personification)

1. Your words and actions are a mirror of your personal values.
2. Her hands are as small as buttercups.

3. The branch tapped against the window like a stranger at the door.
4. Shakespeare said, "All the world's a stage."
5. The row of school desks stood at attention like obedient soldiers.
6. The flame's long fingers tickled the logs in the grate.
7. Her inflated argument was deflated by the pinprick of truth.
8. The television gabbed nonstop through the night.
9. The immigrants packed hopes and dreams into their suitcases.
10. Life is a wheel, forever turning.

EXERCISE 3

Understanding Formal and Informal English
Revise each of the following sentences so that it is written in formal English. (20 points)

EXAMPLE
Jason is giving me bad vibes.
(Jason makes me feel uncomfortable.)

1. The television is on the fritz again.
2. Her stories about traveling down the Nile River are so bogus.
3. The global economy encourages a twenty-four/seven business world.
4. Why do you always get so hyper?
5. Please don't bad-mouth Linda; I like her.
6. Spaghetti with meatballs is okay by me.
7. There's no way you bombed the test.
8. Let's bury the hatchet and be friends.
9. You really are asking for it this time!
10. Don't flip out; just stay cool and everything will float.

EXERCISE 4
Using Figurative Language in Your Writing
Write a sentence that describes each thing by using a simile, metaphor, or personification as directed. (20 points)

EXAMPLE
river (personification; *The river slowly meandered through the small town.*)
1. window (personification)
2. snow (simile)
3. baseball game (metaphor)
4. friendship (metaphor)
5. whiskers (simile)
6. bicycle (personification)
7. perfume (personification)
8. music (metaphor)
9. old sneaker (personification)
10. laughter (simile)

EXERCISE 5
Understanding the Importance of Grammar and Syntax
Revise the word order in the following sentences so that each makes sense. (20 points)

EXAMPLE
Josh we have months known for three only.
(We have known Josh for three months only.)

1. Rhubarb fresh at market the farmer's we bought.
2. Into the canoe slowly the fishermen their river lowered.
3. The animals of an oil spill environment harms and species many.
4. Pup watched from sunrise we our tent the.
5. Summer house and we paint to this the garage need.
6. Birthday sweatshirt me my gave Paula new a for.
7. Trees tall the behind disappeared moon the pine.
8. Roar down waterfalls thunderous with a rushed the.
9. Dinner she practices night every her after clarinet.
10. Second in the point the team scored other the last winning.

EXERCISE 6

Using Appropriate Language in Your Writing

Write a personal essay to be shared with classmates about a humorous or frustrating experience you had relating to a misunderstanding. As you describe the experience, use formal language and at least two examples of figurative language. Incorporate some dialogue into your essay, in which you can use dialect, slang, idioms, contractions, and other characteristics of informal language to make people's speech sound realistic. (20 points)

PART TWO

Grammar

UNIT 2 THE SENTENCE

THE SENTENCE

THE SENTENCE: THE BASIC BUILDING BLOCK OF THE ENGLISH LANGUAGE

From the time you entered school, you probably have been speaking and writing in sentences. In the English language, the sentence is the basic unit of meaning.

A **sentence** is a group of words that expresses a complete thought. Every sentence has two basic parts: a subject and a predicate. The **subject** tells whom or what the sentence is about. The **predicate** tells information about the subject—what the subject is, what the subject does, or what happens to the subject.

EXAMPLE	
sentence	The old professor | read the dusty manuscript.
	(subject) **(predicate)**

A group of words that does not have both a subject and a predicate is called a **sentence fragment**. A sentence fragment does not express a complete thought.

EXAMPLES	
sentence fragment	The baker. (The fragment does not have a predicate. The group of words does not answer the question *What did the baker do?*)
sentence fragment	Frosted the chocolate cake. (The fragment does not have a subject. The group of words does not answer the question *Who frosted the chocolate cake?*)

CONTINUED

sentence fragment	In his kitchen. (The fragment does not have a subject or predicate. The group of words does not tell what the sentence is about or tell what the subject does.)
complete sentence	The baker frosted the chocolate cake in his kitchen.

Try It Yourself

EXERCISE 1

Identifying Sentences and Sentence Fragments
Identify each of the following groups of words as either a complete sentence or a sentence fragment. Write *S* for sentence or *F* for fragment.

1. James was a guitarist for a garage band.
2. Yelling at the children in the street.
3. Far above the snowcapped mountains.
4. The shark swam silently into the lagoon.
5. On the table in the corner of the living room.
6. His dog barked for three hours.
7. Over the fence she threw the plastic ball.
8. A politician and a lawyer.
9. Flowers add color and cheer on a winter day.
10. The aging queen and her son.

EXERCISE 2

Understanding Sentences and Their Basic Parts
Some of the following groups of words are missing a subject or predicate or both. Tell what part is missing; then revise the sentence to include the missing part. If the group of words contains both a subject and a predicate, write *sentence*.

EXAMPLE
The mysterious man.
(predicate missing; The mysterious man *disappeared in a cloud of fog.*)

1. The girl waited in the long line.
2. Under the sofa.
3. An exciting movie.
4. Fills the pitcher with water.
5. A woman found the stone.
6. On a hastily constructed raft.
7. Read the morning newspaper.
8. Dark mounds of dirt in the yard.
9. He could be in the shed.
10. The painted vase.

EXERCISE 3
Using Complete Sentences in Your Writing
Write a paragraph describing to a friend an unusual occupation that you find interesting. Why do you find this occupation appealing? What do people in this occupation usually do or make? Make sure that each sentence in your paragraph contains a subject and predicate.

FUNCTIONS OF SENTENCES

There are four different kinds of sentences: *declarative, interrogative, imperative,* and *exclamatory.* Each kind of sentence has a different purpose. You can vary the tone and mood of your writing by using the four different sentence types. Read the example sentences aloud and notice how your voice changes to express each sentence's different meaning.

- A **declarative sentence** makes a statement. It ends with a period.

> EXAMPLE
> Your cat would like to eat her supper now.

- An **interrogative sentence** asks a question. It ends with a question mark.

EXAMPLE
When will your cat eat her supper?

- An **imperative sentence** gives an order or makes a request. It ends with a period or an exclamation point. An imperative sentence has an understood subject, *you.*

EXAMPLES
(You) Please feed your cat.
(You) Look in the cupboard for the cat food.

- An **exclamatory sentence** expresses strong feeling. It ends with an exclamation point.

EXAMPLE
Your cat is really hungry!

Try It Yourself

EXERCISE 4
Identifying Different Kinds of Sentences in Literature
Identify each of the nine sentences in the passage below as declarative, interrogative, imperative, or exclamatory.

But even yet I refrained and kept still. I scarcely breathed. I held the lantern motionless. I tried how steadily I could maintain the ray upon the eye. Meantime the hellish tattoo of the heart increased. It grew quicker and quicker, and louder and louder every instant. The old man's terror *must* have been extreme! It grew louder, I say, louder every moment!—do you mark me well?

Literature
M O D E L

from "The Tell-Tale Heart"
Edgar Allan Poe

Understanding the Functions of Sentences
Identify the following sentences as declarative, imperative, interrogative, or exclamatory. Then revise each sentence according to the directions in parentheses.

EXAMPLE
Did you see the horse in the pasture? (Change into an imperative sentence.)
(interrogative; imperative, *Look at the horse in the pasture.*)

1. Will you bring the lantern to me? (Change into an imperative sentence.)
2. Tell me what you ate for breakfast. (Change into an interrogative sentence.)
3. Is the basement flooded? (Change into an exclamatory sentence.)
4. I would like a drink of water. (Change into an interrogative sentence.)
5. Today is the last day of school! (Change into a declarative sentence.)
6. What is missing from your purse? (Change into a declarative sentence.)
7. Walk with me over to the park. (Change into an interrogative sentence.)
8. Are you aware that your car is on fire? (Change into an exclamatory sentence.)
9. Will you please rescue the turtle on the side of the road? (Change into an imperative sentence.)
10. I believe that you will not like this dessert. (Change into an exclamatory sentence.)

EXERCISE 6
Using Different Kinds of Sentences in Your Writing
Write a brief speech about a current event that is important to you and that you think will appeal to your fellow classmates. Your speech may be serious, humorous, or persuasive in tone. To gather ideas, look through recent newspapers and magazines. Use all four kinds of sentences in your speech.

Then take turns with your classmates reading your speeches aloud. Consider how the four kinds of sentences make your speeches more expressive.

SUBJECTS AND PREDICATES: THE BASIC BUILDING BLOCKS IN A SENTENCE

Just as the sentence is the basic building block of the English language, the subject and predicate are the basic building blocks in a sentence. Every sentence has two basic parts: a subject and a predicate. The **subject** tells whom or what the sentence is about. The **predicate** tells information about the subject—what the subject is, what the subject does, or what happens to the subject.

> EXAMPLE
> **sentence**   The speedy athlete | won the track competition.
>   **(subject)**   **(predicate)**

To find the subject, ask who or what performs the action of the verb.

> EXAMPLE
> Who won the track competition? (*the speedy athlete*, subject)
>
> What did the speedy athlete do? (*won the track competition*, predicate)

Try It Yourself

EXERCISE 7
Identifying Subjects and Predicates in Literature
Write each sentence from the literature passage and draw a vertical line between the subject and predicate.

> The man tried to open the umbrella, but its metal ribs were broken. The black fabric dangled flat and limp from the pole. He put the umbrella into the plastic bag and headed for the entrance to the school.

Literature
M O D E L

CONTINUED

> A moment later, Zebra heard the whistle that signaled the end of recess. He followed his classmates at a distance, careful to avoid anyone's bumping against his hand.
>
> from "Zebra"
> Chaim Potok

EXERCISE 8

Understanding Subjects and Predicates

Items 1–5 include a list of subjects; items 6–10 include a list of predicates. Write a sentence for each subject or predicate listed, adding the missing part and any other details to create a clear, complete sentence.

1. Our country's leaders
2. The green and yellow leaves
3. A bright shining star
4. The squad of soldiers
5. The purple beads
6. are seeking to find the treasure
7. stood on the shoulder of the road
8. protected the helpless cubs
9. requires constant maintenance
10. bought a large hat

EXERCISE 9

Using Subjects and Predicates in Your Writing

Write a paragraph to be shared with a classmate in which you describe a person you recently observed engaging in an outside activity, such as flying a kite or shoveling snow. Make sure each sentence includes a subject and predicate and creates a clear picture for a peer reader.

SIMPLE AND COMPLETE SUBJECTS AND PREDICATES

In a sentence, the **simple subject** is the key word or words in the subject. The simple subject is usually a noun or a pronoun and does not include any modifiers. The **complete subject** includes the simple subject and all the words that modify it.

The **simple predicate** is the key verb or verb phrase that tells what the subject does, has, or is. The **complete predicate** includes the verb and all the words that modify it.

In the following sentence, a vertical line separates the complete subject and complete predicate. The simple subject is underlined once. The simple predicate, or verb, is underlined twice.

> EXAMPLE
> (complete subject)   (complete predicate)
> The large black <u>umbrella</u> | <u>shielded</u> my brother and sister from the rain.

Sometimes, the simple subject is also the complete subject, and the simple predicate or verb is also the complete predicate.

> EXAMPLE
> <u>Jesse Owens</u> | <u>ran</u>.

To find the simple subject and simple predicate in a sentence, first break the sentence into its two basic parts: complete subject and complete predicate. Then, identify the simple predicate by asking yourself, "What is the action of this sentence?" Then, identify the simple subject by asking yourself, "Who or what is performing the action?"

In the following sentences, the complete predicate is in brackets. The simple predicate, or verb, appears in boldface. Remember, verbs may have more than one word, and as many as four.

USAGE tip

> Every word in a sentence is part of a complete subject or complete predicate.

USAGE tip

> The complete subject can be replaced by a single pronoun—*I, you, he, she, it, we,* or *they.*

EXAMPLES

one-word verb   Three energetic monkeys (**climbed** up the tree.)

two-word verb   Three energetic monkeys (**are climbing** up the tree.)

three-word verb   Three energetic monkeys (**have been climbing** up the tree.)

four-word verb   Three energetic monkeys (**might have been climbing** up the tree.)

Try It Yourself

EXERCISE 10

Identifying Simple and Complete Subjects and Predicates
Draw a vertical line between the complete subject and predicate in each sentence. Then, underline once the simple subject. Underline twice the simple predicate or verb.

EXAMPLE

The <u>children</u> on the playground | <u>are playing</u> hide and seek.

1. The aging general boldly rode out to the front lines.
2. On the fencepost a yellow wren waits for the wind to subside.
3. A lost sheep might have wandered into the cave.
4. The front porch has been the site of many interesting conversations.
5. Julia is planning to swim across the English Channel.
6. A flock of birds exited the tree in unison.
7. Two boats are tied to the pier.
8. The church bell rings each Sunday at 8:00 A.M.
9. Their son's arraignment will be next Thursday.
10. The new city library branch opened its doors today.

Understanding Simple and Complete Subjects and Predicates

Each of the following sentences contains a simple subject and predicate. Revise each sentence by adding details to the simple subject and predicate to create a more specific and clearer sentence. Then draw a vertical line between the complete subject and predicate you've created. Underline once the original simple subject. Underline twice the original simple predicate.

EXAMPLE

The snakes slithered.

(The two green <u>snakes</u> | <u>slithered</u> into the house through the open door.)

1. A ballerina is dancing.
2. The girl walked.
3. The floor has been creaking.
4. The rabbit hid.
5. Their flowers are growing.
6. A tree fell.
7. Songs delight.
8. The officers talked.
9. The rain might have stopped.
10. The birds fly.

Using Simple and Complete Subjects and Predicates in Your Writing

Write a short story about a crime-fighting superhero, such as Spiderman or Batman. Add details to simple subjects and predicates to help your peer readers visualize the subject and the action that is taking place in the story.

COMPOUND SUBJECTS, COMPOUND PREDICATES, AND COMPOUND SENTENCES

A sentence may have more than one subject or predicate. A **compound subject** has two or more simple subjects that have the same predicate. The subjects are joined by the conjunction *and*, *or*, or *but*. A **compound predicate** has two or more simple predicates, or verbs, that share the same subject. The verbs are connected by the conjunction *and*, *or*, or *but*.

> EXAMPLES
> **compound subject**
> <u>Ice</u> and <u>snow</u> | <u>make</u> travel difficult in the winter.
>
> **compound predicate**
> Some <u>teachers</u> | <u>show</u> videos and <u>play</u> CDs during their classes.

A sentence may have both a compound subject and a compound predicate.

> EXAMPLE
> **compound subject and compound predicate**
> <u>John</u> and <u>Diane</u> | <u>drove</u> to the lake and <u>fished</u> all afternoon.

A **compound sentence** consists of two sentences joined by a semicolon or by a coordinating conjunction preceded by a comma. Each part of the compound sentence has its own subject and verb. The most common coordinating conjunctions are *and*, *or*, *nor*, *for*, *but*, *so*, and *yet*.

> EXAMPLES
> **compound sentence**
> Grover Cleveland served as president from 1885 to 1889; he served a second term in the White House from 1893 to 1897.
>
> **compound sentence**
> An economic downturn gripped the nation during Cleveland's second term, **and** his popularity with Americans dwindled.

EXERCISE 13

Identifying Compound Subjects, Compound Predicates, and Compound Sentences

Underline once all of the simple subjects in each sentence. Underline twice all of the simple predicates in each sentence. Then tell whether the sentence has a compound subject, compound predicate, compound subject and predicate, and whether the sentence is a compound sentence.

EXAMPLE

Jesse and his brother robbed the bank, and they rode quickly out of town.
(compound subject, compound predicate, compound sentence)

1. A raccoon knocked over the garbage can and spread trash all over the lawn.
2. Father's retirement party will be at the Legion hall; he worked at the factory for 38 years.
3. Andy and Tim wanted to buy a new baseball, but they did not have enough money.
4. The bear's claws and teeth terrified the campers.
5. Amy worked 62 hours last week, yet her boss was unimpressed.
6. Tiffany picked flowers in the meadow and made a bouquet for her mother.
7. The owl and the mouse eyed each other carefully in the bright moonlight.
8. For years, the old man in the mansion has been feared and has been loathed by the townspeople.
9. The winning lottery ticket brought wealth to Thomas; it also ended his friendship with Carl.
10. An eagle landed and rested on a fencepost in our backyard.

Understanding Compound Subjects, Compound Predicates, and Compound Sentences

Write sentences containing the elements described in each of the directions below.

1. compound subject
2. compound predicate
3. compound subject and compound predicate
4. compound sentence using conjunction *or*
5. compound sentence using conjunction *yet*
6. compound sentence using conjunction *for*
7. compound sentence using semicolon
8. compound subject and compound sentence
9. compound predicate and compound sentence
10. compound subject, compound predicate, and compound sentence

Using Compound Subjects, Compound Predicates, and Compound Sentences in Your Writing

Assume that you are a screenwriter. For your agent, write a scene for the pilot episode of a new television drama. Keep in mind that you'll need to establish the setting, introduce characters, and set up the episode's conflict. Include in your scene five of the different combinations of compound elements listed in Exercise 14.

UNIT 2 REVIEW

TEST YOUR KNOWLEDGE

Identifying Sentences
Identify each of the following groups of words as either a sentence or a sentence fragment. (10 points)

EXAMPLE
Surprisingly picked up his room. (sentence fragment)

1. At dawn, the opossum waddled back into its hole.
2. Into the ominous mist.
3. Abruptly the bus stopped at the railroad crossing.
4. Her stern look told the boys she knew what they had done.
5. Take the garbage out to the curb.
6. This revolutionary new appliance.
7. Believed we were the culprits.
8. Who is there?
9. With a wink and a nod.
10. The sun returned and hope increased.

Identifying the Functions of Sentences
Identify each of the following sentences as declarative, imperative, interrogative, or exclamatory. (10 points)

EXAMPLE
Douglas Southall Freeman was known for his biographies of Lee and Washington. (declarative)

1. We are going to fall!
2. Inform us about your trip.
3. Our teacher is taking a job at another school.
4. Where did you go last night?
5. The tarantula is loose in the house!
6. It often rains here in April.

7. Did you see that green glow in the trees?
8. Please don't climb on the furniture.
9. Although unpopular, your choice was the right one.
10. Find the missing ring.

Identifying Simple and Complete Subjects and Predicates

Draw a vertical line between the complete subject and predicate. Then underline once the simple subject, and underline twice the simple predicate. (20 points)

EXAMPLE

The <u>man</u> in the tower | <u><u>shouts</u></u> orders to the players.

1. The dog buries her bones in the backyard.
2. Gene Hackman has appeared in many movies.
3. Sara's writing is passionate and intense.
4. An article in the newspaper recounted the accomplishments of this administration.
5. The painting inspires a variety of different emotions.
6. He was the only person to stand up for the environment.
7. The man in the painting appears to be longing for something.
8. Songs during a church service can inspire people to worship.
9. A loud thunderstorm frightens our pet hamster.
10. The three soldiers behind enemy lines split up to avoid capture.

EXERCISE 4
Understanding Subjects and Predicates

Tell whether the subject, predicate, or both subject and predicate are missing from the following groups of words. Then revise each sentence to include the missing part or parts. (20 points)

EXAMPLES
Usually hides behind the tree.
(missing subject; *My little sister* usually hides behind the tree.)

1. A thin piece of red string.
2. On the first day of summer.
3. Swiftly scurried into the attic.
4. From the office.
5. The towering, majestic elephant in the clearing.
6. Seeks to find a new job.
7. Over the creaky wooden bridge.
8. Suddenly from under the chair.
9. A red brick with a note attached.
10. Might be traveling to this town.

EXERCISE 5

Using Compound Subjects, Compound Predicates, and Compound Sentences in Your Writing
Write sentences containing the elements described in each of the directions below. Underline subjects once, and underline predicates twice. (20 points)

EXAMPLE
compound subject
(The fresh <u>broccoli</u> and <u>cauliflower</u> on the table <u>looks</u> tasty.)

1. compound subject
2. compound predicate
3. compound subject and compound predicate
4. compound sentence using conjunction *so*
5. compound sentence using conjunction *and*
6. compound sentence using conjunction *but*
7. compound sentence using semicolon
8. compound subject and compound sentence
9. compound predicate and compound sentence
10. compound subject, compound predicate, and compound sentence

EXERCISE 6

Using Different Kinds of Sentences in Your Writing
Imagine that you could step into any setting or dramatic scene in literature. Then describe your experience for a school literary club. What fictional characters did you meet? How did your presence alter the action of the story? What did you gain from the experience? In your description, include at least two examples of each of the four different kinds of sentences: declarative, interrogative, imperative, and exclamatory.
(20 points)

UNIT 3 THE PARTS OF SPEECH

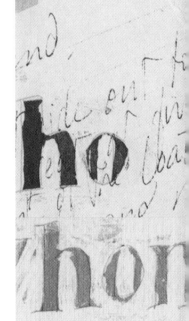

THE PARTS OF SPEECH

IDENTIFYING THE PARTS OF SPEECH

Each word in a sentence performs a basic function or task. Words perform four basic tasks: they name, modify, express action or state of being, or link. By the arrangement of words in a sentence and the task that each word performs within a sentence, you can understand a sentence's meaning. To illustrate how parts of speech work together, try to decipher the following nonsense sentence.

> **EXAMPLE**
> The darhmy, tramk puffums skeggered swin and swain.

What nonsense noun is the subject of the sentence? What adjectives modify the word *puffums?* Which nonsense verb expresses the action in the sentence?

If you substitute real words for the nonsense words, but keep the same arrangement of words, you can identify the nouns, verb, and adjectives in the sentence.

> **EXAMPLE**
> The heavy, dark clouds threatened wind and rain.

There are eight different parts of speech. Each part of speech is defined in the following chart.

Part of Speech	Definition
noun	A **noun** names a person, place, thing, or idea.
pronoun	A **pronoun** is used in place of a noun.
verb	A **verb** expresses action or a state of being.

CONTINUED

adjective	An **adjective** modifies a noun or pronoun. The most common adjectives are the articles *a, an,* and *the.*
adverb	An **adverb** modifies a verb, an adjective, or another adverb.
preposition	A **preposition** shows the relationship between its object—a noun or a pronoun—and another word in a sentence. Common prepositions include *after, around, at, behind, beside, off, through, until, upon,* and *with.*
conjunction	A **conjunction** joins words or groups of words. Common conjunctions are *and, but, for, nor, or, so,* and *yet.*
interjection	An **interjection** is a word used to express emotion. Common interjections are *oh, ah, well, hey,* and *wow.*

EXAMPLES

noun	**Felix** the **cat** curled up in my **lap,** shedding his **fur** all over my **pants.**
pronoun	**We** remember how well **you** treated **our** grandmother when **she** visited.
verb	The mischievous squirrels **scrambled** up the tree and **chased** each other in circles.
adjective	On **the dark** and **dreary** day, they watched **old classic** movies on television.
adverb	Max jumped **quickly** into the pool, **nearly** landing on the raft.
preposition	**Beside** the edge **of** the ravine, the hikers waited **for** the others **in** their group.
conjunction	**Neither** Kim **nor** Betsy wanted to be late, **so** they ran as fast as they could.
interjection	**Hey!** Wait for me!

EXERCISE 1
Identifying the Parts of Speech in Literature
Identify the part of speech of each underlined word in the
following excerpt.

MODEL

Directly in front of the bench where we sat, a little girl
with blond curls was trying to handle a bottle of Coke.
Now and then, she'd manage to turn herself and the
bottle around and watch me with big gray eyes that
seemed to know quite well how badly I wanted a pop. I
thought of asking Momma for fifteen cents so I could get
one from the machine in the back but I was afraid she'd
still say no so I just kept planning more and more
convincing ways to ask. Besides, there was a water
fountain near the door if I could make myself rise and
walk to it.

from "Getting the Facts of Life"
Paulette Childress

EXERCISE 2
Understanding the Parts of Speech
Use each word and its designated part of speech in a sentence.

EXAMPLES

snored (verb)	The black bear snored while deep in hibernation.
snoring (adjective)	The snoring bear will not wake from its hibernation until spring.

1. them (pronoun)
2. courage (noun)
3. request (verb)
4. honestly (adverb)
5. beneath (preposition)
6. but (conjunction)

7. oh (interjection)
8. cunning (adjective)
9. green (adjective)
10. laughter (noun)

EXERCISE 3
Using the Parts of Speech in Your Writing
Write a paragraph to be shared with classmates in which you
describe your idea of Utopia, a place where all people would
live together in peace and harmony. What would the place
look like? What would people do there? Include in your
paragraph at least three examples of each part of speech.

GRAMMAR REFERENCE CHARTS
Parts of Speech Overview
Use these charts as a quick reference guide to different parts of
speech, definitions, and examples.

Type of Noun	Definition	Examples
common noun	names a person, place, idea, or thing	orchestra, sister, mountain, candle
proper noun	names a specific person, place, or thing; begins with a capital letter	Uncle Bernie, Statue of Liberty, Kilimanjaro
concrete noun	names a thing that can be touched, seen, heard, smelled, or tasted	sunrise, dust, music, basket, water
abstract noun	names an idea, quality, concept, or feeling	truth, relativity, Romanticism, fear
singular noun	names one person, place, idea, or thing	goose, idea, feather, cheese
plural noun	names more than one person, place, idea, or thing	geese, ideas, feathers, cheeses

CONTINUED

possessive noun	shows ownership or possession of things or qualities	Holly's necklace, winter's cold, Mr. Fullbright's attention, friend's loyalty
compound noun	made up of two or more words	sidewalk, mousetrap, short story, sister-in-law
collective noun	names groups	family, flock, team

Type of Pronoun	Definition	Examples
personal pronoun	used in place of the name of a person or thing	I, me, we, us, he, she, it, him, her, you, they, them
singular pronoun	used in place of the name of one person or thing	I, me, you, he, she, it, him, her
plural pronoun	used in place of more than one person or thing	us, you, we, they, them
possessive pronoun	shows ownership or possession	my, mine, your, yours, his, her, hers, its, our, ours, their, theirs
demonstrative pronoun	points out a specific person, place, idea, or thing	this, that, these, those
indefinite pronoun	points out a person, place, or thing, but not a particular or definite one	anyone, someone, anything, everyone, nobody, nothing many, any, some, none
reflexive pronoun	refers back to a noun previously used; adds –self and –selves to other pronoun forms	myself, herself, himself, itself, yourself, themselves, ourselves
intensive pronoun	emphasizes a noun or pronoun	me *myself,* he *himself,* you *yourself,* they *themselves,* we *ourselves*

CONTINUED

interrogative pronoun	asks a question	who, whom, whose, which, what
relative pronoun	introduces an adjective clause	that, which, who, whom, whose, what

Type of Verb	Definition	Examples
action verb	names an action	climb, remember, chase, admire, detect
helping verb	helps a main verb express action or a state of being	A dog *can* detect thousands of smells with its nose. Our dog *has been* chasing squirrels in the backyard.
linking verb	connects a noun with another noun, pronoun, or adjective that describes or identifies it; the most common linking verbs are formed from the verb *to be*	My mother *is* the owner of her own business. She *seems* eager to handle the day's challenges.
transitive verb	has a direct object	My dad accidentally locked his keys in the car.
intransitive verb	does not have a direct object	The keys are inside the locked car.
irregular verb	has a different past tense form and spelling	begin/began choose/chose bring/brought

Type of Adjective	Definition	Examples
adjective	modifies nouns and pronouns; answers the questions *what kind? which one? how many?* and *how much?*	*raspberry* yogurt *broken* window *three* children *twenty-five* cents
article	*a* and *an* refer to an unspecified person, place, thing, or idea; *the* refers to a specific person, place, thing, or idea	Please pour me *a* glass of water. *An* empty glass is on the counter. *The* pitcher is filled with water.
proper adjective	is formed from proper nouns; is capitalized; often ends in *–n, –an, –ian, –ese,* or *–ish*	*American* folksong *Jeffersonian* architecture *Japanese* lantern *British* accent

Type of Conjunction	Definition	Examples
coordinating conjunction	joins words or groups of words of equal importance; coordinating conjunctions are *and, but, for, nor, or, so, yet*	Angel *and* Enrico walked to the grocery store. They were hungry, *so* they bought milk, cheese, and bread.
correlative conjunction	word pairs that join words or groups of words; correlative conjunctions include *both/and, neither/nor, either/or*	*Either* Paul *or* Marie will drive you to the airport.
subordinating conjunction	introduces a subordinate clause and joins it to an independent clause; subordinating conjunctions include *after, although, as, as if, because, before, if, since, unless, till, when* and *while*	*Unless* it rains, the picnic will be on Saturday.

UNIT 3 REVIEW

TEST YOUR KNOWLEDGE

E X E R C I S E 1
Identifying the Parts of Speech
Identify the part of speech of the underlined word in each sentence. (20 points)

EXAMPLE
Suzanne <u>always</u> remembers to send me a birthday card.
(adverb)

1. The chef whipped up a <u>dreamy</u> concoction of strawberries and cream.
2. I <u>almost</u> forgot to meet Jennie at the gym.
3. Will <u>they</u> bring their children with them?
4. Slowly, the fisherman lowered the hook <u>into</u> the icy water.
5. It is wise to tell the <u>truth</u>.
6. Waiting for the light to turn, the <u>crowd</u> stood on the curb.
7. Our favorite old movie <u>is</u> *Casablanca*.
8. <u>Well</u>, we can clean up the kitchen later.
9. The speaker was frustrated by the <u>many</u> interruptions.
10. Samuel stayed up too late, <u>so</u> he feels tired today.
11. The group of tourists <u>completely</u> enjoyed the tour.
12. Fortunately, the contestant was a <u>very</u> fast thinker.
13. The wet socks and boots in the hallway are <u>mine</u>.
14. Here's the Empire State Building and, <u>wow</u>, is it tall!
15. The odds of winning are not in their favor, <u>yet</u> the team remains hopeful.
16. <u>Between</u> the two of us, I think we can get the job done.
17. Eric brought the <u>steaming</u> platter of food to the table.
18. The hikers hoped to complete their trek before <u>nightfall</u>.
19. We <u>were</u> relieved to get out of the rain.
20. Water <u>becomes</u> ice when the temperature drops below 32 degrees.

Identifying Nouns and Adjectives
Identify the nouns in the following sentences and any adjectives that modify them. (20 points)

EXAMPLE
Among the ancient ruins live many stray cats. (noun, *ruins,* adjectives, *the, ancient;* noun, *cat,* adjective, *stray*)

1. His old, tattered robe hung in the musty closet.
2. After the lengthy speech, the tired audience responded with weak applause.
3. Several friends met at the court and played basketball.
4. We saw an awful accident over the holiday weekend.
5. The twitching dog was having a dream while it slept.
6. The lottery winner is a very lucky woman.
7. Most people treat others in a respectable way.
8. A heavy snow fell on the midwestern plains.
9. The misbehaving child disrupted a lovely meal.
10. The lemon cake is made with equal amounts of flour and sugar.

Understanding Adverbs
Tell whether the underlined adverb in each of the following sentences modifies a verb, an adjective, or another adverb. (20 points)

EXAMPLE
The novice skier <u>suddenly</u> fell down the icy slope. (modifies verb *fell*)

1. She <u>often</u> called us in the evenings after work.
2. The anxious contestant pressed the buzzer <u>too</u> quickly.
3. A bouquet of flowers will be delivered to your mother <u>tomorrow</u>.
4. This must be a <u>wonderfully</u> happy occasion for you.
5. The northern part of the state is <u>extremely</u> cold in the winter.

6. Megan <u>already</u> doubts whether she'll be able to attend the party.
7. The carpenter hit his thumb with the hammer <u>quite</u> accidentally.
8. Her photography <u>still</u> hangs in the most popular museums.
9. We <u>gingerly</u> picked up the broken glass from the floor.
10. To fly to the moon would be a <u>truly</u> amazing experience.

EXERCISE 4
Understanding the Parts of Speech
Use each word and its designated part of speech in a sentence. (20 points)

EXAMPLES

spoiled (verb)   *Unfortunately, the seafood salad spoiled in the hot sun.*

spoiled (adjective) *The spoiled seafood salad was unsafe to eat.*

1. but (conjunction)
2. somewhat (adverb)
3. glittery (adjective)
4. idea (noun)
5. you (pronoun)
6. causes (verb)
7. cause (noun)
8. billowing (adjective)
9. underneath (preposition)
10. and (conjunction)
11. yikes (interjection)
12. walking (noun)
13. with (preposition)
14. their (pronoun)
15. struggle (noun)
16. White House (noun)
17. fascinated (verb)
18. strongly (adverb)
19. pond (noun)
20. risky (adjective)

EXERCISE 5

Using Appropriate Language in Your Writing
Create for a foreign pen pal a portrait in words of one of the people you admire most in American history. Describe the historical figure's life, actions, personality, physical features, and habits in vivid detail, using each of the eight parts of speech at least three times. (20 points)

UNIT 4 NAMERS
Nouns

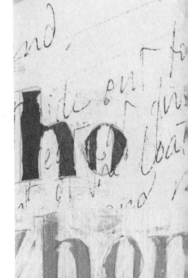

NAMERS: NOUNS

NOUNS

A **noun** is a part of speech that names a person, place, idea, or thing. In this unit, you'll learn about the different kinds of nouns and what they name.

EXAMPLES	
people	Sidney, teacher, mother, photographer
places	city, Wrigley Field, Kentucky
ideas	admiration, addition, relief, plan
things	checkerboard, butterfly, flight, ring

Types of Nouns	Definition	Examples
common noun	names a person, place, idea, or thing	uncle, street, truth, pencil
proper noun	names a specific person, place, or thing; begins with capital letter	Jefferson, Monticello, Declaration of Independence
concrete noun	names a thing that can be touched, seen, heard, smelled, or tasted	shirt, picture, conversation, smoke, apple
abstract noun	names an idea, a theory, a concept, or a feeling	criticism, relativity, Modernism, happiness
singular noun	names one person, place, idea, or thing	referee, lake, wisdom, door
plural noun	names more than one thing	referees, lakes, opinions, doors
possessive noun	shows ownership or possession of things or qualities	Matt's, Mrs. Thompson's, men's, doctor's
compound noun	made up of two or more words	supermarket, apple pie, daughter-in-law
collective noun	names groups	team, council, legislature

USAGE tip

Every noun is:
• common or proper
• concrete or abstract
• singular or plural

COMMON AND PROPER NOUNS

The two basic kinds of nouns are common nouns and proper nouns. A **common noun** names *any* person, place, thing, or idea. Common nouns are usually not capitalized.

> **EXAMPLES**
> **common nouns**
> any person   The **quarterback** signed autographs for his fans.
> any place   A **valley** is located between two hills or mountains.
> any thing   A **padlock** prevented thieves from opening the door.
> any idea   The **beauty** of the sunset awed the onlookers.

A **proper noun** names a *specific* person, place, or thing, and begins with a capital letter.

> **EXAMPLES**
> **common nouns**   governor, statue, street
> **proper nouns**   Jesse, Statue of Liberty, Pennsylvania Avenue

Try It Yourself

EXERCISE 1
Identifying Common and Proper Nouns in Literature
Identify the underlined nouns in the passage below as either common or proper.

> Albert left home as soon as he got out of the hospital. He worked as a stevedore in Halifax for a number of years, and when he got enough money saved, he bought a little run-down house close to Digby, with a view of the Bay of Fundy. He's got a small chunk of land that's so black and rich that it doesn't take any pushing at all to make the flowers and vegetables grow.
>
> from "Be-ers and Doers"
> Budge Wilson

Understanding Common and Proper Nouns
For each common noun listed below, write two proper nouns
on your own paper.

1. newspaper
2. musician
3. ocean
4. town
5. ballplayer
6. sibling
7. journal
8. lake
9. star
10. restaurant
11. capital
12. nation
13. movie
14. legislator
15. student
16. island
17. college
18. store
19. song
20. lawyer

Using Common and Proper Nouns in Your Writing
Write a paragraph to be shared with classmates in which you
describe a trip that you have taken. Include in your description
some of the interesting sites you visited. Underline and label
five common nouns and five proper nouns in your paragraph.
Notice how the use of proper nouns helps to make your
description more specific.

CONCRETE AND ABSTRACT NOUNS

A **concrete noun** names a thing than can be touched, seen, heard, smelled, or tasted—something that can be perceived with any of your five senses.

An **abstract noun** names an idea, a quality, a theory, a concept, or a feeling—something that *cannot* be touched or seen.

EXAMPLES	
concrete nouns	shirt, picture, conversation, smoke, apple
abstract nouns	criticism, relativity, Modernism, happiness

Try It Yourself

EXERCISE 4
Identifying Concrete and Abstract Nouns in Literature
Identify the underlined nouns in the following passage and indicate whether each is concrete or abstract.

Literature
M O D E L

Presently I heard a slight <u>groan</u>, and I knew it was the groan of mortal <u>terror</u>. It was not a groan of <u>pain</u> or <u>grief</u>—oh, no!—it was the low, stifled <u>sound</u> that arises from the bottom of the <u>soul</u> when overcharged with <u>awe</u>. I knew the sound well. Many a <u>night</u>, just at midnight, when all the <u>world</u> slept, it has welled up from my own <u>bosom</u>, deepening, with its dreadful <u>echo</u>, the <u>terrors</u> that distracted me.

from "The Tell-Tale Heart"
Edgar Allan Poe

EXERCISE 5
Identifying Concrete and Abstract Nouns
Identify the underlined word in each sentence as either a concrete noun or an abstract noun.

1. The narrator felt <u>love</u> for the old man.
2. He had no <u>desire</u> for his gold.
3. The old man had a pale blue <u>eye</u>.
4. Whenever the eye fell upon the narrator, his <u>blood</u> ran cold.
5. During the week, he showed the old man <u>kindness</u>.
6. The narrator opened the <u>door</u> slowly, so as not to disturb the old man's sleep.
7. The old man's <u>fears</u> had been growing.
8. The narrator could hear the beating of the old man's <u>heart</u>.
9. The sound increased his <u>fury</u>.
10. He hid the <u>body</u> under the floorboards.

EXERCISE 6

Understanding Concrete and Abstract Nouns

For each concrete noun in items 1–10, write an abstract noun that names an idea, quality, or characteristic with which the concrete noun can be associated. For each abstract noun in items 11–20, write a concrete noun that has the quality of the abstract noun. Look at the example exercises.

EXAMPLES
shark (concrete)—fear (abstract)
courage (abstract)—firefighter (concrete)

1. book
2. hamburger
3. library
4. rain
5. parents
6. car
7. baseball
8. army
9. computer
10. picture
11. faith
12. hate

13. love
14. sarcasm
15. charm
16. honesty
17. integrity
18. pride
19. bitterness
20. joy

EXERCISE 7
Using Concrete and Abstract Nouns in Your Writing
Write a paragraph about a hobby or activity that you would
like to try. In the paragraph, explain why you would like to
pursue this particular hobby or activity. You can choose any
pursuit that sounds interesting to you, such as skydiving, chess,
stamp collecting, or horseback riding. Use five different
concrete nouns and five different abstract nouns in the
paragraph.

SINGULAR AND PLURAL NOUNS

Nouns that represent one person, place, idea, or thing are
called **singular nouns.** Nouns that represent more than one
person, place, idea, or thing are called **plural nouns.**

Most nouns can be made plural simply by adding –*s* to the end
of the word. The spelling of some nouns changes slightly
when the words are made plural, depending on how the word
ends.

USAGE tip

Some nouns have
the same spelling in
both the singular
and the plural
forms, such as *deer,
sheep, series,* or
species. Other
nouns form plurals
in special ways,
such as *children,
women,* or *teeth.*

EXAMPLES
plural nouns
For most nouns, to form the plural add –*s* to the end of the
word.
building = buildings   taco = tacos
paper = papers   thing = things

CONTINUED

If a noun ends in *s*, *sh*, *ch*, *x*, or *z*, add *–es*.

pass = passes   dish = dishes   catch = catches

fox = foxes   topaz = topazes

If a noun ends in *o* preceded by a consonant, add *–es*.

hero = heroes   dodo = dodoes   potato = potatoes

If a noun ends in *y* preceded by a consonant, change the *y* to *i* and add *–es*.

berry = berries   dairy = dairies   poppy = poppies

For some nouns that end in *f* or *fe*, change the *f* to *v* and add *–es* or *–s*.

loaf = loaves   life = lives   half = halves

Try It Yourself

EXERCISE 8

Identifying Singular and Plural Nouns in Literature
Identify the nouns in the following passage. Indicate whether they are singular or plural. Keep in mind that some nouns have the same spelling in both the singular and the plural forms.

MODEL

> Eve Hubbard had a passion for pets. Her entire life had been filled with gerbils, hamsters, a rat, turtles, a dog, a salamander, and most recently, cats. In the beginning there was Chase. He was the dog Eve's parents got before she was born.
>
> from "Pets"
> Avi

EXERCISE 9

Correcting Singular and Plural Nouns
For each singular noun in items 1–10, write the correct plural form. In items 11–20 correct the error in the plural nouns listed. Write *correct* if the plural form is correct.

1. writer
2. key
3. volcano
4. gazebo
5. canary
6. lottery
7. elf
8. knife
9. calf
10. jellyfish
11. roachs
12. burritos
13. potatos
14. factorys
15. dwarfs
16. rice
17. wolfs
18. wheats
19. datums
20. cods

EXERCISE 10
Using Singular and Plural Nouns in Your Writing
Write a paragraph describing the town or city you live in to
someone who has never seen it. Use at least five singular and
five plural nouns.

POSSESSIVE NOUNS

Nouns that show ownership or possession of things or
qualities are called **possessive nouns.** A possessive noun
names who or what has something. Possessive nouns can also
be singular or plural.

An apostrophe is used to form the possessive of nouns. To
form the possessive of a singular noun, add an apostrophe and
an *s* to the end of the word.

USAGE tip

Singular nouns that
end in *s* still need
an apostrophe and
an *s* added at the
end of the word.

glass   glass's

James   James's

Mrs. Fields
Mrs. Fields's

USAGE tip

Both common nouns and proper nouns can be possessive in form.

common nouns
The *house's* doors were all shut and locked.
The *coaches'* meeting was postponed until Wednesday.

proper nouns
Sammy's batting average continued to drop through the summer.
Germany's most famous musician will be touring America in May.

EXAMPLES

singular possessive nouns
Jim's game is on Friday. (Jim + 's = Jim's)
Mr. Taylor's car needs an oil change. (Taylor + 's = Taylor's)

The possessive of a plural noun is formed two different ways. If the plural noun does not end in *s*, you add an apostrophe and an *s* to the end of the word. If the plural noun ends with an *s*, add only an apostrophe.

EXAMPLES

plural possessive nouns
The men's books are located on the second floor of the library. (men + 's = men's)

The dogs' hunger drove them to eat the birthday cake. (dogs + ' = dogs')

Try It Yourself

EXERCISE 11

Identifying Possessive Nouns

Indicate whether the underlined nouns in the following sentences are plural or possessive, or both plural and possessive.

1. Author Milton Meltzer has written about the <u>lives</u> of several queens.
2. <u>Meltzer's</u> book, *Ten Queens: Portraits of Women in Power*, has a section on Elizabeth.
3. Elizabeth I became <u>England's</u> queen in 1558.
4. Elizabeth took the throne after her half <u>sister's</u> death.
5. Many <u>Protestants</u> were happy Elizabeth became queen.
6. The <u>Catholics'</u> anger toward the queen led to conflict.
7. Spanish <u>leaders</u> sent ships to attack England.
8. The English <u>sailors'</u> bravery helped lead to victory in battle.
9. Several family members tried to end the <u>monarch's</u> reign.
10. Elizabeth responded by having her cousin, the <u>Scots'</u> queen, beheaded.

EXERCISE 12

Understanding How to Form Possessive Nouns
Write the correct possessive form of each underlined word or
group of words.

1. <u>bear</u> paw
2. <u>friend</u> loyalty
3. <u>children</u> books
4. <u>rabbits</u> cages
5. <u>bike</u> tire
6. <u>Gorbachev</u> speech
7. <u>desert</u> heat
8. <u>Los Angeles</u> smog
9. <u>computer</u> keyboard
10. <u>fish</u> bowl
11. <u>Jesus</u> parables
12. <u>Twain</u> novels
13. <u>city</u> government
14. <u>ballplayers</u> grievances
15. <u>population</u> unemployment rate
16. <u>cavemen</u> caves
17. <u>hens</u> eggs
18. <u>Phil</u> opinion
19. <u>lion</u> roar
20. <u>tides</u> risings

EXERCISE 13

Using Possessive Nouns
For each sentence write the correct possessive form of the
underlined noun.

1. Roberto Clemente was one of <u>Puerto Rico</u> most famous
   athletes.
2. A <u>ballplayers</u> dream is to play in the Major Leagues.
3. The best competitors earn their <u>teammates</u> respect.
4. <u>Clemente</u> teacher encouraged him to play baseball.
5. He later paid his <u>teacher</u> doctor bills.
6. Clemente starred as one of the <u>league</u> best right fielders.

7. The <u>Pirates</u> success increased after Clemente joined the team.
8. The <u>team</u> World Series victory in 1971 put Clemente in the national spotlight.
9. <u>Pittsburgh</u> left fielder Willie Stargell was his close friend.
10. Clemente died a <u>hero</u> death in 1972.

COMPOUND NOUNS

A **compound noun** is a noun made up of two or more words. Some compound nouns are written as one word, some as two or more words, and some as hyphenated words.

EXAMPLES	
one word	godfather, seahorse, rosebud
two or more words	Washington Monument, San Antonio, flying circus, chief of staff
hyphenated	father-in-law, aide-de-camp, space-time continuum

Try It Yourself

EXERCISE 14
Identifying Compound Nouns
Identify the compound nouns in the following sentences.

1. My uncle Bob is a district attorney.
2. Joel was happy he had the chance to meet the Speaker of the House.
3. My great-grandmother Agnes keeps leaving her purse in the refrigerator.
4. The detective did a lot of spadework to solve the case.
5. We went to the museum to see the crossbow on display.
6. At night, Lynda becomes a masked superhero who fights crime in the city.
7. The painter was a popular neo-impressionist.
8. Jessica often works with hydrochloric acid in the research lab.

USAGE tip

To form the plural of compound nouns made up of one word, add –s or –es.

scorecards
pickaxes

To form the plural of compound nouns written as more than one word or hyphenated, make the most important part plural.

head coaches
daughters-in-law

9. In the 1980s, the world's top female weightlifters were usually East Germans.
10. The soldiers used flamethrowers to keep ground squirrels off the firing range.
11. I learned the flutter kick when I was a ninth-grader.
12. Earl ran a fly-by-night insurance company in New Mexico.
13. Ken waved the baseball bat through the air like it was a broadsword.
14. The party ended when we ran out of ice cubes.
15. Our team's wide receivers keep running into the goalposts.
16. Prime Minister Blair met with the secretary of defense today.
17. We bought a house on a cul-de-sac.
18. Pickup trucks are useful for hauling firewood.
19. I read a book about a field marshall from Austria-Hungary.
20. My sister used to like to ride on merry-go-rounds.

EXERCISE 15

Understanding Plural Compound Nouns
Use the plural form of the compound noun in parentheses to complete each sentence.

1. We saw several (silverfish) in the water.
2. The meeting of the (joint chief of staff) was top secret.
3. Several countries in the world have (merchant marine).
4. The buildup of (natural gas) in the basement could be dangerous.
5. Did you remember to feed the (Yorkshire terrier) last night?
6. Our vacation took a turn for the worse after we offended the (witch doctor).
7. Generals from several (standing army) were present at the conference.
8. The warriors were all armed with (battle axe).
9. (Creampuff) are among my favorite desserts.
10. My grandfather has installed (public-address system) at many stadiums.

EXERCISE 16
Using Compound Nouns
Write a sentence using each of the compound nouns listed below.

1. dragonfly
2. know-it-all
3. fire station
4. powder room
5. right-of-way
6. great-granddaughter
7. station wagon
8. sunglasses
9. wildcat
10. grizzly bear

COLLECTIVE NOUNS

USAGE tip

If you can substitute the word *it* for a collective noun, it is singular. If you can substitute the word *they,* the collective noun is plural.

Collective nouns name groups—such as *family, committee,* and *class*—that are made up of individuals. A collective noun may be either singular or plural, depending on how the group acts. When the group acts together as one unit to do something, the group is considered **singular.** When individuals within the group act differently or do different things at the same time, the collective noun is **plural.**

EXAMPLES

singular   The **team** plays better in night games.
The **herd** sleeps for seven hours each night.

plural   The **team** can't agree about where to eat.
The **herd** often fight among themselves.

EXERCISE 17
Identifying Collective Nouns
Identify the five collective nouns in the following paragraph.

> Our class recently took a trip to Washington, D.C. We had an opportunity to watch the legislature debate an important bill. The press was especially interested in the outcome of the debate. When the session ended the bill was sent back to a Senate committee. The Congress worked very hard that day.

EXERCISE 18
Understanding Collective Noun-Verb Agreement
Identify the collective noun in each of the following sentences. Then complete each sentence by using the correct form of the verb in parentheses.

1. The crowd (expresses, express) its disapproval of the play.
2. The band (plays, play) their solos to warm up for the show.
3. A platoon (attacks, attack) the hill north of the town.
4. Our fleet (sails, sail) south today.
5. The gang of thieves (fights, fight) each other over the money they stole.
6. That cluster of stars (shines, shine) brightest after midnight.
7. A murder of crows (targets, target) my car after I wash it.
8. The coven (casts, cast) their most devious spells on Halloween.
9. Each party (nominates, nominate) a candidate to run for president.
10. The tribunal (rules, rule) on cases that involve military officers.

EXERCISE **19**

Using Collective Nouns in Your Writing

Write a paragraph about one of the following groups: an association, a league, an organization, a squad, or a group of your own choosing. Describe the group, including its activities. In your description use at least two collective nouns that are singular and at least two collective nouns that are plural.

UNIT 4 REVIEW

TEST YOUR KNOWLEDGE

EXERCISE 1
Identifying Nouns
Identify the nouns in each sentence. (10 points)

EXAMPLE
The <u>athletes</u> arrived at the <u>gym</u> after <u>supper</u>.

1. I like to play basketball every Friday.
2. Five players are needed to form a basketball team.
3. Only one person on our team can jump high enough to touch the rim.
4. My team has played in five tournaments this year.
5. I hope to someday play like Michael Jordan.
6. My favorite pro teams are the Bulls and the Wizards.
7. The fans like players who have great intensity.
8. It takes talent and dedication to play the game well.
9. Many students attend tryouts to make the varsity team at school.
10. The coach says maybe I should consider playing chess.

EXERCISE 2
Identifying Common, Proper, Concrete, and Abstract Nouns
Identify each underlined noun as either common or proper.
Then tell whether it is either concrete or abstract. (10 points)

EXAMPLE
At this critical time, England needed a leader with <u>integrity</u>.
(common, abstract)

1. Queen Elizabeth's mother was <u>Anne Boleyn</u>.
2. As a girl, Elizabeth learned to speak four <u>languages</u>.
3. Even as a teenager, she had developed great <u>confidence</u>.

4. After her sister died, <u>Elizabeth</u> became queen.
5. Members of the royal family usually did not marry for <u>love</u>.
6. Elizabeth wanted to bring <u>peace</u> to England.
7. The queen often threw <u>parties</u> and invited many guests.
8. Elizabeth faced <u>opposition</u> from some of England's Catholics.
9. <u>Spain</u> sent an armada of ships to invade England.
10. Spanish <u>aggression</u> against England did not succeed.

EXERCISE 3
Identifying Singular, Plural, and Possessive Nouns
Identify the type of noun underlined in each sentence as either singular, plural, singular possessive, or plural possessive.
(10 points)

EXAMPLES
The appearance of the <u>shark's</u> fin in the water frightened the swimmers. (possessive)

The <u>leaves'</u> colors are especially beautiful in the fall.
(plural possessive)

1. Governor Redford toured the <u>city's</u> new factory.
2. He gave a speech to a large crowd of <u>workers</u> at the plant.
3. <u>Children</u> at the elementary school waited for the candidate to arrive.
4. Mr. Redford told them a <u>story</u> about two cowboys.
5. In the story, the <u>cowboys'</u> horses ran away.
6. The <u>governor's</u> story was a parable about opportunity.
7. He later explained his point to improve the <u>students'</u> understanding of the story.
8. Some of the <u>teachers</u> spoke to the governor before he left.
9. The <u>newspaper's</u> lead reporter was sent to cover the visit.
10. Mr. Redford had a busy <u>schedule</u> every day that week.

EXERCISE 4
Identifying Compound Nouns
Identify the compound nouns in the following sentences.
(10 points)

EXAMPLE
Our <u>bookcase</u> is filled with <u>boardgames</u>.

1. The battleship fired a shot that blew off the yacht's masthead.
2. Our neighbor's backyard is filled with hedgehogs.
3. Their team's base-runner was tagged out at third base.
4. Shelly wrote a guidebook about traveling in Great Britain.
5. My great-grandniece is a sixth-grader this year.
6. For supper I ate a cheeseburger and French fries.
7. I often wear sunglasses during the summertime.
8. We saw a totem pole on our field trip.
9. One privilege that eighteen-year-olds are given is the right to vote.
10. Our German Shepard greets the mail carrier each day at noon.

EXERCISE 5
Understanding Plural and Possessive Nouns
Write the word in parentheses that correctly completes the sentence. (10 points)

EXAMPLE
The (explorers, explorer's) life was full of adventure and difficulty. *(explorer's)*

1. General Lee led the (Confederacies, Confederacy's) last major invasion of the North.
2. At Gettysburg, his (plans, plan's) included taking the hills at the south end of the ridge.
3. General Longstreet disagreed with his (commanders, commander's) strategy.
4. The Rebels continued their (attacks, attack's) for three days.

5. The battle tested the (soldiers, soldiers') resolve.
6. Cannons from both (sides, sides') fired all morning.
7. On the third day the (generals, general's) goal was to break through the center of the Union line.
8. Each side lost many (casualties, casualty's) in the battle.
9. A rainstorm added to the gloom of the (troops, troops') retreat.
10. President Lincoln later praised his (armies, army's) valor at Gettysburg.

EXERCISE 6
Understanding Compound Nouns
Write the plural form of each compound noun below.
(10 points)

1. rattlesnake
2. great-granddaughter
3. guinea pig
4. man-of-war
5. drill bit
6. Medal of Honor
7. rosebush
8. surgeon general
9. heir apparent
10. driver's license

EXERCISE 7
Understanding Collective Nouns
Identify the collective noun in each of the following sentences. Then choose the form of the verb in parentheses that agrees with the collective noun. (10 points)

EXAMPLE
The troop (sells, sell) cookies in the neighborhood.
(troop, sells)

1. The flock (swoops, swoop) down, one-by-one, on the hapless cat.
2. Our division (ships, ship) out at six o'clock tomorrow morning.
3. The school of fish (swims, swim) away from the shark at varying intervals.
4. A pride of lions (sleeps, sleep) in the savannah.
5. The squadron (bombs, bomb) the enemy capital each night after dark.
6. The pack of wolves (fights, fight) each other over the meat.
7. My class (dislikes, dislike) the new math teacher.
8. Her team (selects, select) their favorite ice cream flavors after the game.
9. A gaggle of geese (flies, fly) overhead.
10. The fleet (closes, close) in on the port.

EXERCISE 8

Using Nouns

Write a sentence using each of the types of nouns listed below. Underline the noun in each sentence. (10 points)

1. common noun
2. proper noun
3. concrete noun
4. abstract noun
5. singular noun
6. plural noun
7. singular possessive noun
8. plural possessive noun
9. compound noun
10. collective noun

EXERCISE 9
Using Nouns in Your Writing
Write a descriptive paragraph for a fan-club magazine about one of your favorite actors or actresses. In your description, use at least once each of the types of nouns listed in Exercise 8. Underline and label one example of each of the types of nouns in your paragraph. (20 points)

UNIT *5* NAMERS
Pronouns

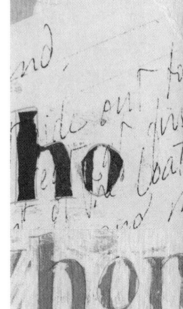

NAMERS: PRONOUNS

PRONOUNS

A **pronoun** is used in place of a noun. Sometimes a pronoun refers to a specific person or thing.

Pronouns can help your writing flow more smoothly. Without pronouns, your writing can sound awkward and repetitive. Take a look at the following examples, which show the same sentence written without and with pronouns.

EXAMPLES	
without pronouns	Terry went for a walk on **Terry's** farm to inspect **Terry's** peach trees and apple trees and later decided to pick some fruit from **the peach trees and apple trees**.
with pronouns	Terry went for a walk on **his** farm to inspect **his** peach trees and apple trees and later decided to pick some fruit from **them**.

The most commonly used pronouns are *personal pronouns, reflexive and intensive pronouns, possessive pronouns, demonstrative pronouns, indefinite pronouns, interrogative pronouns,* and *relative pronouns.*

Types of Pronouns	Definition	Examples
personal pronoun	used in place of the name of a person or thing	I, me, we, us, he, she, it, him, her, you, they, them
indefinite pronoun	points out a person, place, or thing, but not a specific or definite one	one, someone, anything, other, all, few, nobody
reflexive pronoun	refers back to a noun previously used; adds *–self* and *–selves* to other pronoun forms	myself, herself, yourself, themselves, ourselves

CONTINUED

intensive pronoun	emphasizes a noun or pronoun	me *myself*, he *himself*, you *yourself*, they *themselves*, we *ourselves*
interrogative pronoun	asks a question	who, whose, whom, what, which
demonstrative pronoun	points out a specific person, place, idea, or thing	this, these, that, those
relative pronoun	introduces an adjective clause	that, which, who, whose, whom
singular pronoun	used in place of the name of one person or thing	I, me, you, he, she, it, him, her
plural pronoun	used in place of more than one person or thing	we, us, you, they, them
possessive pronoun	shows ownership or possession	mine, yours, his, hers, ours, theirs

A **personal pronoun** is used in place of the name of a person or thing. Personal pronouns are singular, plural, or possessive.

EXAMPLES
personal pronouns
singular   I, me, you, he, she, it, him, her
plural   we, us, you, they, them
possessive   mine, yours, his, hers, ours, theirs

Use personal pronouns to refer to yourself (first person), to refer to people to whom you are talking (second person), and to refer to other people, places, and things (third person).

EXAMPLES
first person   the speaker or speakers talk about themselves: *I, me, my, mine, we, us, our, ours*

second person   the speaker talks about the person talked to: *you, your, yours*

third person   the speaker talks about someone or something else: *he, him, his, she, her, hers, it, its, they, them, their, theirs*

USAGE tip

If subjects are of different numbers, the verb should agree with the subject nearest the verb.

EXERCISE 1
Identifying Pronouns in Literature
Identify the eleven pronouns in the following passage.

Literature
MODEL

> Our father frowned upon the cotton balls. If he saw them, he would make us remove them. He claimed that they diminished the experience of flying and were in any case unnecessary: The engine noise was not so terribly loud that one couldn't get used to it: he certainly had done so.
>
> from "Flying"
> Reeve Lindbergh

EXERCISE 2
Understanding Pronouns
Rewrite each of the following sentences or sentence pairs. Use pronouns in place of any repetitive nouns or groups of nouns.

USAGE tip

> When pronouns replace common nouns, they replace the common noun and all of the modifiers of the common noun.

1. Adam and Geoff gave many speeches appealing to the voters. Adam and Geoff both wanted the voters' support.
2. Adam wants to debate Geoff. Adam and Geoff disagree on many issues.
3. Bill said that Adam and Geoff could use Bill's television show as a forum for Adam and Geoff's debate.
4. In October the two opponents held a debate. The two opponents realized that it would take the two opponents three more debates to cover all of the issues.
5. Lori told Lori's father that Geoff needed a good campaign advisor. Lori's father brought Lori's father's former advisor to Geoff's campaign headquarters.
6. Adam and I read articles about Geoff's campaign advisor. Adam and I wondered if Geoff's campaign advisor was from Adam's home state.
7. "Yes," Adam's wife said, "Geoff's campaign advisor is from Adam and Adam's wife's home state."

8. Joel asked Adam and Adam's wife: "Do Adam and Adam's wife want to campaign in Florida this weekend?" Joel wanted Adam and Adam's wife to go with Joel to Disney World.
9. Joel liked Disney World's many attractions. Disney World's rides bought Joel much happiness.
10. The candidates reserved a flight for the candidates to travel to Orlando.

EXERCISE 3
Using Pronouns in Your Writing
Write a paragraph for a classmate describing a round in a boxing match. Begin your paragraph with this sentence: "The tired champion stepped slowly out to the middle of the ring." Use at least five different pronouns in your descriptive paragraph.

PRONOUNS AND ANTECEDENTS

As you know, a **pronoun** is a word used in place of one noun or more than one noun. The word that a pronoun stands for is called its **antecedent.** The antecedent clarifies the meaning of the pronoun. The pronoun may appear in the same sentence as its antecedent or in a following sentence.

EXAMPLES
Where is **Michael**? **He** is at the library.
(*Michael* is the antecedent of *He*.)

Amy's black **dog** barks loudly because **he** is hungry.
(*Dog* is the antecedent of *he*.)

USAGE tip

When you use a pronoun be sure that it refers clearly to its antecedent and agrees in number (singular or plural) and gender (masculine, feminine, or neutral).

EXERCISE 4
Identifying Pronouns and Antecedents
Identify the personal pronoun(s) in each of the following sentences or sentence pairs. Then identify the antecedent to which each pronoun refers.

1. Edward Estlin Cummings was born in Cambridge, Massachusetts. He was the son of a minister.
2. Cummings attended Harvard College, studying language and literature in its classrooms.
3. He served in World War I and wrote letters critical of the war. They led to his arrest by the French.
4. Cummings's imprisonment provided material for his first book, *The Enormous Room*.
5. Cummings wrote many poems after the war, and they reflected a unique writing style.
6. Critics responded to Cummings's work, but at first they were unsure about him.
7. Cummings also painted many pictures. Have you seen any of them?
8. My family went to the city library yesterday. We found that it contained many works by Cummings.
9. Cummings was frequently imitated by other poets. They were influenced by his writing.
10. Robert Frost was another twentieth-century poet. He was even more popular than Cummings.

EXERCISE 5
Understanding Pronouns and Antecedents
Complete the second sentence in each of the following sentence pairs with the correct pronoun. Then write the pronoun's antecedent.

1. I recently watched a movie called *61**. _____ is about baseball.
2. The movie focuses on two ballplayers, Roger Maris and Mickey Mantle. _____ played for the New York Yankees.

3. The plot focuses on the quest to break a record held by Babe Ruth. _____ also played for the Yankees.
4. Mantle and Maris were both famous ballplayers. I had read many books about _____.
5. My friend James enjoyed watching *61**. The drama of the movie captivated _____.
6. Jeff and Cynthia also liked *61**. It is one of _____ favorite movies.
7. Cynthia does not like the Yankees. Jeff likes to tease _____ when they win the World Series.
8. Jeff and Cynthia decided to write a review of the movie. _____ took notes while watching it.
9. James and I offered to proofread the review. _____ like to read their work.
10. Jeff and Cynthia were grateful for the help James and I provided. They took _____ out to dinner.

EXERCISE 6
Using Pronouns and Antecedents in Your Writing
Write a brief description of a recent family activity to be read by your grandchildren. In your description, you might include who was present, where you went, and what you did. Use at least five different pronouns in your description. Check your writing for correct pronoun-antecedent agreement. Then draw an arrow from each pronoun to the antecedent to which it refers.

SUBJECT AND OBJECT PRONOUNS

Personal pronouns are sometimes used as the subjects of sentences. Personal pronouns are also used as the objects of verbs or prepositions.

A **subject pronoun** is used as the subject of a sentence. An **object pronoun** is used as the object of a verb or a preposition.

EXAMPLES	
subject pronoun	Betty likes to read. **She** often shops at the bookstore. (subject of sentence)
object pronoun	Suspense novels sometimes scare **her**. (direct object of the verb *scare*)
object pronoun	Betty's friend sent **her** a suspense novel. (indirect object of the verb *sent*)
object pronoun	Betty might offer the book to **you**. (object of the preposition *to*)

Personal Pronouns

	Singular	Plural
used as subjects	I you he, she, it	we you they
used as objects	me you him, her, it	us you them

Try It Yourself

EXERCISE 7
Identifying Subject and Object Pronouns in Literature
Identify each of the underlined words as either a subject pronoun or an object pronoun.

Literature
M O D E L

When <u>they</u> were passing the Kemp place <u>they</u> saw the old man sitting on the veranda and Luke stopped. All <u>he</u> could think about was that Mr. Kemp had liked <u>them</u> both and it had been a pleasure to help <u>him</u> get the cows in the evening. Dan had always been with <u>them</u>.

from "Luke Baldwin's Vow"
Morley Callaghan

Subject and object pronouns are also used in compound subjects and compound objects.

EXAMPLES
Mark and Claire walked quickly down the road.
He and **she** walked quickly down the road.
(*He* and *she* form the compound subject.)

Several flowers along the road looked pretty to Mark and Claire.

Several flowers along the road looked pretty to **him** and **her**.
(*Him* and *her* form the compound object.)

Use the subject pronoun *I* and the object pronoun *me* last when they are part of the compound subject or object.

EXAMPLES
compound subject
incorrect   I and Fred decided to climb the mountain.
correct   **Fred and I** decided to climb the mountain.

compound object
incorrect   Shelly wanted me and Sidney to finish the brief today.
correct   Shelly wanted **Sidney and me** to finish the brief today.

E X E R C I S E 8
Understanding Subject and Object Pronouns
Use the correct subject or object pronoun(s) in parentheses to complete each sentence. Then identify each pronoun as either a subject pronoun or an object pronoun.

1. Fred sent (we, us) to the store to buy milk.
2. Julie and (I, me) finished addressing the invitations.
3. Because of Kenneth's incompetence, the boss gave (he, him) a pink slip.
4. Dorian discovered the gold coins and stuffed (they, them) into his bag.
5. Candace, needing a ride, got in the car with (she, her).
6. It is so exciting that they selected (I, me) to be on the game show.

7. How many times have (they, them) tried to rob that bank?
8. (She, her) and (he, him) will be getting married today.
9. (He, him) helped (we, us) hide the evidence before the police arrived.
10. Will you allow (I, me) the honor of introducing you?

EXERCISE 9
Using Subject and Object Pronouns in Your Writing
Write a paragraph recommending to a classmate a story or book that you have recently read. Provide details about the story or book, and correctly use subject and object pronouns in the paragraph.

POSSESSIVE PRONOUNS

A **possessive pronoun** is a kind of pronoun that shows who or what has something. Possessive pronouns have two forms. When a possessive pronoun stands alone, it acts as a pronoun. When a possessive pronoun is used before a noun, it acts as an adjective.

EXAMPLES

used alone
The flowers are **yours**.
Sink this putt and victory will be **ours**.
The blue car in that lot is **mine**.

used before nouns
I already put the saddle on **his** *horse*.
My *paper* is delivered each day at 6:00 A.M.
Please send me **their** *ideas* this afternoon.

Possessive Pronouns	Singular	Plural
used alone	mine yours hers, his, its	ours yours theirs
used as adjectives	my your her, his, its	our yours theirs

USAGE tip

Do not confuse possessive pronouns and contractions. Some possessive pronouns and contractions sound alike, but they have different meanings and spellings. Possessive pronouns do not contain an apostrophe.

**your/you're
their/they're
theirs/there's
its/it's**

EXERCISE 10
Identifying Possessive Pronouns in Literature
Identify the possessive pronouns in the following passage.

Literature
M O D E L

My father carried a sack of rice, which had to last us the whole day. My mother carried one extra change of clothing for each of us, a few personal belongings, and my baby sister on her back. My older sister and I helped carry pots and pans. My stepuncle carried water, dried meat, and his personal belongings.

from "An Unforgettable Journey"
Maijue Xiong

EXERCISE 11
Understanding Possessive Pronouns
Write a sentence using each of the following possessive pronouns.

1. mine
2. yours (used alone)
3. hers
4. its
5. ours
6. theirs
7. his (used before a noun)
8. my
9. their
10. our

EXERCISE 12
Using Possessive Pronouns in Your Writing
Write a paragraph to a pen pal in which you describe a friend. What are some of his or her best qualities? What is one of your favorite memories of time spent with your friend? Use five different possessive pronouns in your paragraph.

INDEFINITE PRONOUNS

An **indefinite pronoun** points out a person, place, or thing, but not a particular or definite one. The indefinite pronouns are listed below.

Singular		Plural
someone	everything	many
somebody	another	few
something	either	both
anyone	neither	several
anybody	each	others
anything	one	
everyone	nobody	
everybody	nothing	

USAGE tip

The indefinite pronouns *all, any, most, none,* and *some* may be singular or plural, depending on their meaning in the sentence.

EXAMPLES
Everyone stops talking once class begins.
Something is out there making that noise.

Don't be confused if a phrase comes between an indefinite pronoun and the verb in a sentence. When an indefinite pronoun is the subject of a sentence, it must agree in number with the verb. In these two examples, the indefinite pronoun and its verb are now in boldface. The interrupting phrase is between them.

EXAMPLES
Some of the work **was** done. (singular)
Some of the deputies **serve** all year long. (plural)

Try It Yourself

EXERCISE 13
Identifying Indefinite Pronouns
Underline the indefinite pronouns in the following sentences.

1. After the shark was sited, few of the swimmers went back into the ocean.
2. The lifeguard said that anyone who went back in would be at risk.

3. Everybody in my group decided to stay on the land.
4. One of the swimmers went back into the water.
5. After seeing him back out there, both of the swimmers' brothers yelled at him.
6. Most of the crowd on the beach watched with anticipation.
7. Several lifeguards discussed whether they should go get the swimmer.
8. After talking it over, none of the lifeguards wanted to take the risk.
9. The tension caused several people on the beach to pass out.
10. Nothing could have prepared us for what we saw next.

E X E R C I S E 1 4
Understanding Indefinite Pronouns
Identify the indefinite pronoun in each of the following sentences. Then choose the word or words in parentheses that correctly complete the sentence. Tell whether the indefinite pronoun is singular or plural.

EXAMPLE
Anyone who (swim, swims) well can make it across the river.
(*Anyone, swims*, singular)

1. When I enter the room, everything (moves, move) to a different location.
2. Several explorers (describes, describe) similar experiences.
3. Each object (seems, seem) to be alive for a moment.
4. Upon closer examination, none of the items (looks, look) unusual.
5. Others down the hall (feels, feel) that magic is at work among us.
6. Some of my courage (flits, flit) away when I hear such talk.
7. Nothing they say (keeps, keep) me from my task, however.
8. I know that most of my friends (believes, believe) I am crazy for coming here.
9. If any of them (asks, ask) why I explore, I try to explain.
10. Nobody truly (understands, understand) what motivates me to take such risks.

Using Indefinite Pronouns

Write ten sentences using the indefinite pronouns below.

1. another
2. someone
3. one
4. anything
5. all
6. some
7. much
8. both
9. everybody
10. others

REFLEXIVE AND INTENSIVE PRONOUNS

A **reflexive pronoun** refers back to a noun previously used and can be recognized because *–self* and *–selves* have been added to other pronoun forms.

> EXAMPLES
> You had better ask **yourself** if you feel lucky.
> Although others doubted her, Carrie believed in **herself**.
> The team watched **themselves** on the television.

An **intensive pronoun** immediately follows and emphasizes a noun or pronoun already named in a sentence. Intensive pronouns and reflexive pronouns use the same forms.

> EXAMPLE
> The author **herself** answered the reporters' questions.

Adding *herself* to *author* emphasizes that the author answered the questions; she didn't have somebody else answer the questions.

> EXAMPLE
> I **myself** believe the book is poorly written.

Adding *myself* stresses that I believe the book is poorly written while recognizing that others may disagree.

Reflexive and Intensive Pronouns	
Singular	**Plural**
myself	ourselves
yourself	yourselves
himself, herself, itself	themselves

USAGE tip

Note that intensive pronouns do not need to be set off from the rest of the sentence by the use of commas.

Try It Yourself

USAGE tip

Reflexive and intensive pronouns should never be used as the subject of a sentence.

incorrect
Jack and myself need to get out of the building.
correct
Jack and I need to get out of the building.

EXERCISE 16
Identifying Reflexive and Intensive Pronouns
Identify the intensive pronouns in each of the following sentences and indicate whether they are reflexive or intensive.

1. We concluded that it would be better if we fixed the car ourselves.
2. The Vikings helped themselves to the king's gold.
3. You need to decide for yourself what you will do tomorrow.
4. I myself figured out the answer to the riddle.
5. After the game, the players themselves passed out candy to the young fans.
6. The pitcher fielded the bunt andtagged out the runner himself.
7. The tree itself is moving across the field.
8. I can't believe the pianist herself is in the front lobby.
9. The governor himself will push the button.
10. How about if we ourselves come up with a solution to the problem?

EXERCISE 17
Understanding Reflexive and Intensive Pronouns
Complete each of the following sentences with the correct reflexive or intensive pronoun. Then identify the pronoun as either reflexive or intensive.

USAGE tip

Do not mistakenly use *hisself* for *himself* and *theirselves* for *themselves*.

EXAMPLE
I learned that Sheila _____ fixed the car.
I learned that Sheila <u>herself</u> fixed the car. (intensive)

1. The robot _____ shut down the power to the space station.
2. We learned a lot about _____ at the seminar.
3. It is the doctors _____ who are the source of the problem.
4. Mr. Lazerri _____ will be teaching the class today.
5. The five sisters _____ are on their way over to discuss the contract.
6. Robert found _____ lost in the woods again.
7. Betsy sometimes thinks of _____ too highly.
8. You need to imagine _____ flying over the obstacle.
9. Somehow the computer fixed _____ while we were gone.
10. Jamie and I _____ will be presenting the slide show.

E X E R C I S E   1 8
Using Reflexive and Intensive Pronouns in Your Writing
Write a paragraph for a parent or guardian about a difficult task that you completed in school. Correctly use at least five examples of reflexive and intensive pronouns in your paragraph.

USAGE tip

The interrogative pronouns *who, whose,* and *whom* refer to people. *What* and *which* refer to things or ideas.

INTERROGATIVE AND DEMONSTRATIVE PRONOUNS

An **interrogative pronoun** asks a question. *Who, whom, whose, what,* and *which* are interrogative pronouns.

USAGE tip

Who is used when the interrogative pronoun is the subject of a sentence. *Whom* is used when the interrogative pronoun is the object of a verb or a preposition.

EXAMPLES
Who will be driving? (subject)
Whom do you want to invite you? (direct object)
Whom will he climb over on his way to the top? (object of preposition)

Whose pants are at the top of the flagpole?
What do you think of my new car?
Which castle should we raid today?

A **demonstrative pronoun** points out a specific person, place, thing, or idea. The demonstrative pronouns are *this, that, these,* and *those.*

USAGE tip

The demonstrative pronouns *this* and *these* point to persons or things that are near. *That* and *those* refer to persons or things that are farther away.

EXAMPLES	
singular	**This** is the finest horse in the state.
plural	**These** are the finest horses in the state.
singular	**That** is a good idea.
plural	**Those** are good ideas.

Try It Yourself

EXERCISE 19
Identifying Interrogative and Demonstrative Pronouns
Identify and label the interrogative and demonstrative pronouns in the following sentences.

1. Whom did Thomas Jefferson and James Madison run against for president?
2. These early presidents were from Virginia.
3. Which of the early presidents commanded the Continental Army?
4. This is the first dumbwaiter invented by Jefferson.
5. Those were the notes he used to write the Declaration of Independence.
6. You will be asking whom to help you lead the tour?
7. From whom did you get that original copy of the Bill of Rights?
8. Whose musket is standing in the corner?
9. What is the best book you have read about American history?
10. Those included Washington, Jefferson, Madison, and Monroe.

EXERCISE 20
Understanding Interrogative and Demonstrative Pronouns
Complete each sentence with the correct word in parentheses.

1. (Who, Whom) did Washington want to replace him?
2. (This, That) was not part of his agenda in his first term.
3. (Who, Whom) do you believe is the best president?
4. (What, Which) does the Bill of Rights say about free speech?
5. I decided (this, that) was the most important idea Madison had.
6. You believe that Jefferson was smarter than (who, whom)?
7. (These, Those) leaders created a new nation over 200 years ago.
8. (This, These) is my favorite monument to visit.
9. Will (these, those) names mean anything to you a year from now?
10. (What, Which) state produced the most American presidents?

EXERCISE 21
Using Interrogative and Demonstrative Pronouns in Your Writing
Choose an American president whom you have learned about. Then write a set of questions to ask this president. Next write a list of statements about the time period in which the president lived. Use each of the interrogative and demonstrative pronouns listed below.

1. who
2. whom
3. whose
4. what
5. which
6. this
7. these
8. that
9. those

RELATIVE PRONOUNS

A **relative pronoun** introduces an adjective clause that modifies a noun or pronoun in the main clause. (Remember that a clause has both a subject and a verb.) The relative pronouns are *who, whom, whose, which,* and *that.*

USAGE tip

Relative pronouns use some of the same words as interrogative pronouns, but they do not ask a question.

> **EXAMPLES**
> Your neighbor, **whose** dog barks all night, is head of the committee **that** passed the city's pet ordinance.

Try It Yourself

EXERCISE 22
Identifying Relative Pronouns
Identify the relative pronoun and the adjective clause it introduces in each of the following sentences. Be careful not to confuse relative pronouns and interrogative pronouns.

USAGE tip

Relative pronouns indicate that a clause is a subordinate clause. A subordinate clause cannot stand by itself.

1. The neighborhood cats hunt in the pond that is filled with goldfish.
2. My grandpa, who served in World War II, will be honored by the American Legion today.
3. I found the bat that Mark McGwire used to hit his seventieth home run.
4. He still drives the blue car, which he bought while in high school.
5. Jennifer's foreign language skills, which she developed in college, helped her get the job.
6. The police officer, whom we often run away from, actually has little interest in us.
7. Of all the books that you have read, which did you like the best?
8. My boss, who oversees the whole unit, cannot remember my name.
9. When you reach the pond that glows red in the moonlight, turn left and walk 200 paces.
10. My friend George, whose uncle is a senator, is running for class president.

Understanding Relative Pronouns
Complete each of the following sentences using the relative pronoun in parentheses and an adjective clause.

1. This is the town (that) _____.
2. Wesley is the notorious outlaw, (who) _____.
3. I found the golden ring, (which) _____.
4. The musician, (whose) _____, will be going on tour this year.
5. By the time we finished the movie, (which) _____, I did not have time to work on my paper.
6. My aunt Hattie, (who) _____, is world famous.
7. The bag of fire crackers (that) _____ will come in handy at the recital.
8. The ex-ballplayer, (whom) _____, is moving out of town.
9. His collection of old bicycles (that) _____ will be sold at an auction.
10. A little girl, (who) _____, sold us five boxes of cookies.

Using Relative Pronouns
Write a sentence using each of the relative pronouns listed below.

1. who
2. whom
3. whose
4. which
5. that

UNIT 5 REVIEW

TEST YOUR KNOWLEDGE

EXERCISE 1
Identifying Types of Pronouns
Identify the type of pronoun underlined in each sentence by writing *personal, possessive, indefinite, reflexive, intensive, interrogative, demonstrative,* or *relative.* (10 points)

EXAMPLE
<u>This</u> is the best day of my life? (demonstrative)

1. Ask the server to bring <u>our</u> check to us.
2. I <u>myself</u> cannot wait for the opening day of baseball season.
3. The old woman, <u>whom</u> you are afraid of, was once a famous actor.
4. I believe <u>he</u> wants your wallet and your jewelry.
5. The outlaw, <u>whose</u> reputation precedes him, is actually a nice guy.
6. Our dogs cannot stop <u>themselves</u> when they smell a pie cooling on the counter.
7. Unbeknown to the partygoers, <u>somebody</u> had been stealing the purses.
8. <u>Who</u> dares to disturb the sleep of the great mummy?
9. <u>Those</u> were worst employees who ever worked here.
10. You have told <u>her</u> enough already.

EXERCISE 2
Identifying Pronouns and Antecedents
Identify the pronoun or pronouns in each sentence. Then identify the antecedent that each pronoun refers to. (20 points)

EXAMPLE
Karl ran into Sid and talked to him after class.
(pronoun, *him;* antecedent, *Sid*)

1. The wolf found itself alone, separated from the pack.
2. Even though Dawn prepared six months for the event, she did not win.
3. Marie asked Robert, "Do you know how to get back home?"
4. After Charlie spotted the children, he talked to them about climbing the tree.
5. The team threw a party for their coach after his 500th victory.
6. The car slid into the ditch and snapped its front axle.
7. After Arthur and Henry won the match, they were congratulated by the queen.
8. Are you sure that all of these cars are yours?
9. Marie could not remember if she had ever seen the man before.
10. The Wildcats are an average team, but they always play hard.

EXERCISE 3

Understanding Subject and Object Pronouns

Write the pronoun you could use in place of the underlined word or words. Then identify whether the pronoun is a subject pronoun or an object pronoun. (20 points)

EXAMPLE
The principal noticed Kyle and (I, me) skipping class this morning. (*me*, object pronoun)

1. I believe that John and (she, her) will be singing a duet.
2. The boss wants to take (he, him) for a little ride.
3. (She, Her) and her sister want to go to Disneyland.
4. The last person to get off the bus is (he, him).
5. (We, Us) did not want to talk with (they, them) for that long.
6. Carl showed (he, him) and (I, me) his stamp collection.
7. What is taking (they, them) so long in there?
8. I will never forget the sight of Peggy and (she, her) on the stage.

9. Paul and (I, me) will win fifty games this year.
10. Should (we, us) or (they, them) bring the cake to the party?

EXERCISE 4
Understanding Possessive Pronouns
Replace each underlined word or group of words with the correct possessive pronoun. (10 points)

EXAMPLE
Todd and Tony's show was popular. (*Their*)

1. The ship's hull has a gaping hole that is letting water in.
2. Some of Julio's friends offered to join him.
3. The horse in the stable is Roy's and Dale's.
4. You will never believe Sheila's and Sherry's idea for the play.
5. If you see Jim's and my post-hole digger, please return it.
6. The responsibility for this fiasco is Henry's.
7. I told Sara, "The keys on the red ring are Sara's."
8. Jimmy looked out at the field and said, "This land is all Jimmy's."
9. Phil asked Jessie, "Did you know that Jessie's headlights are on?"
10. When Cory's book was due, Cory returned it to the library.

EXERCISE 5
Correcting Pronouns
Rewrite the following sentences, correcting any errors in pronouns or pronoun use. If the sentence correctly uses pronouns, write *correct*. (20 points)

EXAMPLE
Joe and me built the shed. (*Joe and I built the shed.*)

1. Whom is going to provide me with the answer?
2. Gail and myself are going to a movie today.
3. Who did you ask to speak at the reception?
4. The lawyers talked among theirselves about the case.

5. Is anybody in here?
6. The doctor, which car was in the shop, took the bus to work.
7. Does these pencil belong to you?
8. He is kinder and gentler than who?
9. The building, whom hosted many events, is scheduled for demolition.
10. Luis is the batter whom is out there practicing.
11. I gave they a new van to use on their trip.
12. The coach had to think to hisself about what was going wrong out there.
13. The movie was pleasing to she and him.
14. Sheriff Taylor gave them a warning to leave the county.
15. Jeff and him are going to the lake.
16. One more jump and the gold medal will be her's.
17. Her and Jamie like to go to the mall on Saturday.
18. Every person should express their opinion at the forum today.
19. Jody Samuelson, who I once met, will be signing books at the store.
20. Frieda herself does not like the fried fish.

EXERCISE 6

Using Pronouns in Your Writing
Write a sentence using each of the types of pronoun listed below. Underline the pronoun in each sentence. (20 points)

1. personal pronoun
2. subject pronoun
3. object pronoun
4. possessive pronoun
5. indefinite pronoun
6. reflexive pronoun
7. intensive pronoun
8. interrogative pronoun
9. demonstrative pronoun
10. relative pronoun

UNIT *6* EXPRESSERS
Verbs

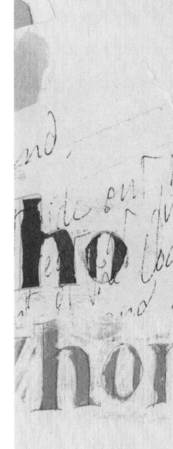

EXPRESSERS: VERBS

PREDICATES—VERBS

In Unit 2 you learned that subjects and predicates are the two basic building blocks in a sentence. Every sentence can be divided into two parts: the **subject** and the **predicate**. The following sentence is divided between the complete subject and the complete predicate.

> EXAMPLE
> The barn **owl** | **glided** slowly over the cornfield.

The subject of a sentence names whom or what the sentence is about. The predicate tells what the subject does, is, or has. A verb is the **predicate** without any complements, linkers, or modifiers. In other words the verb is the simple predicate.

Verbs are the **expressers** of the English language. **Verbs** are used to express action or a state of being. They work hard to tell whether the action is completed, continuing, or will happen in the future. Verbs also express all kinds of conditions for the action. Verbs in the English language can be from one to four words long.

USAGE tip

Remember: A sentence can have more than one verb.

The horse *galloped* around the corral, *jumped* the fence, and *raced* across the pasture.

> EXAMPLE
> Dale **mows** his neighbors' lawns.
> Dale **is mowing** his neighbors' lawns.
> Dale **has been mowing** his neighbors' lawns.
> Dale **might have been mowing** his neighbors' lawns.

Try It Yourself

EXERCISE 1
Identifying Verbs
Identify each of the verbs in the following sentences.

1. During the day our cat sleeps underneath my bed.
2. Some townspeople view tourists as a nuisance.
3. My little brother will listen to the radio all afternoon.

4. Many children awake in the dark and have asked for a nightlight.
5. Samuel reads many of his favorite books in the summer.
6. Arthur is being tutored in math by a couple of students at school.
7. After Dawn packs her suitcase, she will load it into the minivan.
8. In a matter of seconds, the computer screen froze and then the hard drive crashed.
9. Cookies and pies have been cooling on the table for an hour.
10. Before the show, Casey checks the lights, sweeps the stage, and opens the curtain.

ACTION VERBS AND STATE OF BEING VERBS

A **verb** is a word used to express action or a state of being. An **action verb** may express physical action or mental action. The action may or may not be one that you see—but, either way, an action verb tells you that something is happening, has happened, or will happen.

EXAMPLES

physical action My thirsty horse **drinks** water from the stream.
The angry bull **charged** at the farm hands.

mental action Finally, I **memorized** the list of names.
Richard **worries** too much about problems.

USAGE tip

Use action verbs in your writing to create strong images and convey a clear picture for your readers.

A state of being verb does not tell about an action. A **state of being verb** tells you when and where someone or something exists. State of being verbs are formed from the verb *to be*.

Forms of *Be*							
am	be	being	was	are	been	is	were

EXAMPLES
The red pen **is** on the table.
My sisters **were** in the garage.

Try It Yourself

EXERCISE 2

Identifying Action Verbs and State of Being Verbs in Literature

Tell whether each of the underlined verbs is an action verb or a state of being verb.

Literature
M O D E L

After the first moments of strangeness Lucy was glad to be alone. No one [was] <u>breathing</u> down her neck. She <u>looked</u> round the office with pleasure. Hers.

Sunlight <u>streamed</u> through the window. The curtains <u>shifted</u> a little in the spring breeze. There <u>was</u> a small blue-and-green rug on the floor.

from "QWERTYUIOP"
Vivien Alcock

EXERCISE 3

Understanding Action Verbs and State of Being Verbs

Complete each of the following sentences. Include in the predicate an action verb or state of being verb, as indicated.

EXAMPLES
The chocolate chip cookies (state of being verb)
(The chocolate chip cookies *are* in the oven.)

A wary lion (action verb)
(A wary lion *growled* at the safari tourists.)

1. The small kittens (state of being verb)
2. A curious squirrel (action verb)
3. My brother's attorney (state of being verb)
4. To escape, we (action verb)

5. An apple and an orange (state of being verb)
6. The yellow canoe (action verb)
7. A good fishing creek (state of being verb)
8. Beside the gray elephant (state of being verb)
9. The alert baby (action verb)
10. Her mother's parakeet (action verb)

EXERCISE 4
Using Action Verbs and State of Being Verbs in Your Writing

Imagine that you are participating in some sort of competition. The competition can be in any sport or activity. Imagine that you are at a break in the competition—halftime, for example. Write a brief description for a relative of your experience thus far in the competition. Use three different state of being verbs and three different action verbs in your description. Carefully choose your action verbs to make your description vivid.

LINKING VERBS

Like a state of being verb, a linking verb does not express an action. A **linking verb** links, or connects, the subject with a word or words in the predicate that describe or rename the subject.

EXAMPLES

The chocolate cake **was** rich. (The verb *was* connects the subject *cake* with a word that describes it—*rich*.)

The wind and rain **are** cold. (The verb *are* connects the compound subject *wind and rain* with a word that describes it—*cold*.)

Linking verbs can be formed from the verb *to be*.

EXAMPLES

| am | be | being | was | are | been | is | were |

USAGE tip

Some linking verbs are formed from the verb *to be*, but do not confuse a linking verb with a state of being verb. Remember: A linking verb describes or renames the subject.

state of being verb
She *was* outside the classroom.

linking verb
She *was* a popular teacher.

The common linking verbs are listed below.

Linking Verbs			
forms of *be*	feel	remain	sound
become	grow	seem	taste
appear	look	smell	

EXAMPLES

The apple pie **tastes** tart. (The linking verb *tastes* connects the subject *pie* with a word that describes the pie—*tart*.)

Our dance instructor **became** frustrated with the class. (The linking verb *became* connects the subject *instructor* with a word that describes the instructor—*frustrated*.)

Note that some linking verbs can also be used as action verbs.

EXAMPLES

linking verb   Shelly **remained** optimistic about the trip.
action verb   Three fish **remained** in the pond.

linking verb   The ice cream **tasted** smooth and sweet.
action verb   The cat **tasted** tuna in the bowl.

linking verb   Our basement no longer **feels** damp and cold.
action verb   He **feels** a hole in the exhaust pipe.

Try It Yourself

EXERCISE 5
Identifying Linking Verbs in Literature
Identify the six linking verbs in the following literature passage.

MODEL

But, of course, he couldn't always be watching and learning from his Uncle Henry, for too often when he watched him he thought of his own father; then he was lonely. So he began to build up another secret life for himself around the sawmill, and his companion was the eleven-year-old collie, Dan, a dog blind in one eye and

CONTINUED

with a slight limp in his left hind leg. Dan was a fat slow-moving old dog. He was very affectionate and his eye was the color of amber. His fur was amber too.

from "Luke Baldwin's Vow"
Morley Callaghan

EXERCISE 6
Understanding Linking Verbs
Use each of the following linking verbs in a sentence. If you wish, you may change the form of the verbs.

EXAMPLE
is (form of *be*)   *(She is very tired right now.)*

1. seem
2. was (form of *be*)
3. taste
4. smell
5. become
6. grow
7. sound
8. appear
9. feel
10. look

EXERCISE 7
Using Linking Verbs in Your Writing

Imagine that you have discovered a new type of vegetable growing in your garden. Write a paragraph describing this unique and surprising plant. Include each of the following verbs. (You may include other verbs as well.) Use one of these verbs twice, once as an action verb and once as a linking verb.

taste   smell   sound   seem   grow

HELPING VERBS

A **helping verb** helps the main verb to tell about an action. One or more helping verbs followed by a main verb is called a **verb phrase**. In the following examples, the verb phrases are underlined and the helping verbs appear in boldface.

EXAMPLES
I **am** walking to the store.
The children **will be** playing soccer after school.
You **must have been** sleeping when the fire truck drove by.

The common helping verbs and their forms are listed in the following chart.

Helping Verbs				
Forms of *be*	**Forms of *do***	**Forms of *have***	**Other helping verbs**	
am	do	have	can	shall
is	does	has	could	should
are	did	had	may	will
was			might	would
were			must	
be				
being				
been				

Sometimes helping verbs and main verbs are separated by other words.

EXAMPLES
I **did** not **wash** our car today. (The helping verb *did* and the main verb *wash* are separated by the word *not*.)

The rabbits **had** obviously **eaten** all of our flowers. (The helping verb *had* and the main verb *eaten* are separated by the word *obviously*.)

Note that some helping verbs can also be used as main verbs.

EXAMPLES
main verb   I **had** an apple yesterday.
helping verb   I **had eaten** an apple yesterday.

Sometimes a helping verb becomes part of a contraction with a pronoun or a negative word.

EXAMPLES
I have been studying each day after school.
I've been studying each day after school.

We will be flying to Phoenix this weekend.
We'll be flying to Phoenix this weekend.

She does not like to eat anything with caramel in it.
She doesn't like to eat anything with caramel in it.

Try It Yourself

EXERCISE 8
Identifying Helping Verbs in Literature
Identify the seven verb phrases that contain a helping verb and a main verb in the following literature passage. Remember that a word or group of words might separate a helping verb and main verb.

Jed looked at him. Joseph Sabael had always been a tall man, but never one whose frame put on bulk. His shoulders had been broad, but not heavy. His arms had always been long and sinewy like the others in the town who worked the land or the big woods, not the ham-thick sort of arm which turned to softness with age. Like an ash tree's limbs, that was how his grandfather's arms had seemed. But now there was a different look to the old man. His eyes had fallen back into their sockets and one could see the bones beneath the skin in his arms. As he sat hands clasping the blanket about him, it seemed as if his shoulders were folding in around his chest.

Literature
MODEL

from "Jed's Grandfather"
Joseph Bruchac

EXERCISE 9

Understanding Helping Verbs

Complete the following sentences by adding one or more helping verbs that fit the meaning. Then identify the complete verb phrase.

EXAMPLE

Those three convicts _____ always found a way to escape from their cells. *(have, have found)*

1. Our neighbor _____ spotted a rare bird flying in this area.
2. The soldiers _____ stationed at a base in Germany.
3. Frankie _____ _____ joined us when he had the chance.
4. Before driving to work in the morning, Father _____ try to complete a crossword puzzle.
5. I _____ hoping to finish my work in time to watch the start of the game.
6. Hanna is not a good fielder yet, but she _____ try to stay in front of the ball.
7. The incident down by the lake _____ frequently recounted by the townspeople.
8. The fish in this lake _____ _____ biting all afternoon.
9. Your cousins _____ _____ attending the party next month.
10. A police officer _____ directed traffic at the intersection all day.

EXERCISE 10

Using Helping Verbs in Your Writing

Write a paragraph for a history teacher in which you describe a current event that you've been following in the news. Use at least five different helping verbs in your paragraph.

TRANSITIVE AND INTRANSITIVE VERBS

An action verb that has a direct object is called a **transitive verb.** An action verb that does not have a direct object is called an **intransitive verb.**

USAGE tip

Don't confuse a direct object with an object of a preposition. A direct object never appears in a prepositional phrase.

direct object of a verb
Karl **shoveled** the **dirt** into the hole.
object of a preposition
Karl **shoveled** the dirt *into the* **hole**.

EXAMPLES

transitive verb	Jeff **put** the **trophy** on the shelf. (The trophy receives the action, therefore it is the direct object of the transitive verb *put*.)
intransitive verb	The shiny trophy **gleamed** under the light. (There is no direct object, therefore *gleamed* is an intransitive verb.)

Try It Yourself

EXERCISE 11

Identifying Transitive and Intransitive Verbs in Literature
Identify the underlined verbs in the following literature passage as either transitive or intransitive. If a verb is transitive, identify its direct object.

Literature MODEL

> I <u>opened</u> the window, the hummingbird <u>stirred</u> about here and there, feeling the cold from the outside, <u>suspended</u> itself in the area of the open window, stirring this way and that, and then it was gone.
> "<u>Close</u> the window," the old man <u>said</u>.
> We <u>talked</u> a minute or two and then I <u>went</u> home.
> The old man <u>claimed</u> the hummingbird lived through that winter, but I never <u>knew</u> for sure. I <u>saw</u> hummingbirds again when the summer came, but I couldn't tell one from the other.
>
> from "The Hummingbird That Lived through Winter"
> William Saroyan

Understanding Transitive and Intransitive Verbs
Write a sentence using the transitive or intransitive verb indicated. Underline the verb. If the verb is transitive, then underline its direct object as well.

EXAMPLES
lifted (transitive)   *(His brother <u>lifted</u> the <u>hood</u> to look at the engine.)*

talks (intransitive)   *(Bob <u>talks</u> too much in class.)*

1. took (intransitive)
2. believe (transitive)
3. started (intransitive)
4. is humming (intransitive)
5. leaves (transitive)
6. bought (transitive)
7. hear (transitive)
8. cooked (intransitive)
9. close (transitive)
10. had lost (transitive)

Using Transitive and Intransitive Verbs in Your Writing
Write a descriptive paragraph to a pen pal about a form of transportation you have taken at least once during the past week. Use at least three transitive verbs and three intransitive verbs in your paragraph.

VERB TENSES
The Simple Tenses

Verbs have different forms, called **tenses**, which are used to tell the time in which an action takes place. In your writing and speaking, you most commonly use the simple tenses. The **simple tenses** of the verb are **present, past,** and **future.**

The **present tense** tells that an action happens now—in the present time.

EXAMPLES	
present tense singular	The green frog **jumps** into the pond.
present tense plural	The green frogs **jump** into the pond.
present tense singular	The teacher **walks** down the hall.
present tense plural	The teachers **walk** down the hall.

The **past tense** tells that an action happened in the past—prior to the present time. The past tense of a regular verb is formed by adding *–d* or *–ed* to the present verb form.

EXAMPLES	
past tense singular	The green frog **jumped** into the pond.
past tense plural	The green frogs **jumped** into the pond.
past tense singular	The teacher **walked** down the hall.
past tense plural	The teachers **walked** down the hall.

The **future tense** tells that an action will happen in the future. The future tense is formed by adding the word *will* or *shall* before the present verb form.

EXAMPLES	
future tense singular	The green frog **will jump** into the pond.
future tense plural	The green frogs **will jump** into the pond.
future tense singular	The teacher **shall walk** down the hall.
future tense plural	The teachers **shall walk** down the hall.

The Perfect Tenses

The **perfect tenses** of verbs also express present, past, and future time, but they show that the action continued and was completed over a period of time or that the action will be completed in the present or future. The perfect tense is formed by using *have*, *has*, or *had* with the past participle.

EXAMPLES

present perfect singular	Vera **has baked** the birthday cake.
	The birthday cake **has been baked** by Vera.
present perfect plural	Vera and Hans **have baked** the birthday cake. (*have* or *has* + past participle)
past perfect singular	Vera **had baked** the birthday cake.
	The birthday cake **had been baked** by Vera.
past perfect plural	Vera and Hans **had baked** the birthday cake. (*had* + past participle)
future perfect singular	Vera **will have baked** the birthday cake.
	The birthday cake **will have been baked** by Vera.
future perfect plural	Vera and Hans **will have baked** the birthday cake. (*will have* or *shall have* + past participle)

Try It Yourself

EXERCISE 14

Identifying Verb Tenses in Literature
Identify the tenses of the underlined verbs in the following literature passage.

A similar apparition <u>lies</u> just beneath the ocean. While scuba diving in the Caribbean, I <u>have seen</u> and touched the white bones of a dead coral reef. All over the earth, coral reefs have suddenly started to "bleach" as warmer ocean temperatures <u>put</u> unaccustomed stress on the tiny organisms that normally <u>live</u> in the skin of the coral and <u>give</u> the reef its natural coloration. As these organisms— nicknamed "zooks"—<u>leave</u> the membrane of the coral, the coral itself becomes transparent, allowing its white limestone skeleton to shine through…. In the last few years, scientists <u>have been shocked</u> at the sudden occurrence of extensive worldwide bleaching episodes from which increasing numbers of coral reefs <u>have failed</u> to recover.

from "Ships in the Desert"
Al Gore

Literature
M O D E L

EXERCISE 15
Understanding Verb Tenses
Complete each of the following sentences with the form of the verb given in parentheses.

EXAMPLE
A cake baked by my grandmother usually (present of *have*) a pleasant taste. (A cake baked by my grandmother usually *has* a pleasant taste.)

1. Thomas (past of *hope*) that the show would be over by ten o'clock tonight.
2. Jenny (present of *recite*) a poem to the class each day.
3. The bear (past perfect of *hibernate*) for the past several months.
4. Tomorrow at this time, we (future of *be*) in New Orleans.
5. When we return from our trip, do you think that Joe (future perfect of *decide*) what to do with his money?
6. I wonder if Greg (future of *work*) for this firm again.
7. With little trouble, Mickey (present of *deceive*) the goalie.

8. Kelly (present perfect of *fix*) the bicycle petal.
9. By the time they know who did it, Garret (future perfect of *disappear*).
10. While preparing to make a move, Roger noticed that the flag on his clock (past perfect of *drop*).

E X E R C I S E   1 6
Using Verb Tenses Correctly in Your Writing
Imagine that you are an explorer who has been searching for a lost treasure in the mountains for several months. Write a paragraph to a fellow explorer in which you describe a sequence of events that leads finally to your discovery of the treasure. Include at least one example of each of the six verb tenses: present, past, future, present perfect, past perfect, and future perfect.

PASSIVE VOICE AND ACTIVE VOICE

Did you know that verbs have voices? The **voice** of an action verb tells whether the subject of the sentence performs or receives the action. When the subject performs the action of the verb, the verb is in the **active voice**. When the subject receives the action of the verb, the verb is in the **passive voice**.

USAGE tip
A sentence written in the passive voice uses some form of *be* as a helping verb.

EXAMPLES
active voice   Professor Higginbotham **read** a passage from the textbook.
passive voice   He **was found** studying in the library.

The active voice is used more frequently than the passive voice. Active verbs express your ideas more directly. The passive voice is usually used when the receiver of the action is emphasized or the performer of the action is unknown or indefinite. In the following example sentence, the persons who notice the new painting on the wall are indefinite.

> **EXAMPLE**
> The new painting on the museum **is noticed** at the gala event.

A sentence written in the passive voice can usually be revised to the active voice.

> **EXAMPLES**
> **passive voice**   Three of Sally's short stories **were written** last summer.
> **active voice**   Sally **wrote** three short stories last summer.

Try It Yourself

EXERCISE 17
Identifying Passive and Active Verbs
Identify the underlined verbs as either active or passive.

1. Andrew <u>was imprisoned</u> for income tax evasion.
2. Their grandfather <u>drives</u> a bright red pickup truck.
3. Kim <u>bought</u> food and beverages for the publications meeting.
4. The captain <u>joins</u> his crew on the deck.
5. An annoying bee <u>flew</u> in through the open window.
6. I <u>have been called</u> about that noise three times today.
7. He <u>has been praised</u> for his unique portrayal of modern life.
8. A family of raccoons <u>cross</u> the stream.
9. That house on the hill <u>is believed</u> to be haunted.
10. Last Monday Laura <u>started</u> her marathon training.

EXERCISE 18
Understanding Passive and Active Verbs
Revise the following sentences so the verbs are in the active voice.

EXAMPLE

passive verb Writing courses *are* sometimes *taught* by famous authors.

active verb Famous authors sometimes *teach* writing courses.

1. Joey was lectured by his parents about keeping his cat off of the furniture.
2. Whiskers, his cat, is petted by Grandmother during the lecture.
3. Mother and Father were concerned about Whiskers's claws.
4. Joey was reassured by Grandmother that the cat would behave.
5. Whiskers was taken outside by Joey after the conversations ended.
6. The cat was fed by Joey later in the day.
7. Whiskers was talked to by the neighbor's cat after he finished eating.
8. Joey was surprised by the felines' conversation, since he thought that cats could not talk.
9. The boy was watched by the cats as he stared in disbelief.
10. Joey was told by Whiskers, "Of course we can talk, but let's keep this our little secret."

E X E R C I S E   1 9

Using Passive and Active Verbs in Your Writing

For classmates, write a description of a funny turn of events that you either took part in or witnessed. Use at least three passive verbs and three active verbs to describe this event.

IRREGULAR VERBS

As you know, verb forms change to show when an action happened. The many forms of the verb are based on its three principal parts: the present, the past, and the past participle. For all regular verbs, *–d* or *–ed* are added to form the past and the past participle.

EXAMPLES		
present	walk	scratch
past	walked	scratched
past participle	(has, have) walked	(has, have) scratched

Some regular verbs change their spelling when *–d* or *–ed* is added. (See Unit 17 Spelling, pages 392–402.)

EXAMPLES		
present	carry	nap
past	carried	napped
past participle	(has, have) carried	(has, have) napped

Verbs that do not follow the regular pattern of adding *–d* or *–ed* are called **irregular verbs**. Some of these irregular verbs have the same spelling for their past and past participle forms. Some have the same spelling in all three principal forms. Other irregular verbs have three different forms.

EXAMPLES			
present	fight	knit	take
past	fought	knit	took
past participle	(has, have) fought	(has, have) knit	(has, have) taken

When you're not sure whether a verb is regular or irregular, look up the verb in a dictionary. Many of the common irregular verbs are listed in the following chart.

Pattern	Present	Past	Past Participle
Three different forms	begin	began	(has, have) begun
	drink	drank	(has, have) drunk
	grow	grew	(has, have) grown
	know	knew	(has, have) known
	ring	rang	(has, have) rung
	shrink	shrank or shrunk	(has, have) shrunk
	sing	sang	(has, have) sung
	spring	sprang or sprung	(has, have) sprung
	swim	swam	(has, have) swum
	throw	threw	(has, have) thrown
	write	wrote	(has, have) written
Same past and past participle form	bring	brought	(has, have) brought
	buy	bought	(has, have) bought
	catch	caught	(has, have) caught
	creep	crept	(has, have) crept
	feel	felt	(has, have) felt
	get	got	(has, have) got/gotten
	keep	kept	(has, have) kept
	lay	laid	(has, have) laid
	lead	led	(has, have) led
	leave	left	(has, have) left
	lend	lent	(has, have) lent
	lose	lost	(has, have) lost
	make	made	(has, have) made
	pay	paid	(has, have) paid
	say	said	(has, have) said
	seek	sought	(has, have) sought
	sell	sold	(has, have) sold
	sit	sat	(has, have) sat
	sleep	slept	(has, have) slept
	swing	swung	(has, have) swung
	teach	taught	(has, have) taught
	think	thought	(has, have) thought
	win	won	(has, have) won

EXERCISE 20
Identifying Regular and Irregular Verbs in Literature
Identify each of the underlined verbs as either regular or irregular.

That night, Zebra <u>lay</u> in bed looking at his hand. It was a dread and a mystery to him, his own hand. The fingers were all there, but like dead leaves that never <u>fell</u>, the ring and little fingers were rigid and curled, the others barely <u>moved</u>. The doctors <u>said</u> it would take time to <u>bring</u> them back to life. So many broken bones. So many torn muscles and tendons. So many injured nerves. The dark shadow had <u>sprung</u> upon him so suddenly.

from "Zebra"
Chaim Potok

Literature
M O D E L

EXERCISE 21
Understanding Irregular Verbs
Write the correct past or past participle form of the irregular verb given in parentheses.

EXAMPLE
The cheerful goldfinch has (sing) in the tree all morning. *(sung)*

1. She has (buy) a toy for her best friend's child.
2. Julia has (make) a mobile at school today.
3. It is too bad that our team has not (hit) well during this series.
4. I have (seek) that ring of power for over three centuries.
5. Darryl has (sweep) the dusty front porch.
6. The tiger has (creep) quietly in the bushes behind the hunters.
7. The computer listed for sale in the paper has been (sell).
8. Winifred has (take) the figurine from off the shelf.
9. Vincent has (pay) the man with gold coins.
10. What he has (say) will never be forgotten.

EXERCISE 22

Using Irregular Verbs in Your Writing

Choose an occupation that you think might be interesting to have. Pretend that you are employed in this particular occupation. Write a paragraph to a friend describing what you think a typical morning would be like for you in this job. Use at least five irregular verbs in the past and past participle forms in your paragraph.

UNIT 6 REVIEW

TEST YOUR KNOWLEDGE

EXERCISE 1
Identifying Verbs
Identify each of the underlined verbs in the following sentences as either an action, state of being, linking, or helping verb. (10 points)

EXAMPLE
Since it had rained for three days, the water barrel <u>was</u> full.
(linking verb)

1. Her father <u>had</u> served on the council before being elected mayor.
2. This outbreak of criminal activity <u>frustrates</u> the sheriff.
3. After working ten hours today, Sheryl <u>appears</u> tired.
4. I <u>was</u> on the roof when the alarm went off.
5. The children <u>smelled</u> the cookies baking in the oven.
6. My mule <u>grows</u> weary after a long day of walking.
7. You <u>have been</u> spotted out on the golf course several times this week.
8. They <u>were</u> a great team back in the 1970s.
9. After arriving, the colonel <u>looks</u> across the battlefield.
10. Your acoustic guitar <u>sounds</u> mellow.

EXERCISE 2
Identifying Transitive and Intransitive Verbs
Identify the verb in each of the following sentences. Tell whether the verb is transitive or intransitive. If a verb is transitive, identify its direct object. (20 points)

EXAMPLE
The runners all drank water after the race.
(*drank,* verb, transitive; *water,* direct object)

1. Erin's dog begs her for a treat.
2. Her mother drove quickly to the school.
3. Karen works at a nearby hospital.
4. My friends shot clay pigeons at the range.
5. He reads the newspaper each day before breakfast.
6. She always sends cards for her friends' birthdays.
7. Ben usually sleeps during the day.
8. Our new dog runs swiftly around the yard.
9. In the evening Jeremy looks at the sunset.
10. Yesterday, she sang songs with her children.

EXERCISE 3
Identifying Verb Tenses
Identify the tense of each of the underlined verbs as present, past, future, present perfect, past perfect, or future perfect. (10 points)

EXAMPLE
Tomorrow's rain <u>will wash</u> the dirt off my car. (future)

1. Legions of soldiers <u>march</u> toward the castle.
2. One of the players <u>has registered</u> for the draft.
3. Every one of the buses <u>will have departed</u> by 10:00 P.M.
4. We <u>had decided</u> to pursue an alternative plan.
5. The city <u>will fall</u> once the catapults are put into action.
6. Elle's dogs <u>have barked</u> each time the mail carrier walks by.
7. A computer <u>calculates</u> your interest in a matter of seconds.
8. She <u>salted</u> the French fries before she ate them.
9. Unfortunately, we <u>had been warned</u> by that same officer once before.
10. I <u>shall</u> gloriously <u>win</u> the marathon later this month.

EXERCISE 4
Understanding Verbs
Complete each of the following sentences using in the predicate the type of verb indicated in parentheses. (20 points)

The noble eagle (action verb)
(The noble eagle *soared high above the earth.*)

1. The falcon's sharp talons (action verb)
2. A lone wolf (linking verb)
3. My brother's ferret (helping verb)
4. The snowman (intransitive verb)
5. A fat shark (linking verb)
6. I (action verb)
7. An employee from the factory (transitive verb)
8. The snake's scales (linking verb)
9. Sadly, the governor (state of being verb)
10. We (helping verb)

E X E R C I S E 5
Understanding Verb Tenses
Complete each of the following sentences with the form of the verb given in parentheses. (10 points)

EXAMPLE
Happily, the lost dog (past perfect of *found*) its way home.
(Happily, the lost dog *had found* its way home.)

1. Someday you (future of *see*) the foolishness of your decision.
2. The bear (present of *eat*) whatever is in her path.
3. Next week they (future of *think*) differently about not studying before a test.
4. Every month, Dave (present perfect of *be*) late to the vice-president's meeting.
5. In a three-month period of time, Charles (past perfect of *fly*) to six continents.
6. Hanson (past of *take*) two sandwiches from the buffet line.
7. We (past of *talk*) a lot to each other in class last year.
8. By the time you return home, your wife (future perfect of *throw*) your clothes out on the lawn.

9. After six innings, he (present perfect of *pitch*) a brilliant game so far.
10. Serving in the Navy (past of *give*) Tim an affinity for the ocean.

EXERCISE 6
Understanding Passive Voice and Active Voice
Revise the following paragraph, changing any passive verbs to active verbs. (10 points)

The two bank robbers were spotted by Jack, a traveling salesman. Jack was questioned by the police about the robbers' descriptions. He had been asked to look at several pictures of wanted criminals. Jack was made uneasy by all the attention he received. Finally, Jack is told by an officer that the robbers have been captured by the police.

EXERCISE 7
Using Irregular Verbs in Your Writing
Write a paragraph for a parent or guardian describing your activities during a typical day at school. Use the present, past, and past participle forms of each of the following irregular verbs in your paragraph: write, sit, teach, know, and leave. (20 points)

UNIT 7 SENTENCE COMPLETERS
Complements

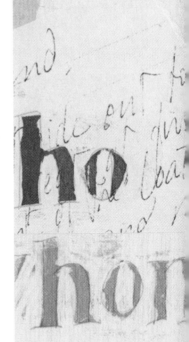

UNIT OVERVIEW

SENTENCE COMPLETERS: COMPLEMENTS

COMPLETERS FOR ACTION VERBS

A sentence must have a subject and a verb to communicate its basic meaning. In the following sentences, the subject and verb express the total concept. There is no receiver of the verb's action.

> EXAMPLES
> We talked.
> I never lose.
> The tree fell.

Many sentences that include action verbs, however, need an additional word or group of words to complete the meaning.

> EXAMPLES
> The soldiers climbed.
> The soldiers climbed the wall.

The group of words *The soldiers climbed* contains a subject (*soldiers*) and a verb (*climbed*). Although the group of words may be considered a sentence, it does not express a complete thought. A word is needed to tell what the soldiers climbed, such as *The soldiers climbed the wall*. The word *wall* completes the meaning expressed by the verb *climbed*. Therefore, *wall* is called a **complement** or a completing word. The **completers** for action verbs are **direct objects** and **indirect objects.**

Direct Objects

A **direct object** receives the action in the sentence. It usually answers the question *what?* or *whom?* To find the direct object, find the action verb in the sentence. Then ask *what?* or *whom?* about the verb.

EXAMPLES

I **found** a **coin** in the pond. (*Found* is the action verb. What did I find? *Coin* is the direct object.)

The dog **jumped** the **fence**. (*Jumped* is the action verb. What did the dog jump? *Fence* is the direct object.)

Remember to use object pronouns for a direct object.

singular	me, you, him, her, it
plural	us, you, them

EXAMPLES

Betty told **us** to drive west.
Evan questioned **him** about the wallet.

USAGE tip

A direct object is usually a noun or a pronoun. It is never an adjective or an adverb. It is never in a prepositional phrase.

Try It Yourself

EXERCISE 1
Identifying Completers for Action Verbs: Direct Objects

Write the direct object in each of the following sentences. If the sentence does not contain a direct object, write *none*.

1. The professor tapped the microphone before starting her talk.
2. She stepped over the cords on the stage.
3. Teachers encouraged students to attend the lecture.
4. Students brought their notebooks to the hall.
5. The professor provided a long discussion about Great Plains history.
6. She presented many interesting facts to think about.
7. Both of my classmates took notes at the lecture.
8. Teachers discuss policy before returning to class.
9. We smelled the cake sitting on the table in the lobby.
10. Three rabbits ran into their hole outside the lecture hall.

EXERCISE 2

Understanding Completers for Action Verbs: Direct Objects

Supply a direct object to complete each of the following sentences. You may need to provide a group of words so that the sentence makes sense.

1. After entering the room, I spotted ___.
2. Can you believe ___?
3. Allison sent her friends several ___ for Christmas.
4. Snow covered the ___.
5. A hailstorm pelted our ___.
6. Ants invaded the ___.
7. Did you turn off the ___ last night?
8. The pig eats ___ and ___ each evening.
9. Candace recorded a ___ of beautiful songs.
10. The professor gave me a ___.

EXERCISE 3

Using Direct Objects in Your Writing

Think about a public figure who interests you. Write a paragraph describing why you want to write a book about this person. Explain how you find the public figure to be interesting or important. Use at least five direct objects in your proposal.

Indirect Objects

Sometimes someone or something receives the direct object. This receiver is called the **indirect object**. It comes before the direct object and tells *to whom* the action is directed or *for whom* the action is performed. Only verbs that have direct objects can have indirect objects.

> **EXAMPLE**
> Seth **sold** Karl a **car.** (*Sold* is the action verb. *Car* is the direct object because it tells what Seth sold. *Karl* is an indirect object. It tells to whom Seth sold a car.)

There are two tests that you can use to identify the indirect object: (1) Look for a noun or pronoun that precedes the direct object. (2) Determine whether the word you think is an indirect object seems to be the understood object of the preposition *to* or *for.*

> **USAGE** tip
>
> An indirect object is used after certain verbs, such as *get, give, lend, offer, read, tell, buy, send, show, make,* and *pay.*

> **EXAMPLE**
> The teacher **gave** the **student** a pencil. (The noun *pencil* answers the question *What did the teacher give?* so it is the direct object. The understood preposition *to* can be inserted into the sentence before the noun *student: The teacher gave (to) the student a pencil.* Therefore, *student* is the indirect object of the sentence.)

Do not confuse direct and indirect objects with objects of prepositions. For example, the words *to* and *for* are prepositions. If the word order of the above sentence was changed to include the preposition *to,* then the sentence would read this way: *The teacher gave a pencil to the student.* In this new sentence, the word *student* is the object of the preposition *to;* it is not the indirect object.

Remember to use object pronouns for indirect objects.

singular	me, you, him, her, it
plural	us, you, them

> **EXAMPLES**
> Your sister sent **me** an invitation to the party.
> Read **her** a story before bedtime.

Try It Yourself

EXERCISE 4

Identifying Completers for Action Verbs: Indirect Objects
Write the indirect object in each of the following sentences. If the sentence does not contain an indirect object, write *none*.

1. Casey hopes to sell Grandpa a box of cookies.
2. The camp provided young athletes a chance to improve their skills.
3. The inmates fled to the cave up in the mountains.
4. Iowa farmers plant their crops in the spring.
5. Sam lent his brother the money to buy the house.
6. She told listeners a story about Abraham Lincoln.
7. My uncle bought me a collection of Mark Twain's books.
8. The upcoming history test gave me many fears.
9. The bald eagle flew over the canyon.
10. I gave the king all of my gold.

EXERCISE 5

Understanding Completers for Action Verbs: Indirect and Direct Objects
Supply an indirect and direct object to complete each of the following sentences. You may need to provide more than one word for the sentence to make sense.

1. Joel paid the ___ a large ___.
2. Bill sent ___ a ___.
3. Sandi gave ___ his ___.
4. The banker lent ___ the ___ to buy the car.
5. Our official web page provides ____ the ___ to learn about the city.
6. I offered ___ ___ in studying for the exam.
7. A real estate agent showed ___ ___ of houses I might like.
8. He bought ___ a beautiful ___.
9. The storm sent ___ an unwelcome ___.
10. After much discussion, she read her ___ several ___.

EXERCISE 6
Using Indirect Objects in Your Writing

Assume that you keep a diary. Write a paragraph describing an activity that you took part in with your friends. Include who participated and some interesting highlights from the activity. Use at least five indirect objects in your paragraph.

COMPLETERS FOR LINKING VERBS

A **linking verb** connects a subject with a noun, pronoun, or adjective that describes or identifies it. Linking verbs do not express action. Instead, they express state of being and need a noun, pronoun, or adjective to complete the sentence meaning. In each of the following sentences, the subject and verb by themselves would not be complete without the words that follow them.

> EXAMPLES
> Jack **is** the head coach.
> He **looked** upset and disturbed.

Most linking verbs are forms of the verb *to be*, including *am, are, is, was,* and *been.* Other words that can be used as linking verbs include *appear, feel, grow, smell, taste, seem, sound, look, stay, feel, remain,* and *become.* When *to be* verbs are part of an action verb, they are helpers.

Predicate Nouns and Predicate Pronouns

A **predicate noun** is a noun that completes a sentence that uses a form of the verb *to be.* Similarly, a **predicate pronoun** is a pronoun that completes a sentence that uses a form of the verb *to be.* In fact, the relationship between the subject and the predicate noun or pronoun is so close that the sentence usually suggests an equation. Such sentences can often be reordered without changing the meaning.

USAGE tip

> Some verbs can be linking or action verbs, depending on their meaning. *Grow, look, feel, sound, smell, taste, appear, remain,* and *stay* can be both. By mentally supplying the verb *to be* after the verb, you tell whether it has a linking or action function. *The plant grew (to be) tall. The apple tasted better than before.*

EXAMPLES
predicate noun
Francine is the first girl to solve the puzzle. (Francine = girl)
The first girl to solve the puzzle is Francine. (girl = Francine)

predicate pronoun
That noise outside could have been made by anything. (noise = anything)

Anything could have made that noise outside. (Anything = noise)

To find a predicate noun or pronoun, ask the same question you would ask to find a direct object.

EXAMPLES
Our car is a sedan. (Our car is a what? *Sedan* is the predicate noun that renames or identifies *car*, the subject of the sentence.)

The villain is probably he. (The villain is probably who? *He* is the predicate pronoun that renames or identifies villain, the subject of the sentence.)

Remember to use subject pronouns after linking verbs.

singular	I, you, he, she, it
plural	we, you, they

EXAMPLES
The top scorer was I. (Think: I was the top scorer.)

The last-place finishers were Tom and Tony. (Think: Tom and Tony were the last-place finishers.)

Predicate Adjectives

A **predicate adjective** completes a sentence by modifying, or describing, the subject of a sentence. To find a predicate adjective, ask the same question you would ask to find a direct object.

EXAMPLE
The wind is cold. (The wind is what? *Cold* is the predicate adjective that describes *wind,* the subject of the sentence.)

Try It Yourself

EXERCISE 7
Identifying Predicate Nouns and Predicate Adjectives in Literature
First read the following passage. Then identify the underlined words as predicate nouns or predicate adjectives.

My sister and I were <u>lucky</u>. We enjoyed singing and dancing, we were natural <u>hams</u>, and our parents never discouraged us. In fact, they were our biggest <u>fans</u>. My mother chauffeured us to all our dance lessons, lessons we begged to take. She drove us to interviews, took us to studios, went on location with us, drilled us on our lines, made sure we kept up our schoolwork and didn't sass back the tutors hired by studios to teach us for three hours a day. She never complained about being a <u>stage mother</u>. She said that we made her <u>proud.</u>

from "Hollywood and the Pits"
Cherylene Lee

Literature
MODEL

EXERCISE 8
Identifying Completers for Linking Verbs: Predicate Nouns, Predicate Pronouns, and Predicate Adjectives
Write the predicate nouns, predicate pronouns, or predicate adjectives in each of the following sentences. If a sentence does not contain a predicate noun, predicate pronoun, or a predicate adjective, write *none.*

1. Pizza is popular with children and adults.
2. It is a tasty treat at almost any time of the day.
3. Many pizza-lovers say that it is good for you.
4. Pizza is often called a pie because of its shape.

5. It is a big seller at restaurants in college towns.
6. Pizza can be hot or cold.
7. Italy is the birthplace of pizza.
8. Pizza is often the food of choice for sports fans.
9. The friend who bought me a pizza yesterday was he.
10. Pizza tastes cheesy and meaty at the same time.

EXERCISE 9

Understanding Completers for Linking Verbs: Predicate Nouns, Predicate Pronouns, and Predicate Adjectives
Complete each of the following sentences with a predicate noun, predicate pronoun, or predicate adjective. You may add a word or a group of words to help the sentence make sense. Identify your addition to the sentence as a predicate noun, predicate pronoun, or predicate adjective.

1. The song sounds _____.
2. The squirrels in the yard are often _____.
3. The assignment for math class could be _____.
4. That pasta sauce you are cooking smells _____.
5. The agency's primary means of support is _____.
6. Could he be the new _____ ?
7. By the afternoon, I grew _____.
8. Your house is _____.
9. The smartest delegates are _____.
10. Those ancient artifacts seemed _____.

EXERCISE 10

Using Predicate Nouns, Predicate Pronouns, and Predicate Adjectives in Your Writing
Write a paragraph to be shared with classmates about one of your favorite television shows. Describe the show's setting, characters, and storyline. Complete some of your sentences with predicate nouns, predicate pronouns, and predicate adjectives to help your readers understand why the show is one of your favorites.

UNIT 7 REVIEW

TEST YOUR KNOWLEDGE

EXERCISE 1
Identifying Direct and Indirect Objects

Identify the direct and indirect objects in the following sentences. If a sentence does not have a direct or indirect object, write *none*. (10 points)

EXAMPLE
The coach passed the basketball to the new guard. (*basketball*, direct object)

1. The new guard brought hope to his school's fans.
2. The team's losing streak caused attendance at the games to drop.
3. The athlete's jump shot is unbelievable!
4. His dribbling skills inspired the coach to put him in the starting lineup.
5. The guard's scoring brought his team an opening day victory.
6. Most sportswriters gave him total credit for the win.
7. Television coverage of the game showcased his talents to fans across the state.
8. When the player appears, the fans stand and cheer.
9. Many people are already making plans to attend the championship tournament.
10. We all felt great happiness at having a winning basketball team again.

EXERCISE 2
Identifying Predicate Nouns, Predicate Pronouns, and Predicate Adjectives

Identify the predicate nouns, predicate pronouns, and predicate adjectives in the following sentences. If there are no predicate nouns, predicate pronouns, or predicate adjectives in the sentence, write *none*. (10 points)

EXAMPLE

Chess is a game that uses many different pieces. (*game,* predicate noun)

1. The deep thought that chess requires is appealing to many.
2. You might have seen chess matches being played at your school.
3. Chess players are often very focused.
4. Gary Kasparov, the former world champion, is brilliant and cool under pressure.
5. The Russians often win the top prizes at international tournaments.
6. The complexity of chess makes it popular with many intellectuals.
7. Today, the game is a favorite activity on the Internet.
8. Many games played online are intense and competitive.
9. Chess can be addictive for its enthusiasts.
10. Many people do not know how to play the game, but more learn each day.

EXERCISE 3

Identifying Sentence Completers: Complements

Identify the direct and indirect objects, predicate nouns, predicate pronouns, and predicate adjectives in the following sentences. (20 points)

EXAMPLE

In 1903, the Wright brothers flew an airplane for the first time. (*airplane,* direct object)

1. Charles Lindbergh saw his first airplane at the age of seven or eight.
2. As a boy, he loved the outdoors and science.
3. His grandfather's laboratory provided Charles a fascinating education.
4. By age twenty-one, Lindbergh was a flyer in the U.S. Army and a pilot on a mail route.
5. A New York hotel owner gave Lindbergh motivation to fly across the Atlantic.

6. An aircraft company built the *Spirit of St. Louis,* Lindbergh's airplane.
7. The trans-Atlantic flight was dangerous and risky, since the distance was very long.
8. Lindbergh was courageous and brave, and became a national hero.
9. Thousands of fans were impressed, and Lindbergh gave crowds across the nation many speeches about his flight.
10. The *Spirit of St. Louis* was a special airplane that carried the hopes of a nation in 1927.

EXERCISE 4
Correcting Pronouns Used in Complements
Correct pronoun errors made in the following sentences. If there are no errors, write *correct*. (10 points)

EXAMPLE
The boss gave he an evaluation today. (The boss gave *him* an evaluation today.)

1. Stress provided he and her the chance to grow closer
2. He and I will drive into town tomorrow.
3. The officer asked she to get out of the car.
4. Can you help we figure out the combination?
5. Give I all of your money.
6. One of the most popular girls in class is her.
7. Do you believe it was they who found the gold?
8. The professor sent we a letter outlining the assignment.
9. Give I a chance and you won't be disappointed.
10. A bear followed us down the mountain.

EXERCISE 5
Understanding Indirect Objects
Choose ten of the following verbs and write a sentence for each that contains both a direct and an indirect object. You may change the tense of the verb. Identify the direct and indirect object in each sentence. (10 points)

EXAMPLE

give   *The mysterious elf gave Jason the magic cookie of invisibility.*
        (cookie, direct object; *Jason,* indirect object)

award	promise	save	take	get	present
lend	offer	read	tell	buy	send
show	make	pay	provide	ask	bought

EXERCISE 6

Using Complements in Your Writing

Write a sentence for each of the following kinds of complements. Underline the complement in each sentence that you write. (20 points)

EXAMPLE
Compound predicate adjective
(*The electric blanket was* <u>warm and toasty</u>.)

1. direct object
2. indirect object
3. predicate noun
4. predicate adjective
5. predicate pronoun
6. pronoun as a direct object
7. compound predicate noun
8. compound indirect object
9. pronoun as an indirect object
10. compound predicate adjective

EXERCISE 7

Using Predicate Nouns and Predicate Adjectives in Your Writing

Write a description of a person who is inspiring to you, to be shared with classmates. For example, you might describe a parent or sibling, a governmental leader, or a favorite author. Use metaphors in your description to help your readers understand the inspiring qualities of this person. Use at least five predicate nouns and predicate adjectives to enhance your description. (20 points)

UNIT *8* SUBJECT-VERB AGREEMENT AND USAGE

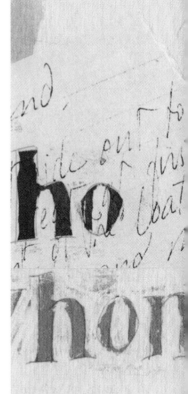

UNIT OVERVIEW

SUBJECT-VERB AGREEMENT AND USAGE

SUBJECT AND VERB AGREEMENT

A **singular** noun describes or stands for *one* person, place, thing, or idea. A **plural noun** describes or stands for *more than one* person, place, thing, or idea.

EXAMPLES					
singular nouns	book	apple	rose	mouse	child
plural nouns	books	apples	roses	mice	children

In a sentence, a verb must be singular if its subject is singular and plural if its subject is plural. In other words, a verb must agree in number with its subject.

EXAMPLES	
singular subject and verb	The **apple seems** ripe.
plural subject and verb	The **apples seem** ripe.
singular subject and verb	A **rose smells** lovely in the evening.
plural subject and verb	The **roses smell** lovely in the evening.
singular subject and verb	A **mouse runs** across the room.
plural subject and verb	The **mice run** across the room.

USAGE tip

When a phrase or clause separates a subject and verb, mentally delete or cover up the phrase or clause so that you can more easily identify subject-verb agreement.

Usually a verb directly follows the subject in a sentence. Sometimes, however, a prepositional phrase or a clause will separate the subject and verb. Even though the subject and verb may be separated, they must still agree in number.

EXAMPLES
The **apple** on the counter **seems** ripe.
The **apples**, which are red, **seem** ripe.

EXERCISE 1
Identifying Subject-Verb Agreement in Literature
Read the following passage. Identify the underlined subjects as either singular or plural. Then identify the subject's verb. Note how the verb agrees in number with its subject.

Like horses with their swerved necks,
I concentrate on grass.
<u>Earthworms</u> insert themselves into the earth
like glossy, pink pins!

Against the green, a yellow <u>shrub</u>
furiously sprouts
in a trance of burning stars.

<u>Branches</u> are suns
that glimmer from within
taking life
here, under the apple tree,
where a <u>crowd</u> of petals close their eyes,
where scraggly <u>layers</u> of trunk
seem to slowly come apart.

At sunset the <u>branch</u> I sit
on snaps and coils.
The <u>blue jay</u> hastily darts, and disappears.

from "Under the Apple Tree"
Diana Rivera

Literature
M O D E L

EXERCISE 2
Understanding Subject-Verb Agreement
Write the correct verb form in parentheses that agrees in number with the subject of the sentence.

1. Seven judges (selects, select) the winner.
2. Our coach (stomps, stomp) onto the court to yell at the referee.
3. One knight (battles, battle) the enemies of the throne.
4. Richard, a brilliant mathematician, often (lectures, lecture) at the university.
5. The famous teammates, Joe Montana and Jerry Rice, (is headed, are headed) for the Hall of Fame.
6. Her dogs (remains, remain) alert, looking for any intruders.
7. Mr. Morales (hates, hate) to see you leave the neighborhood.
8. A pair of lions (sits, sit) in the tall grass waiting for the zebras.
9. Three falcons (swoops, swoop) down upon the luckless rabbits.
10. Can you believe the principal (has contacted, have contacted) my parents?

EXERCISE 3

Correcting Subject-Verb Agreement

Read each of the following sentences. If the subject and verb in a sentence agree in number, write *correct*. If the subject and verb do not agree in number, correct the sentence.

1. A collection of different creatures crawls out of the hole.
2. Our cars needs to be washed today.
3. Tigers from the jungle rests quietly in the cage.
4. The Andes Mountains in South America is beautiful to visit.
5. The cause of this disaster remain undetermined.
6. Diverse groups of people settle in this state every year.
7. Her enemies is gathering around the fortress's perimeter.
8. As the driver of many cars, Jeff know how to shift gears.
9. We can reads the treaty for ourselves.
10. Our family look at the magazines at the store.

EXERCISE 4

Using Subject-Verb Agreement in Your Writing
Imagine that you could travel back or forward in time. What century would you like to visit? Write a paragraph describing a day spent in the century of your choice. Explain the sights, sounds, and activities. Make sure that each of your verbs agrees with its subject.

INDEFINITE PRONOUN AND VERB AGREEMENT

In Unit 5 you learned about different types of pronouns, including indefinite pronouns. An **indefinite pronoun** does not refer to a specific person, place, or thing. Some indefinite pronouns are always singular and take singular verbs: *anybody, anyone, anything, each, either, everybody, everyone, everything, much, neither, nobody, no one, nothing, one, somebody, someone, something.*

> EXAMPLES
> **singular**
> **Nobody** knows the size of the universe.
> **Something** occurs at noon every day.

Some indefinite pronouns are always plural and take plural verbs: *both, few, many, others, several.*

> EXAMPLES
> **plural**
> **Many** of our presidents **were** military officers.
> **Both understand** that this must never happen again.

Some indefinite pronouns can be either singular or plural, depending on their use in the sentence: *all, any, most, none, some.* They are singular when they refer to a portion or to a single person, place, or thing. They are plural when they refer to a number of individual persons, places, or things.

EXAMPLES

singular   **None** of the wall **requires** more paint.
plural   **None** of the teachers **sit** together.

Try It Yourself

EXERCISE 5

Identifying Correct Indefinite Pronoun-Verb Agreement
Complete each sentence by identifying the correct form of the verb in parentheses.

1. Most of the flowers (grows, grow) better in sunlight.
2. Many of the candidates (campaigns, campaign) on Sunday.
3. I found that all of the house (creaks, creak) at night.
4. One never (chooses, choose) to serve in the pit.
5. Nothing (resists, resist) scratches like Teflon.
6. Everything in this room (collects, collect) dust.
7. None (understands, understand) the directions to the town.
8. Most of the city (burns, burn) through the night.
9. Neither of the boys (is, are) going to play in the game.
10. Others in the class (has, have) finished the test already.

EXERCISE 6

Correcting Indefinite Pronoun-Verb Agreement
Write the verb form that agrees in number with the indefinite pronoun of each sentence. If a sentence contains no errors in indefinite pronoun-verb agreement, write *correct*.

1. All of the obstacles was removed from the track.
2. All hope rest on the shoulders of one brave guinea pig.
3. Several of the kangaroos in the park jumps over to see us.
4. Nothing in the garage smell like gasoline.
5. No one at the table suspect that I am the real culprit.
6. None of the buildings remains standing after the blast.
7. Both tacos is in the microwave oven.
8. Everything crumble if you reveal the secret to just one person.
9. Nothing you did changes our overall situation.
10. If either of the sisters win, the fans will be happy.

EXERCISE 7

Using Indefinite Pronoun-Verb Agreement in Your Writing

Write a paragraph to be shared with classmates in which you describe a suspenseful or exciting moment, such as the final minute of a basketball game. Use at least three different indefinite pronouns in your paragraph. Check your paragraph to make sure that the verbs agree in number with the indefinite pronouns.

COMPOUND SUBJECT AND VERB AGREEMENT

A **compound subject** consists of two or more subjects that share the same verb.

> EXAMPLE
> Frank and Wyatt ride horses in the corral. (The compound subject—*Frank and Wyatt*—shares the verb *ride*.)

A compound subject may have either a singular or a plural verb, depending on how the parts of the subject are connected.

Use a singular verb:
- when the compound subject is made up of singular nouns or pronouns connected by *either/or* or *neither/nor*.

> EXAMPLES
> **singular**
> Either Tom or Jesse **looks** like a good choice to start the game.
> Neither sword nor axe **prevents** me from finishing this quest.

Use a plural verb:
- when the compound subject is connected by the coordinating conjunction *and*.
- when the compound subject is formed from plural nouns or pronouns.

EXAMPLES
plural
Cars and trucks **park** in the field.

Either cats or dogs **provide** good companionship.

Neither the Americans nor the Russians **comprehend** the final treaty.

When a compound subject consists of a both singular subject and a plural subject connected by *or* or *nor*, use a verb that agrees in number with the subject closer to it in the sentence.

EXAMPLES
Either Kevin or his sisters **watch** the children in the park. (*sisters watch*—plural)

Neither the players nor their coach **endorses** the statement of the owner. (*coach endorses*—singular)

Try It Yourself

EXERCISE 8
Identifying Compound Subject-Verb Agreement
Identify the correct verb in parentheses to agree with the compound subject in each sentence.

1. A fire truck and a police car (races, race) to the accident.
2. Both the St. Louis Cardinals and the Chicago Cubs (is, are) hopeful for a pennant this year.
3. Sandi and Marie (works, work) hard on the project.
4. Neither lions nor tigers (enjoys, enjoy) captivity.
5. Neither the kittens nor their mother (eats, eat) much in the morning.
6. Either angels or devils (rules, rule) twists of fate.
7. Both Sara and Matt (understands, understand) the consequences of their behavior.

8. Either the dictionary or the encyclopedia (provides, provide) the answer.
9. Neither the chief nor the tribal members (is, are) amused at my joke.
10. Bob, Nancy, or Tim (appears, appear) at my door each day.

EXERCISE 9
Understanding Compound Subject-Verb Agreement
Write a sentence for each of the compound subjects and verbs listed below. Make sure that you use the correct verb form to agree with the compound subject.

1. Either wind or rain (prevents)
2. Sharks and dolphins (swims)
3. Neither the president nor the staff members (agrees)
4. Tom Clancy, Stephen King, and Toni Morrison (writes)
5. The planet and its moons (rotates)
6. Flies and grasshoppers (swarms)
7. Neither Amy nor Laura (talks)
8. Both fleas and ticks (causes)
9. Either the musicians or the conductor (receives)
10. Either mountains or forests (offers)

EXERCISE 10
Using Compound Subject-Verb Agreement in Your Writing

Write a paragraph to a pen pal describing two of your best friends. Use at least three different compound subjects in your paragraph. Make sure that each compound subject and its verb agree in number.

INVERTED SENTENCES

Usually, the subject appears *before* the verb in a sentence. The subject-verb word order is called **natural order**. In an **inverted sentence**, the subject comes after the verb.

EXAMPLES

| natural order | The large **whale swam** over the sunken ship. |
| **inverted sentence** | Over the sunken ship **swam** the large **whale**. |

USAGE tip

Inverted sentences often begin with a prepositional phrase.

When working with inverted sentences, you must first identify the subject and then make the verb agree with it in number. Saying the sentence aloud or rewriting the sentence in natural order often helps.

Most sentences that begin with *Here* or *There* are inverted sentences. The subject of the sentence is never *Here* or *There*. As with other inverted sentences, you can rearrange the words into natural order so that the subject comes first.

USAGE tip

To make it easier to find the subject and verb in an inverted sentence or question, rearrange the words into natural order.

EXAMPLES

inverted sentence	Here **is** the first **bus**.
	Riding to town **are** notorious **outlaws**.
natural order	The first **bus is** here.
	Notorious **outlaws are** riding to town.

Some questions—interrogative sentences—are written in inverted order. Usually a helping verb appears before the subject. You'll find the subject between the helping verb and the main verb.

EXAMPLES

Will you please **fix** the car? (The subject *you* appears between the helping verb *Will* and the main verb *fix*.)

Did Joseph and Bobby **trim** the shrubs? (The compound subject *Joseph and Bobby* appears between the helping verb *Did* and the main verb *trim*.)

EXERCISE 11

Identifying Subjects and Verbs in Inverted Sentences
Underline and label the subjects and verbs in each of the
following inverted sentences.

1. Under the tree sits the lonely young man.
2. There is a school of piranha in the river.
3. Over the hill waits the enemy army.
4. Did Charles purchase the refreshments?
5. In the abyss lurks something more foul than we can
   imagine.
6. Here are your defending champions.
7. Do you understand the charges?
8. Inside the fort are stationed three platoons.
9. Here in the chest is the ancient sword.
10. There rests the most dangerous cat in the jungle.

EXERCISE 12

**Understanding Subject-Verb Agreement in Inverted
Sentences**
Complete each of the inverted sentences by choosing the
correct form of the verb in parentheses.

1. Here in the city (patrols, patrol) the dedicated officer.
2. Next to the statue (stands, stand) the rest of the horses.
3. Beyond the river (grows, grow) the tallest trees in the
   world.
4. There (hides, hide) the elusive mouse.
5. (Does, Do) your dogs bite?
6. Out in the wilderness (wanders, wander) the old
   philosopher.
7. Here (is, are) several varieties of grass.
8. During the night (creeps, creep) many beasts toward the
   house.
9. There on the horse (rides, ride) the famous movie star.
10. Upon this mountain (waves, wave) our tattered flag.

EXERCISE 13

Using Inverted Sentences in Your Writing
Write a paragraph describing your neighborhood to an acquaintance who would like to visit. In your paragraph, use three inverted sentences to provide variety and interest. As one of the inverted sentences, write a question.

UNIT 8 REVIEW

TEST YOUR KNOWLEDGE

EXERCISE 1
Identifying Subject-Verb Agreement
Choose the verb in parentheses that agrees in number with the subject or compound subject in each of the following sentences. (10 points)

EXAMPLES
The paint on the house (looks, look) worn and faded. *(looks)*
The children (runs, run) around the house every day. *(run)*

1. The roof of the building (bears, bear) the weight of the snow.
2. Noise from the street (grows, grow) louder at rush hour.
3. Neither my cat nor my dogs (listens, listen) to a word I say.
4. Ants and a wasp (ruins, ruin) the picnic.
5. Maps, passports, and a cell phone (is, are) in the glove compartment.
6. Birds flying overhead (annoys, annoy) my cat.
7. Tracks from the bear (circles, circle) our camp.
8. Fish or steak (sounds, sound) good for supper.
9. Either Mitch or his sons (handles, handle) cases of disloyalty.
10. Cameras and camcorders (distracts, distract) the performers.

EXERCISE 2
Identifying Indefinite Pronoun-Verb Agreement
Identify the indefinite pronoun in each of the following sentences. Then choose the verb in parentheses that agrees in number with the indefinite pronoun in the sentence. (20 points)

EXAMPLE
Something in the trees (moves, move) about each night.
(*Something,* indefinite pronoun; *moves,* correct verb)

1. Few of the buffalo (remains, remain) on the plains.
2. One (runs, run) free in the park.
3. Everybody in the office (loves, love) to bowl.
4. None of the tomato plants (survives, survive) the cold.
5. Some of the sailors (is, are) eager to reach shore.
6. Most of the forest (has been, have been) cleared.
7. All of our effort (is, are) being wasted.
8. Anything you find (needs, need) to be cataloged.
9. Several in our band (perceives, perceive) the danger we are facing.
10. Others among us (loses, lose) sight of the larger objective.

E X E R C I S E 3
Identifying Inverted Sentences
Underline the subject and its verb in each of the following sentences. Then identify each of the sentences as either natural or inverted. (20 points)

EXAMPLES
Bridget usually jogs in the morning. (*Bridget,* subject; *jogs,* verb; natural)

Across the river dwells an unhappy family. (*family,* subject; *dwells,* verb; inverted)

1. Before lunch Samuel always checks his e-mail.
2. There sits the heir to the English throne.
3. Over the carnage flew the helicopter.
4. Here in this envelope is the mysterious letter.
5. Below the surface of the earth lives a horde of goblins.
6. Inside the boardroom, I presented my ambitious plan.
7. Occasionally the team meets after the games.
8. Uncle Ted, who is plagued by gout, plays cards every night.
9. There are too many holes in this boat.
10. A few soldiers remain behind enemy lines.

Understanding Subject-Verb Agreement in Inverted Sentences

Underline the subject in each of the following inverted sentences. Then choose the correct form of verb in parentheses to complete each sentence. (20 points)

EXAMPLE
Under the surface (swims, swim) a giant <u>eel</u>. *(swims)*

1. Next to the bleachers (sits, sit) the former coach.
2. Over the trees (hovers, hover) several alien spacecraft.
3. Across the lake (floats, float) a collection of boats.
4. In front of the television (is, are) that lazy cat of yours.
5. Above the clouds (orbits, orbit) numerous satellites.
6. Here in the safe (is, are) the stolen knives.
7. There (is, are) few choices left for you right now.
8. Past the edge of the city (grows, grow) a field of corn.
9. At the end of the show (performs, perform) the clowns.
10. Into the pit (jumps, jump) the brave pair of warriors.

EXERCISE 5
Correcting Subject-Verb Agreement

If the subject and verb in each of the following sentences agree in number, write *correct*. If they do not agree, correct the verb. (10 points)

EXAMPLES
A lone sentry patrols the fence during the cold night. (correct)
Several racers speeds into the home stretch. *(speed)*

1. The bears are either black or brown.
2. Monsters under your bed sleeps during the daytime.
3. Each of your exams reflect a lack of preparation.
4. That chicken sitting on the fence produce several eggs a day.

5. Few of the guards has packs of gum to pass out anymore.
6. All of the flock decide to fly south.
7. Pizza or fried chicken sound good for supper tonight.
8. Someone in the audience know whom to call.
9. The snakes slithers away from the lawnmower.
10. Today we builds a structure for shelter.

EXERCISE 6
Using Subject-Verb Agreement in Your Writing
For your school paper, write a paragraph describing a
humorous event. In your paragraph, include at least five
different examples of subject-verb agreement with indefinite
pronouns, compound subjects, and inverted sentences.
(20 points)

UNIT 9 MODIFIERS

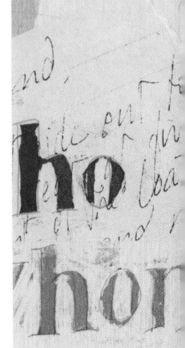

MODIFIERS

ADJECTIVES AND ADVERBS

Adjectives and adverbs—two kinds of **modifiers**—add meaning to nouns, adjectives, verbs, and adverbs.

An **adjective** modifies a noun or pronoun. An **adverb** is a word that modifies a verb, an adjective, or another adverb.

EXAMPLES	
adjective	Hockey is a **confusing** game for **inexperienced** players. (*Confusing* modifies the noun *game;* *inexperienced* modifies the noun *players.*)
adverb	My uncle is **already late** for the play. (*Already* modifies the adjective *late.*)

To determine whether a modifier is an adjective or an adverb, you can follow these steps.
1. Look at the word that is modified.
2. Ask yourself, "Is this modified word a noun or a pronoun?" If the answer is *yes*, the modifier is an adjective. If the answer is *no*, the modifier is an adverb.

In the following example, the word *house* is modified by the word *old*. The word *house* is a noun so, the word *old* is an adjective.

EXAMPLE
The **old house** collapsed during the windstorm.

In the next example, the word *hissed* is modified by the word *angrily*. The word *hissed* is a verb, therefore, the word *angrily* is an adverb.

EXAMPLE
The snake **hissed angrily** at us.

Try It Yourself

EXERCISE 1
Identifying Adjectives and Adverbs in Literature
Identify each of the underlined words in the literature passage as either an adjective or adverb.

> The inside was <u>almost</u> the same as it was before but the differences were there when I looked <u>closely</u>. We entered the <u>same</u> room with the alcove and the pair of <u>painted</u> doors. The vase I admired was no longer there, but the doors showed the same landscapes painted by a master. I peered <u>closely</u> at the pictures and saw that the colors looked <u>faded</u>. What was more, the <u>left</u> panel, the one depicting a <u>winter</u> scene, had a <u>long</u> tear in one corner.
>
> from "The Inn of Lost Time"
> Lensey Namioka

Literature
M O D E L

EXERCISE 2
Using Adjectives and Adverbs in Your Writing
Write a short paragraph to a friend about another friend or a relative who has an interesting or unusual hobby or occupation. Use adjectives and adverbs in your paragraph to describe the person and the way he or she does her job.

ADJECTIVES

Adjectives modify nouns by telling specific details about them.

EXAMPLES	
noun	a car
a little more specific	an orange car
more specific yet	the fast orange car
even more specific	a sporty, fast orange car

USAGE tip

Use a comma between multiple adjectives if the word *and* makes sense between them: *a sporty and fast orange car.*

The articles *a*, *an*, and *the* are the most commonly occurring adjectives. *A* and *an* refer to any person, place, or thing in general. *The* refers to a specific person, place, or thing.

> **EXAMPLES**
> Would you like **a** football as **a** present? (*A* refers to a ball and a present in general.)
>
> **The** bridge over **the** river is closed. (*The* refers to a specific bridge over a specific river.)

Some adjectives tell *how many* or *what kind* about the nouns or pronouns they modify.

> **EXAMPLES**
> There were **several** cars in the lot.
> They chose the car with the **tinted** windows.

Other adjectives tell *which one* or *which ones*.

> **EXAMPLES**
> **Our** car has rust spots.
> **Those** cars in the junkyard were once very expensive.

Adjectives usually precede the words they modify, but they may also follow linking verbs.

> **EXAMPLES**
> **preceding noun**   The **sleek, shiny** car raced down the road.
> **following linking verb**   The car was **sleek** and **shiny**.

Try It Yourself

EXERCISE 3
Identifying Adjectives in Literature
Identify the twenty-one adjectives in the passage below. Tell which noun or pronoun each adjective modifies.

He was standing bent over, very close to Zebra. The words LAND ROVER on his cap shone in the afternoon sunlight. As he worked, he glanced often at Zebra. His tongue kept pushing up against the insides of his cheeks, making hills rise and fall on his face. Wrinkles formed intricate spidery webs in the skin below his gray eyes. On his smooth forehead, in the blue and purple shadows beneath the peak of his cap, lay glistening beads of sweat.

from "Zebra"
Chaim Potok

EXERCISE 4
Understanding Adjectives
Rewrite the paragraph below, replacing general, overused adjectives with more colorful and precise choices and adding adjectives that bring the scene to life.

We saw the large dragon off in the distance. She breathed hot fire into the air. The sight gave me a bad feeling. I was grateful that my strong companion Ironbeard was good with an axe. We slowly crept up the long path toward the dragon's lair. The beast's wings were big. We knew our quest was dangerous, but the dragon guarded a pile of wonderful treasure. The warm wind blew in our faces. When the ugly creature looked in our direction, we stopped in our tracks. If attacked, I felt that our big shields might not protect us from the hot fire. Just then, we spotted a small hole in the rocks alongside the road. Ironbeard and I ran into the hole. It opened into a large dark cave. Our torches provided light that illuminated a small area around us. Here, we planned our strategy.

EXERCISE 5
Using Adjectives in Your Writing
Write a short paragraph for a students' book club about one of your favorite fictional characters. Use vivid adjectives to create a portrait in words of how you envision the character.

ADVERBS

Adverbs modify anything that isn't a *namer* (noun or pronoun). Adverbs can modify verbs, adjectives, or other adverbs. Many times they will tell us *how, when, where,* or *to what extent;* nouns and pronouns tell us *who* or *what.*

EXAMPLES	
adverbs modify verbs	The children sing **cheerfully**. (*Cheerfully* tells how they sing.)
	Eagles **usually** fly **high** in the summer sky. (*Usually* tells when they fly in the sky; *high* tells where they fly.)
adverbs modify adjectives	These noble birds are **especially** graceful. (*Especially* tells to what extent they are graceful.)
	Some rare birds are **nearly** extinct. (*Nearly* tells to what extent the birds are extinct.)
adverbs modify adverbs	The eagles swoop down on their prey **very** quickly. (*Very* tells to what extent they swoop down on their prey quickly.)
	The birds grip **so** strongly, few animals can escape their clutches. (*So* tells how strongly they grip.)

Many adverbs are formed by adding *–ly* to adjectives, such as *quickly, fortunately, poorly,* and *sadly.* Note, though, that you cannot depend on *–ly* to identify adverbs, since some adjectives have the same ending, as in *brotherly, comely, manly,* and *wily.* Also, many common adverbs do not have a consistent ending, such as *always, forever, here, not, now,* and *far.* The only sure way to distinguish between adjectives and adverbs is to determine how the individual word functions in its sentence.

EXERCISE 6

Identifying Adverbs in Literature

Identify the eight adverbs in the passage below.

> Before that summer my mother had always claimed she
> wanted me to be normal. She didn't want me to become
> spoiled by the attention I received when I was working at
> the studios. I still had chores to do at home, went to
> public school when I wasn't working, was punished
> severely when I behaved badly. She didn't want me to feel
> I was different just because I was in the movies. . . . But
> when she was sitting silently in all those waiting rooms
> while I was being turned down for one job after another, I
> could almost feel her wanting to shout, "Use her. Use
> her. What is wrong with her? Doesn't she have it
> anymore?"
>
> from "Hollywood and the Pits"
> Cherylene Lee

Literature
M O D E L

EXERCISE 7

Identifying Adverbs

Identify each adverb in the following sentences and tell
whether it modifies a verb, an adjective, or another adverb.

1. Sue, my neighbor, usually plants her flowers in April.
2. Sometimes she buys seeds at Flowers-R-Us, where she
   also shops for houseplants.
3. Sue plans her garden carefully, but she is not especially
   knowledgeable about flowers.
4. She is probably most pleased when her plants bloom in a
   variety of colors.
5. Her friends are always impressed with her garden.
6. The weather rarely creates problems for Sue in the spring.
7. While Sue is busily planting, her cats romp playfully in
   the lawn.
8. She thinks highly of her cats and her flowers.

9. Sue is quite proud that her garden is always the subject of neighborly conversation.
10. Her flowers are often the most impressive on the block.

EXERCISE 8
Understanding Adverbs
For each incorrectly used adverb in the following sentences, write the correct form. Write *correct* if the adverb in a sentence is used correctly.

1. The cheetah can move very quick when it wants to.
2. I believe the coil is wound too tight.
3. All of the musicians performed marvelous that night.
4. Most bank robberies need to be planned deft to succeed.
5. He made sure all of the products were handled careful.
6. Her reaction was swift and she rightly identified the problem.
7. The engine roared powerful after the tune-up.
8. It is hard to find someone who can paint a house competent.
9. The teacher read the textbook knowledgeable to the class.
10. I am glad he told her about the mix-up tactfully.

EXERCISE 9
Using Adverbs in Your Writing
Write a paragraph for a nature magazine about an animal that lives in the wild, describing its movements and habits. In your paragraph, use adverbs to modify verbs, adjectives, and other adverbs.

APPOSITIVES

An **appositive** is a noun that is placed next to another noun to identify it or add information about it. In these examples, the noun *Larry* identifies the noun *uncle*, and the noun *chef* gives more information about the noun *Rita*. Both *Larry* and *chef* are appositives.

EXAMPLES
The car belongs to my uncle **Larry**.
Rita, the head **chef**, has 30 years of experience.

An **appositive phrase** is a group of words that includes an appositive and other words that modify it, such as adjectives and prepositional phrases. The group of words adds information about the noun it modifies. In the next example, the appositive phrase *a state in the Midwest* gives further information about the noun *Iowa*.

EXAMPLE
Iowa, **a state in the Midwest**, is a leader in agricultural production.

An appositive or an appositive phrase that provides extra information about the noun is set off from the rest of the sentence with one or more commas. If, however, the appositive is needed to identify the noun, it is not set off with commas.

USAGE tip

Ask yourself this question before punctuating appositives: *Is the appositive essential or not essential to the meaning of the sentence?* If it is essential, do not use commas. If it is not essential to the meaning, set off the appositive with commas.

EXAMPLES
Your brother, **a very intelligent student**, won the essay contest. (The appositive *a very intelligent student* further identifies your brother.)

The pitcher **Roger Clemens** won the Cy Young Award. (The appositive *Roger Clemens* identifies which pitcher won the Cy Young Award.)

Try It Yourself

EXERCISE 10
Identifying Appositives
Identify the appositives and appositive phrases in the sentences below. Then write the noun or pronoun the appositive identifies or adds information about.

1. Ray Bradbury, a famous science fiction writer, is the author of *The Martian Chronicles*.
2. He also wrote "The Foghorn," a short story.

3. The narrator of the story, Johnny, works in a lighthouse.
4. Johnny's friend McDunn also works in the lighthouse.
5. The foghorn sound, a mournful moan, comes every fifteen seconds.
6. Johnny and McDunn spot the monster, a hundred-foot dinosaur.
7. The monster's cry, a lonely echo of the foghorn, rang out in the night.
8. The lighthouse, a tall stone tower, collapsed after the monster rammed it.
9. A new lighthouse, a steel-reinforced concrete structure, was built the next year.
10. Bradbury's novel *Fahrenheit 451* is one of his most famous works.

EXERCISE 11

Understanding Appositives

On your paper, copy the following sentences. Identify the appositive or appositive phrase in each sentence by underlining it. Then insert a comma or commas where they are needed to show information that is not essential to the meaning of the sentence.

1. Virginia one of the original thirteen colonies was home to the first English settlement in North America.
2. President George Washington lived in Mount Vernon, Virginia.
3. Washington the father of our country was the first U.S. president.
4. Thomas Jefferson another early president was also from Virginia.
5. During his term the United States purchased a great area of land the Louisiana Territory from France.
6. Jefferson's home Monticello is a tourist attraction today.
7. The commonwealth Virginia set up its own government in the 1770s.
8. In 1863 part of Virginia broke off to be a separate state West Virginia.

9. Richmond Virginia's capital was also the capital of the Confederacy.
10. The state's highest point Mount Rogers is over 5,700 feet high.

EXERCISE 12

Using Appositives in Your Writing

Appositives are often used by advertising or marketing departments to promote their products. Write a promotional headline that is an appositive, such as *"Scrubs," a new soap that is serious about teenage acne.* Then write a short paragraph to convince consumers to purchase the new product. Use appositives and appositive phrases to identify and provide more information about the product. Be sure to punctuate your appositives correctly.

POSITIVES, COMPARATIVES, AND SUPERLATIVES

The form of an adjective or adverb is often changed to show the extent or degree to which a certain quality is present.

EXAMPLES
Will is **tall** for a seventh-grader. (The adjective *tall* shows that the quality is present.)

Will is **taller** than Elijah. (The quality expressed by the adjective *taller* exists to a greater degree in one of the two people or things being compared.)

Will is the **tallest** boy in the seventh grade. (The quality expressed by the adjective *tallest* exists to a greater degree in one of more than two people or things being compared.)

USAGE tip

Use *than*, not *then*, when making comparisons. *Then* tells when.

Each modifier has a **positive, comparative**, and **superlative** form of comparison. Most one-syllable modifiers and some two-syllable modifiers form their comparative and superlative degrees by adding *–er* or *–est*. Other two-syllable modifiers and all modifiers of more than two syllables use *more* and *most*.

	Positive	Comparative	Superlative
Adjectives	happy	happier	happiest
	dull	duller	dullest
	light	lighter	lightest
	frightening	more frightening	most frightening
Adverbs	early	earlier	earliest
	fast	faster	fastest
	close	closer	closest
	completely	more completely	most completely

To show a decrease in the quality of any modifier, form the comparative and superlative degrees by using *less* and *least*.

USAGE tip

Some words are absolute and cannot logically be compared. The positive form of such words as *ideal, exclusive, deceased, unfeasible, unique,* and *eternal* describes their only state. They are not capable of greater or lesser degrees.

EXAMPLES

solid	less solid	least solid
analytical	less analytical	least analytical

Some modifiers form the comparative and superlative degrees irregularly. Check the dictionary if you are unsure about the comparison of a modifier.

EXAMPLES

good	better	best
well	better	best
bad	worse	worst

Try It Yourself

EXERCISE 13
Identifying Positives, Comparatives, and Superlatives
Identify the underlined words in the following sentences as positive, comparative, or superlative.

1. Robert E. Lee and Ulysses S. Grant are two of the <u>most</u> famous American generals.
2. Grant was several years <u>younger</u> than Lee.
3. The two generals opposed each other in the Civil War, the <u>bloodiest</u> war in U.S. history.
4. Grant had <u>more</u> soldiers and a <u>greater</u> amount of supplies for his army.

5. In 1864, the <u>wisest</u> strategy for Lee was to go on the defensive.
6. Lee had earned his reputation early in the war with a series of <u>daring</u> attacks on the Union Army.
7. Grant had a <u>better</u> understanding of how to win the war than his Northern colleagues.
8. Thousands of <u>brave</u> soldiers served in the armies of both generals.
9. After four years, the <u>bitterly</u> contested war <u>finally</u> came to an end.
10. Grant later ascended to the presidency, the <u>highest</u> office in the land.

EXERCISE 14

Understanding Degrees of Comparison

For each incorrectly used adjective or adverb in the following sentences, write the correct positive, comparative, or superlative form. Write *correct* if the adjective or adverb comparison is used correctly.

1. Alaska is the farther north of all states in the union.
2. We had hoped to arrive at the checkpoint earliest than our rivals.
3. I am a slow reader, but I always finish my homework on time.
4. My prank was daringer than those of my coworkers.
5. I can't figure out which is worst, your laziness or your arrogance.
6. The deep valley in New Mexico is larger enough to hide the spaceship.
7. Of all the players on the team, Edgar is the better.
8. George is the most fuller developed intellectual in the group.
9. We played more better than they did and won the game.
10. The crowd engaged in the most riotous behavior in the town's history.

EXERCISE 15
Using Comparisons Correctly in Your Writing
Write a review of a novel or short story you have recently read for a classmate who has not read the selection. Highlight the main conflict and the way the characters solve it. To help your classmate understand what he or she will be reading, compare the book or short story to others of its type. Use the positive, comparative, and superlative forms of adjectives and adverbs to express your opinion about the film.

NEGATIVES AND DOUBLE NEGATIVES

Negatives such as *not* and *never* are adverbs because they add to the meaning of the verb. The verb tells what an action is, and the negative says that the writer or speaker means the opposite of that.

> EXAMPLE
> I like hot fudge sundaes.
> I do **not** like hot fudge sundaes.

Make sure to use only one negative in each sentence. A **double negative** is the use of two negative words together when only one is needed. Check your writing to be sure that you have not used a negative word such as *not, nobody, none, nothing, hardly, can't, doesn't, won't, isn't,* or *aren't* with another negative word. Correct double negatives by removing one of the negative words or by replacing one of the negative words with a positive word.

> EXAMPLES
> **double negative**   Not nobody will show up on time.
> **corrected sentence**   Nobody will show up on time.
>
> **double negative**   He doesn't do no work after six o'clock.
> **corrected sentence**   He doesn't do any work after six o'clock.
> **corrected sentence**   He does no work after six o'clock.
>
> *CONTINUED*

double negative	Shelly isn't feeling no better than before.
corrected sentence	Shelly isn't feeling any better than before.
corrected sentence	Shelly is feeling no better than before.

Try It Yourself

EXERCISE 16
Identifying Negatives
Write the negative words in the following sentences.

1. The governor would not issue a pardon.
2. Nobody had any sympathy for the convicted felon.
3. After the police surrounded his house, he had nowhere to hide.
4. The criminal hardly tried to avoid capture after assessing his situation.
5. In court he tried to convince the jury that he was not guilty by reason of insanity.
6. His lawyer knew that nothing would convince any sane person that his client was innocent.
7. We had never witnessed a trial conclude that quickly.
8. Every time I think about him, I don't understand why he turned to crime.
9. When the sentence was carried out, no one said a word.
10. The man would be free today, if he hadn't tried stealing that pack of gum.

EXERCISE 17
Understanding Double Negatives
Rewrite the following sentences to remove the double negatives. Remember that you can either remove one of the negative words or replace it with a positive word. If a sentence does not contain a double negative, write *correct*.

1. No one did nothing to help solve the traffic problems in the town.
2. The citizens hadn't talked about no solutions at the meeting.
3. Unfortunately, Mayor Crimmins was not no bold leader.

4. No one hadn't surveyed the streets in the town.
5. There wasn't hardly a street in town that was easily traversable.
6. The townspeople concluded that the situation was not likely to change anytime soon.
7. They couldn't hardly figure out what needed to be done.
8. We ourselves don't talk to no one about traffic in this town.
9. Visitors aren't likely to stop in this town if no solution is found.
10. I'll bet you've never seen nothing like all those cows piled up in a traffic jam.

E X E R C I S E **1 8**
Using Negatives in Your Writing
Write a sentence for each of the five negative words below. Be careful to avoid using any double negatives.

1. not
2. won't
3. none
4. isn't
5. no

CONTRACTIONS

Contractions combine two words by shortening and joining them with an apostrophe. When you are trying to determine subjects and verbs in a sentence, write out contractions into the two words that they represent. After the contraction is written out, each word should be considered separately. Remember that a negative is never part of a verb but is an adverb.

USAGE tip

Don't confuse the possessive pronouns *its, their, your,* and *whose* with the contractions *it's, they're, you're,* and *who's.*

EXAMPLES
Todd **wasn't** home yesterday. (*was* = verb; *not* = adverb)

He'll be arriving next week. (*he* = subject; *will be* = helping verb and verb)

CONTINUED

I couldn't decide what to do. (*I* = subject; *could decide* = helping verb and verb; *not*=adverb)

USAGE tip

Contractions are common in speech and in informal writing. Your teacher may want you to write out the words represented by contractions when your topic, purpose, and audience are formal.

Try It Yourself

EXERCISE 19

Identifying Contractions

Write the contraction in each of the following sentences. Write out each contraction as the two words it represents. Then write the verb or verb phrase.

1. I'll tell you about the author Shel Silverstein.
2. I've read most of Silverstein's works, including his poems, cartoons, stories, and plays.
3. Many believe he might've been the most versatile.
4. Some people think that he could've become a great magazine writer.
5. Instead he's remembered as one of the best authors of children's books.
6. If Silverstein hadn't written books for children, many readers would've missed out on his wonderful stories.
7. It's always fun to read his stories to the children.
8. I first read *Where the Sidewalk Ends* because that's one of his most famous books.
9. What've you read lately?
10. Who's your favorite author of children's books?

EXERCISE 20

Understanding Contractions

Revise the following paragraph to make it more formal by removing all contractions.

When Opening Day arrives in April, it's like a holiday for baseball fans. For several months they've waited with anticipation for the first pitch. It doesn't matter which team they root for, on Opening Day all fans have hope. Whether they're pulling for the world champs or last year's cellar-dwellers, these fans view the start of the

CONTINUED

season with excitement. A team can't be counted out of the pennant race on Opening Day. If the fans didn't believe in their teams, no underdogs would've ever made it to the World Series. People shouldn't underestimate how much their support means to the players. Playing on Opening Day in stadiums packed with excited, hopeful fans creates memories that the players won't ever forget.

EXERCISE 21
Using Contractions in Your Writing

Write a paragraph about a bad habit you have that you would like to break. For example, maybe you'd like to stop biting your fingernails, or perhaps you'd like to stop procrastinating about studying for tests. Describe when the habit started, what causes you to do it, and why you would like to stop doing it. Write with an informal tone and use at least five contractions in your paragraph.

USAGE tip

Sometimes when you move the misplaced or dangling phrase or clause closer to the word it modifies, you may have to do some additional rewording of the sentence.

DANGLING AND MISPLACED MODIFIERS

Dangling modifiers and misplaced modifiers are phrases or clauses that confuse the meaning of a sentence. A **dangling modifier** seems to modify the wrong word or no word at all because the word it should modify does not appear in the sentence. A **misplaced modifier** is located so far from the word it should modify that it appears to be modifying an inappropriate word. You can edit dangling and misplaced modifiers by moving the modifier within the sentence or by rewording the sentence.

EXAMPLES
dangling modifier   Gazing across the field, a deer stopped at the creek to take a drink. (It sounds as if the deer is simultaneously gazing across the field and stopping to take a drink.)

CONTINUED

corrected sentence	Gazing across the field, I saw a deer stop at the creek to take a drink. (*Gazing across the field* now modifies what *I* am doing. Notice how the wording of the sentence changes slightly.)
dangling modifier	After departing from work, a new restaurant attracted his attention. (It sounds as if the new restaurant is departing from work.)
corrected sentence	A new restaurant attracted his attention after he departed from work. (He noticed a new restaurant after he departed from work.)
misplaced modifier	The newspaper has an article describing woodchucks on the table. (It sounds as if woodchucks are on the table.)
corrected sentence	The newspaper on the table has an article describing woodchucks. (The woodchucks are in an article in the newspaper on the table.)
misplaced modifier	The owl looked down at the scurrying mice in the tree. (It sounds as if the scurrying mice are in the tree.)
corrected sentence	The owl in the tree looked down at the scurrying mice. (The owl is in the tree, and it looks down at the scurrying mice.)

Try It Yourself

EXERCISE 22

Identifying Dangling and Misplaced Modifiers

Identify the dangling modifiers in the following sentences by writing *DM*. Identify the misplaced modifiers by writing *MM*.

1. Leaving clues in the bank, the police are hot on the trail of the robbers.
2. Detective Silas is a brash, arrogant crime fighter from the Bronx with no hair.
3. Convicted criminals were always following Silas's investigations.
4. Deciding to first question the witnesses, a plan developed to solve the case.
5. Also part of the interrogation, Silas additionally questioned known friends of the robbers.
6. Hook, the leader of the bank robbers, had a hook-shaped scar from a car accident on his face.
7. Silas methodically gathered evidence, never deviating from the task at hand or making the case personal like a robot.
8. Hook started spending his money while on the run continually.
9. As with most crimes, Hook's gang left clues to help solve the case.
10. In the article Silas described how he tracked down the criminals in the newspaper.

EXERCISE 23
Understanding Dangling and Misplaced Modifiers
Revise the sentences in Exercise 22 so that the modifiers are placed as close as possible to the words they modify.

EXERCISE 24
Correcting Dangling and Misplaced Modifiers
Revise any sentences that contain dangling and misplaced modifiers. If a sentence does not contain errors in modifier use, write *correct*.

1. Barking and growling, Dave gave a sausage to his dog.
2. The car nearly used a quart of oil on the trip to the coast.
3. To fly the kite, great skill and dexterity were needed.
4. We noticed the green trees jogging through the park.

5. The company Christmas party is at Misty's, a favorite annual event of the employees.
6. Judy located the missing disk cleaning out her desk.
7. When visiting the pubs in the village, proper etiquette must be observed.
8. A number of wild animals and birds inhabit this jungle.
9. Finally separating itself from the pack, the greyhound raced toward the finish line.
10. Dark and damp, the hikers continued their trek on the trail.

EXERCISE 25

Understanding Dangling and Misplaced Modifiers
Combine each pair of sentences below by making one sentence into a modifier. Check your sentences to be sure that you didn't create any dangling or misplaced modifiers.

1. Jill unwrapped the present. She giggled with glee.
2. The puppy chewed on the shoes. He was filled with mischief.
3. The enemy cannons were not visible. We were stationed in a valley.
4. I received advice on how to pay less tax. The advice was from my barber.
5. Billy climbed up the side of the mountain. A fear of failure compelled him to go further.
6. Jim and John worked on the car for three hours. It still would not run.
7. I looked out and saw the Pacific Ocean. I flew in a jet.
8. Garfield painted his house this afternoon. A cat watched him.
9. My nieces competed in a dance competition this weekend. They are twins.
10. We drove the car two miles down the road. Its engine started smoking.

CHOOSING THE CORRECT MODIFIER

In everyday conversation, people often use adjectives in place of adverbs. For example, someone might say, "Go quick!" instead of "Go quickly!" When you write, make sure that you use adjectives to modify nouns and pronouns and adverbs to modify verbs, adjectives, and other adverbs. In the following sentence, the choice between the adjective and adverb affects the meaning of the sentence.

EXAMPLE	
adjective	Sara found an unpleasant, crunchy object in her cereal. (The object was both unpleasant and crunchy. The adjective *unpleasant* modifies the noun *object*.)
adverb	Sara found an unpleasantly crunchy object in her cereal. (The crunchiness was unpleasant. The adverb *unpleasantly* modifies the adjective *crunchy*.)

Try It Yourself

EXERCISE 26
Identifying Modifiers in Literature
In the following literature model, identify the underlined modifiers as either adjectives or adverbs.

Literature
M O D E L

Eve was too far gone to notice these attacks. "Chase," she whispered in a trembling voice, "please come back. I need you <u>badly</u>. I want you to chase these cats away."

So saying, she squeezed her hands together and repeated her words <u>passionately</u>.

Suddenly there was a bark. Eve looked around. It was <u>dim</u>, her vision was fogged, but there before her— <u>unmistakably</u>—was Chase. In her delirium Eve saw him in reverse: where he had been white, he was now black, and his black spots were now white.

Chase paid no attention to her, but was galloping <u>madly</u> toward the cats. Behind him followed a <u>ragged</u>

CONTINUED

parade of salamanders, turtles, hamsters, gerbils, and many flopping goldfish. All were ghosts.

from "Pets"
Avi

EXERCISE 27
Understanding Modifiers

Rewrite the following sentences so that the adjectives and adverbs are used correctly. If the modifier or modifiers are used correctly, write *correct*.

1. This prison is the most secure facility in the nation.
2. He spoke so rapid, I could not understand him.
3. If you go quick, you can still catch them.
4. The tank destroyed each building in the town methodical.
5. A fawn ran graceful through the meadow.
6. With long strides, Fred started his slow walk down the street.
7. She looked at me coldly after I asked for her phone number.
8. Upon taking the podium, he spoke bold.
9. Your history report was outstandingly written.
10. He thought sad about the opportunity he missed.

EXERCISE 28
Using Modifiers in Your Writing

Write for classmates a paragraph about a recent accomplishment of yours that makes you feel proud. As you write about your achievement, make sure to use modifiers correctly.

COMMONLY CONFUSED WORDS

The modifiers *good, well, bad,* and *badly* can be confusing because the distinctions between *good* and *well* and between *bad* and *badly* are often not followed in conversation. Confusion can also occur because *well* can function as either an adjective or an adverb.

EXAMPLES

The cheese smelled **bad** after it had set out all night. (*Bad* is an adjective. It follows a linking verb like *smelled*.)

Mike skied **badly** after his accident. (*Badly* is an adverb that modifies *skied*.)

Ken is a **good** bowler. (*Good* is an adjective that modifies a noun like *bowler*.)

Ken bowls **well**. (*Well* is an adverb meaning "skillfully." It modifies a verb like *bowls*.)

Ken was ill, but now he seems **well** enough to bowl. (*Well* is an adjective meaning "healthy" or "state of satisfactory condition." It follows a linking verb like *seems*.)

USAGE tip

Good, well, and bad form their comparative and superlative degrees irregularly: *good, better, best; well, better, best;* and *bad, worse, worst. Badly* becomes *more badly* and *most badly* in the comparative and superlative degrees.

Try It Yourself

EXERCISE 29

Identifying Commonly Confused Words

Choose the correct form of *good, well, bad,* and *badly* in the sentences below.

1. The children behave (bad, badly) each day after school.
2. She skates (good, well), but success comes with a price.
3. These burritos you brought home taste really (good, well).
4. We had some (good, well) times when we were in high school.
5. The skunk carries a (bad, badly) odor with it.
6. That child does not play (good, well) with others.
7. I told you that the car performs (bad, badly) under pressure.
8. He has not been (good, well) since receiving his quarterly stock report.
9. The exterminator felt (bad, badly) when he realized he sprayed the wrong house.
10. You put on a (good, well) performance for the others, but I can see right through you.

EXERCISE 30

Understanding Commonly Confused Words

Correct any misuse of *good*, *well*, *bad*, and *badly* in the following sentences. If no modifiers are misused in the sentence, write *correct*.

1. With three of its starters out, the team lost bad last night.
2. The lawn looks well after it rains.
3. The chicken soup you made helped her feel well again.
4. Whatever is rotting in your locker smells badly.
5. I shot good enough to earn a marksmanship award.
6. I know it looks bad, but it tastes good.
7. Those houses look good now that they have been painted.
8. You need to practice if you want to sing good next week.
9. He golfed well enough to make the cut.
10. I hate to tell you this, but you have a bad cat.

EXERCISE 31

Using Commonly Confused Words in Your Writing

Write a short review of a television show, movie, or play you recently watched. Check to be sure that you have used the modifiers *good*, *well*, *bad*, and *badly* correctly.

VERBALS: PARTICIPLES, GERUNDS, AND INFINITIVES

Verbals are verb forms that act as namers or modifiers. There are three different forms of verbals: participles, gerunds, and infinitives.

Participles are verb forms that are action adjectives. There are two kinds of participles: *present participles* and *past participles*. Present participles end in *–ing*. Past participles end in *–ed*. Even though they are verb forms, participles act as modifiers.

> EXAMPLES
> I put the **ironing** board away before the guests arrived.
> Place the **cooked** goose into the boiling pot.

USAGE tip

Do not confuse a participle used as an adjective with a participle used as the main verb in a verb phrase.

Singing, Jamie did not hear the alarm. (participle)
Jamie *is singing* a song. (verb phrase)

USAGE tip

Both participles and gerunds end in –*ing*. To tell whether the word is a participle or a gerund, determine how the word is used in a sentence. When it is used as a noun, it is a gerund. When it is used as an adjective, it is a participle.

Reading can be a powerful skill.
I'd like to take a *reading* seminar next semester.

USAGE tip

In an infinitive, *to* is followed by a verb. In a prepositional phrase, *to* is followed by a noun or a pronoun that is its object.

Gerunds are verb forms ending in –*ing* that are action nouns. They can act as the subject, direct object, predicate nominative, or object of a preposition in a sentence.

> EXAMPLES
> **Boating** is a fun activity.
> Jane has greatly improved her **cooking**.

Infinitives are formed by adding the word *to* a verb. They can act like nouns, adjectives, or adverbs in a sentence.

> EXAMPLES
> I want **to play** that game.
> Will you dare **to fly** that plane again?

Try It Yourself

EXERCISE 32

Identifying Participles, Gerunds, and Infinitives

Identify each underlined word in the following sentences as a participle, gerund, or infinitive.

1. Alan went to buy the tickets.
2. Sawing wood is good exercise.
3. Catching this criminal was more luck than skill.
4. I hope that selling the farm will be the blessing we've hoped for.
5. The lighting of the torch is the most important part of the ceremony.
6. Hiding the cake, Shelly went outside to feed the barking dog.
7. Your concerns appear to stem from the dying fish in your pool.
8. I looked out and saw the flying, singing bird up in the sky.
9. The beating our team took last week is nothing compared to what is coming this Friday.
10. My intense longing makes the wait even more difficult.

EXERCISE 33
Understanding Participles, Gerunds, and Infinitives
Write the verbals in the following sentences. Then label each one *participle*, *gerund*, or *infinitive*.

1. Learning these truths now will help your later understanding of life's twists.
2. The captain planned to go boldly into space to find new forms of life.
3. Our last experience discouraged me from driving to do any shopping.
4. The outlaw was unflinching as he and the sheriff had their meeting.
5. I can't decide whether to buy or to sell.
6. Take that melted iron over to the pile of ruined metal.
7. Jerry tried to work out a planned solution to the running water problem.
8. When you decide to crawl out of your shell, you will be talking all the time.
9. To find happiness, has been their goal all along.
10. The beaching of the craft left us with no more options.

EXERCISE 34
Using Participles, Gerunds, and Infinitives in Your Writing

Write sentences using the following participles, gerunds, and infinitives in the way specified. Be sure to place these modifiers as close as possible to the words they modify.

1. singing on the stage (participle used as an adjective)
2. to build a growing consensus (infinitive used as an adverb)
3. drinking lemonade (gerund used as a noun)
4. selling the car later (gerund used as the object of a preposition)
5. to prepare for the future (infinitive used as an adjective)
6. cleaned and oiled (participle used as an adjective)
7. arrived early (participle used as an adjective)
8. riding across the street (gerund used as a noun)
9. folded in the basket (participle used as an adjective)
10. to fly (infinitive used as a noun)

UNIT 9 REVIEW

TEST YOUR KNOWLEDGE

EXERCISE 1
Identifying Adjectives and Adverbs
Identify the underlined words in each of the following
sentences as either an adjective or an adverb. (10 points)

EXAMPLE
The size of our galaxy is <u>enormous</u>. (adjective)

1. The <u>dedicated</u> scientists at NASA study the <u>extremely</u> vast size of space.
2. The <u>expanding</u> universe is <u>nearly</u> <u>incomprehensible</u> to any human.
3. Gravity binds <u>large</u> clusters of stars into <u>rotating</u> galaxies.
4. Many <u>brightly</u> <u>shining</u> stars blend together into bands.
5. We can see only a <u>small</u> part of the <u>visible</u> universe.
6. Other galaxies are <u>so</u> <u>far</u> <u>away</u> that a <u>large</u> telescope is needed to see them.
7. The size of the earth is <u>surprisingly</u> small compared to the <u>giant</u> planet Jupiter.
8. Pluto <u>distantly</u> orbits our sun at the edge of the solar system.
9. Much of space is <u>eerily</u> void of any <u>perceptible</u> objects.
10. Like the <u>vast</u> universe, our knowledge of space is <u>ever</u> growing.

EXERCISE 2
Identifying Appositives
Identify the appositives and appositive phrases in the sentences
below. Then tell which noun or pronoun the appositive
identifies or modifies. (10 points)

EXAMPLE
Lou Gehrig, a famous baseball player, was born in 1903.
(a famous baseball player, Lou Gehrig)

1. Gehrig's parents were born in Germany, a country in Europe.
2. An excellent young athlete, Gehrig was on the baseball, football, and swimming teams in high school.
3. In 1921 Gehrig enrolled at Columbia University, a school in New York.
4. The New York Yankees, the top professional baseball team, signed Gehrig to a contract in 1923.
5. Babe Ruth, Gehrig's teammate, was the most popular of the Yankees.
6. "The Iron Horse," one of Gehrig's nicknames, came from his streak of playing in over 2,000 consecutive games.
7. In 1927 and 1936, he won the Most Valuable Player award, one of the league's most prestigious honors.
8. In 1939 Gehrig contracted amyothropic lateral sclerosis, a rare muscle disease.
9. Mayor Fiorello LaGuardia appointed Gehrig New York City Parole Commissioner.
10. Gehrig received baseball's highest honor, election into the Hall of Fame, in 1939.

EXERCISE 3

Identifying Positives, Comparatives, and Superlatives

Identify the underlined words in the following sentences as positive, comparative, or superlative. (10 points)

EXAMPLE
The Pacific Ocean is the world's <u>largest</u> body of water. (superlative)

1. I don't think you <u>fully</u> understand the consequences of your actions.
2. The Ford Escort is <u>less expensive</u> than that Cadillac you bought.
3. How many teams have a player <u>taller</u> than our center?
4. His goal was to become the <u>greatest</u> boxer of all time.
5. That was the <u>worst</u> movie of the year.
6. We cannot play because it is <u>dark</u> outside.
7. The rebuke was <u>sharply</u> worded.

8. Lucy is the <u>wisest</u> of all the owls in the forest.
9. There has to be a <u>better</u> way to fix the sink.
10. Gray Lightning is a <u>faster</u> dog when he races on Saturdays.

E X E R C I S E   4
Identifying Verbals

Identify each underlined word in the following sentences as a participle, gerund, or infinitive. (10 points)

EXAMPLE

The <u>hissing</u> skunk was his favorite pet. (participle)

1. I think we should agree <u>to part</u> as friends.
2. We put our car in the <u>heated</u> garage.
3. He spends too much time watching <u>boxing</u> on the television.
4. <u>Adjusting</u> go-carts <u>to roll</u> faster is illegal on the day of the race.
5. <u>To build</u> a consensus is a difficult task in this county.
6. He wrote a <u>dazzling</u> book about the <u>heralded</u> king.
7. That bird <u>flying</u> overhead keeps circling our position.
8. We asked the judge <u>to grant</u> us more time to prepare.
9. <u>Reading</u> the book, I suddenly realized my destiny.
10. He was the best at <u>diving</u> and <u>swimming</u>.

E X E R C I S E   5
Understanding Modifiers

Rewrite the following sentences so that the adjectives and adverbs are used correctly. If the modifiers are used correctly in a sentence, write *correct*. (10 points)

EXAMPLE

Hank rode gallant into battle. (Hank rode *gallantly* into battle.)

1. I performed the stunt gooder than anyone else in the class.
2. If you are going to make it in time, you'd better run fast.
3. The battle is remembered as a gloriously event in our nation's history.

4. Her illness became worst and required further treatment.
5. Can you be any more busier than you are now?
6. All through the performance, she sang sad.
7. Joel writes good for a second-grader.
8. Ira felt badly about losing the account.
9. After you see all of the flowers, I think you will agree that the rose is the prettier.
10. The soup you made today tastes really good.

EXERCISE 6

Correcting Dangling and Misplaced Modifiers

Rewrite the following sentences so that the modifiers are placed as close as possible to the words they modify. (10 points)

EXAMPLE
The cat jumped up on the car with black spots. (The cat with black spots jumped up on the car.)

1. On top of the refrigerator, in the morning we located the insurance papers.
2. Deciding to solve the problem today, the children were scolded by Bill.
3. While still a child, Harold taught his son how to fly a kite.
4. Jordan bought a turtle with a green shell named Speedy.
5. We trudged off to the camp with heavy hearts.
6. Before leaving the park, the tree was climbed one more time by me.
7. Wyatt had several dreams about tigers napping in his hammock.
8. Riding up to the summit, Bryan's thoughts became jumbled.
9. After capturing him in the field, Frank sought a way to escape from the police.
10. In seventh grade, my favorite team won the World Series.

Correcting Modifier Use
Rewrite the following sentences to eliminate double negatives and commonly confused modifiers. (10 points)

EXAMPLE
Tammy didn't want no chocolate on her ice cream. (Tammy didn't want *any* chocolate on her ice cream.)

1. I can't find not one pair of socks that match.
2. The teacher couldn't barely understand the excited student.
3. There aren't none of the same buildings here anymore.
4. Sally sings good when she tries.
5. The transaction went bad, and the alliance crumbled rapidly in the following week.
6. They don't require no help getting back on their feet.
7. After recovering from the flu, Sheila is good again.
8. He isn't nobody important.
9. After she saved the bear, everyone knew she was a well person.
10. Julie won't hardly say anything to Tom.

Using Modifiers
Expand each of the following sentences with modifiers. Choose colorful and precise adjectives and adverbs as well as appositives and verbals to bring your sentences to life. Be sure to place your modifiers as close as possible to the word or words they modify. (10 points)

EXAMPLE
The dog walked over to the visitor. *(Wagging its tail, the happy dog trotted quickly over to the kind visitor.)*

1. Locusts are among those guests a farmer does not want.
2. The baker frosted the cake.
3. Mountains, deserts, and wind hindered the travelers.
4. That book is long.
5. Joe heard the conversation.

6. Lori's dress is pretty.
7. The police officer directed traffic.
8. Jennifer sang.
9. Matt threw the ball.
10. The tree grew.

EXERCISE 9

Using Appositives

Combine each pair of sentences below so that one of the two is used as an appositive. In combining the sentences, you may change the wording slightly. (10 points)

EXAMPLE

Michael Jordan is a Washington Wizard. His is one of the greatest players in basketball history. *(Michael Jordan, a Washington Wizard, is one of the greatest players in basketball history.)*

1. The senator announced his candidacy. He is the youngest politician to chair a committee.
2. The lion is the "king of the jungle." Its roar strikes terror into the other animals.
3. *Moby Dick* describes a man consumed by his desire for revenge. It is Herman Melville's best-known book.
4. Her favorite television show is *Friends*. It portrays the lives of six fictional characters who live in New York.
5. Atlantis is "the lost continent" to some people. They believe it was once a real island in the Mediterranean Sea.
6. Only two U.S. presidents had fathers who were president. They are John Quincy Adams and George W. Bush.
7. Chicago is known as "the windy city." It reflects the powerful gusts that rip through the city.
8. In college Charles Barkley was nicknamed "the round mound of rebound." He starred for Philadelphia, Phoenix, and Houston in the NBA.
9. Masada was a Jewish fortress in the first century AD. It took the Romans many months to capture it.
10. Rhode Island was one of the thirteen original colonies. It did not send delegates to the Constitutional Convention.

EXERCISE **10**

Using Verbals

Combine the following pairs of sentences by turning one sentence into a participle, gerund, or infinitive. Be sure to place the verbal as close as possible to the word that it modifies. (10 points)

EXAMPLE

Softball is a popular summer activity. It provides exercise and entertainment to many families. *(Softball is a popular summer activity, providing exercise and entertainment to many families.)*

1. The aspiring novelist wrote dozens of manuscripts. They were submitted to several different publishers.
2. If she has the V6 engine, find all six plugs. You can replace the plugs quickly if you have the right tools.
3. The library allows you to spend two hours on the Internet. It is useful for finding information about cars.
4. A laptop computer is another item you will want to take. It can hold a large amount of data.
5. Computers are manufactured by several different companies. The least expensive computers are priced under $1,000.
6. Your route covers Elm, Main, Grand, and Cherry Streets. It forms a big square.
7. Many carriers have made a lot of money delivering papers. They have discovered the early morning hours are well-suited to them.
8. Some speed-readers can read over 1,000 words a minute. They can finish several books in a week.
9. Running a campaign requires fund-raising, public speaking, and advertising. It is an ordeal that I wouldn't want to go through very often.
10. Candidates need to have an answer ready for every question. They must look prepared at all times.

UNIT *10* LINKERS AND JOINERS
Prepositions and Conjunctions

LINKERS AND JOINERS: PREPOSITIONS AND CONJUCTIONS

PREPOSITIONS AND CONJUNCTIONS

Prepositions and conjunctions are the linkers of the English language. They are used to join words and phrases to the rest of a sentence. They also show the relationships between ideas. Prepositions and conjunctions help writers vary their sentences by connecting sentence parts in different ways.

A **preposition** is used to show how a noun or a pronoun used as its object is related to other words in the sentence. Some commonly used prepositions include *above, after, against, among, around, at, behind, beneath, beside, between, down, for, from, in, on, off, toward, through, to, until, upon,* and *with*.

> **EXAMPLES**
> A whale swam **under** our boat.
>
> We had to crawl **through** the tunnel **between** the two buildings.

A **conjunction** is a word used to link related words, groups of words, or sentences. Like a preposition, a conjunction shows the relationship between the words it links. Some of the most commonly used conjunctions are *and, but, for, nor, or, yet, so, if, after, because, before, although, unless, while,* and *when*. Some conjunctions are used in pairs, such as *both/and, neither/nor,* and *not only/but also*.

> **EXAMPLES**
> I found leaves **and** twigs in the yard.
>
> He stopped running **after** he twisted his ankle.
>
> **Neither** the plaintiffs **nor** the defendants understand the ruling.

Certain words can function as either conjunctions or prepositions. There are two important differences between a word used as a preposition and one used as a conjunction.

1. A preposition is always followed by an object, but a conjunction is not.

EXAMPLES	
preposition	They sat **beside** a roaring fire. (The noun *fire* is the object of the preposition *beside*.)
conjunction	**Because** they ate lunch, the students were not hungry. (*Because* is not followed by an object. It introduces a group of words that depends on the rest of the sentence for meaning.)

2. A preposition introduces a prepositional phrase that connects parts of a sentence. A conjunction connects words or groups of words.

EXAMPLES	
preposition	I drove to the airport **before** the storm. (*Before* introduces the prepositional phrase *before the storm*.)
conjunction	Call her **before** the deadline passes. (*Before* connects two groups of words, *call her* and *the deadline passes*.)

Try It Yourself

EXERCISE 1
Identifying Prepositions and Conjunctions in Literature
Identify the underlined words in the literature passage as prepositions or conjunctions.

One day a hunter (and there were now hunters among the Binis) was returning <u>from</u> a hunt. Listen <u>to</u> this. He had an elephant <u>on</u> his back, an antelope in his bag, <u>and</u> a rabbit in each hand. When he heard a small cricket chirping <u>in</u> the sand, he wanted that as well! He started

Literature
MODEL

CONTINUED

digging <u>for</u> it <u>with</u> his big toe. This was too much for Eshu, the mischievous one. He caused the hunter to stumble and fall <u>under</u> the weight of the elephant. He was crushed <u>by</u> the elephant <u>and</u> died immediately.

from "Why the Sky Is Far Away from the Earth"
Fitzgerald Iyamabo

EXERCISE 2
Using Prepositions and Conjunctions
Write a sentence for each preposition or conjunction below.

1. and (conjunction)
2. onto (preposition)
3. beside (preposition)
4. while (conjunction)
5. neither/nor (conjunction)
6. after (preposition)
7. after (conjunction)
8. because (conjunction)
9. through (preposition)
10. over (preposition)

PREPOSITIONS

A **preposition** shows the relationship that exists between its object, a noun or pronoun, and another word in a sentence. Notice in the following sentences the number of different relationships shown between the noun *overpass* and the verb *happened*.

EXAMPLES
The multicar accident happened **under** the overpass.
The multicar accident happened **near** the overpass.
The multicar accident happened **on** the overpass.
The multicar accident happened **behind** the overpass.
The multicar accident happened **beside** the overpass.

The noun or pronoun that follows the preposition is called the **object of the preposition**. Together, the preposition, the object of the preposition, and the modifiers of that object form a **prepositional phrase**. In the following sentence, *in the bowl*, *against the glass*, and *during feeding time* are all prepositional phrases.

The goldfish **in** the bowl brushed its fantail **against** the glass **during** feeding time.

To test a word to see if it is a preposition, ask questions like "in what?","against what?",or "during what?" The answers are "bowl," "glass," and "feeding time." All three are objects of the preposition. Therefore, there are three prepositional phrases in the sentence.

These are the most commonly used prepositions. Remember, though, that any word on this list may not always be used as a preposition. If it is a preposition, it will always have an object.

USAGE tip

In some sentences, particularly those that ask a question, the preposition follows the object: *Whom are you rooting for to win the game? Whom* is the object, and *for* is the preposition. Think: *For whom are you rooting to win the game?*

Prepositions

aboard	behind	during	since
about	below	except	through
above	beside	for	throughout
across	besides	from	to
after	between	in	under
against	beyond	into	underneath
along	but	like	until
amid	(meaning	of	up
among	"except")	off	upon
around	by	on	with
at	concerning	over	within
before	down	past	without

Try It Yourself

EXERCISE 3
Identifying Prepositional Phrases in Literature
Identify the thirteen prepositional phrases in the literature passage below.

Back in the mists of time there lived a boy called Susanoo. His father and mother were the first people on earth, but then his father became Lord of the Heavens and his mother Lady of the Underworld.

Susanoo himself lived with his brothers and sisters on the bridge which linked heaven and earth, but he was always complaining. He complained about not being able to visit his mother, even though his father explained to him that if he once went to the underworld he would never be able to come back, and he complained even more when his sister Amaterasu was given the jeweled necklace of heaven and made goddess of the sun, while he was given only corals and made god of the sea.

from "Amaterasu"
Carolyn Swift

EXERCISE 4
Understanding Prepositional Phrases
Rewrite each of the following sentences, supplying a preposition and an object of the preposition in each blank. Some objects of the preposition may be more than one word.

1. Jerry ran ___ the ___.
2. She studied less ___ the ___.
3. Are you going to go ___ the ___?
4. ___ the ___ a frightened bunny scampered.
5. It was decided ___ the ___ of ___.
6. Your team stood anxiously ___ the ___.
7. Frank bowled a strike ___ the ___.
8. Julie was praised ___ her ___.
9. This country used to be blanketed___ ___.
10. The wrapped package was sent ___ ___.

Using Prepositional Phrases in Your Writing
Write a description of an interesting historical site that you have visited or would like to visit. Use prepositional phrases to help locate your readers at the site so that they can visualize the place as you walk them through it.

COORDINATING CONJUNCTIONS

A **coordinating conjunction** is a word used to join words or groups of words of equal importance in a sentence. The most common coordinating conjunctions are *and, or, nor, for, but, yet,* and *so*.

Coordinating conjunctions can connect nouns, verbs, adjectives, adverbs, prepositional phrases, other sentence elements, and sentences themselves. Each coordinating conjunction shows a different relationship between the words that it connects.

When a coordinating conjunction joins two or more complete thoughts that could be independent sentences, then a **compound sentence** is formed. A comma is placed before the coordinating conjunction that joins the two complete thoughts.

USAGE tip

By using coordinating conjunctions to connect words and groups of words, you can express the clear relationships between ideas without needless repetition. These three sentences can be rewritten as one by using a coordinating conjunction between the nouns: *Gary played baseball at recess. Mary also played baseball. Darryl played baseball, too. Gary, Mary, and Darryl played baseball at recess.*

EXAMPLES
The car is elegant **yet** affordable. (*Yet* shows the contrast between *elegant* and *affordable*. The coordinating conjunction joins two adjectives.)

He will hide in the closet **or** under the bed. (*Or* shows choice. The coordinating conjunction joins two prepositional phrases.)

The enemy will not prevail, **for** we have not yet begun to fight. (*For* shows a cause and effect relationship. The coordinating conjunction joints two complete sentences.)

Be careful not to confuse the coordinating conjunction *for* with the subordinate conjunction *because*. The latter can introduce a sentence: *Because we have not yet begun to fight, the enemy will not prevail.* The former cannot. *For we have not yet begun to fight, the enemy will not prevail.*

Try It Yourself

EXERCISE 6

Identifying Coordinating Conjunctions in Literature
Write the six coordinating conjunctions you locate in the literature passage below.

Literature MODEL

All he could think of was that Mr. Kemp had liked them both and it had been a pleasure to help him get the cows in the evening. Dan had always been with them. Staring at the figure of the old man on the veranda, he said in a worried tone, "I wish I could be sure of him, Dan. I wish he was a dumb, stupid man who wouldn't know or care whether you were worth anything. . . . Well, come on." He opened the gate bravely, but he felt shy and unimportant.

"Hello, son. What's on your mind?" Mr. Kemp called from the veranda. He was a thin, wiry man in a tan-colored shirt. He had a gray, untidy moustache, his skin was wrinkled and leathery, but his eyes were always friendly and amused.

from "Luke Baldwin's Vow"
Morley Callaghan

EXERCISE 7

Understanding Coordinating Conjunctions
Write the coordinating conjunction that best fits the blank in each item below by linking the words, phrases, or sentences.

1. The fish ___ the chicken is tastier than the steak.
2. The opposing center was tall, ___ Dan was much quicker.

3. Germany won a series of victories in 1942, ___ the Allies would turn the tide the next year.
4. This production requires a lot of money, ___ the props are very expensive.
5. Our car gasped, wheezed, ___ coughed before it finally died in the middle of the road.
6. Sally, dreaming of winning, ___ not sure if her score was high enough, sat and waited for the judges' decision.
7. My cat is afraid of the neighbor's dog, ___ we have to leave him inside.
8. The network tried to decide if it should go with Ted ___ Dave.
9. That pretty flower looks harmless, ___ it has hundreds of poisonous thorns.
10. We did not eat ___ did we sleep yesterday.

EXERCISE 8
Using Coordinating Conjunctions in Your Writing
Write five sentences about a class that you liked because of what you learned or because of the teacher. Use in your sentences each of the seven coordinating conjunctions at least once. Check to be sure that you use a comma and a coordinating conjunction between two complete sentences.

CORRELATIVE CONJUNCTIONS

Correlative conjunctions are words used in pairs to join parts of a sentence. The most common correlative conjunctions include *both/and, either/or, neither/nor,* and *not only/but also.*

> EXAMPLES
> **Both** the players **and** the coaches were pleased with the decision.
> **Neither** George **nor** Al could have expected such a long ordeal.
> Ted can **either** cut his calorie intake **or** increase his exercise time.
> France is **not only** beautiful **but also** rich in history.

Because correlative conjunctions emphasize the equal relationship between items or ideas, it is important that all the sentence elements are parallel. The order of the elements after the second connection should match the elements after the first connector.

incorrect
I asked you *either to buy* the felt-tipped ink pens *or wait* until next week for the sale.

correct
I asked you *either to buy* the felt-tipped ink pens *or to wait* until next week for the sale.

Try It Yourself

EXERCISE 9
Identifying Correlative Conjunctions
Write the correlative conjunctions you find in the following sentences.

1. Neither Simon nor this large crowd truly understands the nature of power.
2. At the antique store I found not only George Washington's first sword, but also the uniform he wore while in the Virginia militia.
3. Reading either Melville or Orwell would be better than reading that pulp fiction you have been buying.
4. Both *The Lord of the Rings* and *The Chronicles of Narnia* were written decades ago.
5. Not only did your cousin burn down the barn, but he also wrecked the car.
6. Those representatives attended both Grinnell College and Yale Law School.
7. I can see neither the mountains nor the foothills from my vantage point.
8. If you must go, either ride the bus or take the taxi to reach your destination.
9. Both softball and fishing are popular summer activities in this area.
10. If you buy now, you get not only the JuiceMaster 9000 but also a set of six juice glasses.

EXERCISE 10
Understanding Correlative Conjunctions
Combine each pair of sentences below with the correlative conjunction indicated in parentheses.

1. I like to play Monopoly. My cousin also likes to play Monopoly. (both/and)
2. The dog did not jump over the barrier. It did not jump though the hoop. (neither/nor)

3. Your book could be on the table. It could be under the sofa. (either/or)
4. We found the movie to be boring. We also thought it was interminably long. (not only/but also)
5. That boy isn't a good hitter. He isn't a good fielder either. (neither/nor)
6. Dave's aspiration is to be a writer. His other aspiration is to be a painter. (not only/but also)
7. To be a Navy Seal you must be physically fit. You must be mentally sharp too. (both/and)
8. Before the performance Tina was excited. She was also nervous. (not only/but also)
9. Cake could be served at the party. Pie could be served at the party. (either/or)
10. Tom can't figure out the problem. Cameron can't figure out the problem. Thelma can't figure out the problem. (neither/nor)

EXERCISE 11
Using Correlative Conjunctions in Your Writing
Choose two or three musicians whose music you like. Write five sentences in which you discuss their style or their songs. Use each of the pairs of correlative conjunctions at least once. Check your sentences for parallelism, making sure that the order of the elements that follows the second part of the pair of conjunctions is the same as the order of elements that follows the first part.

SUBORDINATING CONJUNCTIONS

Subordinating conjunctions introduce subordinate clauses—clauses that cannot stand alone. Subordinating conjunctions connect the clauses to independent clauses, which can stand alone as complete sentences.

In the example sentence, the subordinating conjunction *because* introduces the subordinate clause *they contained precious jewels.* *Because* connects the subordinate clause to the independent clause, *Many ancient pyramids were raided.* The subordinating conjunction adds important information about why the pyramids were raided.

USAGE tip

Keep in mind that many of the words in this list can be used as other parts of speech. For example, *after, as, before, since,* and *until* can also be used as prepositions.

EXAMPLE
Many ancient pyramids were raided **because** they contained precious jewels.

Subordinating conjunctions usually express relationships like these:

time	after, as, as long as, as soon as, before, since, until, when, whenever, while
place	where, wherever
manner	as, as if, as though
cause	because, as, since
condition	although, as long as, even if, even though, if, provided that, though, unless, while, wherever
comparison	as, than
purpose	in order that, so that, that

USAGE tip

A subordinate clause may precede, interrupt, or follow an independent clause.

Wherever there is smoke, a fire is burning.

A fire, *wherever there is smoke,* is burning.

A fire is burning *wherever there is smoke.*

EXAMPLES
If you are late, we will not be able to see the show. (*If* introduces the subordinate clause and expresses condition.)

Do you want to see the show **after** we finish dinner? (*After* introduces the subordinate clause and expresses a time relationship.)

Try It Yourself

EXERCISE 12
Identifying Subordinating Conjunctions in Literature
Write the two subordinating conjunctions found in the literature passage below. Then identify both the subordinate clause and the independent clause in each sentence.

Literature
M O D E L

The eyes also play a vital role in timing. People are right-eyed and left-eyed, just as they are right-handed, and left-handed, right-footed and left-footed. When someone focuses on a tennis ball, one eye—and one eye alone—does the focusing. In turning aside during a backswing, the dominant eye can lose contact with the ball momentarily. At 120 miles an hour, a tennis ball can elude the best eyes. From the beginning, I had no trouble waiting for just the right moment. Because of my lack of size and weight, however, I had to develop a semi-lob off the forehand as a form of survival.

from *Off the Court*
Arthur Ashe

EXERCISE 13
Understanding Subordinating Conjunctions
Combine each pair of sentences below with the subordinating conjunction indicated in parentheses. You may need to reword the sentences slightly so that they make sense when combined. Try to express main ideas in independent clauses and less important ideas in subordinate clauses.

1. I called for an ambulance. There was an accident. (because)
2. The kicker sat in the locker room with his head held low. He had lost the game by himself. (as if)
3. You stay out too late. You will be grounded for three months. (if)
4. My dog dropped the newspaper. I would see it this morning. (where)
5. We like to dance. We did not attend the prom. (although)
6. The alarm went off. I finally fell asleep. (as soon as)
7. She returned to teach the class sooner. I had hoped. (than)
8. We will be late. We start running immediately. (unless)
9. I wanted to read the book. I could learn how to fix the computer. (so that)
10. He behaved badly. He nonetheless received a present. (even though)

Using Subordinating Conjunctions
Write a sentence for each subordinating conjunction listed below. Use the kind of conjunction in parentheses as a guide for the relationship between the independent and subordinate clauses. Experiment with different placements of the subordinate clauses.

1. when (time)
2. so that (purpose)
3. because (cause)
4. where (place)
5. even if (condition)

UNIT *10* REVIEW

TEST YOUR KNOWLEDGE

Identifying Prepositions
Write the prepositions and their objects in each of the
following sentences. (10 points)

EXAMPLE
The topic of this speech will include all aspects of James
Garfield's presidency. *(of speech; of presidency)*

1. The exhibits at the Sheldon Art Museum in Lincoln are
   often fine examples of modern art.
2. That painting of dogs playing pool belongs in your
   basement, not mine.
3. He pitched another year for the love of the game.
4. If you find the answer by visiting the website, record your
   success in the report log.
5. Unbelievably, the man in the truck is driving the
   eighteen-wheeler underneath the low bridge.
6. The cake on the platter is to be saved for your birthday.
7. For the last time, stop making fun of my idea to replace
   paper currency with gold coins.
8. In ancient Egypt the cat was revered as a magical spirit by
   most Egyptians.
9. Put the money back in the box, for if you are caught with
   it, you will be arrested.
10. The tarantula is the most feared of all spiders, making
    people run for their lives.

EXERCISE 2

Identifying Conjunctions

Write the conjunctions in the following sentences and then label them as *coordinating*, *correlative*, or *subordinating*. (10 points)

EXAMPLE
I did not find out when the performance began and the band started playing. (*when*, subordinating; *and*, coordinating)

1. I did not fix the stove because I lacked the proper tools.
2. What you saw last night was either a UFO hovering over the treetops or a weather balloon descending back to Earth.
3. Not only does that cereal provide a boost of energy, but it is also sweet and tasty.
4. You're thinking back to another era, when dinosaurs and other giant creatures ruled the earth.
5. I can see that both your dogs and your cats like to destroy furniture.
6. If you enter the compound, you will be facing certain capture or death.
7. That van is used for driving the children to school or soccer practice.
8. You will be punished since you decided to throw the snowball.
9. Although your antics and actions are sometimes funny, making that face when the pastor starts the sermon is not appropriate.
10. The day I need your help may never come, but if it does, I'd like to know where you are living.

EXERCISE 3
Identifying Prepositions and Conjunctions
Identify the underlined words in the following sentences as prepositions or conjunctions. (10 points)

EXAMPLE
You should wash your car <u>before</u> you drive to the restaurant. (conjunction)

1. Would you blow up all of the balloons <u>for</u> the party?
2. I cannot believe how much he has changed <u>since</u> he started taking that class.
3. Doug will not be able to fix the computer <u>until</u> the beginning of next week.
4. The dog will spring into action <u>after</u> the cat races out the back door.
5. You weren't punished very severely <u>for</u> as late as you were in getting home.
6. <u>Since</u> December that house has been on the market.
7. I will meet you in the parking lot <u>after</u> the game.
8. He wakes up every morning <u>before</u> dawn to deliver the papers.
9. We cannot play basketball <u>until</u> my brother knocks the ball out of the tree.
10. The fire wiped out the entire block, <u>for</u> all of the buildings were connected.

EXERCISE 4
Understanding Prepositions
Combine each of the following sets of sentences into one sentence that includes one or two prepositional phrases. You may have to add, delete, or rearrange words. Some items have more than one possible answer. (10 points)

EXAMPLE
The dog barked at the mail carrier. He was walking on the sidewalk. *(The dog barked at the mail carrier walking on the sidewalk.)*

1. High inflation plagued the American economy. This occurred in the 1970s.
2. The movie just kept on going. It lasted over three hours.
3. James disagreed with my proposal. He had many counter-points.
4. Donnie started writing a book. It will be about World War I.
5. Carol Ann likes to travel. She flies in a jet.
6. The board called a meeting. It wanted all thirty staff members to attend.
7. Johnny plays third base. He is a member of the Durham Bulls.
8. We walked to her office. It was time for our orientation.
9. We were asked to draw a cartoon. We need to use black felt-tipped markers.
10. Our teacher gave a lecture. Her topic was Renaissance music. Kimball Hall is where the lecture was given.

EXERCISE 5

Understanding Coordinating and Correlative Conjunctions

Combine each set of sentences below into one sentence that includes one coordinating conjunction or correlative conjunctions. You may have to add, delete, or rearrange words. Some items have more than one possible answer. (10 points)

EXAMPLE

The basketball team lost the tournament. Some believe that the coach will be fired. Others think he will be reassigned to a desk job. *(Because the basketball team lost the tournament, some believe that the coach will be fired or reassigned to a desk job.)*

1. Julie could become a strong player. She needs to practice.
2. Fans often like to carpool to distant road games. This saves money on gas.
3. The team won their conference this year. They won every game played at home.

4. Angela, the point guard, is a good ball handler. She also shoots well.
5. Occasionally the team plays flat on the road. Sometimes the opposing crowd inspires the players.
6. The team won twenty-three games this season. It was ranked only fourteenth in the final poll.
7. Jessica has been called one of the top centers in the nation. She shoots only about 60 percent from the free-throw line.
8. Coach Gaines is one of the wisest and most experienced coaches in the league. He always carefully scouts the team's next opponent.
9. Over 6,000 people crowded into the gymnasium for the game. This number does not include the players. It does not include the media.
10. The Ravens won their first tournament game because they were quicker than their opponents. The Ravens won their first tournament game because their opponents lacked determination.

EXERCISE 6

Correcting Subordinate Clauses

Each of the subordinate clauses below is a sentence fragment. Even though each group of words has a subject and a verb, it is introduced by a subordinating conjunction, which means that it must be combined with an independent or main clause to make sense. Rewrite each of the following clauses by attaching it to an independent clause that can stand alone. Try to vary the placement of the subordinate clauses. (10 points)

EXAMPLE
If you study *(You will pass your algebra test, if you study.)*

1. While the snow is falling
2. After the holidays end
3. Whenever the can-opener starts
4. Because of your track record
5. Before the holiday season arrives

6. Although your paper is well researched
7. If we both work together
8. So that we will be free from worry
9. As far as the eye can see
10. Even though the batteries are new

EXERCISE 7

Using Prepositional Phrases in Your Writing

In your journal, write a travel guide for an imaginary vacation spot that you would like to visit. In addition to creating a location and places of amusement, describe its residents, as well as any unique attractions that will catch the interest of potential vacationers like yourself. Underline all the prepositional phrases you use. (20 points)

EXERCISE 8

Using Conjunctions in Your Writing

Choose a person who has had an important positive impact on your life. You can select a relative, friend, or a teacher who has been a role model for you, or even an author or public figure who has inspired you. Describe this person to a pen pal and then explain his or her importance in your life. Use coordinating, correlative, and subordinating conjunctions in your essay to vary your sentence structure and to show the relationship between ideas. Underline the conjunctions that you use. (20 points)

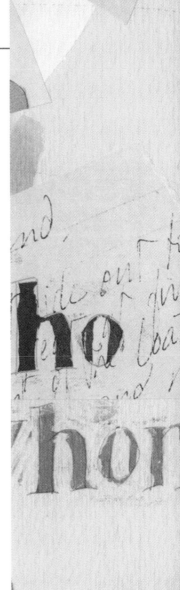

UNIT *11* INTERRUPTERS

INTERRUPTERS

INTERRUPTERS

An **interrupter** is a word or phrase that breaks, or interrupts, the flow of thought in a sentence. In your writing, you will sometimes want to use an interrupter to emphasize a point.

An interrupter is usually set off by commas from the rest of the sentence because it is not a basic part of the sentence or essential to its meaning. The commas that set off an interrupter indicate a pause before and after the interruption.

USAGE tip

Sometimes dashes are used to set off interrupters.

EXAMPLES
You will find, **however**, that first impressions are not always accurate.

Her latest book, **of course**, is on the bestseller list.

My uncle—**the one you met last summer**—collects bugs.

Try It Yourself

EXERCISE **1**
Identifying Interrupters in Literature
Identify the four interrupters in the passage below.

Literature
M O D E L

Across the street lived old Dikran, who was almost blind. He was past eighty and his wife was only a few years younger. They had a little house that was as neat inside as it was ordinary outside—except for old Dikran's garden, which was the best thing of its kind in the world. Plants, bushes, trees—all strong, in sweet black moist earth whose guardian was old Dikran. All things from the sky loved this spot in our poor neighborhood, and old Dikran loved *them*.

CONTINUED

One freezing Sunday, in the dead of winter, as I came home from Sunday School I saw old Dikran standing in the middle of the street trying to distinguish what was in his hand. Instead of going into our house to the fire, as I had wanted to do, I stood on the steps of the front porch and watched the old man.

from "The Hummingbird That Lived through Winter"
William Saroyan

EXERCISE 2

Understanding Interrupters

Identify the interrupters in the following sentences. Then rewrite each sentence, correctly adding commas or dashes to set off each interrupter from the rest of the sentence.

1. Porcupines have quills stiff and sharp that they use to defend themselves.
2. There is a porcupine I believe living in the brush behind the shed.
3. Children of course should not wander into that area alone.
4. Joey for example was pricked twice in the leg last week.
5. The porcupine however is not dangerous unless it feels threatened.
6. The animals according to our teacher really want to be left alone.
7. If you happen to spot a porcupine a disturbing sight stop and slowly back away.
8. Porcupines like opossums will not try to chase you.
9. Some groups nonetheless believe the animals should be protected.
10. Did you know that the porcupine is actually a rodent a small gnawing mammal and has some similarities to a rat?

Using Interrupters in Your Writing
Write a paragraph to be shared with classmates in which you describe the characteristics and movements of a particular animal, perhaps a pet, if you have one. Remember to set off each interrupter with commas or dashes.

INTERJECTIONS

An **interjection** is a part of speech that expresses feeling, such as surprise, joy, relief, urgency, pain, or anger. Common interjections include *ah, aha, alas, bravo, dear me, goodness, great, ha, help, hey, hooray, hush, indeed, mercy, of course, oh, oops, ouch, phooey, really, say, see, ugh,* and *whew.*

Interjections actually indicate different degrees of emotion. They may express intense or sudden emotion, as in *Wow! I can't believe it.* Notice that the strong expression of emotion stands alone in the sentence and is followed by an exclamation point.

Interjections can also express mild emotion, as in *Well, I suppose it has to be this way.* In this sentence, the interjection is part of the sentence and is set off with only a comma. Even when interjections are part of a sentence, they do not relate grammatically to the rest of the sentence.

Try It Yourself

EXERCISE 4
Identifying Interjections in Literature
Identify the four interjections in the following passage. Explain why the interjections are punctuated with commas.

The class was silent. "Very nice, Laura." Things remained quiet as other students droned through their speeches. Then Miss Merrill looked briskly around the room. "Now, Rachel, I believe you're next."

There was a ripple of dry, humorless laughter—almost, Laura thought, like the sound of a rattlesnake. Rachel stood before the class now, her face red, her heavy arms piled with boxes.

Diane Goddard tossed back her head and winked at Steve.

"Well, well, don't we have lots of things to show," said Miss Merrill. "But aren't you going to put those boxes down, Rachel? No, no, not there!"

"Man, that kid's dumb," Steve muttered, and his voice could be clearly heard all through the room.

With a brisk rattle, Miss Merrill's pen tapped the desk for silence.

from "The Fan Club"
Rona Maynard

Literature
MODEL

EXERCISE 5
Understanding Interjections
For each emotion listed below, write a sentence that expresses the emotion. Include an appropriate interjection, and use either a comma or an exclamation point to set off the interjection from the sentence.

1. happiness
2. shock
3. rage
4. glee
5. terror
6. extreme exhaustion
7. mild discomfort
8. disbelief
9. annoyance
10. sadness

Using Interjections in Your Writing
Write a dialogue for a conversation that might occur between two teammates on the practice field, a principal and a student in the principal's office, or a musician and his or her teacher after a performance. Try to make your conversation realistic by using interjections to convey the emotion of the people involved. Use commas or exclamation points to punctuate your interjections correctly.

PARENTHETICAL EXPRESSIONS

Parenthetical expressions are those words or groups of words that may explain, comment on, or qualify the ideas contained in a sentence. Expressions such as *of course, after all, however, mind you, for instance, for example, by the way, furthermore, besides, in fact, to tell the truth, in my opinion, on the other hand, in addition,* and *as I was saying* may aid understanding but are not essential to basic meaning. They are set off from the rest of the sentence with a comma or commas.

> EXAMPLES
> Tomorrow, **after all**, is another day.
> This picture, **to tell the truth**, is not visually appealing.

Try It Yourself

EXERCISE 7
Identifying Parenthetical Expressions in Literature
Write the three parenthetical expressions that you find in the passage below.

Literature
M O D E L

What he secretly yearned to do during the flying years, though, was to jump right out of an airplane altogether, with a parachute. Finally, many years later, he had his chance and told me about it afterward. He stood at the open door of the airplane, with the parachute strapped to his back, wobbling back and forth at first, like a baby bird

CONTINUED

afraid to leave the nest. Then he jumped, fell about a hundred feet through the air, and only then pulled the cord that caused the chute to blossom around him like a great circular sail. Swaying under it, he floated toward the ground until he landed, fairly hard. I listened with astonishment; my brother's daring thrilled me to the bone.

My father on the other hand, along with most of the early aviators, was not impressed by the growing enthusiasm for parachute jumping as a sport.

from "Flying"
Reeve Lindbergh

EXERCISE 8
Understanding Parenthetical Expressions
Rewrite each of the following sentences by inserting a parenthetical expression into each. Try to vary your placement of these expressions, and be sure to punctuate them correctly with commas.

1. Our teacher did always show up to class on time.
2. The car was in the garage.
3. His singing tonight was much better than in his concert last week.
4. Barry Bonds hit the ball well in 2001.
5. The turtle in the zoo is over 100 years old.
6. This may be the best way out of the valley.
7. Tomorrow the weather will be warm and sunny.
8. Your dog buries my newspaper in the garden.
9. Principal Smiley called about you today.
10. Cats sleep more than half the day.

EXERCISE 9
Using Parenthetical Expressions
Write a sentence for each of the parenthetical expressions below. Try to vary your placement of the expressions, and be sure to punctuate them correctly with commas.

1. after all
2. for example
3. in fact
4. thus
5. to be honest
6. I believe
7. at most
8. furthermore
9. on the other hand
10. in my opinion

NOUNS OF DIRECT ADDRESS

Nouns of direct address name the person or group spoken to. A noun of direct address is *never* the subject of the sentence. When the subject of a sentence is understood, or not stated, be careful not to confuse the understood subject with the noun of direct address.

> EXAMPLES
> Jeffrey, take out the garbage. (*Jeffrey* is the noun of direct address. *You* [understood] is the subject of the sentence.)
>
> Betty, will Wally be moving soon? (*Betty* is the noun of direct address. *Wally* is the subject of the sentence.)

A noun of direct address can appear at any place in a sentence. Notice in the following examples where the nouns of direct address appear and how commas are used to set them off from the rest of the sentence.

> EXAMPLES
> Your homework had better be finished, John, or you will be staying home Friday night. (*John* is the noun of direct address. *Homework* and *you* are the subjects of the two independent clauses.)
>
> Stand at attention, soldier. (*Soldier* is the noun of direct address. *You* is the understood subject of the sentence.)

Try It Yourself

EXERCISE 10

Identifying Nouns of Direct Address

Write the nouns of direct address used in the sentences below. Then write the subject of the main clause in each sentence.

1. The telephone is for you, Josh.
2. Would you tell me, ma'am, did you see anything unusual here?
3. Students, you are about to explore the fun and exciting world of calculus.
4. Yolanda, would you like to share your note with the rest of the class?
5. Ladies, one more victory is needed for you to be national champions.
6. Not all Roman emperors, Sam, were good role models.
7. This discovery could change your life forever, Phil.
8. You must remember that practice, Mark, makes you a better musician.
9. When your oil light comes on, Kevin, you need to pull over immediately.
10. Rachel, your cartoon will be understood by only a few people.

EXERCISE 11

Understanding Nouns of Direct Address

Insert commas where needed to set off the nouns of direct address from the rest of the sentence.

1. Why did you leave the front door unlocked Cleo?
2. Students please pass your papers to the front of the class.
3. Stuart you left the lights on in the basement again.
4. Where did you see the UFO Seth?
5. Few basketball players Kelvin have the talent to play in the NBA.
6. There have been others Ian who have tried to climb this mountain.

7. Family it's time to have a discussion about finances.
8. Mr. Summers I did not realize that you were driving that car.
9. My fellow Americans I am proud to lead this country for the next four years.
10. You should probably remove the lens cover first Carolyn.

E X E R C I S E   1 2
Using Nouns of Direct Address in Your Writing
Sometimes a speaker will directly address the audience. This can help the speaker communicate with his or her listeners. Write a paragraph for a speech in which you address an audience of third-graders to inspire or motivate them. The speech can cover any topic. Be sure to punctuate nouns of direct address correctly.

USAGE tip

Before you examine appositives as interrupters, you may want to review appositives as modifiers in Unit 9 on pages 166–169.

APPOSITIVES

An **appositive** is a word or a group of words that renames a noun. In the following sentence, the appositive *Herman Melville* renames the noun *writer*.

> EXAMPLE
> The American writer Herman Melville lived in the nineteenth century.

If the information in an appositive specifically identifies the noun that proceeds it, then the appositive is called **essential** and not set off with commas. In the sentence above, *Herman Melville* identifies which American writer lived in the nineteenth century.

If the information in the appositive is not necessary to identify the noun that precedes it, then the appositive is called **nonessential** and is set off with commas. The following two sentences will help you see the difference between essential and nonessential information in an appositive.

EXAMPLES

essential appositive   Your sister Tina is a good singer. (The appositive *Tina* renames the noun *sister*. The appositive *Tina* is essential to the meaning of the sentence. Without the appositive, you would not know which sister is a good singer.)

nonessential appositive   Your oldest sister, Tina, is a good singer. (The appositive *Tina* is not essential to the meaning of the sentence. The adjective *oldest* tells you which sister. You do not need the information in the appositive to tell you which sister.)

USAGE tip

Do not use commas with an appositive when it is part of a proper name or when it is needed to identify the noun it follows: *my brother Dave, my friend Sue, King Henry VIII.*

Try It Yourself

EXERCISE 13

Identifying Appositives

Identify the appositives in the sentences below. Then write the noun or pronoun that the appositive or appositive phrases identify or modify.

1. Morley Callaghan met Ernest Hemingway in 1923 while working for a Toronto newspaper, the *Daily Star*.
2. Callaghan published his story "A Girl With Ambition" in 1926.
3. Callaghan's short story "Luke Baldwin's Vow" is about a boy and his dog.
4. In the story, Luke's dog, a collie, is eleven years old.
5. Luke's uncle, Henry, decides that the dog is not worth keeping around.
6. Henry asked Sam Carter, a mill hand, to get rid of the dog.
7. Luke saved his dog Dan from drowning.
8. Luke asked a neighbor, Mr. Kemp, if Dan could live with him.
9. The boy listened to Mr. Kemp, a wise man, and took his advice.
10. Helen, Luke's aunt, helped him convince Henry to let him keep the dog.

Correcting Sentences with Appositives

Rewrite the sentences below, adding commas where necessary. If a sentence has no errors, write *correct*.

1. My uncle recently bought a restored Model T a car built in the early 1900s.
2. The automobile manufacturer Henry Ford revolutionized the car industry.
3. Today, the company he started the Ford Motor Company is one of the largest manufacturing organizations in the United States.
4. My uncle an antique car collector owns many old cars.
5. He even owns a Model A the automobile that replaced the Model T.
6. General Motors Ford's competitor made big gains in car sales in the 1920s.
7. The major automobile manufacturers sold fewer cars during the Great Depression a severe economic downturn.
8. Antique cars now sell for large amounts of money thousands of dollars if they are in good condition.
9. The center of automobile industry is Detroit a city in Michigan.
10. Because of this distinction, Detroit was given the nickname "the Motor City."

Using Appositives in Your Writing

Write a brief paragraph about your favorite music group for a school newspaper. Use at least three appositives in your description to identify and provide more information about the band and their songs. Be sure to punctuate your appositives correctly.

UNIT 11 REVIEW

TEST YOUR KNOWLEDGE

EXERCISE 1
Identifying Interrupters
Write the interrupters in the following sentences. Then indicate whether the interrupter is an interjection, a parenthetical expression, a noun of direct address, or an appositive. (10 points)

EXAMPLE
The dog, a springer spaniel, is a devoted companion.
(*a springer spaniel*, appositive)

1. The disk, I believe, contains all the files you need to start the project.
2. Grandma will be cooking your favorite dish, spaghetti and meatballs.
3. Santa Fe, the capital of New Mexico, is where you must go.
4. Felix, do you have any idea what you are doing?
5. That plant, as I was saying, is the most dangerous of its kind in the forest.
6. The movie you rented, in fact, could be the worst movie I have ever seen.
7. Goodness, that was a loud noise.
8. By the way, that cheese you are eating sat out all night.
9. I come home early and, aha, I find you watching soap operas.
10. Mr. Worf, will you please throw Wesley off the bridge?

EXERCISE 2
Identifying Interjections and Nouns of Direct Address
Write the interjections and nouns of direct address in the following sentences. Then label the kind of interrupter it is. (10 points)

EXAMPLE

Hush! We don't want them to find us. (*Hush!,* interjection)

1. Hurry up and get the cows into the barn, James.
2. Oops! I just about dropped the glass bowl.
3. Whew! That was a close call.
4. Say, Bill, did you know that the Braves are playing tonight?
5. Wow! Phil, look at the tornado funnel heading this way!
6. Gentlemen, really, I'm surprised by your rude behavior.
7. We should take care of the business at hand, Melinda.
8. Rats! Somebody just tripped the car alarm again.
9. Well, I guess it's supposed to rain tomorrow.
10. Karen, hey, turn down the stereo!

EXERCISE 3

Identifying Parenthetical Expressions and Appositives
Identify the underlined words or groups of words in the sentences below as parenthetical expressions or appositive phrases. (10 points)

EXAMPLE

This success, on the other hand, comes with a price. (parenthetical expression)

1. Tim, the best hitter on the team, likes to eat strawberry yogurt before each game.
2. Our opponent's best player, Johnson, for example, also has a unique pregame diet.
3. If it helps mental readiness, the key factor in winning, then I am all for it.
4. The Dragons, last year's league champion, have several superstitious players.
5. Keeping your players happy, after all, can have great benefits.
6. The umpire Pullman, by the way, parks in the same spot for every game.
7. As for me, to tell the truth, I don't believe in any of that stuff.

8. Practice, <u>the best pregame ritual</u>, is what I rely on for success.
9. It has worked for me so far, <u>luckily</u>, since I don't like yogurt.
10. In my opinion, the entire starting lineup, <u>hitters one through nine</u>, could use some extra batting practice.

EXERCISE 4
Understanding Interjections
Choose an appropriate interjection for the emotions expressed in the following sentences. Rewrite each sentence so that the interjection is punctuated correctly. (10 points)

EXAMPLE
I'm so glad that test is over. *(Whew! I'm so glad that test is over.)*

1. That man ate three large pizzas at one sitting.
2. We are not going to have enough money to replace the broken vase.
3. I have to study both Friday and Saturday night.
4. I don't know what to do about this annoying problem.
5. It's raining again today.
6. The catcher's mitt is under the sofa.
7. The stove is still hot.
8. The children will be out of school at 3:00 P.M.
9. I dropped my keys down the elevator shaft.
10. You are stepping on my foot.

EXERCISE 5
Correcting Sentences with Interrupters
Rewrite the following sentences so that nouns of direct address, parenthetical expressions, and appositives are punctuated correctly with commas or occasionally dashes. (10 points)

EXAMPLE
After all Justin what goes up must come down. *(After all, Justin, what goes up must come down.)*

1. Looking through all these files marriage licenses and birth certificates gave me a headache.
2. Jamie the store will be closing in five minutes.
3. Naturally the solution to this mystery was right under our noses.
4. Most of your relatives aunts, uncles, and cousins showed up at the reunion.
5. These artifacts relics from another age have a great deal to tell us.
6. The red dress in my opinion looks better on you.
7. I found the culprit a raccoon digging through the garbage.
8. Mr. Hall to say the least is a dedicated man.
9. Sandra is today your last day of school?
10. Furthermore Bill painted the entire barn yesterday.

EXERCISE 6

Understanding Appositives

Combine each group of sentences below, creating one sentence that contains essential or nonessential appositives. Be sure to punctuate the appositives correctly. (20 points)

EXAMPLE

John Steinbeck was a twentieth-century author. He wrote *The Grapes of Wrath*. *The Grapes of Wrath* is a classic book in American literature. *(John Steinbeck, a twentieth-century author, wrote* The Grapes of Wrath, *a classic book in American literature.)*

1. The time period prior to the Civil War is also called the antebellum period in American history. It lasted for about four decades.
2. Several presidents served in the antebellum period. They were Whigs or Democrats. This was the second two-party era in American history.
3. The presidents tried to avoid dealing with slavery. The issue of slavery divided the nation.
4. Most southerners were small farmers. They did not own slaves. These farmers worked their own land.

5. The large planters in the South owned slaves. They were a small part of the population. Plantation owners believed the Constitution allowed them to own slaves.
6. Abolitionists slowly gained strength in the North. Abolitionists wanted to free the slaves. They gave speeches and published newspapers to promote their cause.
7. Small white farmers in the South also supported slavery. They did not believe that African Americans were citizens. These farmers feared living alongside freed slaves.
8. The issue was intensified after the addition of the western territories. These were new lands acquired by the United States from Mexico.
9. Most southern political leaders were slave owners. They wanted to open the territories to slavery.
10. Most northern political leaders opposed the expansion of slavery in the West. This was the area where new states would be formed. These leaders did not oppose slavery in the South. This was the area where it already existed.

EXERCISE 7

Using Interrupters
Write a sentence for each of the interrupters listed below.
(10 points)

EXAMPLE
a noun of direct address for the beginning of a sentence
(Andy, you are the most talented artist in the state.)

1. an interjection showing mild emotion
2. an interjection showing sudden, intense emotion
3. a parenthetical expression for the beginning of a sentence
4. a parenthetical expression for the middle of a sentence
5. a noun of direct address for the end of a sentence
6. an essential appositive
7. a nonessential appositive
8. a noun of direct address and a parenthetical expression
9. a parenthetical expression and an appositive
10. an interjection and an appositive

EXERCISE 8

Using Interrupters in Your Writing

Write a short essay for a teen mystery magazine about the mysterious disappearance of an ordinary object, such as a pair of ice skates, keys, or a catcher's mitt. Use interjections, parenthetical expressions, nouns of direct address, and appositives in your paragraph. Be sure to punctuate correctly the interrupters you use. (20 points)

UNIT *12* PHRASES, CLAUSES, AND COMPLEX SENTENCES

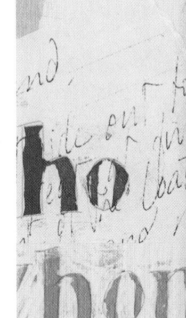

PHRASES, CLAUSES, AND COMPLEX SENTENCES

PHRASES AND CLAUSES

Sometimes groups of words function as one part of speech. These groups of words are either *phrases* or *clauses*. Clauses have both subjects and verbs; phrases do not.

EXAMPLES	
phrase	I want **to eat one more slice of pizza.**
phrase	He is being taken **to the county jail.**
clause	You can have dessert **after you finish your spinach.**
clause	Could you find out **what is making that terrible noise?**

Try It Yourself

EXERCISE 1
Identifying Phrases and Clauses in Literature
Identify the underlined groups of words in the literature passage as phrases or clauses.

Literature MODEL

When he was home, he was so grouchy we were afraid to speak. Now when we saw him coming, we got lost. Even our friends ran for cover.

At the railroad tracks, we sped up. The tracks were as far across as a block was long. Silently, I counted the rails by the heat of the steel bars through my thin soles. On the other side, I felt something heavy rise up in my chest and I knew that I wanted to cry. I wanted to cry or run or kiss the dusty ground.

from "Getting the Facts of Life"
Paulette Childress

Using Phrases and Clauses
Write a complete sentence incorporating each of the following
phrases or clauses.

1. about what happened on the boat
2. when you discover the problem
3. that I could understand
4. who the teacher is
5. in fifteen minutes
6. beyond the third hill
7. at the top of the mountain
8. among the farmers
9. if we could figure it out
10. without any distractions

PHRASES

A **phrase** is a group of words used as a single part of speech. A
phrase lacks a subject, a verb, or both. Therefore, it cannot be
a sentence. There are three common kinds of phrases:
prepositional phrases, verbal phrases, and appositive phrases

PREPOSITIONAL PHRASES

A **prepositional phrase** consists of a preposition, its object,
and any modifiers of that object. A prepositional phrase adds
information to a sentence by modifying another word in the
sentence. It may function as an adjective or an adverb.

USAGE tip

You may want to
review prepositions
and prepositional
phrases on pages
196–199 in Unit 10.

EXAMPLES
adjectives   Ted bought a car **with a sunroof**. (The
prepositional phrase *with a sunroof* tells what kind
of car Ted bought. The phrase is an adjective,
modifying the noun *car*.)

He bought the car from a dealership **on
Washington Street**. (The prepositional phrase *on*

CONTINUED

Remember that some words function as either an adverb or a preposition, depending on the sentence. Prepositions never stand alone. They always have an object and are part of a prepositional phrase. If the word stands alone, it is an adverb.

Washington Street tells at which dealership Ted bought the car. The phrase is an adjective, modifying the object of the prepositional phrase *from a dealership*.)

adverbs   The fog drifted **over the hill**. (The prepositional phrase *over the hill* tells where the fog drifted. The phrase is an adverb, modifying the verb *drifted*.)

The soldier is accurate **with a rifle**. (The prepositional phrase *with a rifle* tells how the soldier is accurate. The phrase is an adverb, modifying the adjective *accurate*.)

Use prepositional phrases to create sentence variety. When every sentence in a paragraph starts with its subject, the rhythm of the sentences becomes boring. Revise your sentences, where it is appropriate, to start some with prepositional phrases.

EXAMPLE
The professor lectured about economic theory **for two hours**. **For two hours** the professor lectured about economic theory.

Try It Yourself

EXERCISE 3
Identifying Prepositional Phrases in Literature
Write the word that each underlined group of words modifies. Then label each prepositional phrase as an adjective or an adverb phrase.

Literature
MODEL

There was a hummingbird once which <u>in the wintertime</u> did not leave our neighborhood <u>in Fresno, California</u>. I'll tell you about it.

<u>Across the street</u> lived old Dikran, who was almost blind. He was past eighty and his wife was only a few years younger. They had a little house that was as neat inside as it was ordinary outside—except for old Dikran's

CONTINUED

garden, which was the best thing <u>of its kind</u> <u>in the world</u>. Plants, bushes, trees—all strong, in sweet black moist earth whose guardian was old Dikran. All things <u>from the sky</u> loved this spot <u>in our poor neighborhood</u>, and old Dikran loved *them*.

from "The Hummingbird That Lived through Winter"
William Saroyan

E X E R C I S E 4
Understanding Prepositional Phrases
Rewrite the following sentences so that each begins with a prepositional phrase.

1. An argument about the future of the town rages inside the meeting hall.
2. The thief removed the diamond without a trace of evidence.
3. Your dog will come wandering in the house with his supper dish in his mouth.
4. Coach Gaines watched the practice from the observation tower.
5. The shots were fired from the abandoned house.
6. My house sits on a hill across the lake.
7. Sheri finished her Christmas shopping at the mall.
8. I believe you will find the evidence you are looking for underneath the rug.
9. The frightened cat climbed up the tree in the middle of the backyard.
10. Your friend is resting in the shade under the awning.

E X E R C I S E 5
Using Prepositional Phrases in Your Writing

For a school newspaper, write a human-events story about an event that recently happened in your life. Make sure that your story answers the journalists' questions *Who? What? Where? When? Why?* and *How?* Use prepositional phrases in the story to help your readers visualize what happened, and try to vary the placement in your sentences.

USAGE tip

You may want to review the material on verbals on pages 183–185 in Unit 9.

VERBAL PHRASES

Verbals are verb forms that act as namers or modifiers. There are three kinds of verbals: participles, gerunds, and infinitives.

Participial Phrases

A **participle** is a verb form ending in *–ing*, *–d*, or *–ed* that acts as an adjective, modifying a noun or a pronoun. A **participial phrase** is made up of a participle and all of its modifiers, which may include objects, nouns, adjectives, adverbs, and prepositional phrases. The entire phrase acts as an adjective.

EXAMPLES

Climbing carefully up the tree, Elijah was able to reach the cat. (The participle *climbing*, the adverb *carefully*, and the prepositional phrase *up the tree* make up the participial phrase that modifies *Elijah*.)

Jim came up with the idea for the mural **painted on the building**. (The participle *painted* and the prepositional phrase *on the building* make up the participial phrase that modifies *mural*.)

For variety, begin some of your sentences with participial phrases. However, be sure to place the participial phrase close to the word it modifies. Otherwise, you may say something you do not mean.

EXAMPLES

misplaced participial phrase	We discussed what to do about the bird **standing at the water cooler**.
revised sentence	Standing at the water cooler, we discussed what to do about the bird.

EXERCISE 6

Identifying Participial Phrases in Literature
Identify the five participial phrases in the literature passage below. Beside each, identify the noun or pronoun the participial phrase modifies.

Literature
M O D E L

Some of the covey lit in trees but most of them scattered into brush piles and it was necessary to jump on the ice-coated mounds of brush several times before they would flush. Coming out while you were poised unsteadily on the icy, springy brush they made difficult shooting, and I killed two, missed five and started back pleased to have found a covey close to the house and happy there were so many left to find on another day.

At the house they said the boy had refused to let anyone come into the room.

"You can't come in" he said. "You mustn't get what I have."

I went up to him and found him in exactly the position I had left him, white-faced, but with the tops of his cheeks flushed by the fever, staring still as he had stared at the foot of the bed.

from "A Day's Wait"
Ernest Hemingway

EXERCISE 7

Understanding Participial Phrases
For each of the following participial phrases, write a complete sentence. Try to vary your sentence structure, but be sure to place the participial phrase close to the word it modifies.

1. remembered each year
2. scribbled on the menu
3. borrowing from his sister
4. spotted over the trees
5. shocked at the outcome

6. diving into the pool
7. traveling across the state
8. talking of trouble
9. flying near the ground
10. operated by the boss

Using Participial Phrases in Your Writing
Imagine that you are writing a letter to a business as part of a summer job application. To let your potential employers know what qualities you would bring to the job, describe in the letter your skills. Use participial phrases in your letter to explain your abilities and experience.

Gerund Phrases

A **gerund phrase** is a phrase made up of a gerund (a verb a form ending in –*ing*) and all of its modifiers and complements. The entire phrase functions as a noun. This means that it may be the subject, predicate nominative, direct object, indirect object, or object of the preposition in a sentence. Adjectives, adverbs, and prepositional phrases can all modify a gerund.

> EXAMPLES
> **Waiting for the bus** is boring for Tracy. (The gerund phrase functions as the subject of the sentence.)
>
> Tracy's least favorite activity is **waiting for the bus**. (The gerund phrase functions as the predicate nominative of the sentence.)
>
> Tracy hates **waiting for the bus** at the corner. (The gerund phrase functions as the direct object of the sentence.)
>
> Tracy called a taxi instead of **waiting for the bus**. (The gerund phrase functions as the object of the preposition.)

EXERCISE 9

Identifying Gerund Phrases in Literature

Identify the three gerund phrases in the literature passage below. Beside each phrase, tell whether the gerund phrase is used as a subject, predicate nominative, direct object, indirect object, or object of the preposition.

Literature
M O D E L

Wondering what all the noise was about, Amaterasu peeped out of the cave and at once saw her own face reflected in the mirror. She had never seen a looking-glass before, so she thought the people must have found another sun to replace her and ran from the cave in a rage. The others immediately stretched ropes across the mouth of the cave to stop her from going back into it again, but there was no need. By then she had discovered that it was her own shining face looking back at her. She was delighted by this and by the necklaces, as well as the singing and dancing for, truth to tell, she had begun to feel lonely in her cave.

from "Amaterasu"
Carolyn Swift

EXERCISE 10

Understanding Gerund Phrases

Write a sentence for each of the following gerund phrases. Be sure to use each phrase as the subject, predicate nominative, direct object, indirect object, or object of the preposition.

1. carrying the books
2. dancing on the stage
3. writing a report each day
4. completing the requirements
5. cracking his knuckles

6. pulling my hair
7. polling the voters
8. beginning the speech with a joke
9. jogging each weekend
10. sleeping in the afternoon

EXERCISE 11
Using Gerund Phrases in Your Writing
Write a short passage for an instruction manual about fixing an object, putting something together, or setting something up. Potential topics for this exercise could include how to fix a bicycle tire, how to set up a VCR, how to put up a volleyball net, or how to build a model airplane. In your passage, use at least four gerund phrases.

Infinitive Phrases

An **infinitive phrase** is made up of an infinitive (a verb form preceded by the word *to*) and all its modifiers and complements. Infinitive phrases can function as nouns, adjectives, or adverbs.

EXAMPLES
It is fun **to fly in a balloon far above the ground**. (The infinitive phrase functions as an adverb.)

The snake likes **to slither through the grass**. (The infinitive phrase functions as a noun.)

Sometimes the *to* of an infinitive phrase is left out; it is understood.

EXAMPLES
Jerry helped [**to**] paint the house.
I'll go [**to**] feed the cat.

USAGE tip

When a modifier comes between *to* and the verb, the infinitive is said to be *split*. Avoid split infinitives, unless by not doing so the result is awkward or sounds unnatural.

EXERCISE 12

Identifying Infinitive Phrases in Literature

Identify the five infinitive phrases in the literature passage
below. Beside each phrase, tell whether it is used as a noun,
adjective, or adverb.

In the darkness, Lester looked over the yard, picking out
familiar shapes—the *Hummingbird*, the *Zephyr*. He'd
worked on them both. Train travel wasn't anything like it
used to be in the old days—not since people had begun to
ride airplanes. "Progress," he scoffed. "Those contraptions
will never take the place of a train. No sir!"

Suddenly he felt a sharp pain in his chest. At exactly
the same moment he heard the mournful sound of a train
whistle, which the wind seemed to carry from some faraway
place. Ignoring his pain, Lester looked at the old station.
He knew nothing was scheduled to come in or out till early
morning. Nervously he lit a match to check the time. 11:59!

from "The 11:59"
Patricia McKissack

Literature
M O D E L

EXERCISE 13

Understanding Infinitive Phrases

Complete each of the following sentences with an infinitive
phrase.

1. ___ might help ease the tension.
2. Gerry decided ___.
3. Harry's plan for the summer is ___.
4. Tomorrow will be the day ___.
5. The kitten hid under the chair ___.
6. Joann had an idea ___.
7. You never had the ability ___.
8. Judy should be commended for her work ___.
9. I hate ___ when there is too much to do.
10. Our brother looked in the book ___.

EXERCISE **14**

Using Infinitive Phrases in Your Writing

Write a paragraph to a pen pal describing one of your friends. Describe his or her likes and dislikes and any favorite activities. Use at least five infinitive phrases in your paragraph.

APPOSITIVE PHRASES

An **appositive phrase** is a group of words made up of an appositive and all its modifiers. The phrase renames or identifies a noun or pronoun.

USAGE tip

Before reading this section, you may want to review coverage of appositives on pages 166–169 in Unit 9.

EXAMPLES

Dr. George, **the former football coach**, is our new professor. (The appositive phrase renames the noun *Dr. George.*)

The television show *Let's Make a Deal* used to be very popular. (The appositive phrase identifies which show used to be very popular.)

The first example above, *the former football coach*, is a **nonessential appositive phrase.** It is not necessary to identify Dr. George, who has already been named. Therefore, it is set off with commas. The second example, *Let's Make a Deal*, is an **essential appositive phrase.** It is necessary for identifying which particular television show. This appositive phrase is not set off with commas.

Appositive phrases add versatility to your writing because they can be placed at the beginning, in the middle, or at the end of a sentence. They also provide variety. Using appositive phrases to combine sentences eliminates unimportant words and creates more fact-filled sentences. When you join two ideas with an appositive phrase, place the idea you wish to stress in the main clause and make the less important idea the appositive.

EXAMPLES

Tammy sings in the church choir. She is a ninth-grader.
Tammy, a ninth-grader, sings in the church choir.

Try It Yourself

EXERCISE 15

Identifying Appositive Phrases

Write the appositive phrases you find in the sentences below.
Then tell the noun or pronoun each appositive phrase
identifies.

1. That man at the bar, Brett Samuels, arrived in town two
   days ago.
2. I've heard that he is from Barren Canyon, a town about
   150 miles northeast of here.
3. The sound of gunshots, three loud cracks, rang out in the
   street.
4. Everyone in the bar, gamblers, miners, and drifters,
   scrambled out the door.
5. A man dressed in a black jacket, a threatening figure,
   stood in the middle of Main Street 100 feet away.
6. Right outside the bar, Cole West, the town sheriff, lay
   face down in the street.
7. Cole had been the only law enforcement in Broken
   Cactus, a small mining community.
8. No one dared to challenge the defiant gunman, a
   menacing presence who stood his ground unmoving.
9. Brett Samuels, a stranger to most in this town, ambled
   out into the street and faced the gunman.
10. Onlookers breathlessly awaited the showdown, a duel
    between two outsiders that would determine the fate of an
    entire town.

EXERCISE 16

Understanding Appositive Phrases

Combine each pair of sentences with an appositive or an
appositive phrase.

1. Alaska is the largest state in the union. It has the fewest people per square mile.
2. The state's total area is nearly 600,000 square miles. Alaska is over one-fifth the size of the entire lower forty-eight states.
3. Alaska is the northernmost state in the union. It has only one city with a population greater than 100,000.
4. Mount McKinley is in Alaska. It is the highest mountain in North America.
5. America bought Alaska in 1867 from Russia for $7.2 million. The price was two cents an acre.
6. Alaska's population grew by more than 10 percent in the 1990s. The state has fewer than 1.5 people per square mile.
7. Oil was discovered in Alaska in 1968. Oil became a major part of the state's economy.
8. In 1989, ten million gallons of oil were spilled into Prince William Sound in the *Exxon Valdez* disaster. This was the worst oil spill in U.S. history.
9. Included as part of Alaska are the Aleutian Islands. Three of these islands were occupied by the Japanese during World War II.
10. Alaska has been known for several economic pursuits throughout its history. Hunting for furs, fishing, whaling, and gold mining have all been part of the state's economy.

EXERCISE 17
Using Appositives in Your Writing
Choose an ordinary object, such as an apple, a bowling ball, or a snowflake. Write a poem, to be shared with classmates, in praise of the object. Use at least five appositive phrases to describe the object in detail.

CLAUSES WITHIN A SENTENCE

A **clause** is a group of words that contains a subject and verb and that functions as one part of speech. There are two types of clauses—independent and subordinate.

An **independent clause,** sometimes called a *main clause*, has a subject and a verb and expresses a complete thought. Since it can stand alone as a sentence, it is called *independent*.

> EXAMPLE
> Abraham Lincoln is often called the "Great Emancipator."

A **subordinate clause** has a subject and a verb, but it doesn't express a complete thought. It can't stand alone. It must be attached to or inserted into an independent clause. That's why subordinate clauses are also called *dependent clauses*. When you combine subordinate clauses with independent clauses, you form complete sentences.

> EXAMPLES
> **When the bell rang**, the students ran out of the room. (The subordinate clause *when the bell rang* is attached to an independent clause.)
>
> The dog **that barked all night** slept throughout the day. (The subordinate clause *that barked all night* is inserted into the independent clause *The dog slept throughout the day.*)

There are three types of subordinate clauses: adjective clauses, adverb clauses, and noun clauses.

Try It Yourself

EXERCISE 18
Identifying Independent and Subordinate Clauses in Literature
Write the subordinate and independent clauses you find in the following passage.

The American does not join in the argument but watches the other guests. As he looks, he sees a strange expression come over the face of the hostess. She is staring straight ahead, her muscles contracting slightly. With a slight gesture she summons the native boy standing behind her chair and whispers to him. The boy's eye's widen: he quickly leaves the room.

from "The Dinner Party"
Mona Gardner

EXERCISE 19
Understanding Independent and Subordinate Clauses
Label the following clauses as *independent* or *subordinate*. Then rewrite the subordinate clauses so that they are attached to or inserted into an independent clause.

1. James entered the room
2. when the first horse runs out of the barn
3. wherever we look for the cat
4. since it gets cold outside at night
5. I understand
6. although they passed the class
7. that crashed into the building
8. this ordeal is over
9. run for cover
10. if you cannot sit still

ADJECTIVE CLAUSES

An **adjective clause** is a subordinate clause that functions as an adjective. It modifies a noun or pronoun. Adjective clauses are introduced most frequently with words like the following: *that, which, who, whom, whose, after, before, since, than, when, why,* and *where.* An adjective clause follows the word it modifies.

EXAMPLES
Julie, **who is fourteen years old**, will be playing in the golf tournament.

Tomorrow is the day **when the season starts**.

When an adjective clause is essential to the meaning of a sentence, it should not be set off from the rest of the sentence with commas. When an adjective clause is nonessential, it is set off with commas.

EXAMPLES

essential We found the couch spring **that had been squeaking**.

Each person **who enrolls in the class** receives a green notebook.

nonessential Our car, **which we bought last year**, has 65,000 miles on the odometer.

Our camp counselor, **who frowns upon practical jokes**, should not find out about this.

Try It Yourself

EXERCISE 20
Identifying Adjective Clauses in Literature
Write the five adjective clauses found in the poem.

Branches are suns
that glimmer from within
taking life
here, under the apple tree,
where a crowd of petals close their eyes,
where scraggly layers of trunk
seem to slowly come apart.

Literature
M O D E L

CONTINUED

At sunset the branch I sit
on snaps and coils.
The blue jay hastily darts, and disappears.
I like it
here
where birds now nestle and sleep,
where little, high-pitched, cricketed chirps
rise like tiny bells towards the ageless moon.

from "Under the Apple Tree"
Diana Rivera

EXERCISE 21

Correcting Adjective Clauses

Correct the punctuation of the adjective clauses in the following sentences. If a sentence has no punctuation errors, write *correct*.

1. That car, that is in the garage, is a priceless antique.
2. Is Bernice the girl who is having a birthday party?
3. This book, which can be purchased at any bookstore, will change your life.
4. The center needs a volunteer who knows how to speak Spanish.
5. The snowman that you built in the backyard is melting.
6. Saturday is the day, when all of our hard work will pay off.
7. Bill is the player, whom you will be guarding in the game.
8. Dawn whose cat frequently visits lives three houses down the street.
9. Your table which is made of oak is over 100 years old.
10. They will fly to Seattle where the convention is being held.

EXERCISE 22
Using Adjective Clauses in Your Writing
Write a description for a peer of your favorite mode of
transportation. Tell about what it is, how it functions, and
what you especially like about it. Use at least four adjective
clauses in your description.

ADVERB CLAUSES

An **adverb clause** is a subordinate clause that functions as an
adverb. It modifies a verb, an adjective, or another adverb.

USAGE tip

You may want to
review the section
on subordinating
conjunctions on
pages 203–206 in
Unit 10.

EXAMPLES
Marlene played the flute **whenever she had the time**.
(*Whenever she had the time* modifies the verb *played*.)

Your car is faster **than my car**. (*Than my car* modifies the
adjective *faster*.)

The mayor will speak a half-hour longer **than he normally
does**. (*Than he normally does* modifies the adverb *longer*.)

Adverb clauses often, but not always, start with a
subordinating conjunction such as *after, although, because, before,
if, so that, unless, when, whether,* and *while*.

USAGE tip

When you use an
adverb clause at the
beginning of a
sentence, follow it
with a comma. If
you use an adverb
clause at the end of
a sentence, you do
not need to use a
comma before it.

*When you see a
green light*, hit the
gas and go.

Hit the gas and go
*when you see a
green light*.

Try It Yourself

EXERCISE 23
Identifying Adverb Clauses in Literature
Identify the two adverb clauses in the following passage.

> During the next few days, Mark's parents watched
> anxiously to see, Mr. Armitage said, whether Mark would
> start to sprout esparto grass instead of hair. For he
> doggedly ate Brekkfast Brikks for lunch, with soup, or
> sprinkled over his pudding; for tea, with jam; and for
> supper, lightly fried in dripping; not to mention, of
> course, the immense helpings he had for breakfast, with

Literature
M O D E L

CONTINUED

sugar and milk. Mr. Armitage, for his part, soon gave out; he said he wouldn't taste another Brekkfast Brikk even if it were wrapped in an inch-thick layer of *paté de foie gras.* Mark regretted that Harriet, who was a handy and uncritical eater, was still away, convalescing from her measles with an aunt.

In two days, the second packet was finished (sundial, paved garden, and espaliers). Mark cut it out, fastened it together, and joined it on to Section Three with trembling hands. Would the spell work for this section, too? He sang the rhyme in rather a quavering voice, but luckily the plywood door was shut, and there was no one to hear him. Yes! The gate grew again above him, and when he opened it and ran across the lawn through the yew arch, he found himself in a flagged garden full of flowers like huge blue cabbages.

from "The Serial Garden"
Joan Aiken

EXERCISE 24

Understanding Adverb Clauses

Write an independent clause to attach to each of the following adverb clauses. When you write out the complete sentences, be sure to punctuate the adverb clauses correctly.

1. whenever it is possible
2. even though they were confused
3. before the storm hits
4. until we come up with a better idea
5. that we could find such a necklace
6. than the first time we came here
7. if the problem continues
8. whether you choose or not
9. so that our parents won't be mad
10. after the sun goes down

EXERCISE 25

Using Adverb Clauses in Your Writing
Write a paragraph, to be shared with classmates, describing a recent accomplishment of which you are proud. In your paragraph, use at least three adverb clauses.

NOUN CLAUSES

A **noun clause** is a subordinate clause that functions as a noun. This means that it can function as a subject, predicate nominative, direct object, indirect object, object of a preposition, or appositive. Notice that noun clauses can have modifiers and complements. They can come at the beginning, middle, or end of a sentence.

Words like these often introduce noun clauses: *how, if, that, what, whatever, when, where, whether, which, who, whoever, whom, whose,* and *why.*

USAGE tip

Too many noun clauses can make your writing sound wordy and overly formal, especially when the noun clauses are used as subjects.

That smoking cigarettes is unhealthy is something that most people are aware of.

Most people are aware *that smoking cigarettes is unhealthy.*

EXAMPLES	
subject	**That our plan did not work** was obvious to all.
predicate nominative	That is **what happened yesterday**.
direct object	Can you tell me **where my guinea pig is hiding**?
indirect object	Tell **whoever is singing** to stop immediately.
object of the preposition	Katrina earned a trophy for **what she accomplished Saturday**.
appositive	The topic of the lecture, **that wolves can be trained**, grabbed people's attention.

EXERCISE 26

Identifying Noun Clauses in Literature

Write the two noun clauses you find in the literature passage below. Beside each, identify its function in the sentence.

> Ironically, before I understood the mystery, I felt vaguely comforted to imagine that perhaps this urban environment, so similar to the one in which many Americans live, was not so hostile to wild things after all. I briefly supposed that, like the resourceful raccoons and possums and squirrels and pigeons, all of whom have adapted to life in the suburbs, creatures as wild as pheasants might have a fighting chance. Now I remember that pheasant when I take my children to the zoo and see an elephant or a rhinoceros. They too inspire wonder and sadness.
>
> from "Ships in the Desert"
> Al Gore

EXERCISE 27

Understanding Noun Clauses

Write a sentence using each group of words below as a noun clause. Check your work to be sure that you have written a noun clause, not an adjective or adverb clause.

1. how I should ride a bicycle
2. what they did
3. whomever she met
4. why the tree fell
5. whether you like it or not
6. that you studied all night
7. whatever the boss decides
8. what I would like
9. who felt the need to draw on this wall
10. whoever finds the ring first

EXERCISE 28
Using Noun Clauses in Your Writing

Write a paragraph for your journal about an important decision you made recently. Discuss your motives and why you consider the decision important. Use at least five noun clauses in your report, and underline each one.

THE CLAUSES OF A SENTENCE: SIMPLE, COMPOUND, AND COMPLEX SENTENCES

Sentences are classified according to the number and kind of clauses they contain. Three types of sentence structures are *simple*, *compound*, and *complex*.

A **simple sentence** contains one independent clause and no subordinate clauses. It may have any number of phrases. It may also have a compound subject and a compound verb. A simple sentence is sometimes called an independent clause because it can stand by itself.

> EXAMPLES
> The bird flew over the mountain.
> Snow and sleet hampered our travel.
> We loaded the cannon and commenced firing.

A **compound sentence** consists of two or more independent clauses that are joined together with a comma and a coordinating conjunction (*and, but, or, nor, for, yet,* or *so*).

> EXAMPLES
> Occasionally the fox will appear near the edge of the forest, **but** usually he doesn't venture out of the trees.
>
> The gang buried the money, **and** their cars were pushed into the lake.
>
> I feel good about myself today, **for** I figured out the ingredients to the secret formula.

A **complex sentence** consists of one independent clause and one or more subordinate clauses. In the following examples, the independent clauses are italicized.

> EXAMPLES
>
> **After the game was over** but **before the postgame interview,** *the coach sat down and talked to us.*
>
> **When the whistle blew,** *an army of three hundred raced out to their cars.*

Try It Yourself

EXERCISE 29
Identifying Sentence Structures in Literature
Identify the seven sentences in the literature passage below as simple, compound, or complex.

Literature
MODEL

Mr. Fuller and the snake-man got out of the car. The snake-man was small and very old, probably over seventy. He wore leather boots made of thick cowhide and he had long gauntlet-type gloves on his hands made of the same stuff. The gloves reached above his elbows. In his right hand he carried an extraordinary implement, an eight-foot-long wooden pole with a forked end. The two prongs of the fork were made, so it seemed, of black rubber, about an inch thick and quite flexible, and it was clear that if the fork was pressed against the ground the two prongs would bend outwards, allowing the neck of the fork to go down as close to the ground as necessary. In his left hand he carried an ordinary brown sack.

from "The Green Mamba"
Roald Dahl

Understanding How to Use Clauses to Create Different Sentence Structures
Expand each of the following simple sentences into a compound or complex sentence by adding a subordinate clause and/or an independent clause. Label each sentence type that you create.

1. The poodle devoured the cake.
2. Chris fell down.
3. Ben's computer broke.
4. This blanket feels warm.
5. A few of the books are worth reading.
6. Debbie tried to call her.
7. The nightly news will never be the same.
8. Both Peter and Bob played soccer.
9. Jen believed Tim's story.
10. Kenneth wrote the novel.

Using Different Sentence Structures in Your Writing
Check a newspaper, news broadcast, or the Internet to learn about a current event that is happening overseas. For classmates, write a summary in which you describe the important details of this event. In your summary, use a variety of simple, compound, and complex sentences.

UNIT 12 REVIEW

TEST YOUR KNOWLEDGE

EXERCISE 1

Identifying Phrases

Identify each underlined phrase by writing one of these abbreviations. (10 points)

PREP = prepositional phrase   *INF* = infinitive phrase
PART = participial phrase   *APP* = appositive phrase
GER = gerund phrase

> EXAMPLE
> The snake slithered <u>under the table</u> and <u>into the pipe</u> after it saw us. (PREP, PREP)

1. <u>Buying a new car</u> requires research and patience.
2. <u>Bragging about his high school football days,</u> Dirk continued <u>to talk with no end in sight</u>.
3. I want <u>to help you</u> figure out how <u>to fix the problem</u>.
4. Yesterday I sat <u>under the tree</u> and read my book.
5. <u>Walking in the park</u> helped me focus on the task I had been given.
6. <u>Running briskly with long strides,</u> he quickly made it home.
7. <u>To learn this skill now</u>, puts you at a great advantage over the competition.
8. The owl, <u>a merciless hunter of the night</u>, sat poised on the tree branch.
9. His dog, <u>the cocker spaniel</u>, is not going to win the competition.
10. <u>Throughout the voyage</u>, the captain reminded us of who was in charge.

EXERCISE 2

Identifying Independent and Subordinate Clauses
Label each numbered item below as *I* for independent clause
and *S* for subordinate clause. (10 points)

EXAMPLE
Many fish are unable to swim near the surface. (I)

1. His sense of humor is bizarre.
2. When we were kings.
3. As it was creeping up the side of the house.
4. That you figured out the puzzle quickly.
5. Where the corn grows as far as the eye can see.
6. The speaker tapped the microphone.
7. We decided to work.
8. Before they do.
9. Rather than [to] make this job more difficult.
10. Tom wanted to tell them.

EXERCISE 3

Identifying Types of Clauses
Identify the underlined clauses in each sentence by writing
ADJ for an adjective clause, *ADV* for an adverb clause, and *N*
for a noun clause. (10 points)

EXAMPLE
This could be the class <u>that will turn around your academic
career</u>. (ADJ)

1. <u>After you leave the store</u>, you might want to double-check
   the receipt.
2. There is the lion <u>that chased a hunter up a tree</u>.
3. <u>What the historian wrote</u> only confuses the issue further.
4. Is he the advisor with <u>whom you discussed your class
   schedule</u>?
5. Let me know if they consider <u>whether they can fix the
   car</u>.
6. I cannot understand students <u>who do not value their
   education</u>.

7. The barn is a place <u>where bats like to congregate</u>.
8. Marie is meaner <u>when she is figuring out the payroll taxes</u> than at other times.
9. Your teacher discussed <u>why your behavior is disruptive to others</u>.
10. The sunset is brighter <u>when there are fewer clouds in the sky</u>.

EXERCISE 4

Identifying Sentence Structure
Identify each of the following sentences by writing *S* for simple, *CD* for compound, and *CX* for complex. (10 points)

EXAMPLE
I will buy the cake, and Barb will pick up the candles. (CD)

1. Larry just bought the car that is sitting in the street.
2. I find this book to be too long and boring.
3. We won the game, but the coach yelled at us anyway because we were goofing around.
4. You are going to be flying on the jumbo jet, which is faster than the smaller plane.
5. It is a great day for a picnic, although the horde of ants is unpleasant.
6. Rover and Fluffy chewed and clawed the furniture and the drapes.
7. The crowd watched silently as the golfer analyzed her shot.
8. Gary won another tournament, for he is the greatest to ever play the game.
9. We would like to go home for the weekend, but we don't have a car that can get us there.
10. Brad is a good employee who can be trusted to get his work done.

EXERCISE 5
Understanding Phrases
Use different kinds of phrases to combine the sentences in
each numbered item. You may have to change the wording
slightly so that your sentences make sense. Remember to
punctuate your phrases correctly. (10 points)

EXAMPLE
Carl Sandburg is the son of Swedish immigrants. He grew up in
Galesburg, Illinois. *(Carl Sandburg, the son of Swedish
immigrants, grew up in Galesburg, Illinois.)*

1. Sandburg traveled from town to town throughout the
   Midwest. He worked as a brick maker, carpenter's helper,
   a milk wagon driver, and a house painter.
2. Sandburg had a diverse work experience. This allowed
   him to understand the lives of ordinary workers.
3. In 1898 Sandburg served as a soldier in the
   Spanish-American War. This was a short conflict. The
   United States quickly defeated Spain.
4. Sandburg worked as an advertising writer and a journalist.
   He is best known as a poet. He traveled around the
   country reading his poems.
5. Sandburg's poetry was about ordinary people and
   everyday life. He described them as "simple poems for
   simple people."
6. Sandburg is also known as a biographer. He wrote about
   Abraham Lincoln. Two of Sandburg's books are *Abraham
   Lincoln: The Prairie Years* and *Abraham Lincoln: The War
   Years*.
7. Lincoln was the sixteenth president of the United States.
   Many historians consider him to be the greatest president
   in American history.
8. Lincoln lived in Illinois. He was born in Kentucky. He
   spent part of his childhood in Indiana.
9. Carl Sandburg died in 1967. This was 102 years after
   Lincoln was assassinated.
10. Sandburg's books about Lincoln were widely read. They
    helped inspire later biographies of the president.

Understanding Clauses

Use different kinds of clauses to combine the sentences in each numbered item. You may have to change the wording slightly so that your sentences make sense. Remember to punctuate your clauses correctly. (10 points)

EXAMPLE

Tennis is a popular sport that is played by millions of Americans. It reflects the desire of many to play an outdoor sport. *(Tennis, a popular sport played by millions of Americans, reflects the desire of many to play an outdoor sport.)*

1. Tennis players can be so careful in selecting their rackets. They spend a lot of time shopping for them.
2. Tennis started to gain worldwide popularity in 1877. The first Wimbledon tournament was held in England.
3. For many years tennis was a sport played only by the wealthy. Private country clubs in Britain and the United States were the exclusive sites where the game was played.
4. Segregation rules closed tournaments to African Americans. These rules were especially strict in the South. They were excluded from many events in the United States.
5. In the 1960s attitudes began to change. Arthur Ashe developed into one of the world's best tennis players.
6. Ashe was the first African American to become the top-ranked tennis player in the world. He opened opportunities for other minority tennis players in the United States.
7. Many in tennis were uncomfortable with Ashe's success. He rose to the top of his sport.
8. Ashe won singles titles at the U. S. Open, Wimbledon, and the World Championship Tennis tournaments. He was at the top of his game in the 1960s and 1970s.

9. One of the books Ashe has written is *A Hard Road to Glory: A History of the African-American Athlete*. It is a thorough discussion of early black athletes in the United States and Canada.

10. During open-heart surgery, Ashe contracted the HIV virus from a blood transfusion. He died in 1993. Arthur Ashe Stadium was dedicated in his honor in Flushing Meadows, New York.

EXERCISE 7

Understanding How to Use Clauses to Create Different Sentence Structures

Expand each of the following sentences by adding subordinate and/or independent clauses to create compound and complex sentences. Then identify the type of sentence you have written. Write five compound and five complex sentences. (10 points)

EXAMPLE

simple sentence	The New York Yankees won the World Series in 1927.
complex sentence	*The New York Yankees won the World Series in 1927 after they swept the Pittsburgh Pirates in four games.*

1. Public television educates and entertains its viewers.
2. A song can brighten a person's day.
3. Many television shows are poorly written.
4. A few politicians do not care what the polls report.
5. Grover Cleveland is the only president to serve two non-consecutive terms.
6. George Patton was a born leader.
7. Our dog has short hair and a long tail.
8. The play was short but dramatic.
9. Your alarm went off every fifteen minutes.
10. Each day is a new adventure.

Understanding Clauses and Phrases

Write a sentence following the directions for each item. Be sure to punctuate your clauses and phrases correctly. (10 points)

> EXAMPLE
>
> an introductory appositive phrase *(The first state to secede after Lincoln's election, South Carolina led the way for ten other southern states to leave the Union.)*

1. three prepositional phrases
2. a participial phrase
3. a gerund phrase used as a subject
4. an infinitive phrase used as an adjective or adverb
5. an appositive phrase
6. a subordinate clause used as an adjective
7. a subordinate clause used as an adverb
8. a simple sentence with a compound verb
9. a compound sentence
10. a complex sentence

Using Different Sentence Structures in Your Writing

Write a response to the quotation below, with which you can agree or disagree. You may choose to explain how the quotation has applied to your life or to the life of someone you know. Use a variety of sentence structures to respond fully to the ideas expressed in the quotation. (20 points)

> Champions aren't made in gyms. Champions are made from something they have deep inside them—a desire, a dream, a vision.
>
> Mohammed Ali

UNIT *13* DIAGRAMMING SENTENCES

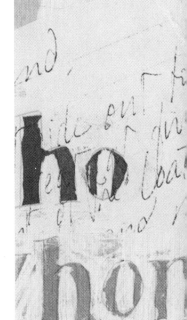

DIAGRAMMING SENTENCES

SENTENCE DIAGRAMS

A sentence consists of different parts of speech that work together to form a complete thought. A good way to see the relationship between these parts of speech is to diagram them. A **sentence diagram** is a picture of the structure of a sentence. Using horizontal, vertical, and slanting lines, the diagram shows the role of every word and phrase in a sentence.

A few general rules apply to all sentence diagrams.

1. Start with a horizontal line. On this line you will write the sentence base.
2. In approximately the center of the line, you will draw a short vertical line cutting the horizontal one. This vertical line is the dividing point between the complete subject, which goes on the left, and the complete predicate, which goes on the right. Use this placement even if the predicate precedes the subject in the sentence, as in interrogative sentences.
3. Always capitalize the first word in the sentence.
4. Do not use sentence punctuation in the diagram.

SIMPLE SUBJECTS AND SIMPLE PREDICATES

Start with the basic diagram—a horizontal line divided approximately in the center by a vertical line. Write the simple subject to the left of the vertical line. Write the simple predicate to the right of the vertical line. Notice that the entire verb phrase is written on the horizontal line.

EXAMPLES
The crowd cheered.

crowed | cheered

He had been sleeping.

He | had been sleeping

CONTINUED

The chipmunk popped out of the hole.

```
chipmunk | popped
```

Try It Yourself

Diagramming Simple Subjects and Simple Predicates
Diagram the simple subject and simple predicate for each
sentence below.

1. The telephone rang.
2. Many lives were lost in the war.
3. Sue parked the car.
4. The package should arrive tomorrow.
5. Diane likes music.
6. Clouds floated above us.
7. The dog snored loudly.
8. Our television set broke.
9. We have been hearing noises in the attic.
10. A squirrel might have broken in.

FOUR TYPES OF SENTENCES

In a sentence diagram, the order of simple subject and simple
predicate is always the same, regardless of the order the words
actually occur in the sentence.

Declarative and Exclamatory Sentences

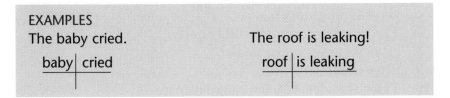

EXAMPLES
The baby cried.   The roof is leaking!

```
baby | cried                       roof | is leaking
```

Interrogative Sentences

Notice that although the subject comes between the two parts of the verb phrase, it is diagrammed just like the declarative sentence.

EXAMPLES

Did the baby cry?

| baby | Did cry |

Has the roof been leaking?

| roof | Has been leaking |

Imperative Sentences

Notice that the simple subject is the understood *you*.

EXAMPLES

Stop!

| (you) | Stop |

Don't do it.

| (you) | Don't do |

Try It Yourself

EXERCISE 2

Diagramming Four Types of Sentences

Diagram the simple subject and simple predicate for each sentence below.

1. Did Andrea stay?
2. That is totally amazing!
3. Come here.
4. Has the car been fixed?
5. Tom played a terrific game.
6. Have some rhubarb.
7. The new frogs are incredibly noisy!
8. Have you ever met a llama?
9. Place them here.
10. The chickadee had an orange throat.

COMPOUND SUBJECTS AND COMPOUND PREDICATES

When a sentence has a compound subject or a compound verb or both, diagram them on separate horizontal lines. Write the conjunction that joins the subjects or verbs on a broken vertical line linking the horizontal lines.

EXAMPLES
compound subject   Boys and girls play.

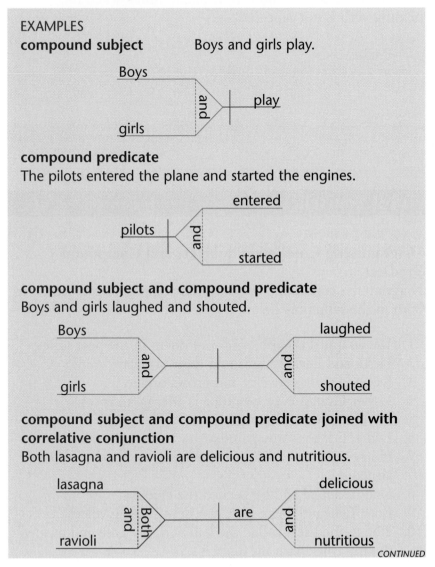

compound predicate
The pilots entered the plane and started the engines.

compound subject and compound predicate
Boys and girls laughed and shouted.

compound subject and compound predicate joined with correlative conjunction
Both lasagna and ravioli are delicious and nutritious.

CONTINUED

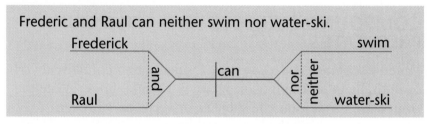

Frederic and Raul can neither swim nor water-ski.

Notice how a compound verb is diagrammed when the helping verb is not repeated.

EXAMPLE

Jason was catching and throwing the ball.

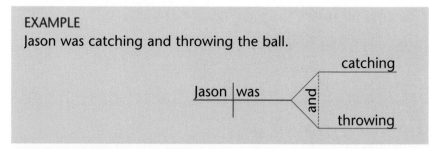

Try It Yourself

EXERCISE 3

Diagramming Compound Subjects and Compound Predicates

Diagram the compound subjects, the compound predicates, or both in the sentences below.

1. We wrapped the gifts and took them to the post office.
2. Heidi and Earl are finishing their project.
3. DeVona makes jewelry and grows orchids.
4. Either Grandma or Grandpa is allergic to roses.
5. Plant and water the begonias.
6. Lydia, Ed, and Amy painted the scenery for the play.
7. Houses and cars look like toys from the window of an airplane.
8. Dad seasoned and barbecued the chicken.
9. Both Lyle and Steve have excellent singing voices.
10. The trained seal rolled the ball with his nose and pushed the toy truck with his flippers.

DIRECT AND INDIRECT OBJECTS

A direct object is part of the predicate and appears on the horizontal line after it. The direct object is separated from the predicate by a short vertical line. Notice that unlike the line that separates subject and predicate, the line that separates the predicate and the direct object does not extend below the horizontal line.

EXAMPLES

The Ninjas lost the game.

We bought olives, cheese, and crackers at the market.

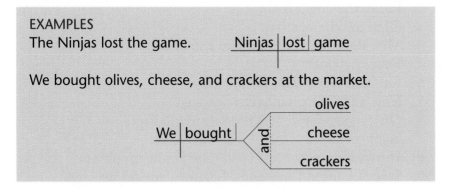

The indirect object is diagrammed on a horizontal line beneath the verb because it tells to whom or for whom the action of a verb is done. An indirect object comes before the direct object in a sentence. Connect the indirect object to the verb with a slanted line. Notice in the second example that the parts of a compound indirect object are diagrammed on horizontal parallel lines. The conjunction is placed on a broken line between them.

EXAMPLES

The veterinarian gave the dog a shot.

Ken showed my brother and me the waterfall.

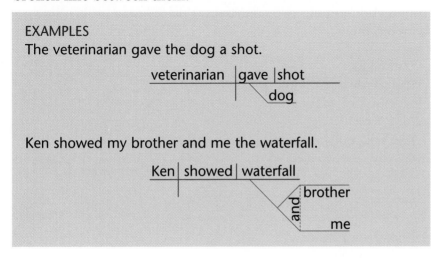

EXERCISE 4

Diagramming Direct and Indirect Objects

Diagram the direct and indirect objects in the following sentences.

1. Dr. Appel fixed the bicycle.
2. I gave the dog a bath.
3. Glen told her a story.
4. Mrs. Ramirez gave the man a dollar.
5. Read this book.
6. Can you teach the bird a trick?
7. Kurt and Ellen stapled the papers.
8. Oliver gave Gretchen and Lenny their pillows and blankets.
9. Her grandmother left Holly the family sapphires.
10. Serena knitted Lucy and Melanie identical sweaters.

ADJECTIVES AND ADVERBS

In a sentence diagram an adjective is written on a slanting line below the noun or pronoun it modifies. When more than one adjective modifies a word, each is written on its own line. The articles *a*, *an*, and *the* and possessive pronouns such as *her* and *their* are also diagrammed in this way. Notice that a conjunction joining two adjectives is placed on a broken line between them.

EXAMPLES
The sturdy pots didn't break.

Tiny pink buds have appeared on the dogwood tree.

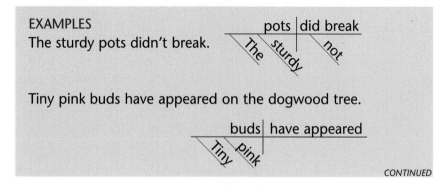

CONTINUED

The shiny black crow drank from the birdbath.

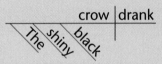

Their old rusted car finally fell apart.

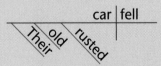

The yellow and white striped wallpaper was a good decision.

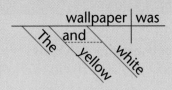

Adverbs are also diagrammed on slanting lines. An adverb modifying a verb is placed below the verb. An adverb modifying an adjective or an adverb is placed on a slanting line attached to the word that is being modified. Notice that *not* and *never* are diagrammed as adverbs modifying the verbs with which they are used.

EXAMPLES
The casserole had been prepared quickly and easily.

I have never liked cauliflower.

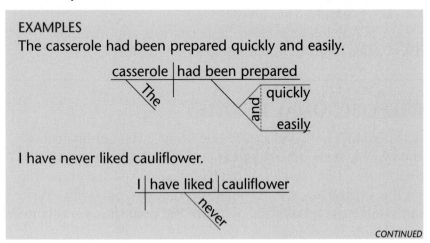

CONTINUED

Many students arrived too late.

Her best friend has always been Margaret.

Try It Yourself

EXERCISE 5
Diagramming Adjectives and Adverbs
Diagram the adjectives and adverbs in the following sentences.

1. The lively fish would not stay in the pond.
2. The sleek new ship sailed yesterday.
3. Young evergreen trees grow quite quickly.
4. The barnyard gradually awakened.
5. A tall, dark man waved excitedly.
6. Three cars passed noisily.
7. A really strange thing happened yesterday.
8. Kayla giggles very loudly.
9. The old and lame pony limped slowly and painfully.
10. Carlos easily defeated his best opponent.

PREPOSITIONAL PHRASES

To diagram a prepositional phrase, draw a slanted line below the word that the phrase modifies. From the bottom of that line, draw a line parallel to the base line. Write the preposition on the slanted line and its object on the horizontal line. Write any words that modify the object of the preposition on slanted lines below the object.

EXAMPLES
James found a dollar in his pocket.

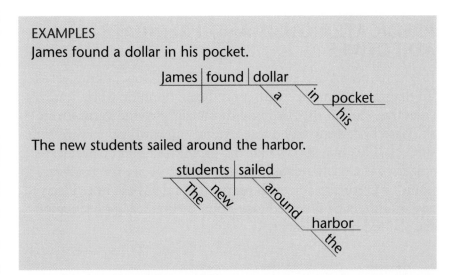

The new students sailed around the harbor.

Try It Yourself

E X E R C I S E 6
Diagramming Prepositional Phrases
Diagram the prepositional phrases in each of the following
sentences.

1. He hit the ball over the fence.
2. We pulled some of the weeds in the garden.
3. The car is parked under the bridge.
4. A dog with a red collar trotted behind Peter.
5. A play about World War II will be performed tonight.
6. The students sketched with charcoal and painted with
   watercolors.
7. Sit beside me.
8. The old trunk was well hidden among the bushes.
9. The University of Virginia was designed by Thomas
   Jefferson.
10. Many acres of trees can burn down during a wildfire.

PREDICATE NOUNS AND PREDICATE ADJECTIVES

Predicate nouns and predicate adjectives follow linking verbs. To diagram a sentence with a predicate noun or a predicate adjective, extend the base line to the right of the verb. From the base line, draw a line that extends upward and toward the subject. This line shows that the predicate noun or predicate adjective is closely related to the subject. Write the predicate noun or predicate adjective on the extended base line. Place any modifiers of the predicate noun or predicate adjective on the slanted lines below it.

EXAMPLES
One famous cathedral in France is Notre Dame.

Notre Dame is famous for its stained glass windows.

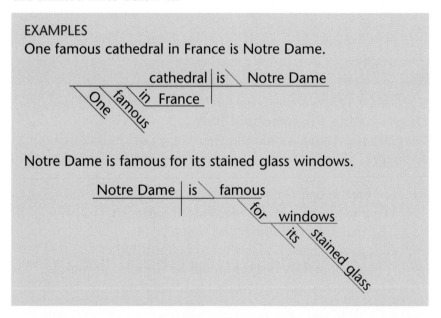

Try It Yourself

EXERCISE 7
Diagramming Predicate Nouns and Predicate Adjectives
Diagram the predicate nouns and predicate adjectives in the sentences below.

1. Soccer may be the world's most popular sport.
2. My pottery bowls and mugs are much too thick.
3. My aunt Beth is a professor of archeology.

4. Rice is a grain from China, India, and Japan.
5. White rice is low in fat.
6. Elias and I were partners for the tennis tournament.
7. April is generally cool and wet.
8. The new student's name is Mick Rubin.
9. That boy is my cousin.
10. The volunteers appear enthusiastic and dedicated.

VERBALS

A participle or a participial phrase acts as an adjective. To diagram a participle or a participial phrase, draw a slanted line and a horizontal line below the word that the participle or participial phrase modifies. Write the participle so that it starts on the slanted line and curves onto the horizontal line. If a direct object follows the participle, separate the two elements with a vertical bar. If a predicate noun follows the participle, separate the two elements with a slanted line.

EXAMPLES
A bouncing yellow ball attracted the dog's attention.

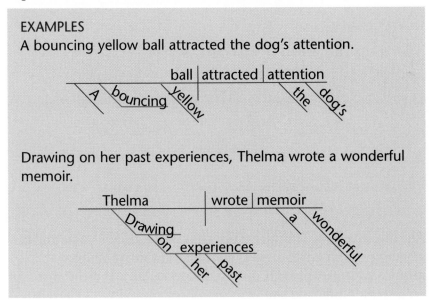

Drawing on her past experiences, Thelma wrote a wonderful memoir.

A gerund or a gerund phrase acts as a noun. To diagram a gerund or a gerund phrase, place the gerund on a step and place the step on a standard or stilt. Write the gerund so that it starts on the slanted line and curves onto the horizontal line. Place the standard or stilt in the position in the main diagram that shows the function of the gerund or gerund phrase in the sentence. If the phrase has modifiers or complements, diagram them on the line extending from the step.

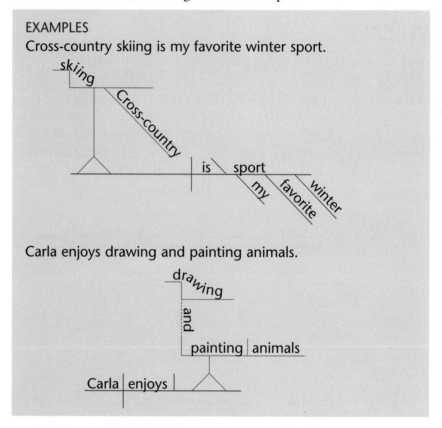

EXAMPLES

Cross-country skiing is my favorite winter sport.

Carla enjoys drawing and painting animals.

An infinitive or an infinitive phrase may be used as a noun, an adjective, or an adverb. To diagram an infinitive or an infinitive phrase, place it on a standard or stilt. Put the word *to* on a slanted line and the verb on a horizontal line. Diagram modifiers and complements as you would in a sentence. Then place the standard or stilt in a position in the main diagram that shows the function of the infinitive phrase in the sentence.

EXAMPLES

infinitive phrase used as a noun

To sail to Alaska is the Marantzes' plan for August.

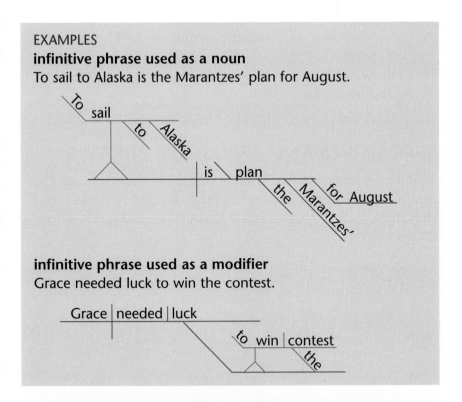

infinitive phrase used as a modifier

Grace needed luck to win the contest.

Try It Yourself

EXERCISE 8

Diagramming Verbals and Verbal Phrases

Diagram the verbals and verbal phrases in the following sentences.

1. Frustrated, Dan thought about a new job.
2. Sporting a pair of purple running shoes, Alicia warmed up on the field.
3. Ruth Furtel had the idea to serve good steaks at reasonable prices.
4. Migrating geese covered the golf course.
5. David, waiting anxiously for the doctor's call, paced the hallway.
6. Sophia's biggest pet peeve is standing in line.
7. Swimming with dolphins or sharks sounds ideal.
8. In many states, dancing or shopping on Sunday was illegal.

9. The play concludes with the signing of the Declaration of Independence.
10. The island, founded for victims of leprosy, never became a destination for tourists.

APPOSITIVES AND APPOSITIVE PHRASES

To diagram an appositive or an appositive phrase, place the appositive in parentheses next to the word that it explains or identifies. Place any modifiers on slanted lines directly below the appositive.

EXAMPLES
David Frank, my pottery teacher, is a well-known local artist.

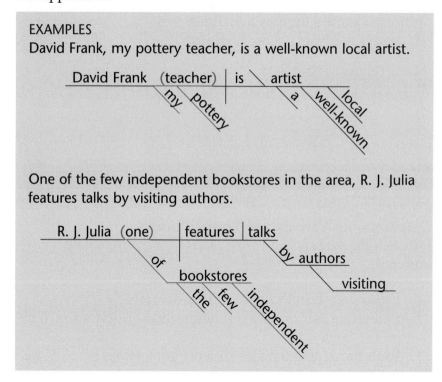

One of the few independent bookstores in the area, R. J. Julia features talks by visiting authors.

EXERCISE 9

Diagramming Appositives and Appositive Phrases
Diagram the appositives and appositive phrases in the
following sentences.

1. Mars, the red planet, is the fourth major planet from the
   sun.
2. The major planets of our solar system are divided into
   two types, terrestrial and giant.
3. Saturn, the sixth planet from the sun, is famous for its
   rings.
4. Satellites, tiny bodies orbiting a planet, make up the rings
   around Saturn, Jupiter, and Uranus.
5. Two satellites of Jupiter, Ganymede and Callisto, are
   almost the size of the planets Mercury and Mars.
6. Meteors, chunks of matter from space, glow in the night
   sky.
7. Galileo, a seventeenth-century scientist, invented the
   telescope.
8. The Big Dipper is the cluster of seven stars in the
   constellation Ursa Major.
9. The constellation Orion contains the star Betelgeuse.
10. Some of the stars of the Pleiades, the Seven Sisters, are
    visible to the naked eye.

UNIT 13 REVIEW

TEST YOUR KNOWLEDGE

EXERCISE 1
Diagramming Subjects and Predicates
Diagram the simple and compound subjects and the simple
and compound predicates in the following sentences.
(20 points)

1. Nothing happened.
2. Can Lorraine and Tisha wait?
3. Answer!
4. Either Leo or Tom called.
5. Come and visit.
6. Has Eleanor returned?
7. Both Radullah and Zuleika howled and hissed.
8. The hawk glides and swoops.
9. Sparrows, wrens, and chickadees danced and twittered.
10. The bassoonist bowed and waved.

EXERCISE 2
Diagramming Modifiers
Diagram the adjectives and adverbs in the following sentences.
(20 points)

1. The expert chess player won easily.
2. The gray and brown forest gradually awakened.
3. Tiny and brilliantly purple violets emerge.
4. The computer's fan whirs constantly.
5. Speak up confidently.
6. Did the opera singer and rock star harmonize well?
7. The quaint, twisted candlesticks had been sold already.
8. The expensive crystal vase cracked immediately.
9. The rough stone path curved slightly and then stopped.
10. Do not rub so hard.

EXERCISE 3
Diagramming Direct and Indirect Objects, Predicate Nouns, and Predicate Adjectives
Diagram the direct and indirect objects and the predicate nouns and predicate adjectives in the following sentences. (20 points)

1. The little boy gave his mother a bunch of daffodils.
2. The spacecraft is a complicated machine.
3. Bill Gates has given schools many computers.
4. Did Mom ever find her wallet?
5. The visitors seemed curious but undisturbed.
6. The main character tests his brother's loyalty.
7. Her lengthy explanation was unbelievable.
8. Michael is courteous and considerate.
9. Jerkface Clothing Company has terrific T-shirts.
10. Amidala is a *Star Wars* queen.

EXERCISE 4
Diagramming Phrases
Diagram the prepositional, appositive, and verbal phrases in the following sentences. (20 points)

1. Look at your library or bookstore in the travel section for the new book about Belize.
2. Shad, a member of the herring family, is an oily fish.
3. Broiling, baking, or sautéing shad will bring out its flavor.
4. For good shad the secret is in the boning of the fish.
5. William Gillette, a stage actor, was famous during the early 1900s for his portrayals of Sherlock Holmes.
6. His dream was to build a castle in Connecticut.
7. My suggestion was to have a buffet brunch for Mother's Day.
8. Arguing with Ralph does little good.
9. Distracted by the noise, President Hill stopped his address.
10. We stood up to see better.

EXERCISE 5

Diagramming Sentences

The following sentences contain various sentence parts and parts of speech that you have studied. Diagram each sentence to show where subjects, predicates, modifiers, phrases, objects, and complements go. (20 points)

1. Thor Heyerdahl, a Norwegian adventurer, crossed the Pacific on a balsa log raft.
2. Reaching Polynesia from Peru after 101 days, Heyerdahl proved his theory.
3. The purpose of his raft voyage was to show the possibility of ancient trips from the Old World to the New World.
4. He was a hero in his homeland.
5. His book *Kon Tiki* was made into a movie.
6. In 1951 it won an Academy Award for best documentary.
7. His theories about ancient seafaring migrations were very controversial.
8. He made other voyages in papyrus and reed boats patterned after those of ancient people.
9. He was fascinated with pyramid building.
10. Part of the challenge of his work involved raising money and overcoming obstacles.

UNIT *14* COMMON USAGE PROBLEMS

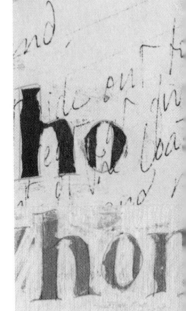

COMMON USAGE PROBLEMS

USAGE tip

Before beginning this section, you may want to review Unit 8, "Subject-Verb Agreement and Usage," pages 149–151.

INCORRECT SUBJECT-VERB AGREEMENT

A subject and its verb must agree in number. Use singular verb forms with singular subjects and plural verb forms with plural subjects.

Intervening Words

A prepositional phrase that comes between a subject and a verb does not determine whether the subject is singular or plural.

> EXAMPLES
>
> The **captain** on the bridge **gazes** across the sea. (*captain gazes*, singular)
>
> The **detective**, in addition to the police, **looks** for clues at the house. (*detective looks*, singular)
>
> The **players** on the team **practice** diligently. (*players practice*, plural)
>
> The **books** in the back of the store **are** only half price. (*books are*, plural)

Compound Subjects

Use a plural verb with most compound subjects connected by *and*.

> EXAMPLES
>
> <u>Jim and his brother</u> **plan** strategy before each game.
> <u>Cars, trucks, and motorcycles</u> **roar** past our house.

Use a singular verb with a compound subject that refers to one person or thing or that generally conveys the idea of a unit.

EXAMPLES
Pork and beans **is** my favorite menu item at this restaurant. (one selection)

The same song and dance **comes** from this sales clerk every time we visit here. (one technique)

Use a singular verb with a compound subject made up of singular nouns or pronouns connected by *or* or *nor*. Use a plural verb with a compound subject formed from plural nouns or pronouns.

EXAMPLES
singular
Neither rain nor snow **keeps** me from attending the opera.
Either Joe or Mary **needs** to address the audience.

plural
Either hot dogs or hamburgers **are** on the menu.
Neither the players nor the coaches **like** the new chancellor.

When a compound subject consists of a singular subject and a plural subject connected by *or* or *nor*, use a verb that agrees in number with the subject that is closer to it in the sentence.

EXAMPLES
Either Jamie or her friends **cause** trouble at school each day. (*friends cause,* plural)

Neither the workers nor the supervisor **understands** the new regulation. (*supervisor understands,* singular)

Indefinite Pronouns as Subjects

Indefinite pronouns are pronouns that refer to people or things in general. Some indefinite pronouns are always singular and take singular verbs: *anybody, anyone, anything, each, either, everybody, everyone, everything, much, neither, nobody, no one, nothing, one, other, somebody, someone, something.*

EXAMPLES
Nobody sings well in this town. (*nobody sings,* singular)

Everything seems to be in order here. (*everything seems,* singular)

Some indefinite pronouns are always plural and take plural verbs: *several, both, few, many.*

EXAMPLES
Several are hidden in the backyard. (*several are hidden,* plural)

Few were seen outside before six o'clock. (*few were seen,* plural)

Some indefinite pronouns can be either singular or plural, depending on their use in the sentence: *all, any, enough, more, most, none, plenty, some.* They are singular when they refer to a portion or to a single person, place, or thing. They are plural when they refer to a number of individual persons, places, or things. The verb form may be controlled by the object of the preposition.

EXAMPLES
None of the cake was eaten yesterday. (*None* refers to a portion of the cake and is therefore singular.)

None of the apples remain in the barrel. (*None* refers to multiple apples and is therefore plural.)

Inverted Word Order

In questions and in sentences beginning with *Here* or *There,* the verb appears before the subject. In these sentences with inverted word order, you must identify the subject and then make the verb agree with it in number. Saying the sentence to yourself in normal order often helps.

EXAMPLES

Over the hill **were** seven angry dwarves. (*dwarves were,* plural)

Here **is** the solution for the problem. (*solution is,* singular)

Where **are** the keys to this old car? (*keys are,* plural)

There **are** three whales and a shark swimming below us.
(*whales and shark are swimming,* plural)

Try It Yourself

EXERCISE 1
Identifying Problems with Subject-Verb Agreement
Write the correct verb form in parentheses that agrees in
number with the subject of the sentence.

1. The baseball season (begins, begin) in April for most
   major league teams.
2. Fans in America, as well as other nations, (roots, root) for
   their favorite team.
3. Sports (provides, provide) identity, pride, and
   entertainment to cities that (has, have) a professional
   team.
4. The players in major league baseball often (quarrels,
   quarrel) with the owners.
5. The average fan (gets, get) annoyed with these labor
   disputes which (is, are) too frequent.
6. Arbitrators sometimes (resolves, resolve) salary issues
   between a player and an owner.
7. In smaller cities, free agency and low revenue (causes,
   cause) teams to lose top players.
8. New York and Atlanta (was, were) dominant franchises in
   the 1990s.
9. Everyone who (studies, study) baseball economics
   (concludes, conclude) that success is related to spending.
10. The top teams in the game (spends, spend) more money
    on players than the other franchises.

Correcting Subject-Verb Agreement Problems
Write the verb form that agrees in number with the subject of each sentence. If there are no subject-verb agreement problems in the sentence, write *correct*.

1. The possum, along with his rodent followers, have staked out a claim in my backyard.
2. Your plant between the trees seem bigger this year.
3. The cars in the driveway needs to be washed today.
4. An officer, plus two reporters, was looking for you.
5. Stan, Stew, and their father believes that the weather will change soon.
6. I tried to buy a couple of rakes, but the store were out of them.
7. Neither the dog nor the cats want to come back inside.
8. No one in the audience seem eager to volunteer.
9. Hidden among the rocks was a cleverly disguised chameleon.
10. Here sit either Tom or his twin brother.

Using Correct Subject-Verb Agreement
Some of the following phrases are singular and some are plural. Write five interesting sentences using each of the phrases. Then change each phrase from singular to plural or from plural to singular and write five new sentences.

1. bird flies
2. pretty flowers were
3. teachers meet and discuss
4. many are
5. either Paul or Jesse runs

INCORRECT USE OF APOSTROPHES

Use an apostrophe to replace letters that have been left out in a contraction.

USAGE tip

You may also want to refer to "Apostrophes" in Unit 15, pages 330–332.

EXAMPLES		
it's = it is	don't = do not	I'll = I will

Use an apostrophe to show possession.

Singular Nouns

Use an apostrophe and an *s* (*'s*) to form the possessive of a singular noun, even if it ends in *s*, *x*, or *z*.

EXAMPLES		
Rachel's notebook	Frank's lizard	Conan's ring

Plural Nouns

Use an apostrophe and an *s* (*'s*) to form the possessive of a plural noun that does not end in *s*.

EXAMPLES		
women's shirts	children's books	people's candidate

Use an apostrophe alone to form the possessive of plural noun that ends in *s*.

EXAMPLES		
rodents' food	the boys' locker room	the ships' sails

Do not add an apostrophe or *'s* to possessive personal pronouns: *mine, yours, his, hers, its, ours,* or *theirs*. They already show ownership.

EXAMPLES
Our cars are painted; **theirs** are still rusty.
The shark opened **its** mouth.

Try It Yourself

EXERCISE 4

Identifying Problems with Apostrophes

Choose the word in parentheses that represents the correct use of an apostrophe.

1. The book (dealers', dealers's) convention will be held this Saturday.
2. Is the blue bicycle (his, his's)?
3. Jerome slowly climbed the steps of the high (priestesses' priestesses's) temple.
4. The (dress's, dresse's) buttons are green.
5. Your (oxes', ox's) horns seem to be longer than usual.
6. We (wo'nt, won't) take (its, it's) tires off until later.
7. Several (mouse's, mice's) holes were found in the house.
8. Alyssa saw the (trees's, trees') leaves change before her eyes.
9. The (deer's, deers') tracks crisscrossed the snow.
10. Cheri decided to count all of the (potatoe's, potatoes') eyes.

EXERCISE 5

Correcting the Use of Apostrophes

Rewrite the following sentences to correct the use of apostrophes. If there are no errors in a sentence, write *correct*.

1. If were to find the house, well have to take a map so we wont get lost.
2. Sams' speech about economics was longer than his' talk about politics.
3. Is anyone's car parked in the street?
4. Thirteen counties judges were at the conference.
5. A days' pay doesnt buy as much as it used to.
6. When I performed here the mens' dressing room was painted pink.
7. Your flowers stems are less leafy than I expected.
8. Thats the first time well be across the Canadian border.
9. Jess' hat flew off his head into the fans section of the stadium.
10. A childrens museum is located somewhere in the citys downtown area.

EXERCISE 6
Using Apostrophes Correctly
Write two sentences for the following words. The first sentence should use the singular possessive form of each noun. The second sentence should use the plural possessive form of each noun.

1. carnival
2. doe
3. bill
4. principal
5. man
6. table
7. idea
8. member
9. sister
10. sock

AVOIDING DOUBLE NEGATIVES

Make sure that you use only one of the following negatives in each sentence: *not, nobody, none, nothing, hardly, can't, doesn't, won't, isn't, aren't.* A **double negative** is the use of two negative words together when only one is needed. Correct double negatives by removing one of the negative words or by replacing one of the negative words with a positive word.

USAGE tip

Before reading this section, you may want to review "Negatives and Double Negatives" in Unit 9, pages 172–176.

EXAMPLES

double negative	We won't hardly make it in time.
corrected sentence	We will hardly make it in time.
	We won't make it in time.
double negative	Nell wasn't never able to win the big prize.
corrected sentence	Nell was never able to win the big prize.
	Nell wasn't ever able to win the big prize.

EXERCISE 7

Identifying Double Negatives

Choose the correct word in parentheses to complete each sentence. After you have completed the exercise, read each sentence aloud with the correct word in place.

1. She (is, isn't) hardly able to see the signals from the ship.
2. Our coach didn't take (no, any) time to think about the call.
3. I've never smelled (nothing, anything) like my grandmother's cookies.
4. You haven't (never, ever) finished a book that you started.
5. Her poodles (were, weren't) hardly able to climb the stairs.
6. It's unbelievable that (somebody, nobody) didn't figure out what happened.
7. Couldn't you (ever, never) decide what to do about the truck?
8. We (couldn't, could) barely hear the person at the drive-up window.
9. The gym coach didn't have (any, no) idea when class was supposed to end.
10. There isn't (anything, nothing) here that we are interested in.

EXERCISE 8

Correcting Double Negatives

Rewrite the following sentences to remove the double negative. Remember that you can either remove one of the negative words or replace it with a positive word. If a sentence does not contain a double negative, write *correct*.

1. We don't see nobody at the gas station.
2. Hans won't eat no ice cream with sprinkles on it.
3. There wasn't barely a trace of dust in the room.
4. I can't hardly see the ship out there.
5. Greg and Nancy didn't do no proofreading of their assignments.
6. Fred couldn't find no one in the backyard.
7. Julie can't believe you didn't ever win a trophy.

8. I haven't never heard anything like that before.
9. Carrie never did nothing wrong at school.
10. His voice didn't make barely a whisper.

EXERCISE 9
Using Negatives Correctly
Write a sentence using each of the following negative words.
Avoid using any double negatives in your sentences.

1. no
2. not
3. no one
4. nobody
5. never
6. nowhere
7. nothing
8. scarcely
9. barely
10. hardly

AVOIDING DANGLING AND MISPLACED MODIFIERS

Place modifying phrases and clauses as close as possible to the words they modify; otherwise, your sentences may be unclear or unintentionally humorous.

A **dangling modifier** has nothing to modify because the word it would logically modify is not present in the sentence. In the following sentence, the modifying phrase has no logical object. The sentence says that a whale was flying.

USAGE tip

Before reading this section, you may want to review "Dangling and Misplaced Modifiers" in Unit 9, pages 176–179.

EXAMPLE
Flying above the ocean, a whale was spotted.

You can eliminate dangling modifiers by rewriting the sentence so that an appropriate word is provided for the modifier to modify. You can also expand a dangling phrase into a full subordinate clause.

EXAMPLES
Flying above the ocean, we saw a whale.
As we flew above the ocean, we spotted a whale.

A **misplaced modifier** is located too far from the word it should modify.

EXAMPLE
I found a penny during my morning jog on a park bench.

You can revise a misplaced modifier by moving it closer to the word it modifies.

EXAMPLES
I found a penny on a park bench during my morning jog.
On a park bench I found a penny during my morning jog.
During my morning jog, I found a penny on a park bench.

Try It Yourself

EXERCISE 10
Identifying Dangling and Misplaced Modifiers
Identify the dangling modifiers in the following sentences by writing *DM*. Identify the misplaced modifiers by writing *MM*.

1. The rusty old car is in the garage missing two tires.
2. Joe fell into the newly filled swimming pool with a splash.
3. The city has an old bridge over the river made entirely of wood.
4. Arriving after 8:00 A.M., the meeting had already started.
5. Your cat jumped over the fence from the picnic table, which is ten feet high.
6. After settling into the room, a fire alarm sounded.
7. To sell your house, the outside walls need to be painted.
8. Ending with a flurry, applause shook the concert hall.
9. I adopted a dog from the humane society with black and white spots.
10. Before reading the report, the cats wanted to be fed.

EXERCISE 11
Correcting Dangling and Misplaced Modifiers
Revise the sentences in Exercise 10 so that the modifiers are placed as close as possible to the words they modify.

EXERCISE 12
Using Modifiers Correctly
Expand each of the following sentences by adding a phrase or clause that provides detail. Be sure to place your phrases and clauses as close as possible to the words they modify.

1. The sharks swam toward their prey.
2. Jim declined the invitation to speak.
3. Water poured into the ship.
4. The tall tree fell to the ground.
5. Each line needs to be memorized.
6. It's best to study for the test alone.
7. This movie is easy to sleep through.
8. The counselor discussed three options.
9. I believed it to be the artifact we had been searching for.
10. The police arrived on the scene to disperse the crowd.

AVOIDING SPLIT INFINITIVES

An infinitive, the base verb combined with *to*, should not be split under most circumstances. Infinitives such as *to buy*, *to teach*, and *to stop* should not be interrupted by adverbs or other sentence components.

EXAMPLES	
nonstandard	Wally is not able to clearly hear the speech.
standard	Wally is not able to hear the speech clearly.

In some cases, a modifier sounds awkward if it does not split the infinitive. In these situations, it may be best to reword the sentence to eliminate the infinitive.

EXAMPLES	
nonstandard	Jim wants to nearly match his win total from last season.
revised	Jim wants to win nearly as many games as he did last season.

Try It Yourself

EXERCISE 13

Correcting Split Infinitives

Revise the following sentences to eliminate any split infinitives.

1. I would like to someday visit the Netherlands.
2. Jeff decided to later discuss the movie with his children.
3. The burglar's plan was to silently open the back window.
4. We need to seriously talk about fixing the car.
5. The rabbit tried to quickly cross the neighbor's yard.
6. I paused to calmly gather my thoughts.
7. Your uncles began to humorously joke about the show.
8. The birds started to gleefully sing when the sun came out.
9. Pam sought to diligently work on finding the answer to the equation.
10. After searching the restaurant, I was able to fortunately find my missing watch.

EXERCISE 14

Using Infinitives Correctly

Create a sentence for each of the following infinitives. Be careful not to split the infinitives.

1. to run
2. to think
3. to fly
4. to sing
5. to gain

COMMONLY MISUSED WORDS

The following pages contain an alphabetic list of words and phrases that often cause usage problems.

a, an   Use *a* before words beginning with a consonant sound. Use *an* before words beginning with a vowel sound, including a silent *h*.

> **EXAMPLES**
> I want to buy **a** present for my sister.
> **An** elk was spotted in this area.
> You should give **an** honest answer.

accept, except   *Accept* is a verb meaning "to receive willingly" or "to agree." *Except* is a preposition that means "leaving out" or "but."

> **EXAMPLES**
> I cannot **accept** this present from you.
> Gary found all of the eggs **except** the one in the tree.

affect, effect   *Affect* is a verb that means "to influence." The noun *effect* means "the result of an action." The verb *effect* means "to cause" or "to bring about."

> **EXAMPLES**
> The mood of the teacher will **affect** her students.
> You still don't understand the **effects** of your decision.
> Susan will **effect** the needed changes.

ain't   This word is nonstandard English. Avoid using it in speaking and writing.

> **EXAMPLES**
> **nonstandard**   I ain't going to church today.
> **standard**   I **am not** going to church today.

all ready, already   *All ready* means "entirely ready or prepared." *Already* means "previously."

> **EXAMPLES**
> The students in the class are **all ready** for the geometry test.
> We **already** discussed what to do about the pickup truck.

all right *All right* means "satisfactory," "unhurt," "correct," or "yes, very well." The word *alright* is not acceptable in formal written English.

> **EXAMPLES**
> **All right**, I am happy to see all of you here tonight.
> The cow is **all right** she won't be going near that fence again.

a lot *A lot* means "a great number or amount" and is always two words. Because it is imprecise, you should avoid it except in informal usage. *Alot* is not a word.

> **EXAMPLE**
> There were **a lot** of children at the movie last night.

altogether, all together *Altogether* is an adverb meaning "thoroughly." Something done *all together* is done as a group or mass.

> **EXAMPLES**
> He was **altogether** frustrated waiting all afternoon.
> We were **all together** awaiting news of our test scores.

anywheres, everywheres, somewheres, nowheres Use these words and others like them without the *s: anywhere, everywhere, somewhere, nowhere.*

> **EXAMPLE**
> There is green grass **everywhere** in this state.

at Don't use this word after *where.*

> **EXAMPLE**
> Where are your pencils?

bad, badly *Bad* is always an adjective, and *badly* is always an adverb, Use *bad* after linking verbs.

> **EXAMPLES**
> Dave proposed one **bad** idea after another.
> She feels **bad** because you failed the test.
> Rachel needs that medicine **badly**.

beside, besides *Beside* means "next to." *Besides* means "in addition to." *Besides* can also be an adverb meaning "moreover."

EXAMPLES
The book is **beside** the lamp on the table.
This house has a two-stall garage **besides** a large storage shed.
Besides not having any money, we don't know where the concert is being held.

between, among   Use *between* when referring to two people or things. Use *among* when you are discussing three or more people or things.

EXAMPLES
I divided what was left of the fruitcake **between** my two dogs.
He will divide his fortune **among** the four siblings.

bring, take   Use *bring* when you mean "to carry to." It refers to movement toward the speaker. Use *take* when you mean "to carry away." It refers to movement away from the speaker.

EXAMPLES
I would like you to **bring** the goblet to me.
Please **take** this foul-smelling sock down to the laundry room.

bust, busted   Do not used these nonstandard words as verbs to substitute for *break* or *burst*.

EXAMPLES
nonstandard   Your toy car is busted.
                     The barrel busted open.
standard   Your toy car is **broken**.
                     The barrel **burst** open.

can, may   The word *can* means "able to do something." The word **may** is used to ask or give permission.

EXAMPLES
Can you swim across Square Lake?
You **may** go swimming when you finish weeding the garden.

choose, chose   *Choose* is the present tense and *chose* is the past tense.

EXAMPLES
I **choose** a different pair of shoes each day.
Randy **chose** a chocolate donut with frosting.

could of   Use the helping verb *have* (which may sound like *could of*) with *could, might, must, should, ought,* and *would.*

> **EXAMPLES**
> **nonstandard**   You might of been able to jump over the pond.
> **standard**   You **might have** been able to jump over the pond.

doesn't, don't   *Doesn't* is the contraction of *does not*. It is used with singular nouns and the pronouns *he, she, it, this,* and *that. Don't* is the contraction of *do not*. Use it with plural nouns and the pronouns *I, we, they, you, these,* and *those.*

> **EXAMPLES**
> Mike **doesn't** understand what is at stake here today.
> These people **don't** know what the speech will be about.

farther, further   Use *farther* to refer to physical distance. Use *further* to refer to greater extent in time or degree or to mean "additional."

> **EXAMPLES**
> Greg hit the ball **farther** this time.
> We need to talk about this issue **further**.
> The story needs **further** revision before it can be published.

fewer, less   Use *fewer*, which tells "how many," to refer to things that you can count individually. *Fewer* is used with plural words. Use *less* to refer to quantities that you cannot count. It is used with singular words and tells "how much."

> **EXAMPLES**
> I see **fewer** stars in the sky tonight than last night.
> The car has **less** gas in the tank after being driven all afternoon.

good, well   *Good* is always an adjective. *Well* is an adverb meaning "ably" or "capably." *Well* is also a predicate adjective meaning "satisfactory" or "in good health." Don't confuse *feel good*, which means "to feel happy or pleased," with *feel well*, which means "to feel healthy."

> **EXAMPLES**
> Bill is a **good** bowler.
> Dale felt **good** [happy] after winning the lottery.
> Peggy sings quite **well**.
> Bobby missed school because he didn't feel **well**.

had ought, hadn't ought The verb *ought* should never be used with the helping verb *had*.

EXAMPLES	
nonstandard	We had ought to leave if we're going to make it in time.
standard	We **ought** to leave if we're going to make it in time.
nonstandard	They hadn't ought disturb that alligator.
standard	They **ought** not disturb that alligator.

hardly, scarcely Since both of these words have negative meanings, do not use them with other negative words such as *not*, *no*, *nothing*, and *none*.

EXAMPLES	
incorrect	We can't hardly see the stage from here.
correct	We can **hardly** see the stage from here.
incorrect	Tammy hadn't scarcely enough time to finish her report.
correct	Tammy had **scarcely** enough time to finish her report.

he, she, they Do not use these pronouns after a noun. This error is called a double subject.

EXAMPLES	
incorrect	Jeff's sister she went to college this year.
correct	Jeff's sister went to college this year.

hisself, theirselves These are incorrect forms. Use *himself* and *themselves*.

EXAMPLES	
incorrect	Our son Juan bought hisself a new car last week.
correct	Our son Juan bought **himself** a new car last week.
incorrect	They decided for theirselves to confess what they had done.
correct	They decided for **themselves** to confess what they had done.

how come Do not use in place of *why*.

EXAMPLES	
nonstandard	How come you stopped watering the plant?
standard	**Why** did you stop watering the plant?

in, into   Use *in* to mean "within" or "inside." Use *into* to suggest movement toward the inside from the outside.

> EXAMPLES
> Sean is **in** the house.
> Sean walked **into** the house.

its, it's   *Its* is a possessive pronoun. *It's* is the contraction for *it is*.

> EXAMPLES
> The bird flapped **its** wings.
> **It's** the first day of the month today.

kind, sort, type   Use *this* or *that* to modify the singular nouns *kind*, *sort*, and *type*. Use *these* and *those* to modify the plural nouns *kinds*, *sorts*, and *types*. *Kind* should be singular when the object of the preposition following it is singular. It should be plural when the object of the preposition is plural.

> EXAMPLES
> This **type** of snake is usually the most dangerous.
> Do you understand these **kinds** of problems?

kind of, sort of   Do not use these terms to mean "somewhat" or "rather."

> EXAMPLES
> **nonstandard**   He's kind of lazy.
> **standard**   He's **somewhat** lazy.

lay, lie   *Lay* means "to put" or "to place." *Lay* usually takes a direct object. *Lie* means "to rest" or "to be in a lying position." *Lie* never takes a direct object. (Note that the past tense of *lie* is *lay*.)

> EXAMPLES
> **Lay** the book on the shelf.
> Gretchen **laid** the book on the shelf.
> **Lie** down and keep still.
> Betsy **lay** down and kept still.

learn, teach   *Learn* means "to gain knowledge." *Teach* means "to give knowledge." Do not use them interchangeably.

EXAMPLES
I will **learn** to speak Spanish this summer.
I hope my friend Marie will **teach** me in her spare time.

like, as   *Like* is usually a preposition followed by an object. It generally means "similar to." *As, as if*, and *as though* are conjunctions used to introduce subordinate clauses.

EXAMPLES
The wind felt **like** an icy dagger.
Mark looked at me, **as if** he knew what was going on.
Holly laughs **as though** she's really happy.

of   This word is unnecessary after the prepositions *inside*, *outside*, and *off*.

EXAMPLES
The car drove **off** the road.
A menacing crowd gathered **outside** the jail.
Would you look **inside** the garage for the rake?

precede, proceed   *Precede* means "to go or come before." *Proceed* means "to go forward."

EXAMPLES
An artillery barrage will **precede** the infantry attack.
If the siren goes off, **proceed** down the hall and out the door.

quiet, quite   Although these words sound alike, they have different meanings. *Quite* is an adverb meaning "positively" or "completely," whereas *quiet* is an adjective that means "making little or no noise."

EXAMPLES
The park was **quiet** and tranquil yesterday.
That ball traveled **quite** far after she hit it.

real, really   *Real* is an adjective meaning "actual." *Really* is an adverb meaning "actually" or "genuinely." Do not use *real* to mean "very" or "extremely."

EXAMPLES
That ring contains a **real** diamond.
This is a **really** (not *real*) important day for your father.

reason . . . because   *Reason is because* is both wordy and redundant. Use *reason is that* or simply *because.*

EXAMPLES
incorrect	The reason for her firing was because of laziness.
correct	The reason for her firing was laziness.
correct	The reason for her firing was that she was lazy.
correct	She was fired because she was lazy.

regardless, irregardless   Use *regardless, unmindful, heedless,* or *anyway. Irregardless* is a double negative.

EXAMPLE
Regardless of who wins this game, the divisional title has already been determined.

rise, raise   *Rise* is an intransitive verb that means "to move upward." It is an irregular verb that does not take a direct object. *Raise* is a transitive verb that means "to lift or make something go upward." It is a regular verb, and it takes a direct object.

EXAMPLES
The cake **rises** after being baked for a period of time.
Duane **raised** the flag at the post office.

scratch, itch   *Scratch* means "to scrape lightly to relieve itching." *Itch* means "to feel a tingling of the skin, with the desire to scratch."

EXAMPLES
My feet **itch** when I try to wear these socks.
I cannot effectively **scratch** my feet through these thick socks.

set, sit   *Set* is a transitive verb meaning "to place something." It always takes a direct object. *Sit* is an intransitive verb meaning "to rest in an upright position." It does not take a direct object.

EXAMPLES
Please **set** my drink on the coffeetable.
I think you should **sit** down before you hear what I have to say.

some, somewhat   *Some* is an adjective meaning "a certain unspecified quantity." *Somewhat* is an adverb meaning "slightly." Do not use *some* as an adverb.

EXAMPLES	
incorrect	The wind has died down some.
correct	That dog is **somewhat** disoriented.
correct	We found **some** gold in those mountains.

than, then   *Than* is a conjunction used in comparisons. *Then* is an adverb that shows a sequence of events.

EXAMPLES
Andy's car is faster **than** Ken's motorcycle.
If I had known **then** what would later happen, I never would have rubbed the lamp.

their, there, they're   *Their* is the possessive form of *they*. *There* points out a place or introduces an independent clause. *They're* is the contracted form of *they are*.

EXAMPLES
The bears decided to go back into **their** caves.
There is the largest tree in the forest.
Wanda and Marylyn said **they're** coming over this weekend.

them   *Them* is a pronoun. It should never be used as an adjective. Use *those*.

EXAMPLES	
incorrect	I think them wolves are looking for something to eat.
correct	I think **those** wolves are looking for something to eat.

this here, that there   Do not use. Simply say *this* or *that*.

EXAMPLES	
incorrect	This here bat is from Cuba.
correct	**This** bat is from Cuba.
incorrect	That there is a genuine Colt revolver.
correct	**That** is a genuine Colt revolver.

to, too, two   *To* is a preposition that can mean "in the direction of." *Too* is an adverb that means both "extremely, overly" and "also." *Two* is the spelling for the number 2.

> EXAMPLES
> Take the money **to** the bank.
> Juan has **too** many incompletes on his report card.
> Cecelia is excused, **too.**
> I have **two** options I can take.

try and   Use *try to* instead.

> EXAMPLES
> **incorrect**   Try and be polite to our guests.
> **correct**   **Try to** be polite to our guests.

use to, used to   Be sure to add the *d* to *used* to form the past participle.

> EXAMPLES
> **incorrect**   Glenn use to be the best teacher in the school.
> **correct**   Glenn **used to** be the best teacher in the school.

way, ways   Do not use *ways* for *way* when referring to distance.

> EXAMPLES
> **incorrect**   We are a long ways from Arizona.
> **correct**   We are a long **way** from Arizona.

when, where   When you define a word, don't use *when* or *where*.

> EXAMPLES
> **incorrect**   A *charley horse* is when you get a cramping pain in your arm or leg.
> **correct**   A *charley horse* is a cramping pain in the arm or leg.

where, that   Do not use *where* to mean "that."

> EXAMPLES
> **incorrect**   I read where a new mall is going to be built in town.
> **correct**   I read **that** a new mall is going to be built in town.

which, that, who, whom   *Which* is used to refer only to things. Use it to introduce nonessential clauses that refer to things or to groups of people. Always use a comma before *which* when it introduces a nonessential clause.

EXAMPLES
His car, **which** was impounded, is a Chevy Nova.
This sled, **which** was built by my grandfather, will slide faster than you can imagine.

That is used to refer either to people or things. Use it to introduce essential clauses that refer to things or groups of people. Do not use a comma before *that* when it introduces an essential clause.

EXAMPLES
The bird **that** built a nest in the tree has come back.
A clock **that** does not work has little value.

Who or *whom* is used to refer only to people. Use *who* or *whom* to introduce essential and nonessential clauses. Use a comma only when the pronoun introduces a nonessential clause.

EXAMPLES
Valerie is the girl **who** is selling cookies in the neighborhood.
That umpire, **whom** you offended earlier, is going to be working our game.

who's, whose   *Who's* is a contraction for *who is* or *who has*. *Whose* is the possessive form of *who*.

EXAMPLES
Who's going to play quarterback for our school this year?
Whose dog keeps barking all night?

without, unless   Do not use the preposition *without* in place of the conjunction *unless*.

EXAMPLES
incorrect   I will not win without I practice.
correct   I will not win **without** practice.
correct   I will not win **unless** I practice.

your, you're *Your* is a possessive pronoun. *You're* is a contraction for the words *you are*.

EXAMPLES
The dog found **your** homework under the table.
You're not going to pass the class unless you redo the work.

Try It Yourself

EXERCISE 15

Identifying Common Usage Problems

Choose the correct word in parentheses to complete the sentence.

1. The players are (already, all ready) for the big game.
2. Our mayor (affected, effected) a very useful policy.
3. (Its, It's) so hot in the summer, the dog rarely leaves (its, it's) shade tree.
4. Everyone on the team, (accept, except) for Tim, will show up to (accept, except) the award.
5. This is a (quite, quiet) neighborhood to live in.
6. Your (rise, raise) up the company ladder is impressive, but you still did not (rise, raise) the support needed to become president.
7. I'm going to (sit, set) on this couch while I decide where to (sit, set) the vase.
8. I think (their, they're) not going to play Friday because they have to paint (there, their) house.
9. If (your, you're) truck is faster (then, than) mine, (then, than) you should drive us to the hospital.
10. Fred (use, used) to sell (use, used) cars to make a living.
11. Abbott and Costello, (whose, who's) comedy routine "(Whose, Who's) on First?" was popular, are considered to be legends by many people today.
12. You are taking (fewer, less) credits this semester.
13. Grandma divided the cookies (between, among) Kyle and Kelsey.
14. Albuquerque is a short (way, ways) down the highway from here.
15. It seems (like, as if) the younger players don't respect the game anymore.
16. Those bears (doesn't, don't) appear amused at (them, those) campers taking pictures.
17. In college Shelly was (learned, taught) macroeconomics before she (learned, taught) how to run (a, an) small business.

18. Paul better (bring, take) that iguana outside before his parents come home.
19. Cockroaches can be found (everywhere, everywheres) in this town because it lacks a (good, well) exterminator.
20. Billy (had ought, ought) to find a different riddle to tell the class.
21. We found the cat (outside, outside of) the house.
22. The doctor removed her appendix before it (busted, burst).
23. Rhonda sits (beside, besides) the tree each day at lunch.
24. I (should of, should have) thought more carefully about that decision.
25. My family (could hardly, couldn't hardly) see the performance from where they were sitting.

EXERCISE 16
Correcting Common Usage Problems
Rewrite the following sentences to correct any mistakes in usage. If a sentence does not have any errors, write *correct*.

1. That dog ain't going to hunt anymore.
2. We will not be going to camp without we raise more money.
3. Will you look and see if our guests have arrived yet?
4. Except for Carl, everyone ought to buy new shoes.
5. There are alot of frogs in this pond.
6. This here guitar was once owned by Les Paul.
7. Put your hands in the air real slow.
8. The governor hisself will be leading the parade.
9. I already finished my homework for tonight.
10. A traffic jam is when a large number of cars are unable to move.
11. We should have guessed that the Sandersons would be bringing their harmonicas.
12. Jeff will be playing today irregardless of the pain.
13. How come weeds can grow in the hot dry summer?
14. Jamie plays the fiddle really good.
15. The wolf which was howling last night is in our backyard.
16. Leslie is kind of grouchy in the morning.
17. My friend Hannah she is going to be singing in the musical.

18. The reason for the UFO sighting is because a weather balloon blew off course.
19. The farther you travel away from here, the more you will miss your home.
20. Please let me know where you will be staying at.
21. Those type of snakes will not attack unless provoked.
22. Josh ran in the garage.
23. Our neighbor read where you will be receiving a big promotion.
24. If you itch that mosquito bite, it will get worse.
25. All right, I believe we can now begin.

EXERCISE 17
Using Commonly Misused Words in Your Writing
Write an original sentence using each of the following groups of words correctly.

1. between the two cats
2. besides Matt
3. as if
4. an effect
5. can accept
6. already here
7. among the audience
8. sings badly
9. take
10. beside the tree
11. except for
12. already arrived
13. affected the outcome
14. like a hawk
15. looked bad
16. a little farther
17. than
18. feeling well
19. more than 90 percent
20. bring a dish

UNIT 14 REVIEW

TEST YOUR KNOWLEDGE

EXERCISE 1
Identifying Problems with Subject-Verb Agreement
Choose the verb in parentheses that agrees in number with the subject. (10 points)

EXAMPLE
The fish (is, are) biting today. *(are)*

1. The guard, along with two dogs, (patrols, patrol) the perimeter each night.
2. Either of the movies (sounds, sound) entertaining to me.
3. One of the horses (is, are) frightened by the storm.
4. A teacher and her students (is, are) touring the factory
5. There (is, are) a group of coyotes up in the hills.
6. Hall and Oates (was, were) a popular musical act in the 1970s and 1980s.
7. Here (is, are) the paper you are looking for.
8. Jackie, as well as her entourage, (was, were) waiting for the limousine.
9. Many of the deer (has, have) left clues about where they were heading.
10. Either the team or the coach (is, are) going to win an award this season.

EXERCISE 2
Identifying Problems with Apostrophes
Choose the word in parentheses that uses the apostrophe correctly. (10 points)

EXAMPLE
(I've, Ive') decided to change careers. *(I've)*

1. We could only spare a (month's, months') wages for the horse.
2. A (robin's, robins) nest is in our tree in the front yard.
3. The (tomato's, tomatoes') ripeness is a key factor in determining their taste.
4. That (actress's, actresses) dress (is'nt, isn't) going to impress anyone.
5. Your (children's, childrens') toys are all neatly put away.
6. When comparing cars, one can see that (our's, ours) is the better value.
7. She (wont', won't) practice anymore this week.
8. The (antelope's, antelopes') tracks led to the place where they like to play.
9. Three (referee's, referees') decisions cannot be overruled.
10. Stay inside to avoid (winter's, winters') icy fury.

EXERCISE 3
Identifying Commonly Misused Words
Choose the word in parentheses to complete each sentence correctly. (10 points)

EXAMPLE
The batter (hisself, himself) did not even see the pitch. *(himself)*

1. I cannot believe the (affect, effect) you have had on the boy.
2. We have (already, all ready) learned about a bear and (its, it's) hibernation patterns.
3. The restaurant is serving chicken and dumplings (beside, besides) the beef and potatoes.
4. You should present (a, an) well-written essay to the instructor.
5. This state has (fewer, less) resources now (than, then) it did ten years ago.

6. After taking the medicine, Karla felt (good, well) enough to attend school.
7. Can you (learn, teach) me to sing (real, really) well?
8. The donkey was (kind of, somewhat) reluctant to travel any (further, farther).
9. Will you (try and, try to) fix the squeaky door?
10. The gorilla looked (like, as though) he was hungry.

EXERCISE 4

Correcting Problems in Usage

Rewrite the following sentences to correct for errors in subject-verb agreement, apostrophes, double negatives, split infinitives, and dangling and misplaced modifiers. If there are no usage errors in the sentence, write *correct*. (10 points)

EXAMPLE
We don't have no plans for this weekend.
(We don't have *any* plans for this weekend.)

1. He is driving the car which ran a couple of red lights.
2. I am asking you to directly go to the grocery store.
3. The computer's keyboard, which are similar to a typewriter's keyboard, is something you should become familiar with.
4. Hugh could not scarcely find a rabbit in the field.
5. Floating down the river, lions' roars were heard.
6. Either Zane or his sons were working in the garage last night trying to further understand the problem with the engine.
7. The captain stood on the ship's bridge in a blue uniform with gold buttons.
8. We cannot understand the computers error messages that keep appearing on the screen.
9. I have found that traveling farther into the wilderness brings greater freedom from civilization's restraints.
10. Let me know where you are living at so I can come visit you.

EXERCISE 5

Writing with Correct Usage

The Internet has revolutionized the way people communicate and gather information. It is unlike anything that was available throughout history. Write a brief essay to be shared with classmates in which you describe ways that the Internet could have been used by people during a past age (e.g., an ancient Romans e-trade network, Jefferson and Adams corresponding via e-mail, abolitionist web sites to stir opposition to slavery). When you revise your essay, look for common usage problems, including subject-verb agreement, double negatives, split infinitives, apostrophe use, and commonly misused words. (10 points)

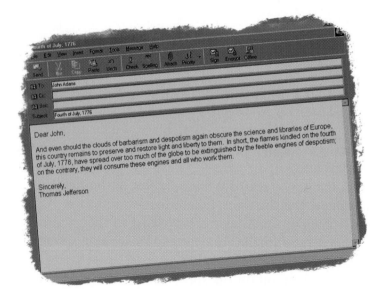

Style

UNIT *15* PUNCTUATION

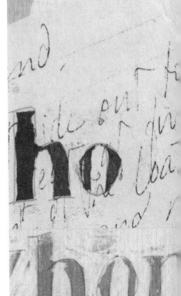

PUNCTUATION

EDITING FOR PUNCTUATION ERRORS

When editing your work, correct all punctuation errors. Several common punctuation errors to avoid are the incorrect use of **end marks**, **commas**, and **semicolons**.

END MARKS

An **end mark** tells the reader where a sentence ends. An end mark also shows the purpose of the sentence. The three end marks are the **period,** the **question mark**, and the **exclamation point.**

EXAMPLES

declarative sentence	I will be attending the play tonight.
imperative sentence	Return the overdue library books.
interrogative sentence	Will you be studying this weekend?
exclamatory sentence	There is a tarantula in the house!

A **declarative sentence** makes a statement and ends with a period.

EXAMPLE
The circus is coming to town next week.

An **imperative sentence** gives a command or makes a request. Often, the understood subject of these sentences is *you*.

EXAMPLE
(You) Take out the garbage.

An **interrogative sentence** asks a question. It ends with a question mark.

EXAMPLE
When will their train arrive at the station?

USAGE tip

An indirect question ends with a period rather than a question mark: *Grant asked me why I draw caricatures.*

An **exclamatory sentence** expresses strong feeling and ends with an exclamation point.

> EXAMPLE
> Watch out for the avalanche!

Try It Yourself

EXERCISE **1**
Identifying Sentence Purposes in Literature
Identify each sentence in the following literature passage as declarative, interrogative, or exclamatory.

It was as silent as the fog through which it swam.
"It's a dinosaur of some sort!" I crouched down holding to the stair rail.
"Yes, one of the tribe."
"But they died out!"
"No, only hid away in the Deeps. . . . Isn't that a word now, Johnny, a real word, it says so much: the Deeps. There's all the coldness and darkness and deepness in the world in a word like that."
"What'll we do?"

from "The Foghorn"
Ray Bradbury

Literature
M O D E L

EXERCISE **2**
Understanding End Marks
Punctuate the end of each sentence with the correct mark of punctuation—a period, question mark, or exclamation point.

1. I believe this hammer belongs to you
2. We just won a million dollars
3. The deadline for paying taxes is April 15
4. This rain cannot last much longer
5. Give me the remote control
6. Should the cat be roaming free in Mrs. Nelson's garden
7. Jack asked me when I would be home

8. The roof is on fire
9. Why can't we stay home today
10. Tomorrow we will go fly a kite

EXERCISE 3
Using End Marks in Your Writing
Choose a household product, for example, a broom, a detergent soap, a can opener. Imagine that you make a living by selling this object door to door. Write out what you would say as part of your sales pitch, noting facts and details that would interest customers in your product. Use sentences that end with periods, exclamation points, and question marks.

COMMAS

A **comma** separates words or groups of words within a sentence. Commas tell the reader to pause at certain spots in the sentence. These pauses help keep the reader from running together certain words and phrases when they should be kept apart.

Use commas to separate items in a series. Three or more items make a series.

> EXAMPLES
> Possums, rabbits, and squirrels invaded my yard.
>
> The school supplies he needs include pencils, erasers, paper, and a ruler.

Use commas when separating adjectives modifying a noun. In this case the comma can be thought of as replacing the word *and*.

> EXAMPLE
> It was a dark, stormy night. (It was a dark [and] stormy night.)

Use commas when you combine sentences using *and, but, or, nor, yet, so,* or *for*. Place the comma before these words.

USAGE tip

When a coordinating conjunction like *and* or *but* connects a series of items, phrases, or clauses, do not add commas. Commas are used only between independent clauses.

Bill spotted a pearl necklace on the ground *and* looked for the owner *but* never found her.

EXAMPLES
You and your mother can drive to the store, but make sure you have enough gas in the tank.

The burglars broke in through the window, or they entered through the cellar door.

Use a comma after an introductory word or phrase.

EXAMPLES
Finally, the semester is over.

Looking across the ocean, Shelly thought back to the previous summer.

Use a comma to set off words or phrases that interrupt sentences. Use two commas if the word or phrase occurs in the middle of the sentence. Use one comma if the word or phrase comes at the beginning or at the end of a sentence.

EXAMPLES
My brother plays for the Iowa Cubs, a minor league baseball team in Des Moines, Iowa.

The Battle of Stalingrad, the turning point of World War II, was fought in late 1942 and early 1943.

Use a comma to set off names used in direct address.

EXAMPLES
James, will you go to the store for me?
Don't forget to check the oven, Sara.

Use commas to separate parts of a date. Do not use a comma between the month and the year.

EXAMPLES
A fire swept through Baltimore on February 7, 1904.
Bill Clinton left office in January 2001.

Use commas to separate items in addresses. Do not use a comma between the state and the ZIP code.

EXAMPLES
The National Baseball Hall of Fame is located in Cooperstown, New York.

My new address is 4487 Starbuck Street, Birmingham, Alabama 35235.

Try It Yourself

EXERCISE 4
Identifying Commas in Literature
Identify the use of the commas in each sentence of the literature passage below as one of the following: series, combining sentences, or interrupters.

Literature
MODEL

This yard was enclosed by a high brick wall, crowded with trees, shrubs, and flowers. It was a shady, often damp place, where the moss grew thick, while strange-looking mushrooms sprang up overnight, and withered and died just as quickly.

Midgarden was a small, murky pool in which, during the summer, fat goldfish swam. As they darted about the dark water, Eve was reminded of summer heat lightning.

from "Pets"
Avi

EXERCISE 5
Correcting Comma Use
Rewrite the following sentences so that they are correctly punctuated with commas. If a sentence is punctuated correctly, write *correct*.

1. The battleship in the harbor has been painted gray so it matches the other ships in the fleet.
2. Indianapolis is the capital and largest city in the state of Indiana.
3. The address for Nebraska Wesleyan University is 5000 Saint Paul Avenue Lincoln Nebraska 68504.

4. Athena one of the Greek gods is the subject of this story.
5. Looking into the old chest I found a musket a cutlass and a uniform.
6. My grandfather told me that September 2 1945 was a special day for him.
7. The town's newspaper founded in 1845 is having financial difficulties.
8. Blankets clothes food and medical supplies are needed for the disaster victims.
9. You might want to buy a new tent and don't forget to bring along a couple of lanterns.
10. Dedication determination and stamina will be needed to finish race for it covers twenty miles of mountains forests and streams.

EXERCISE 6
Using Commas in Your Writing
Write a letter to a pen pal describing an important day in your life. Include information about your age at the time, where you lived, who was with you, and what happened on that day. Choose details that will be interesting to your pen pal and that will help him or her understand why this day is special to you. Be sure that you have used commas correctly in your essay.

SEMICOLONS

A **semicolon** joins two closely related sentences.

> EXAMPLE
> The Nelsons are finished moving in; they are probably exhausted right now.

Conjunctions such as *and, but, so, or, nor, for,* and *yet* can be used to combine two related sentences. A semicolon is a punctuation mark that also joins two closely related sentences. The semicolon can be used in place of the comma and the conjunction. Using a semicolon instead of a comma and a coordinating conjunction adds emphasis to the second clause.

The semicolon signals a pause that is longer than a comma's pause but shorter than a period's.

EXAMPLES	
two separate sentences	The *Titanic* was a majestic 882-foot ship that was believed to be indestructible. It sunk on its first voyage across the Atlantic.
joined with semicolon	The *Titanic* was a majestic 882-foot ship that was believed to be indestructible; it sunk on its first voyage across the Atlantic.

Try It Yourself

EXERCISE 7
Understanding Semicolons
Combine each pair of independent clauses by correctly placing a semicolon between them.

1. The Vietnamese people have been occupied by foreign powers for much of their history the Mongols and Chinese ruled over them hundreds of years ago.
2. European powers dominated much of Asia in the 1800s France established its rule over the Vietnamese and Laotians in the 1860s.
3. During World War II many French colonies were occupied by Japan the Japanese ruled Vietnam for five years.
4. After World War II France reestablished its control over Vietnam the Vietnamese and Laotian people fought to gain their independence.
5. The Vietnamese and Laotians fought with determination in 1954 they defeated the French, who pulled out of Southeast Asia.
6. In 1954 the United States entered Vietnam to oppose its new government this was the start of America's involvement in the Vietnam War.

7. For the Vietnamese the war was a struggle to throw off another foreign power they fought with great determination.

8. The Vietnam War became unpopular in the United States protesters demonstrated against the war on campuses across America.

9. President Lyndon Johnson lost support because of his Vietnam policy he did not choose to run for reelection in 1968.

10. In 1973 the United States pulled its troops out of Southeast Asia two years later Vietnam was united under a Communist government.

EXERCISE 8

Using Semicolons

Each independent clause that follows is the first half of a sentence. Add a semicolon and a second independent clause. Make sure that your second thought is also independent, is related to the first thought, and can stand alone.

1. The hungry tiger prowled in the night
2. Jennifer heard an ominous noise
3. Our car rolled slowly down the hill
4. Soldiers marched toward the town
5. The boss made a decision about the project
6. Beavers built a dam in the river
7. An alarm sounded in the building
8. Betty read half of the book this morning
9. A mist crept in among the houses
10. Snow came down for three days straight

COLONS

A **colon** introduces a list of items. Colons are also used between numbers that tell hours and minutes and after the greeting in a business letter.

EXAMPLES

The speech covered three topics: parking permits, housing, and leash laws.

You will be meeting the boss at 10:00 A.M.

Dear Human Resources: Please send a job application.

A colon may be used when the second clause explains or amplifies the first clause.

USAGE tip

Avoid using a colon after a form of the verb *to be* or after a preposition.

EXAMPLES

I seldom eat dinner: after 6:00 P.M., food doesn't appeal to me.

I was disappointed they left without me: I didn't want to miss the concert.

Try It Yourself

EXERCISE 9
Understanding Colons
Insert colons where they are needed in the following sentences. If no colons are needed, write *correct*.

1. The collection included the work of four nineteenth-century American writers Nathaniel Hawthorne, Herman Melville, Harriet Beecher Stowe, and Mark Twain.
2. Melville wrote about his experiences in three of his well-received books *Typee*, *Omoo*, and *Redburn*.
3. These books are based on his voyages to the Marquesas Islands, Tahiti, and Liverpool.
4. In *Moby Dick*, Melville writes about the experiences of the fictional characters Ishmael, Ahab, Starbuck, Stubb, and Queequeg.
5. The book blends these elements drama, adventure, and a technical treatise on whaling.
6. *Moby Dick* bears the influence of these writers Shakespeare, Hawthorne, and Byron.
7. Melville also wrote these three short stories "Bartleby the Scrivener," "the Encantadas," and "Benito Cereno."

8. Later in his life, he wrote the books *John Marr and Other Sailors*, *Timoleon*, and *Billy Budd*.
9. Melville's siblings included three brothers Gansevoort, Allan, and Tom.
10. Near the end of *Moby Dick*, I became so engrossed in the story that I stayed up reading until 230 A.M.

EXERCISE 10

Using Colons in Your Writing

Write a letter to a company that manufactures a product you use. Ask for information that you could use in a report about the company. Just for practice, try to use a number of colons in your letter.

ELLIPSIS POINTS

Ellipsis points are a series of three spaced points. Ellipsis points are used to show that material from a quotation or a quoted passage has been left out. Read the following literature model. Then note how the underlined material is omitted and replaced with ellipsis points in the second model.

But the most significant change thus far in the earth's atmosphere is the one that began with the industrial revolution early in the last century <u>and has picked up speed ever since</u>. Industry meant coal, and later oil, <u>and we began to burn lots of it</u>—bringing rising levels of carbon dioxide (CO_2), with its ability to trap more heat in the atmosphere and slowly warm the earth. Fewer than a hundred yards from the South Pole, <u>upwind from the ice runway where the ski plane lands and keeps its engines running to prevent the metal parts from freeze-locking together</u>, scientists monitor the air several times every day to chart course of that inexorable change.

Literature
M O D E L

from "Ships in the Desert"
Al Gore

But the most significant change thus far in the earth's atmosphere is the one that began with the industrial revolution early in the last century. . . . Industry meant coal, and later oil . . . bringing rising levels of carbon dioxide (CO_2), with its ability to trap more heat in the atmosphere and slowly warm the earth. Fewer than a hundred yards from the South Pole . . . scientists monitor the air several times every day to chart course of that inexorable change.

from "Ships in the Desert"
Al Gore

To use ellipsis points correctly, follow these guidelines:

- If material is left out at the beginning of a sentence or passage, use three points with a space between each point.

EXAMPLE
. . . I found the dragon asleep in his lair.

- If material is left out in the middle of a sentence, use three points with a space between each point.

EXAMPLE
Above the dragon . . . hovered a golden sphere.

- If material is left out at the end of a sentence, use an end mark after the ellipsis points.

EXAMPLES
The dragon was still sleeping. . . . My eyes had never gazed upon such a fearsome creature.

As I heard the dragon awakening, I ran down the tunnel. . . .

EXERCISE 11

Understanding Ellipsis Points

Rewrite each of the following sentences, correctly adding ellipsis points in place of the underlined material.

1. Though he was the pilot <u>on these flights</u>, he did not own the airplane.
2. It was a sixty-five-horsepower Aeronica, with tandem cockpits, <u>that he rented from a former bomber pilot whose name was Stanley</u>.
3. Stanley managed the airport, <u>including the huge loaf-shaped hangar that served as a garage for repairs and maintenance to the aircraft</u>, and he leased out the groups of small planes tethered near the building like a fleet of fishing boats clustered around a pier.
4. <u>It was Stanley, most often, who stood in front of the airplane and waited for my father to shout "ConTACT!" from the cockpit window, at which time</u>, Stanley gave the propeller a hefty downward shove that sent it spinning into action and started the plane shaking and shuddering on its way.
5. The job of starting the propeller was simple but perilous. <u>My father had warned us many times about the danger of standing anywhere near a propeller in action</u>. We could list almost as well as he did the limbs that had been severed from the bodies of careless individuals "in a split second" by a propeller's whirling force.
6. Therefore, <u>each time that Stanley started the propeller</u>, I would peer through its blinding whir to catch a glimpse of any pieces of him that might be flying through the air.
7. Each time, I saw only Stanley, whole and smiling, waving us onto the asphalt runway with his cap in his hand and his hair blowing in the wind of our passing—<u>"the propwash" my father called it</u>.
8. <u>My sister and</u> my three brothers flew on Saturdays too.

9. The older ones were taught to land and take off, to bank and dip, and even to turn the plane over in midair, although my second-oldest brother confessed that he hated this—<u>it made him feel so dizzy</u>.

10. The youngest of my three brothers, <u>only a few years older than me</u>, remembers my father instructing him to "lean into the curve" as the plane made a steep sideways dive toward the ground.

from "Flying"
Reeve Lindbergh

E X E R C I S E **12**

Using Ellipsis Points in Your Writing

Select a passage from one of your textbooks. Write the passage in its complete form. Then rewrite the passage, deleting some of the text and indicating omissions with ellipsis points.

APOSTROPHES

USAGE tip

To make pronunciation easier, add only an apostrophe after historical names of more than one syllable that end with an *s*: *Damocles' sword, Mephistopheles' curse, Jesus' parables, Augustus' census.*

An **apostrophe** is used to form the possessive of nouns. To form the possessive of a singular noun, add an apostrophe and an *s* to the end of the word.

EXAMPLES

a week's pay	a friend's bicycle	James's cat
the dress's collar		

The possessive of a plural noun is formed two different ways. If the plural noun does not end in –*s*, you add an apostrophe and an *s* to the end of the word. If the plural noun ends with an *s*, add only an apostrophe.

EXAMPLES

women's shoes	geese's flight	children's jokes
fans' cheers	six days' wages	actresses' agents

EXERCISE 13

Identifying Singular and Plural Possessive Nouns

Identify each of the following possessive nouns as singular or plural.

1. Mrs. Talbot's garden
2. Germans' hopes for peace
3. three months' vacation
4. anyone's guess
5. PETA's objective
6. her professors' advice
7. his brothers' cars
8. James's house
9. Socrates' wisdom
10. Zeus's bolts

EXERCISE 14

Correcting the Use of Apostrophes

Complete each of the following sentences by inserting 's or an apostrophe alone to form the possessive case of the underlined words.

1. On the first day of class, the <u>students</u> books had not yet arrived.
2. A <u>teachers</u> job is not done after the last class.
3. Mrs. <u>Jones</u> assignments are always the most difficult.
4. The <u>principals</u> first two years on the job went smoothly.
5. This <u>schools</u> music department needs funding.
6. Pizza was served for the <u>semesters</u> first lunch.
7. Our <u>lockers</u> combinations had all been changed from last year.
8. The <u>city</u> streets had been repaired before the school year started.
9. This <u>weeks</u> assignments had piled up by Friday.
10. The <u>bells</u> ring brought the much welcome sound of freedom.

Using Apostrophes in Your Writing

For your journal, write a paragraph describing a typical Saturday morning in your household. Include details about your activities, meals, and other people with whom you interact. Be sure to use apostrophes correctly in your singular and plural possessive nouns.

UNDERLINING AND ITALICS

Italics are a type of slanted printing used to make a word or phrase stand out. In handwritten documents or in forms of printing in which italics are not available, underlining is used. You should underline or italicize the titles of books, magazines, works of art, movies, and plays.

EXAMPLES	
books	*The Call of the Wild; The Grapes of Wrath; For Whom the Bell Tolls* or <u>The Call of the Wild</u>; <u>The Grapes of Wrath</u>; <u>For Whom the Bell Tolls</u>
magazines	*The Atlantic Monthly; Newsweek; Chess Life* or <u>The Atlantic Monthly</u>; <u>Newsweek</u>; <u>Chess Life</u>
works of art	*Mona Lisa; The Last Supper; The Thinker* or <u>Mona Lisa</u>; <u>The Last Supper</u>; <u>The Thinker</u>
movies and television and radio programs	*A Beautiful Mind; Malcolm in the Middle; All Things Considered* or <u>A Beautiful Mind</u>; <u>Malcolm in the Middle</u>; <u>All Things Considered</u>
plays	*Othello; Death of a Salesman; The Producers* or <u>Othello</u>, <u>Death of a Salesman</u>; <u>The Producers</u>

Try It Yourself

EXERCISE 16

Understanding Correct Usage of Underlining and Italics

Underline the words in the following sentences that should be italicized.

332 *LANGUAGE ESSENTIALS*

1. The lyrics in the musical Joseph and the Amazing Technicolor Dreamcoat are quite clever.
2. I don't know if he will be able to give a speech in front of the David statue.
3. Legend is one of Tom Cruise's lesserknown movies.
4. She first read The Hobbit in seventh grade.
5. I read about someone who went to see the musical Cats thirty-two times.
6. The Des Moines Register provided in-depth coverage of the Iowa Caucus.
7. We saw the painting The Scream when it was on loan to our city's art gallery.
8. My grandmother once appeared in Life Magazine.
9. Christopher Lambert delivers a powerful performance in the movie The Highlander.
10. If you want to learn about the early meatpacking industry, you should read The Jungle.

EXERCISE 17
Using Italics and Underlining in Your Writing
For the school newspaper, compare and contrast two movies, books, or plays that you have recently seen or read. Include plots and characters in your comparison. Think about ways in which the plots and characters are alike and ways in which they are different. Be sure to use either italics or underlining correctly in your review.

QUOTATION MARKS

When you use a person's exact words in your writing, you are using a **direct quotation.** Enclose the words of a direct quotation in **quotation marks**.

EXAMPLES
"Good morning, fans," announced the sports anchor. "It's time to cover last night's games."

CONTINUED

> Hovering above his friends, Ivan teased, "Haven't you seen a boy fly before?"

A direct quotation should always begin with a capital letter. Separate a direct quotation from the rest of the sentence with a comma, question mark, or exclamation point. Do not separate the direct quotation from the rest of the sentence with a period. All punctuation marks that belong to the direct quotation itself should be placed inside the quotation marks.

> **EXAMPLES**
> "You can count on me," Chris replied.
> Bobby roared, "Get your head in the game!"
> "Why did you say that?" Mr. Ross asked.
> "Please," Robin begged, "give me another chance."

Use quotation marks to enclose the titles of short works such as short stories, poems, songs, articles, essays, and parts of books.

> **EXAMPLES**
> | | |
> |---|---|
> | **short stories** | "The Inn of Lost Time," "Zebra" |
> | **poems** | "Basic Black," "The Raven" |
> | **songs** | "Bridge Over Troubled Water," "Again" |
> | **articles, essays,** | |
> | **and parts of books** | "The Public Debt and the Power of the Purse," "On Religion" |

Try It Yourself

EXERCISE 18
Identifying the Correct Use of Quotation Marks
The following sentences include direct quotations and the titles of short works. Add the appropriate quotation marks, commas, question marks, exclamation points, and periods to the sentences.

1. This semester's reading list made me feel like singing I am a man of constant sorrow

2. According to William James Wherever you are it is your own friends who make your world
3. Reeve Lindbergh wrote that in the air her father Charles wasn't flying the airplane, he was being the airplane
4. In the song One Night in Bangkok the arbiter declares One town's very like another when your head's down over your pieces brother
5. Billie Jean King once gave the advice If you're going to make an error, make it a doozy, and don't be afraid to hit the ball.
6. I'll be watching you is Sting's promise in the hit Police song Every Breath You Take
7. When can their glory fade asks Alfred, Lord Tennyson about the soldiers in the Light Brigade in his poem The Charge of the Light Brigade
8. Ronald Reagan's speechwriter Peggy Noonan proclaimed The crew of the space shuttle *Challenger* honored us by the manner in which they lived their lives
9. One's destination is never a place but rather a new way of looking at things is an inspiring quote by Henry Miller.
10. After Paul Harvey told his listeners Now you know the rest of the story he signed off by saying Good day

EXERCISE 19
Using Quotation Marks
Write a sentence in response to each direction below. Be sure to use quotation marks correctly.

1. your favorite short story and why it appeals to you
2. a song you dislike and your thoughts about its lyrics
3. a poet who has written a poem that you like
4. an inspiring quote from a famous person
5. a magazine article that provided you with useful information

HYPHENS AND DASHES

Hyphens are used to make a compound word or compound expression.

USAGE tip

Use a dictionary to find out if a compound word or expression is hyphenated or written as one word or two words.

EXAMPLES
great-grandfather Jones
lift-off
long-winded
cul-de-sac
thirty-eight-year-old man

A **dash** is used to show a sudden break or change in thought. Note that a dash is longer in length than a hyphen. Dashes sometimes replace other marks of punctuation, such as periods, semicolons, or commas.

Literature MODELS

But one day Beltane dragged in something rare and shimmery—a struggling hummingbird.

from "Mute Dancers: How to Watch a Hummingbird"
Diane Ackerman

The disease had sharpened my senses—not destroyed—not dulled them.

from "The Tell-Tale Heart"
Edgar Allan Poe

USAGE tip

Do not use the dash when commas, semicolons, and periods are more appropriate. Too many dashes can create a jumpy quality in writing and draw unnecessary attention to the writer.

Try It Yourself

EXERCISE 20
Identifying the Correct Use of Hyphens and Dashes
Rewrite the following sentences, adding hyphens and dashes where they are appropriate.

1. Running a fifty meter dash will get your blood pumping.
2. Winning a medal at the Olympics is a great feeling earning a gold medal is indescribable.

3. Paying one half of the bill ahead of time might ensure a first rate job.
4. This is a job for Batman and Robin the fearless crime fighting duo.
5. Before he went to prison, my uncle was a top notch safe cracker.
6. She read a book about James Madison the fourth president of the United States.
7. He wrote all of his reports using only lower case letters.
8. You have plenty of apples in your basket only four will be needed for the dessert.
9. I saw your uncle a strange looking man crossing the street downtown.
10. You should be more safety conscious always wear a hard hat at the construction site.

EXERCISE 21
Using Hyphens and Dashes in Your Writing
Write for the dietitian in the school cafeteria a description of an ideal meal that you would like to eat. Include at least three of your favorite foods and a beverage in this meal. Include hyphens and dashes in your description.

PARENTHESES AND BRACKETS

Use **parentheses** around material that is added to a sentence but is not considered of major importance. This material might include explanations, facts, minor digressions, and examples that aid understanding but are not essential to meaning.

USAGE tip

Parentheses are often used in place of dashes or commas.

EXAMPLES
The size of our club (now over 130) indicates a strong interest in the game of backgammon.

You can find many hand-held tools (hammers and screwdrivers, for example) in the storage shed.

Commas, dashes, and parentheses may all be used to enclose words or phrases that interrupt the sentence and are not considered essential to meaning. Notice in the following sentences how each punctuation mark increases the emphasis.

> **EXAMPLES**
> We saw a variety of birds, robins, starlings, and blue jays, in the backyard tree. (a short pause)
>
> We saw a group of birds in the backyard tree—robins only. (a stronger break in the sentence)
>
> We saw a variety of birds (nothing exotic) in the backyard tree. (a minor digression)

Use **brackets** to enclose information that explains or clarifies a detail in quoted material.

> **EXAMPLES**
> The historian noted, "The president [Harry Truman] displayed an unusual level of political courage for someone with so little prior experience in Washington." (The brackets explain who "the president" is in the quote.)
>
> According to another historian, "[Harry] Truman should be remembered as one of our five greatest presidents." (The brackets provide the president's first name.)

Try It Yourself

EXERCISE 22
Understanding Parentheses and Brackets
Rewrite the following sentences, adding parentheses and brackets where they are appropriate.

1. A historical movie such as *Eight Men Out* can be both informative and entertaining.
2. One reviewer declared that, "It *Eight Men Out* is the best sports movie ever made."

3. Several of the actors in the movie including Charlie Sheen and D. B. Sweeney have appeared in other sports films.
4. Other well-known actors such as Christopher Lloyd and John Cusack appear in *Eight Men Out*.
5. The movie portrays the 1919 World Series the Black Sox Series and the events that followed.
6. Several members of the Chicago White Sox being bribed by gamblers worked to lose the Series against the Cincinnati Reds.
7. One historian concluded, "These eight men the Black Sox created the worst scandal in baseball history."
8. After being caught, all eight Black Sox having been banned by Commissioner Landis never played major league baseball again.
9. Several of the players including Buck Weaver claimed they did not throw any games.
10. It did not take long for baseball the national pastime to recover from the Black Sox Scandal.

EXERCISE 23
Using Parentheses and Brackets in Your Writing
Write an informal letter to a friend describing your room. Include comments that other people have made about the room. To set off information, use parentheses and brackets where needed.

UNIT 15 REVIEW

TEST YOUR KNOWLEDGE

EXERCISE 1
Identifying Sentence Purposes
Identify the following sentences as imperative, declarative, interrogative, or exclamatory. (10 points)

EXAMPLE
We need to take out the garbage before our guests arrive.
(declarative)

1. Will you be attending the banquet on Saturday?
2. Set your drink on a coaster.
3. It looks like the cat has found a new friend.
4. Your shirt is on fire!
5. Holy cow! The Cubs are going to the World Series.
6. Do you still believe that plan will work?
7. A new gas station opened down the street.
8. Weather patterns can be hard to predict in this state.
9. Yes, I received a perfect score on my test!
10. Who is going to be singing first tonight?

EXERCISE 2
Understanding Commas and End Marks of Punctuation
Proofread the following sentences to add end punctuation marks and commas where appropriate. (10 points)

1. Did you find that book you were looking for at the library
2. Your new system comes with a keyboard monitor speakers and a mouse
3. The car just rolled over the cliff
4. This forest is full of deer elk and foxes
5. When did you find out that he had been fired

6. Marge Wilma and Peggy will all be receiving awards this evening
7. This product slices dices and purees any type of food
8. I would like to buy eggs and milk when we go to the store
9. Wow I can't believe how fast he runs
10. Shouldn't you be checking on the cake in the oven

Correcting Punctuation Errors
Rewrite the following sentences to correct any errors in end marks, commas, and semicolons. If a sentence is punctuated correctly, write *correct*. (10 points)

1. How can we find out Tom and Sharon's address
2. Oh no, the river is flooding out of it banks
3. Your new friend is intelligent funny and compassionate
4. A hurricane ripped through this town three years ago it caused over a million dollars' worth of damage
5. One of the boys is the leader of the gang the others are his followers
6. It is not always easy to make the right decision when you know it will be unpopular.
7. Hail wind and rain made our trek though the woods very unpleasant
8. Can you find your way back to the path.
9. Yeah, I knew we would win!
10. We looked in the garage but found nothing but dust cobwebs pebbles and an old rake

Understanding Colons and Semicolons
Proofread the following business letter to add colons and semicolons where appropriate. (10 points)

5546 Wolf Street
Olympia, Minnesota 56309
April 5, 2002

Dear Mr. Cain

I recently ordered a CD from your February 2002 catalog. My selection was titled "Country Legends." It had songs from these artists Merle Haggard, Hank Williams Sr., Johnny Cash, and George Jones. The CD I received, "Metal Nightmares," has songs from these groups Metallica, Black Sabbath, Motley Crue, and Poison. I checked the number on my order form and the number on the invoice they do not match.

Here is my original order information Item number 347259; Price $14.95; Category Country. I am returning the CD to you please send me the "Country Legends" CD instead. If you need to contact me about this order, use this number (309) 555-1937. Thank you.

Sincerely,

Phil Sackett

EXERCISE 5
Identifying Singular and Plural Possessive Nouns
Identify each of the following possessive nouns as singular or plural. (10 points)

EXAMPLE
dog's collar   (singular)

1. kittens' paws
2. women's league
3. singers' microphones
4. radio's antenna
5. trees' leaves

6. airplane's wings
7. pen's ink
8. girl's father
9. snakes' skins
10. Jess's apple

EXERCISE 6

Understanding Ellipsis Points

Rewrite each of the following sentences, correctly adding ellipsis points in place of the underlined material. (10 points)

EXAMPLE
I heard the snake's head strike against the thick cowhide boot <u>with a sharp little crack</u>, and then at once the head was back in that same deadly backward-curving position, ready to strike again. —Roald Dahl, from "The Green Mamba"

(I heard the snake's head strike against the thick cowhide boot . . . and then at once the head was back in that same deadly backward-curving position, ready to strike again. —Roald Dahl, from "The Green Mamba")

1. We enjoyed singing and dancing, <u>we were natural hams</u>, and our parents never discouraged us. —Cherylene Lee, from "Hollywood and the Pits"
2. Our family remained in Nongkhai for three agonizing years, <u>with our fate uncertain and our future obscure</u>. —Maijue Xiong, from "An Unforgettable Journey"
3. The lean faces of the two ronin, <u>lit by the fire</u>, suddenly looked fierce and hungry. —Lensey Namioka, from "The Inn of Lost Time"
4. His ears strained to identify the sound, making sure it was a whistle. <u>No mistake</u>. It came again, the same as the night before. —Patricia McKissack, from "The 11:59"
5. <u>Feasting and flying, courting and dueling</u>, hummingbirds consume life at a fever pitch. —Diane Ackerman, from "Mute Dancers: How to Watch a Hummingbird"

6. To see if the waters were receding, I sent a dove which returned to me, <u>seeing no place to stand</u>. Then I sent a swallow out to fly. —Christina Kolb, from her retelling of "The Epic of Gilgamesh"
7. Dan, a dog blind in one eye and with a slight limp in his left hind leg. <u>Dan was a fat slow-moving old dog</u>. He was very affectionate and his eye was the color of amber. —Morley Callaghan, from "Luke Baldwin's Vow"
8. So when the railroad left, he began to do everything wrong. <u>Stayed out all hours. Drank and drank some more.</u> When he was home, he was so grouchy we were afraid to speak. —Paulette Childress, from "Getting the Facts of Life"
9. Firth saw the yellow light of Rhayader's lantern down by his little wharf, <u>and she found him there</u>. —Paul Gallico, from *The Snow Goose*
10. But no king or queen rules alone, <u>no matter how authoritative or arrogant they may be. They usually look to others for advice, advice they may follow or reject.</u> Elizabeth appointed ministers to handle the various departments of government, and made Sir William Cecil, <u>then thirty-eight</u>, her principal advisor. —Milton Meltzer, from *Ten Queens: Portraits of Women of Power*

EXERCISE 7
Understanding Apostrophes, Underlining, Italics, and Quotation Marks
Proofread the following sentences to add apostrophes, underlining or italics, and quotation marks where appropriate. (10 points)

EXAMPLE
Terry never misses an issue of Wall Street Journal. (Terry never misses an issue of *Wall Street Journal*.)

1. I read the article The Dandy and the Mauler in Mexico in the Journal of Sport History.
2. The movie Inherit the Wind is based on a trial that occurred in Tennessee in 1925.

3. Seeing the cat scale the trunk of the tree, Bill cried, Fluffy, no! Get back down here!
4. Searching the students lockers will not yield any answers.
5. Call me Ishmael is the opening line of the classic novel Moby Dick.
6. Cosmopolitan and Glamour are her favorite magazines.
7. Tracys car would not start, so we did not see Titanic at the theater.
8. Have you ever read Beneath the Wheel by Hermann Hesse?
9. The singers duet brought the fans to their feet.
10. Birds nests can be found in every tree in the park.

EXERCISE 8
Understanding Hyphens, Dashes, Parentheses, and Brackets
Proofread the following sentences to add hyphens, dashes, parentheses, or brackets where appropriate. (10 points)

EXAMPLE
Matt looked under the table for the Ping Pong ball. (Matt looked under the table for the *Ping-Pong* ball.)

1. The mouse feeling as bold as a lion approached the cat to demand an explanation.
2. He noticed that she was walking a dog a Boston Terrier and thought of an opening line.
3. The speaker implored, "Every book by this author Mark Twain must be banned."
4. Our full scale model took up one half of the table's surface.
5. Going to a drive in movie a replay of *Star Wars* reminded us of our high school days.
6. Climbing the old oak tree in the backyard a feat his brothers never accomplished was his summer goal.
7. Shelly decided that her age twenty-eight years old put her at too great of a disadvantage to compete.

8. Did you see the saber toothed tiger at the museum?
9. The news anchor reported, "The city London is under a heavy fog this evening."
10. An ill timed comment will provoke a long winded reply from her.

EXERCISE 9
Using Correct Punctuation
Write a sentence for each direction below. (10 points)

EXAMPLE
commas in a series and a semicolon *(There were many old computers at the warehouse; we saw Commodore 64s, Commodore Vic 20s, Apple IIs, and Timex Sinclairs.)*

1. an interrogatory sentence with a plural possessive noun
2. a comma used in a date and quotation marks
3. an exclamatory sentence and a dash or dashes
4. a singular possessive noun and a hyphen
5. two sentences joined by a semicolon
6. a compound sentence and parentheses
7. commas used for an interrupter and a colon
8. underlining or italics and commas in a series
9. quotation marks for a direct quotation and brackets
10. a declarative sentence and a colon

EXERCISE 10
Using Correct Punctuation in Your Writing
Write a fictional conversation between two characters who are trying to overcome or resolve a problem. Explain in the dialogue what the problem is and what the characters decide to do about it. Use end marks, commas, semicolons, colons, apostrophes, underlining or italics, quotation marks, hyphens, dashes, parentheses, and brackets correctly in your dialogue. (10 points)

UNIT *16* CAPITALIZATION

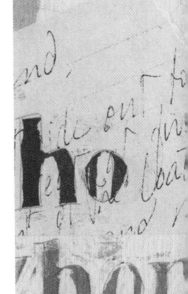

CAPITALIZATION

EDITING FOR CAPITALIZATION ERRORS

To avoid capitalization errors, check your draft for proper nouns and proper adjectives; geographical names, directions, and historical events; and titles of artworks and literary works.

Proper nouns and proper adjectives are capitalized. A **proper noun** names a specific person, place, or thing.

EXAMPLES	
Andrew Jackson	Queen Victoria
Madison Square Garden	Russia

A **proper adjective** is an adjective formed from a proper noun or a proper noun used as an adjective.

EXAMPLES	
Jacksonian democracy	Victorian culture
Russian novelist	

Geographical names of specific places are capitalized, including terms such as *lake, mountain, river* or *valley* if they are used as part of a name. Do not capitalize general names for places.

EXAMPLES		
capitalized	Lake Huron	Kuskokwim Mountains
	Rio Grande River	
not capitalized	a lake	the mountains
	the river	

Geographical directions are capitalized if they are part of a specific name of a commonly recognized region. Do not capitalize such words as *east(ern), west(ern), north(ern),* and *south(ern)* if they are used only to indicate direction.

EXAMPLES		
capitalized	Far East	West Texas
	West Coast	
not capitalized	east of the river	western Canada
	the south bay	

Historical events are capitalized, as are special events and recognized periods of time.

EXAMPLES		
Gilded Age	Super Bowl	Era of Good Feelings

The **titles of artworks and literary works** are capitalized. Note that articles, conjuctions, and prepositions in the title do not need to be capitalized.

EXAMPLES	
Where the Red Fern Grows	*Gabrielle with a Rose*
To Kill a Mockingbird	

Try It Yourself

EXERCISE 1
Identifying Capitalized Words in Literature
For each underlined word in the following passage, identify the capitalization rule.

Literature
MODEL

"Well, whaddaya know!" It was <u>Steve's</u> voice, softer this time, but all mock amazement. Laura jabbed her notebook with her pencil. Why were they so cruel, so thoughtless? Why did they have to laugh?

"This one," <u>Rachel</u> was saying as she opened one of the boxes, "it's one of the best." Off came the layers of paper and there, at last, smooth and pearly and shimmering, was the shell. Rachel turned it over lovingly in her hands. White, fluted sides, like the closecurled petals of a flower; a scrolled coral back. <u>Laura</u> held her breath. It was beautiful. At the back of the room snickers

CONTINUED

had begun again.

"Bet she got it at <u>Woolworth's</u>," somebody whispered.

"Or in a trash dump." That was <u>Diane</u>.

Rachel pretended not to hear, but her face was getting very red and Laura could see she was flustered.

"Here's another that's kind of pretty. I found it last summer at <u>Ogunquit</u>."

from "The Fan Club"
Rona Maynard

EXERCISE 2

Correcting Capitalization

Rewrite each sentence, correcting it for errors in capitalization.

1. Titus smith rode with his brothers, fred and paul, from kansas city to tulsa.
2. During the trip Titus read the famous novel *the hobbit*.
3. Titus is a seventh-grade student at Lincoln middle school; his favorite subject is spanish.
4. He hopes to someday visit spain, france, and other countries in western europe.
5. On the trip, the brothers listened to CDs by diamond rio, sawyer brown, and alabama.
6. Soon after crossing the mississippi river, Fred pulled into a gas station.
7. Paul took over driving and piloted the car down highway 44 toward tulsa.
8. At the university of oklahoma, Paul is studying english literature.
9. After eating in the cafeteria, the smith brothers watched the old television show *bonanza*.
10. Titus once wrote a poem, "the grey box," about the experience of watching television.

EXERCISE 3
Using Capitalization in Your Writing

Write for your classmates a summary of a trip you once took with your family, fellow students, or friends. In your summary note the rule for each capitalized word: proper noun, proper adjective, geographical name, geographical direction, historical name, title of an artwork, title of a literary work, pronoun *I*, first word in a sentence, and title of a person. Try to include at least one capitalized word for each rule listed above.

USAGE tip

Middle initials and the abbreviations *Jr.* and *Sr.* should also be capitalized.

PROPER NOUNS AND PROPER ADJECTIVES
Proper Nouns

A **proper noun** names a specific person, place, or thing. The following kinds of proper nouns should be capitalized.

USAGE tip

Do not capitalize the names of seasons: *spring, summer, fall, winter.*

Names of people

EXAMPLES		
Abigail Adams	Harry S. Truman	Ken Griffey Jr.

Months, days, and holidays

EXAMPLES		
April	Sunday	Thanksgiving

Names of religions, languages, races, and nationalities

USAGE tip

Capitalize words referring to the Diety: *Our Father, God, Adonai, Allah.* Do not capitalize the word *god* referring to deities in ancient mythologies: *Mars was the god of war.*

EXAMPLES	
Judaism	Hinduism
German	Sanskrit
Mexican	Asian American
Caucasian	Latin

Names of clubs, organizations, businesses, and institutions

USAGE tip

Do not capitalize words such as *school, college,* or *theater* unless they are part of a name: *Central College, The Lincoln School of Commerce, Riviera Theater.*

EXAMPLES	
American Cancer Society	Boy Scouts
Franklin Life Insurance Company	Union Bank

Names of awards, prizes, and medals

EXAMPLES		
Tony Award	Pulitzer Prize	Medal of Freedom

Proper Adjectives

A **proper adjective** is either an adjective formed from a proper noun or a proper noun used as an adjective.

Proper adjectives formed from proper nouns

EXAMPLES	
Chinese puzzle	Kafkaesque plot
Canadian pilots	Italian envoy

Proper nouns used as adjectives

EXAMPLES		
House chamber	Hitchcock classic	Torah scholar

Try It Yourself

EXERCISE 4

Identifying Proper Nouns and Proper Adjectives

Identify the proper nouns and proper adjectives in the following sentences.

1. Grant Rollins told me that the math assignment is hanging over him like Damocles sword.
2. He likes to play Whiz Kid, a popular word game that is made by the Smart Games Company.
3. Most of Douglas Southall Freeman's writings are about the South.
4. Sara can't believe that you didn't tell Laura about Mrs. Hartman's pop quiz.
5. Mary said the song "Puff the Magic Dragon" does not contain a hidden meaning.
6. My cousin Jessica decided to attend William and Mary in the fall.

USAGE tip

Some adjectives derived from names or nationalities are no longer capitalized because of common use: *bowie knife, cardigan sweater, french toast, italian dressing, china pattern.* Check a dictionary if you have any questions about whether a proper adjective formed from a proper noun should be capitalized.

USAGE tip

Brand names are used as proper adjectives. Capitalize the name used as an adjective, but do not capitalize the common noun it modifies unless the word is part of the product name: *Tornado vacuum cleaner, Mrs. Jones's pies.*

7. Jesse James had several family members in his gang including Cole Younger, Jim Younger, and Frank James.
8. Scott and Rick will be playing softball on Wednesdays and Fridays through the summer.
9. Marmaduke is a Great Dane who appears each day in the newspaper comics.
10. I think Santa Claus vacations in the Bahamas from New Year's Day until Labor Day.

EXERCISE 5
Correcting Capitalization for Proper Nouns and Proper Adjectives
Correct any capitalization errors in the following sentences.

1. I believe that our tree in the front yard has dutch elm disease.
2. The movie *a beautiful mind* is based on the life of john nash.
3. You leave for your trip on saturday, october 23, and will return from england a week later.
4. uncle seymour studied spanish, french, and romanian in college.
5. William jennings bryan lived in lincoln, nebraska, for many years.
6. I once saw larry bird play basketball at the boston garden.
7. The teacher gave a lecture on james madison's contributions to the federalist papers.
8. She may only be one-eighth irish, but she sure enjoys St. patrick's day.
9. Bill is a member of the kiwanis club and the american legion.
10. Gale, a surveyor from st. louis, used a gunter's chain to mark off the land.

EXERCISE 6

Using Capitalization of Proper Nouns and Proper Adjectives in Your Writing

Write a brief narrative to share with classmates about two friends who visit an unfamiliar city to see the sights. Be sure to furnish specific details so that your readers will know the characters' names, where they are from, where and why they are going, when their trip occurs, with whom they meet, and other details that add interest to the narrative. Be sure to capitalize correctly proper nouns and proper adjectives.

I AND FIRST WORDS

Capitalize the pronoun *I.*

> EXAMPLE
> Yesterday I found a quarter on the sidewalk.

Capitalize the **first word** of each sentence.

> EXAMPLE
> We will be driving to San Antonio later this month.

Capitalize the first word of a **direct quotation**. Do not capitalize the first word of a direct quotation if it continues after an interruption in the quote or the identification of the speaker. Do not capitalize an indirect quotation.

> EXAMPLES
> **direct quotation**
> "That possum will regret the day he dug a hole under my garage," Mr. Rawling said determinedly to his neighbor.
>
> **direct quotation interrupted**
> "The animal sleeps in there during the day," he explained, "but at night he comes out to look for food."
>
> **indirect quotation**
> Mr. Rawling said that the possum will regret digging a hole under his garage.

When citing **poetry**, follow the capitalization of the original poem. Though most poets capitalize the first word of each line in a poem, as is the case in the first set of lines below, some poets do not. The second example shows how the poet uses a combination of uppercase and lowercase letters at the beginning of lines.

Literature
MODELS

Hector the Collector
Collected bits of string,
Collected dolls with broken heads
And rusty bells that would not ring.

from "Hector the Collector"
Shel Silverstein

He hunches over the table, pencil gripped in fist,
shaping the heavy letters
Days later we will write story-poems, sound-poems,
but always the same subject for Carlos

from "The Lost Parrot"
Naomi Shihab Nye

Capitalize the first word in a **letter salutation** and the **name or title of the person** addressed.

EXAMPLES
My dear Bettina   Dear Dave   Dear Sir

Capitalize only the first word in **letter closings**.

EXAMPLES
Sincerely yours   Your pal   Admiringly   Best regards

Try It Yourself

EXERCISE 7
Correcting Capitalization for the Pronoun *I* and First Words
Correct any errors in capitalization you find in the following sentences. If there are no errors in the sentence, write *correct*.

1. The coach yelled, "let's start playing some defense!"
2. I think that leslie will believe Anything I tell her.
3. We noticed that Sally started her letter with "dear John" and closed with "your friend."
4. that was the best movie i've seen in a long time.
5. She is a Professor who teaches at the University.
6. The famous Tennyson poem "the charge of the light brigade" is about a small, but brave, group of british soldiers.
7. Grandma always begins her letters to me with the salutation, "my dear boy."
8. My guidance counselor advised me to join the junior rotary club.
9. "if you look into the cauldron," warned the witch, "You will see more than you can handle."
10. "The mouse is too smart to get caught in the trap," moaned Oscar. "I'm going to buy a cat."

EXERCISE 8

Using Capitalization of *I* and First Words in Your Writing
Write a sentence for each of the directions below. Be sure to capitalize any proper nouns and proper adjectives in addition to the pronoun *I* and first words in sentences, quotations, and lines of poetry.

1. Write a sentence in which you quote a line from a poem or short story.
2. Turn the direct quotation you wrote in item number 1 into an indirect quotation.
3. Write a lyric from your favorite song.
4. Write a sentence about a family member, including his or her birthplace and occupation.
5. Describe in a sentence or two a favorite holiday memory.

FAMILY RELATIONSHIPS AND TITLES OF PERSONS

Capitalize the **titles** or **abbreviations** that come before the names of people.

USAGE tip

Do not capitalize occupations:
John Sanders used to be a sheriff before he retired.
Ten years ago Sheriff Sanders arrested your cousin.

EXAMPLES
General William Sherman   Dr. Spock
Chief Justice Marshall   Ms. Carey Hall

Capitalize a person's title when it is used as a proper noun.

EXAMPLES
This plan will not succeed, General.
Can you translate this passage, Professor?

Capitalize words showing **family relationships** when used as titles or as substitutes for a name.

USAGE tip

Do not capitalize words for family relationships when they are preceded by a possessive noun or pronoun: *my uncle Sid; his father; their daughters Beth and Heidi.*

EXAMPLES
Uncle Ross   Grandmother   Cousin Vito

Try It Yourself

EXERCISE 9
Understanding Capitalization of Titles and Family Relationships
Correct the capitalization in the following items. If the item is correct as written, write *correct*.

1. senator Dole
2. my aunt
3. dr. williams
4. grandma gertrude
5. sammy davis jr.
6. king richard I
7. mayor davidson
8. his brother and father
9. reverend lovejoy
10. a bishop

Using Titles and Family Relationships in Your Writing
Write a story for a school newspaper about a family trip to Washington, D.C. This story can be based on an actual experience or can be completely fictional. Describe who went on the trip with you and the leaders you met (or could potentially meet) in the nation's capital. Use a variety of capitalized and lowercased titles and words for family relationships in your sentences.

TIME DESIGNATIONS

Capitalize the time abbreviations B.C., A.D., A.M., and P.M. When these abbreviations appear in type, they usually are printed in small capital letters.

You may also see *C.E.* (of the common era) and *B.C.E.* (before the common era) used instead of *B.C.*

The abbreviation B.C. refers to the time before Christ. When using the abbreviation B.C., place it after the date.

> **EXAMPLE**
> Nebuchadnezzar II, the King of Babylon, died in 562 B.C.

The abbreviation A.D. refers to the time after Christ. When using the abbreviation A.D., place it before the date.

> **EXAMPLE**
> Roman troops invaded Jerusalem in A.D. 70.

The abbreviation A.M. refers to time within the twelve-hour period from midnight to noon. The abbreviation P.M. refers to time within the twelve-hour period from noon to midnight.

Never use the terms *morning, evening,* or *o'clock* with either *A.M.* or *P.M.*

> **EXAMPLES**
> We will be meeting with our supervisor at 10:30 A.M.
> The movie you want to see will be starting at 9:00 P.M.

EXERCISE 11
Understanding Capitalization of Time Designations
Answer each of the following questions with a time designation. Be sure to capitalize the time abbreviations correctly.

1. What time do you arrive at school each morning?
2. What time does your first class end?
3. What time does your lunch hour begin?
4. What time do you leave school each day?
5. What time do you usually eat supper?
6. From what time to what time do you sleep?
7. What span of time do you set aside to do homework in the evenings?
8. In what year did you celebrate your fifth birthday?
9. What year do you plan to graduate from high school?
10. In what year before Christ do you think Cleopatra was born?

EXERCISE 12
Correcting Capitalization Errors in Time Designations
Correct any capitalization and usage errors in time designations in the following sentences. If the sentences are correct as written, write *correct*.

1. Julius Caesar lived from 100 to 44 b.c.
2. The play begins at 7:00 p.m. and will end around 10:00 p.m.
3. Does the meeting begin at 9:00 a.m. or 10:00 a.m.?
4. Rome's population exceeded one million by 118 a.d.
5. Work began on the Great Wall of China in 214 b.c.
6. Cyrus the Great ruled Persia in the sixth century B.C.
7. I believe that your flight will be taking off at 11:15 a.m.
8. Thutmose I succeeded Amenhotep I as ruler of Egypt in 1525 b.c.
9. The poet Ovid wrote *The Art of Love* in 1 A.D.
10. She will be leaving work at 5:30 P.M. and should be home at 6:00 p.m.

EXERCISE 13
Using Time Designations in Your Writing
Write a paragraph about an important figure from ancient history. Include the dates of this person's life as well as the dates of his or her important achievements. At the bottom of your paper, write down the time you started writing and the time you finished writing your paragraph.

GEOGRAPHICAL NAMES, DIRECTIONS, AND HISTORICAL NAMES

Capitalize the **names of cities, states, countries, islands,** and **continents**.

USAGE tip

Do not capitalize prepositions such as *of* or *upon* used in geographical names: *Mount of Olives, Berwick-upon-Tweed.*

EXAMPLES

cities	Tokyo	Miami	Boise
states	Mississippi	Virginia	Maine
countries	Brazil	Switzerland	China
islands	Aleutian Islands	Crete	Guam
continents	South America	Australia	Asia

Capitalize the **names of bodies of water** and **geographical features**.

EXAMPLES

Red Sea	Ohio River
Gobi Desert	Mount Everest

Capitalize **names of buildings, monuments,** and **bridges**.

EXAMPLES

Independence Hall	Lincoln Memorial
Brooklyn Bridge	

USAGE tip

Do not capitalize general names for places: *Follow the expressway for three miles, then take a right when you reach the river.*

Capitalize the **names of streets** and **highways**.

EXAMPLES

Madison Avenue	Sunset Strip
Massachusetts Turnpike	Route 66

Capitalize **sections of the country**.

EXAMPLES
the Pacific Coast   the Northeast
the Southwest   Southern France

Capitalize the **names of historical events, special events, documents,** and **historical periods.**

EXAMPLES
historical events   VJ-Day   Battle of Shiloh
special events   Pony Penning Day   Art in the Park
documents   Federalist Papers   Treaty of Ghent
historical periods   Renaissance   Gilded Age

USAGE tip

Do not capitalize directions of the compass:
Naomi rode west from Chicago.
The restaurant is east of Washington Avenue.
I like to drive the northern route.

Try It Yourself

EXERCISE 14
Identifying Capitalization in Literature
Identify the rule that applies to each of the underlined words or groups of words in the following literature passage.

Literature
M O D E L

That I can experience this part of history is in large part thanks to the POWs themselves. The <u>American Ex-Prisoners of War</u>, a veterans group of more than 30,000 members, teamed with the <u>National Park Service</u> to raise the money needed to build the museum. Their influence permeates the project, especially in the commemorative courtyard. . . .

"I'm here to try to heal a little bit from what I experienced and what I still experience," says Lloyd, who was captured on <u>December</u> 19, 1944, in <u>Belgium</u> during the <u>Battle of the Bulge</u>. He spent four months in <u>Stalag 9B</u>, a German prison <u>camp</u>.

from "The Price of Freedom"
Cassandra M. Vanhooser

Understanding Capitalization of Geographical and Historic Names and Directions

Rewrite the following using correct capitalization.

1. arch of titus
2. isle of man
3. the dark ages
4. panama canal
5. st. paul, minnesota
6. the southeast
7. death valley
8. the compromise of 1850
9. the national road
10. south america
11. mount hood
12. southwest of montgomery
13. victoria falls
14. kodiak island
15. route 33
16. cook county
17. great dismal swamp
18. bay of pigs
19. the age of reason
20. declaration of independence

Using Capitalization in Your Writing

Write a paragraph for your history teacher about a current event taking place in the world. Explain to him or her why you think this event is important. Include specific people, places, and outcomes of this event. Be sure to check your capitalization when you are editing and proofreading.

TITLES OF ARTWORKS AND LITERARY WORKS

Capitalize the first and last words and all important words in the titles of artworks and literary works, including titles of books, magazines, short stories, poems, songs, movies, plays, paintings, and sculpture. Do not capitalize articles (*a*, *an*, and *the*), conjunctions, and prepositions that are less than five letters long unless they are the first word in the title, as in "A Rose for Emily" or *The Great Santini*.

EXAMPLES
American History (magazine)
King Solomon's Mines (book)
"A Secret for Two" (short story)
"Faun Playing the Pipe" (painting)

Capitalize the titles of **religious works**.

EXAMPLES
Bible   Koran   Old Testament

Try It Yourself

EXERCISE 17
Identifying and Correcting Errors in Capitalization of Titles of Artworks and Literary Works
Write the words that should be capitalized in the following sentences.

1. We read the short story "the serial garden" in class today.
2. John Adams, Benjamin Franklin, and George Washington are three of the main characters in *rise to rebellion*.
3. The principal saved the show when he jumped up on stage and sang "born to be wild."
4. Besides the poem "the raven," Edgar Allan Poe wrote many famous short stories, including "the tell-tale heart" and "the pit and the pendulum."
5. I read about the Stanley Cup finals in the latest issue of *sports illustrated*.

6. My professor has the Georges Roualt painting *the apprentice* in his office.
7. Hugo von Hofmannsthal wrote the libretto for Richard Straus's opera *elektra*.
8. The musicals *jesus christ superstar* and *godspell* both premiered in 1971.
9. "eyes in the heart" is my art teacher's favorite jackson pollock painting.
10. My grandfather used to be a reporter for the *washington post*.

EXERCISE 18

Using Correct Capitalization in Your Writing
Have you ever wanted to learn more about the culture in which your parents or guardians grew up? Make a list of titles of books, movies, television shows, magazines, short stories, albums, songs, poems, and paintings that were popular when your parents or guardians were your age. Beside each reference, write a sentence explaining why it is noteworthy or what your parents or guardians liked about it. You may want to interview one or both of your parents or guardians for this exercise. Be sure to capitalize your references correctly.

UNIT *16* REVIEW

TEST YOUR KNOWLEDGE

EXERCISE 1
Identifying Proper Nouns and Proper Adjectives
Identify the proper nouns and proper adjectives that appear in the following sentences. (10 points)

EXAMPLE
Grandpa Elmer brought German chocolate to share
with the family.
(*Grandpa Elmer,* proper noun; *German,* proper adjective)

1. Samuel led a Bible study for young married couples in the church.
2. You will need Super Duper soap to wash away the smell of the fertilizer.
3. J. R. R. Tolkien invented Elvish languages for *Lord of the Rings* characters such as Legolas and Gildor.
4. In George Orwell's novel *1984* the world is divided into Oceania, Eurasia, and Eastasia.
5. David Letterman hosts *The Late Show* which is produced by his company, Worldwide Pants.
6. My uncle used to own a Gordon setter, a black and tan bird dog with long hair.
7. Her cousin ate a stack of Belgian waffles after she recovered from the German measles.
8. The professor has written three books about Baroque architecture.
9. English fireboats wreaked havoc on the Spanish Armada in 1585.
10. The Lutheran pastor showed the Catholic priest the new windows in the church.

Correcting Errors in Capitalization of Proper Nouns and Proper Adjectives

Rewrite the following sentences to correct any capitalization errors. (10 points)

EXAMPLE
The league of nations failed to keep peace in north Africa in the 1930s. (The *League of Nations* failed to keep peace in *North Africa* in the 1930s.)

1. The woman down the street owns three maltese cats.
2. People in Northern missouri speak with a different dialect than people in Southern missouri.
3. Since today is a Canadian holiday, I decided to watch a toronto blue jays baseball game.
4. Former attorney general Janet Reno will be speaking at andrew jackson high school today.
5. Father promised to take us to the lake on the next hot sunday this Summer.
6. That little boston terrier wants to play with the Belgian Sheep Dog.
7. The american film institute named Humphrey bogart the greatest male screen legend.
8. Fishing in the long island sound, James caught nothing but a rubberall tire.
9. In february, Ted sent flowers to sara for valentine's day.
10. A gila monster is a lizard that lives in the Southwestern United States.

Correcting Errors in Capitalization of Proper Nouns, *I*, and First Words

Rewrite the following sentences to correct any capitalization errors. If no added capitals are needed, write *correct*. (10 points)

1. Last fall, Pete and Dale bought a large section of farmland in northern Iowa.
2. That was the most boring movie i've ever had to sit through.
3. Mr. Barnes looked twice at the letter when he noticed that it began with "dear Frankie-boy" and closed with "your best buddy, theodore."
4. Soon after daybreak we heard Captain Anderson yell, "all hands on deck!"
5. "if you finish the test early, I'll excuse you from the room," Said Mrs. Blode.
6. Sir Arthur Conan Doyle once wrote, "where there is no imagination there is no horror."
7. The letter to my great-grandfather closed with, "your obedient servant, charles."
8. Looking under the sofa, all i found was a nickel.
9. "when will you be home?" My mother yelled as we drove away.
10. I went to his office and asked, "Will we be receiving a Christmas bonus this year?"

EXERCISE 4

Correcting Errors in Capitalizing Family Relationships, Titles, Time Designations, and Geographical and Historical Names

Rewrite the following sentences to correct any capitalization errors. (10 points)

1. Unfortunately, mayor stoltz does not support the plan to repair circle street.
2. Vice president Adams and attorney general Randolph joined Washington for dinner.
3. Our flight leaves Chicago at 10:32 a.m. and lands in Denver at 2:42 p.m.

4. People living in the south miss out on the joy of shoveling snow in subzero weather.
5. My Grandfather owned land near jordan, montana, in the 1930s.
6. Our Company has decided that the services of Mr. hand will no longer be needed.
7. The Bus Driver told Mother that she could not ride without exact change.
8. The doctor and Reverend Steiner were seen walking into the target store on main street.
9. German author Herman Hesse published *Siddhartha* the same year that an irish writer named James Joyce published *Ulysses*.
10. Attila, the leader of the huns, died in a.d. 453.

EXERCISE 5

Correcting Errors in Capitalization

Rewrite the following paragraph, adding capitalization where necessary. (10 points)

On march 4, 1881 James Garfield was inaugurated as president of the united states. He would serve the second shortest term of any to hold that office. At 9:30 a.m. on July 2, 1881, Charles Guiteau shot President Garfield in Washington d.c. Guiteau, who was mentally unstable, said that he did it did it to unite the republican party. A team of surgeons led by Dr. D. W. bliss operated on the president three times after the shooting. On september 6, Garfield requested to be taken to elberon, New Jersey. He was suffering from blood poisoning from being probed by unsterilized instruments. At 10:35 p.m. on September 19, 1881, president Garfield died. Vice president Chester A. Arthur became the new president.

EXERCISE 6
Correcting Errors in Capitalization

Rewrite the following paragraph, adding capitalization where necessary. (10 points)

George Armstrong Custer was born in new rumley, ohio, on december 5, 1839. He graduated from west point in 1861. During the Civil War, he served as an aide to general George McClellan. Custer fought in many battles during the war, including Antietam, Fredericksburg, chancellorsville, and Gettysburg. After the war, he was transferred to the west. Custer fought against native americans in several campaigns. In May 1876 he led his troops in the 7th Cavalry against a large force of warriors led by crazy horse. The battle of little bighorn was Custer's last battle. A horse named comanche was the only member of his unit to survive the engagement.

EXERCISE 7
Using Capitalization in Your Writing

For each item listed below, write the name of someone or something that is your favorite. Then write a short explanation of the importance of the person, place, thing, or idea. Be sure to use capitalization correctly. (20 points)

EXAMPLE
poet *(Edgar Allan Poe was a master of the macabre.)*

1. song
2. subject in school
3. television show
4. movie star
5. state
6. river or creek
7. novel
8. monument
9. past president
10. restaurant

Using Capitalization in Your Writing

You have been selected by classmates to write a brochure that describes your school to pen-pal students overseas. In addition to providing basic information about location, subjects taught, and extracurricular activities, you may want to include interesting information about the teachers and students. Explain the school in detail, and be sure to capitalize correctly. (20 points)

UNIT *17* SPELLING

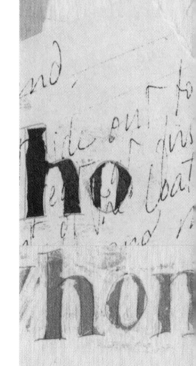

SPELLING

EDITING FOR SPELLING ERRORS

Always check your writing for spelling errors, and try to recognize the words that give you more trouble than others. Use a dictionary when you find you have misspelled a word. Keep a list in a notebook of words that are difficult for you to spell. Write the words several times until you have memorized the correct spelling. Break down the word into syllables, and pronounce each individual syllable carefully.

Some spelling problems occur when adding prefixes or suffixes to words or when making nouns plural. Other spelling problems occur when words follow certain patterns, such as those containing *ie/ei*. The following spelling rules can help you spell many words correctly.

SPELLING RULES I: PREFIXES AND SUFFIXES

Prefixes

A **prefix** is a letter or a group of letters added to the beginning of a word to change its meaning.

When adding a prefix, do not change the spelling of the word itself.

> EXAMPLES
> in– + describable = indescribable
> mis– + handle = mishandle
> over– + take = overtake
> il– + legitimate = illegitimate
> inter– + continental = intercontinental

Suffixes

A **suffix** is a letter or a group of letters added to the end of a word to change its meaning.

The spelling of most words is not changed when the suffix _–ness_ or _–ly_ is added.

> **EXAMPLES**
> fearful + –ly = fearfully
> quick + –ness = quickness
> large + –ly = largely
> hopeful + –ness = hopefulness

If you are adding a suffix to a word that ends with _y_ and that _y_ follows a vowel, usually leave the _y_ in place.

> **EXAMPLES**
> pay   pays   paying   payment
> deploy   deploys   deploying   deployment
> portray   portrays   portrayed   portrayal

If you are adding a suffix to a word that ends with _y_ and that _y_ follows a consonant, change the _y_ to _i_ before adding any ending except _–ing_.

> **EXAMPLES**
> happy   happiness
> hasty   hastily
> tarry   tarried   tarrying
> fly   flied   flying

USAGE tip

Note that this rule will sometimes form _ie_ combinations after _c._ In these cases, it is correct for _ie_ to follow _c._

lacy   lacier
saucy   saucier

Double the final consonant before adding a suffix beginning with a vowel (such as *–ed, –en, –er, –ing, –ence, –ance,* or *–y*) if the word ends in a single consonant preceded by a single vowel and if the word is either a single syllable or ends in a stressed syllable.

EXAMPLES

defer	deferred
mad	madden
begin	beginner
trim	trimming
deter	deterrence
sun	sunny

If you are adding a suffix that begins with a vowel to a word that ends with a silent *e*, usually drop the *e*.

EXAMPLES

taste	tasting
make	makable
note	notify
reuse	reusable

If you are adding a suffix that begins with a consonant to a word that ends with a silent *e*, usually leave the *e* in place.

USAGE tip

With some words, the *e* becomes an *i* when you add the suffix.

malice + –ous = malicious

caprice + –ous = capricious

EXAMPLES

infinite	infinitely
late	lateness
require	requirement
complete	completely

EXCEPTIONS

argue	argument
due	duly
true	truly

If the word ends in a soft *c* (spelled *ce*) or a soft *g* (spelled *ge*) sound, keep the *e* when adding the suffixes *–able* or *–ous*.

EXAMPLES

notice	noticeable
acknowledge	acknowledgeable
outrage	outrageous

Try It Yourself

EXERCISE 1

Identifying Incorrect Spelling with Prefixes and Suffixes
Write the correct spelling of the words that are misspelled in the following sentences. If no words are misspelled in the sentence, write *correct*.

1. Because she could alliterate, Beth happily and immodestly accepted the position writing for the poetry journal.
2. In my judgement you are mistaken about what is causing the occurence.
3. The happyness in the house ended once the arguement began.
4. The Stetsons have a statly home with a nice swiming pool in back.
5. We need to put this trunk in storeage tommorrow.
6. Howard is a knowledgable mechanic who truely understands the business.
7. Forget the senseible dinner, I want a cheeseburger and french fries.
8. He is surelly one of the largeest cats in the suburbs.
9. This luxurious apartment can be yours if you agree to live peacefully with your neighbors.
10. An agent will noteify you about when this spaceous house is going on the market.

E X E R C I S E 2

Understanding Spelling with Prefixes and Suffixes

Combine the prefix and root word or the root word and the suffix. Write each new word, and be sure to spell it correctly.

1. change + –able
2. annoy + –ance
3. like + –ness
4. im– + moral
5. un– + intended
6. grace + –ous
7. home + –ly
8. case + –ment
9. in + –ordinate
10. rue + –ful

E X E R C I S E 3

Using Prefixes and Suffixes Correctly in Your Writing

Describe for classmates an out-of-the-ordinary event that happened to you within the last year. Use at least one word that demonstrates each different spelling rule you have covered thus far in this unit. Be sure to spell each word correctly according to its rule about adding a prefix or suffix.

SPELLING RULES II: PLURAL NOUNS AND SPELLING PATTERNS

Plural Nouns

Most noun plurals are formed by simply adding –*s* to the end of the word.

> **EXAMPLES**
> pencil + –s = pencils
> rake + –s = rakes
> tricycle + s = tricycles
> trumpet + s = trumpets

The plural of nouns that end in *o, s, x, z, ch,* or *sh* should be formed by adding *–es.*

> EXAMPLES
> gas + –es = gases
> box + –es = boxes
> peach + –es = peaches
> mass + es = masses

The exception to the rule above is that musical terms and certain other words that end in *o* are usually made plural by adding *–s.* Check a dictionary if you aren't sure whether to add an *–s* or an *–es.*

> EXAMPLES
> adagio + –s = adagios   hobo + –s = hobos
> patio + –s = patios   piano + –s = pianos
> peso + –s = pesos   cameo + –s = cameos

Form the plural of nouns that end in *y* following a consonant by changing the *y* to an *i* and adding *–es.*

> EXAMPLES
> cab   cabbies
> lady   ladies
> country   countries
> perjury   perjuries
> fry   fries

Nouns that end end *f* or *fe* must be modified, changing the *f* or *fe* to *v,* before adding *–es* to the plural form.

> EXAMPLES
> half   halves
> elf   elves
> knife   knives
> wife   wives

USAGE tip

Some nouns have plural forms that are exceptions to the rules:

woman	women
man	men
child	children
mouse	mice
foot	feet

The *ie/ei* Spelling Pattern

When a word is spelled with the letters *i* and *e* and has a long *e* sound, it is usually spelled *ie* except after the letter *c*.

EXAMPLES

believe	ceilometer
piece	deceive
fief	conceit

EXCEPTIONS

protein	neither	weird

Use *ei* when the sound is not long *e*.

EXAMPLES

forfeit	sleight	stein	counterfeit

EXCEPTIONS

sieve	friend

If the vowel combination has a long *a* sound (as in *eight*), always spell it with *ei*.

EXAMPLES

sleigh	feign	weighty	vein

When two vowels are pronounced separately in a word, spell them in the order of their pronunciation.

EXAMPLES

society	conscience	being

USAGE tip

This rhyme may help you remember the *ie/ei* rule:

Put *i* before *e*
Except after *c*
Or when sounded like *a*,
As in *neighbor* and *weigh*.

The "Seed" Sound Pattern

The "seed" ending sound has three spellings: *–sede*, *–ceed*, and *–cede*.

> EXAMPLES
>
> Only one word ends in *–sede: supersede*
>
> Three words end in *–ceed: proceed, succeed, exceed*
>
> All other words end in *–cede: accede, concede, recede, precede, secede*

Silent Letters

Some spelling problems result from letters that are written but not heard when a word is spoken. Becoming familiar with the patterns in letter combinations containing silent letters will help you identify other words that fit the patterns.

- Silent *b* usually occurs with *m*.

> EXAMPLES
>
> dumb   crumb   jamb   lamb

- Silent *b* also appears in *debt* and *doubt*.

- Silent *c* often appears with *s*.

> EXAMPLES
>
> scepter   scenario   scientist   scintillate

- Silent *g* often appears with *n*.

> EXAMPLES
>
> gnarl   gnome   sign   resign

- Silent *gh* often appears at the end of a word, either alone or in a combination with *t* (*–ght*).

> EXAMPLES
>
> though   slough   fraught   weight

- Silent *h* appears at the beginning of some words.

EXAMPLES			
honesty	heir	honor	hour

- Silent *h* also appears in a few other words, as in *rhythm* and *ghost*.

- Silent *k* occurs with *n*.

EXAMPLES			
knapsack	knowledge	knell	knickknack

- Silent *n* occurs with *m* at the end of some words.

EXAMPLES		
solemn	condemn	autumn

- Silent *p* occurs with *s* at the beginning of some words.

EXAMPLES		
psychiatry	psalm	psychoanalyze

- Silent *s* occurs with *l* in some words.

EXAMPLES		
island	islet	aisle

- Silent *t* occurs with *s* in a few words.

EXAMPLES		
fasten	listen	thistle

- Silent *w* occurs at the beginnings of some words.

EXAMPLES			
wren	wrote	writ	who

- Silent *w* also occurs with *s* in a few words, such as *sword* and *answer*.

Letter Combinations

Some letter combinations can cause spelling problems because when combined the letters have a different pronunciation.

- The letters *ph* produce the *f* sound.

> **EXAMPLES**
> phone   graph   photography

- The letters *gh* produce the *f* sound usually at the end of a word. (Otherwise they are silent.)

> **EXAMPLES**
> rough   enough   cough

- The letter combination *tch* sounds the same as *ch*.

> **EXAMPLES**
> fetch   latch   batch   hitched
> such   lunch   torch   broached

Try It Yourself

EXERCISE 4
Identifying Words with Spelling Patterns
Write the correct spelling for the words that are misspelled in the following sentences. If there are no misspelled words in a sentence, write *correct*.

1. The king's riegn was marred by problems created by the preseeding monarch.
2. My neice wieghed herself on the new scale today.
3. I saw the foxs cautiously approach the bag of french frys.
4. Hans decided to sieze the opportunity to fix the cieling in his house.
5. She used a slieght of hand trick to steal the reciept that was right under thier noses.
6. The vein of gold you found will allow you to buy as many tacos as you can eat.

7. I have switched to a high protien deit to prepare for football season.
8. We heard sliegh bells ringing on top of our freind Jimmy's house.
9. The cacher hached a plan to swich the baseball with a potato.
10. He drove his foriegn car past the stable while the horses nieghed.

EXERCISE 5

Understanding Words with Spelling Patterns

Complete the following words by filling in the blanks with the letters *ie* or *ei*.

1. to give or to rec_ _ ve
2. h_ _ r to the throne
3. writing profic_ _ ncy
4. a v_ _ l of silk
5. the pat_ _ nt waiting room

Add the correct –*sede*, –*ceed*, or –*cede* ending to these words.

6. super_ _ _ _ his authority
7. the se_ _ _ _ _ _ states
8. pro_ _ _ _ to the police station
9. wait for the tide to re_ _ _ _
10. suc_ _ _ _ at all she tries

Complete each word by adding the correct silent letter or letter combination.

11. frei _ _ t
12. _ _ issors
13. cau _ _ t
14. _ _ eudo
15. throu _ _
16. rema _ _ _
17. _ our

18. lim _
19. _ _ awing
20. _ _ ife

EXERCISE 6
Understanding Noun Plurals
Make the following words plural by adding the correct ending.

1. cameo
2. tomato
3. deer
4. ox
5. cargo
6. volcano
7. eddy
8. monkey
9. fairy
10. foot

EXERCISE 7
Using Spelling Patterns in Your Writing

Write a description for a school magazine of how you would like to spend an ideal Saturday. You may write about activities that you have done before and/or activities that you have never done but would like to do. Use as many words from the unit as you can to show your understanding of letter and sound patterns.

COMMON SPELLING ERRORS

Pronunciation is not always a reliable guide for spelling because words are not always spelled the way they are pronounced. However, by paying attention to letters that spell sounds and to letters that are silent, you can improve some aspects of your spelling. Always check a dictionary for the correct pronunciations and spellings of words that are new to your experience.

Extra Syllables

Sometimes people misspell a word because they include an extra syllable in it. For example, *disastrous* is easily misspelled if it is pronounced *disasterous*, with four syllables instead of three. Pay close attention to the number of syllables in these words.

EXAMPLES			
two syllables	athlete	grievous	mischief
three syllables	athletics	grievously	mischievous

Omitted Sounds

Sometimes people misspell a word because they do not sound one or more letters when they pronounce the word. Be sure to include the underlined letters of these words even if you don't pronounce them.

EXAMPLES		
accidentally	February	environment
chocolate	library	particular
groceries	government	Connecticut

Homophones

Words that have the same pronunciation but different spellings and meanings are called **homophones.** An incorrect choice can be confusing to your readers. Knowing the spelling and meaning of these groups of words will improve your spelling.

EXAMPLES	
bridal/bridle	buy/bye/by
capital/capitol	pedal/peddle
their/there/they're	shone/shown
sole/soul	some/sum
who's/whose	two/too/to
your/you're	

Commonly Confused Words

Some other groups of words are not homophones, but they are similar enough in sound and spelling to create confusion. Knowing the spelling and meaning of these groups of words will also improve your writing. You'll find other groups of commonly confused words in Unit 14, pages 297–307.

EXAMPLES

access/excess	accept/except
formally/formerly	allowed/aloud
ascent/assent	site/sight/cite
compliment/complement	principle/principal
affect/effect	

Try It Yourself

EXERCISE 8

Identifying Words with Extra Syllables and Omitted Sounds

Write the word in each group that is spelled correctly.

EXAMPLE

genous   genyous   genius   *(genius)*

1.	artheritis	arthrightis	arthritis
2.	separate	seperate	seprate
3.	frownded	frowned	fround
4.	labratory	laberatory	laboratory
5.	expecially	especially	especielly
6.	prescription	perscripshun	prescription
7.	strength	strenth	streenth
8.	nucular	nuclear	nuclaer
9.	opprate	opereate	operate
10.	lonly	lonely	lownly

EXERCISE 9

Identifying Common Spelling Errors

Choose the correct spelling of the word in parentheses. If necessary, use a dictionary to find the meanings of the two words before making your choice.

1. Jim worked for twenty years at the (foundry, foundary) just outside of town.
2. The doctor asked for the (insterment, instrument) to start the operation.
3. After we pay off the (morgage, mortgage) in twenty-nine years, this house will be all ours.
4. Sara always wears the finest (jewelry, jewlry) to these events.
5. It is always a (privledge, privilege) to have the professor speak at our school.
6. Dana always had a great interest in protecting the (environment, enviroment).
7. Nobody knows what (tommorrow, tomorrow) will bring.
8. My friend's days as a (batchlor, bachelor) are numbered.
9. For dessert, we would like to try the (choclate, chocolate) mousse.
10. I would like to (persue, pursue) this opportunity further.
11. Sam would like you to give him some (advice/advise) about the house.
12. When writing a research paper, you need to (site/cite) every source that you use.
13. The Vikings decided to (raze/raise) the town after they had finished plundering it.
14. There are (to/two) horses out running in the field.
15. If you don't behave, you're going to be sent to the (principle's/principal's) office.
16. We need to move (forward, foreward) if we are going to get out of this mess.
17. Shelly held the horse's bridle with a (lose/loose) grip.

18. An (eminent/imminent) scholar will be presenting a paper at the conference today.
19. Our scout (led, lead) the way through the forest.
20. We went to visit the (capital, capitol) building in Montgomery today.

EXERCISE 10

Using Commonly Confused Words Correctly in Your Writing

Write a letter to the editor of the local newspaper calling for a specific change you would like to see enacted in your neighborhood or community. Choose at least five pairs of commonly confused words, and write your letter using one or both of the words in each pair. Underline the words that you use, and be sure to check your spelling.

COMMONLY MISSPELLED WORDS

Some words are often misspelled. Here is a list of 150 commonly misspelled words. If you master this list, you will avoid many errors in your spelling.

Commonly Misspelled Words		
absence	article	column
abundant	attendance	committee
academically	bankruptcy	conceivable
accessible	beautiful	conscientious
accidentally	beggar	conscious
accommodate	beginning	consistency
accurate	behavior	deceitful
acknowledgment	biscuit	descendant
acquaintance	breathe	desirable
adequately	business	disastrous
adolescent	calendar	discipline
advantageous	camouflage	efficiency
advisable	catastrophe	eighth
ancient	cellar	embarrass
annihilate	cemetery	enormous
anonymous	changeable	enthusiastically
answer	clothes	environment
apparent	colossal	exhaust

CONTINUED

existence	naïve	resources
fascinating	necessity	responsibility
finally	nickel	rhythm
forfeit	niece	schedule
fulfill	noticeable	seize
guerrilla	nucleus	separate
guidance	nuisance	sergeant
hindrance	nutritious	siege
hypocrite	obedience	significance
independent	occasionally	souvenir
influential	occurrence	sponsor
ingenious	orchestra	succeed
institution	outrageous	surprise
interference	pageant	symbol
irrelevant	parallel	synonymous
irresistible	pastime	temperature
judgment	peasant	tomorrow
league	permanent	transparent
leisure	persistent	twelfth
license	phenomenon	undoubtedly
lightning	physician	unmistakable
liquefy	pneumonia	unnecessary
magnificent	prestige	vacuum
manageable	privilege	vehicle
maneuver	procedure	vengeance
meadow	prophesy	villain
mediocre	prove	vinegar
miniature	receipt	weird
mischievous	referred	whistle
misspell	rehearsal	withhold
mortgage	relieve	yacht
mysterious	resistance	yield

Try It Yourself

EXERCISE 11

Identifying Commonly Misspelled Words
Choose the correct spelling of each of the following words.

1. obediance   obedianse   obedience
2. anonimous   anonymous   aynonimous
3. sponser   sponsor   sponsar
4. consistency   consistancy   consestency

5. beginning	begining	begenning
6. irrelevent	irrelivent	irrelevant
7. resistence	resistance	resistince
8. colosal	colossol	colossal
9. acessible	accessible	accessable
10. pneumonia	pnemonia	pnuenomia

EXERCISE 12

Using Commonly Misspelled Words Correctly in Your Writing

Assume that you found a secret treasure. Write a paragraph describing the treasure to classmates. In your description, use ten of the words from the list of Commonly Misspelled Words that you find difficult.

UNIT 17 REVIEW

TEST YOUR KNOWLEDGE

E X E R C I S E 1
Identifying Incorrectly Spelled Words
Find the spelling errors in the following sentences and rewrite the incorrectly spelled words. If there are no misspelled words, write *correct*. (20 points)

EXAMPLE
Grandma cut the cake into several different peaces. *(pieces)*

1. Tommorrow we will take flowers to the cemetary.
2. I need to aks you a question about what happened to the tacoes.
3. It looks like there pateince has run out with the car alarm.
4. Candace decieved the lawyer about where the defendent was that night.
5. Paul began his life of a beggar while still an adolescent.
6. It would be embarassing if you turned in a résumé with a mispelled word.
7. Shane will recieve his new lisence plates next week.
8. We can go shopping for electric pianoes after you finish your potatoe.
9. This occurrance could be a result of the high temparature in this room.
10. The villian in this movie is more mischievious than evil.
11. Victor's quest for vengeance was totally unnecessary.
12. We found alumenum cans in the maedow behind the garage.
13. Tom built a miniture medieval town, complete with little paesant figures, in the basement.
14. I heard a wierd sound while walking through the prarie.
15. Attendence fell dramatically after the team fell into twelf place.
16. Bring a piece of stationary to me so I can start this letter.
17. The hotel can not accommodate all of the people at the bussiness conference.

18. Does your conscious bother you about manuevering your brother into such an undesirible situation?
19. Those tomatos on the table were nothing more than an ilusion.
20. Don't pass judgement until you have herd you neice's side of the story.

EXERCISE 2
Understanding Prefixes and Suffixes
Put the words and their prefixes or suffixes together correctly. Correctly spell the new words. (10 points)

EXAMPLE
immediate + –ly   *(immediately)*

1. please + –ing
2. lackey + –s
3. im + material
4. neigh + –ing
5. droopy + iest
6. dis– + pleased
7. solve + –able
8. destruct + –ive
9. deceit + –ful
10. full + –ly

EXERCISE 3
Understanding Noun Plurals
Write the plural form of each of the following nouns. (20 points)

EXAMPLE
pony   *(ponies)*

1. scratch
2. cameo
3. patio
4. ferry
5. fuzz

6. watch
7. tree
8. cello
9. hanky
10. tornado
11. fax
12. ox
13. muse
14. fly
15. fish
16. artery
17. toe
18. gazebo
19. fray
20. log

EXERCISE 4

Understanding Words with Letter or Sound Patterns

Write each word, adding *ie* or *ei*. (20 points)

EXAMPLE
bel _ _ f   *(belief)*

1. r_ _ gn
2. w_ _ ght
3. gr_ _ f
4. n_ _ ce
5. f_ _ rce
6. s_ _ ve
7. _ _ ther
8. dec_ _ ve
9. f_ _ gn
10. rec_ _ ve

Write each word, adding *–sede*, *–ceed*, or *–cede*.

11. pro_ _ _ _
12. super _ _ _ _
13. suc_ _ _ _
14. pre_ _ _ _

15. ac _ _ _ _
16. se_ _ _ _
17. re_ _ _ _
18. inter_ _ _ _
19. ex_ _ _ _
20. con_ _ _ _

EXERCISE 5
Correcting Words with Silent Letters or Letter Combinations

Using the rules for silent letters or letter combinations, write the correct spelling for each of the following misspelled words. (10 points)

EXAMPLE
bom   (bomb)

1. Febuary
2. sene
3. rugh
4. resin
5. sordfish
6. cach
7. seudo
8. coff
9. rath
10. fone

EXERCISE 6
Understanding Spelling Rules

Make a list of the spelling errors you commonly make. To do so, you might first review writing assignments that your teacher has already graded and check for spelling errors. Once you have a list of twenty-five words or so, group them according to the spelling rules in this unit. Include both the correct and incorrect spelling, the spelling rule, and a memory device that will help you recall the correct spelling. Keep your spelling list in your notebook or writing folder and add to it regularly. Once you feel that you have mastered the spelling of a difficult or unfamiliar word, cross it off your list. (10 points)

Using Correct Spelling in Your Writing

Imagine that you have been hired by a tourism agency to prepare a report on the attractions of your local area. Write a brochure describing in compelling terms why tourists would want to come visit your town or city. Include natural attractions, restaurants, places of amusement, and any other information about your area that you think would be of interest. Use at least ten words from this unit in your brochure. Then proofread carefully to be sure that you've spelled all words correctly. (10 points)

UNIT 18 ELECTRONIC COMMUNICATIONS
Etiquette and Style

ELECTRONIC COMMUNICATIONS: ETIQUETTE AND STYLE

NETIQUETTE FOR COMMUNICATING ON THE INTERNET

Netiquette, a blend of the words *Internet* and *etiquette*, refers to the courtesies writers use when communicating with others online. Given the flexibility, speed, and low cost of communicating on the Net, people sometimes forget how very public and permanent e-mail actually is.

Judith Martin, who writes about etiquette as Miss Manners, highlights some of the reasons for netiquette in cyberspace.

> Freedom without rules doesn't work. And communities do not work unless they are regulated by etiquette. It took about three minutes before some of the brighter people discovered this online. We have just as many ways, if not more, to be obnoxious in cyberspace and fewer ways to regulate them. So, posting etiquette rules and looking for ways to ban people who violate them is the way sensible people are attempting to deal with this.
>
> from "Manners Matter"
> Kevin Kelly and Judith Martin

Whether you're chatting online with a friend, requesting information from an organization, or writing a complaint letter about an order that went awry, use netiquette that is appropriate for your purpose and audience.

Dos and Don'ts

Do use e-mail
- to ask quick questions.
- to exchange information and to send newsy updates to friends.
- to schedule events and activities.
- to praise a group, especially when you want to copy others.

Not all messages should be electronic, however. Don't use e-mail
- to replace a formal thank-you note.
- to share controversial or personal information.
- to send bad news.
- to convey anything that if forwarded or overheard could be harmful or embarrassing.

Guidelines for Communicating on the Internet

Know the rules. Make sure that you understand the policies of the online services you are using. In listservs, chat rooms, and other group discussions, check the new subscriber information or ask other participants for guidance. In a chat room, if you feel your privacy is being compromised, ask a responsible adult for help or simply sign off.

State your topic. Always fill in the subject line. Flag your message with a clear, informative header. If your problem is urgent, write SOS. If it's a quick question, say so. This allows the user to locate and deal with the message quickly.

Be brief. Lengthy e-mails—those longer than one screen—can be daunting and annoying. Even though friendly exchanges can be chatty, a screen filled with solid type can overwhelm readers. If you want a quick reply, be concise. Break long thoughts into separate paragraphs or numbered lists.

Use a limited number of acronyms. Acronyms like the ones listed below are frequently used to shorten communications on the Internet. However, keep in mind that messages filled with these abbreviations can be both confusing and annoying.

IMHO = in my humble (or honest) opinion
LOL = laughing out loud
BTW = by the way
F2F = face to face
BCNU = be seeing you
FWIW = for what it's worth
J/K = just kidding
L8R = later
IOW = in other words

Know what the buttons mean. The most destructive use of e-mail can occur when you reply "back to all" when your intention is to reply to the sender only.

Watch what you say. E-mail can be printed, forwarded, and filed. Even worse, deleted e-mails can be retrieved and used as evidence in a court of law. Use common sense, and try not to put anything in an e-mail that you wouldn't want published in the local newspaper. Avoid writing when angry. Avoid personal attacks, known as **flaming**. Keep in mind that sarcasm and humor may be misinterpreted. Without the benefit of facial expression, body language, and tone of voice, your joke may come across as criticism or an insult.

Use conventional capitalization. Using all capital letters in a message comes across online as SHOUTING and can be irritating or even offensive to your readers. Using all lowercase letters can make a message harder to read. Use **asterisks** before and after a word or phrase to make your point more evident, or use more conventional methods of emphasis, such as boldface and underlining. If your e-mail software doesn't allow type styles such as italic or underlining, it is appropriate to use all caps for titles of books or films, for example.

Edit your writing. Reread your message before sending it to be sure it says what you want it to say. Check for the kinds of careless errors you may make when your mind operates faster than your fingers can type—left-out words and reversed letters. If your e-mail carrier has a spell checker, use it before you press the send button.

Try It Yourself

EXERCISE 1
Identifying Netiquette
For classmates unacquainted with the use of e-mail, write an advice column that illustrates two of the points on the Dos and Don'ts list. Your advice column can be fictional or based on a real-life situation that happened to you or to someone you know.

EXERCISE 2
Understanding Netiquette
For a school newspaper, write an essay about the positives and negatives of e-mail and communicating on the Internet. Indicate to readers what you consider to be your favorite aspect of using e-mail, what you think is the biggest weakness of e-mail communication, and how your life would be different if you did not have e-mail.

EXERCISE 3
Using Netiquette in Your Writing

Write an e-mail message to the members of a sports team that you belong to informing them of a change in the season's schedule. Make sure to include all of the important information, such as the new time, date, and location of the games affected by the change. If you do not have access to e-mail, you may write out the message on a piece of paper.

SEARCHING THE INTERNET

The Internet is an enormous collection of computer networks that can open a whole new world of information. With just a couple of keystrokes, you can access libraries, government agencies, high schools and universities, nonprofit and educational organizations, museums, user groups, and individuals around the world.

Evaluating Your Sources

Keep in mind that no one owns or regulates the Internet. Just because you read something online doesn't mean it's true or accurate. Because anyone can publish something on the Internet without having to verify facts or guarantee quality, it's always a good idea to confirm facts from the Internet against another source. In addition, to become a good judge of Internet materials, do the following:

• **Consider the domain name of the resource.** Be sure to check out the sites you use to see if they are commercial (.com or .firm), educational (.edu), governmental (.gov) or organizational (.org or .net). Ask yourself questions like these: What bias might a commercial site have that would influence its presentation of information? Is the site sponsored by a special-interest group that slants or spins information to its advantage?

Key to Internet Domains	
.com	commercial entity
.edu	educational institution
.firm	business entity
.gov	government agency or department
.org or .net	organization

• **Consider the author's qualifications.** Regardless of the source, ask these questions: Is the author named? What expertise does he or she have? Can I locate other online information about this person?

- **Check the date posted.** Is the information timely? When was the last time the site was updated?

Keeping Track of Your Search Process

Because the Internet allows you to jump from one site to the next, it's easy to lose track of how you got from place to place. A research journal, kept in a separate electronic file or in a notebook, is an excellent tool for mapping how you find information. The example on page 402 shows one way to set up a research log.

- Write a brief statement of the topic of your research.

- Write key words or phrases that will help you search for this information.

- Note the search engines that you will use.

- As you conduct a search, note how many "hits" or Internet sites the search engine has accessed. Determine whether you need to narrow or expand your search. Write down new key words and the results of each new search.

- Write down all promising sites. As you access them, evaluate the source and nature of the information and jot down your assessment.

- As you find the information you need, document it carefully according to the directions in "Citing Internet Resources," pages 406–408.

- Keep a list of favorite websites, either in your research journal or in your browser software. This feature may be called *bookmark* or *favorites*. You can click on the name of the site in your list and return to that page without having to retype the URL (Uniform Resource Locator).

Internet Research Log

Topic:_____

Key words: _____

Search engine: _____

Promising hits (titles and summary of sources): _____

_____

_____

New key words or phrases tried:_____

_____

Promising hits (titles and summary of sources):

_____

_____

Complete web addresses of most promising sites:

_____

_____

_____

_____

_____

Search Tools

A number of popular and free search engines will allow you to find topics of interest. Keep in mind that each service uses slightly different methods of searching, so you may get different results using the same key words.

All the Web at http://www.alltheweb.com
AltaVista at http://www.altavista.com
Go at http://www.go.com
Yahoo at http://www.yahoo.com
Excite at http://www.excite.com
HotBot at http://www.hotbot.com
WebCrawler at http://www.webcrawler.com
Google at http://www.google.com

Search Tips

• To make searching easier, less time consuming, and more directed, narrow your subject to a key word or a group of key words. These key words are your search terms. Key search connectors, or Boolean commands, can help you limit or expand the scope of your topic.

AND (or +) narrows a search by retrieving documents that include both terms. For example: *George Washington* AND *Continental Army.*

OR broadens a search by retrieving documents that include any of the terms. For example, *George Washington* OR *Continental Army* OR *Valley Forge.*

NOT narrows a search by excluding documents containing certain words. For example: *George Washington* NOT *army.*

• If applicable, limit your search by specifying a geographical area by using the word *near*. For example, *chess tournaments near Wichita, Kansas.*

- When entering a group of key words, present them in order, from the most important to the least important key word.

- If the terms of your search are not leading you to the information you need, try using synonyms. For example, if you were looking for information about which gasoline is best to use in your automobile, you might use these terms: *octane*, *unleaded*, *gasohol*, and *mileage*.

- Avoid opening the link to every page in your results list. Search engines typically present pages in descending order of relevancy or importance. The most useful pages will be located at the top of the list. However, skimming the text of lower order sites may give you ideas for other key words.

- If you're not getting the desired results, check your input. Common search mistakes include misspelling search terms and mistyping URLs. Remember that URLs must be typed exactly as they appear, using the exact capital or lowercase letters, spacing, and punctuation.

Try It Yourself

EXERCISE 4
Understanding the Internet
Follow the directions for each item.

1. Use the Internet to locate information about Herman Melville. Write down two URLs that you find.
2. Your topic is opossums. You've found two sites:
   http://www.opossum.org
   http://www.possumnetwork.com
   Evaluate them in terms of where the data comes from, who wrote it, and when it was written.
3. Choose two of the search engines listed on page 403 and do a search on *typhoons*. List two relevant hits you get from each search engine.
4. You are interested in doing a report on whales. What key terms might you use to narrow your search?

5. Where would you expect to get the most unbiased information about which late-model automobiles are the most fuel efficient—a site that has the suffix .com, .edu, .gov, .org, or .net? Why?

EXERCISE 5
Using the Internet
Use the Internet and the search tips in this section of the unit to find the answers to these questions. Cite the sources for your responses.

1. When did George Foreman first win the heavyweight boxing title, and whom did he defeat to win it?
2. What is the population of Greenland?
3. Where do Gila monsters live?
4. What is the URL of a site with a map of Fargo, North Dakota?
5. What are the URLs of two websites with information about the Edsel automobile?

EXERCISE 6

Using the Internet in Your Writing
Imagine you are preparing a report on Mongolia for your geography class. Conduct a search on this topic and create a research journal to track your process. Include key words or phrases for searching, the search engines you use, promising sites and an evaluation of each, and a summary of what each site or article contains.

CITING INTERNET SOURCES

Plagiarism means to claim someone else's words or thoughts as your own. Whenever you use someone else's words or ideas, you must be careful either to put the ideas in your own words or to use quotation marks. In either case, you must give credit to the person whose ideas you are using. This is as true for Internet resources as it is for print resources, such as encyclopedias, books, and magazines. Giving such credit to others is called documenting your sources.

To document your sources, use your research journal to record each site you visit, or make bibliography cards as you search. An entry should include the following general pieces of information:

- Name of the author, if available, last name first, followed by a period.
- Title of the source, document, file, or page in quotation marks, followed by a period.
- Date of the material, if available, followed by a period.
- Name of the database or online source, underlined, and followed by a period.
- Date that the source was accessed (day month year), followed by a period. Although MLA (Modern Language Association) style does not require the insertion of the words *retrieved* or *accessed* before the access date, you may want to include one of these words to distinguish a retrieval date from a publication date.
- Electronic address, enclosed in angle brackets (< >), followed by a period. MLA style suggests that writers avoid showing network and e-mail addresses as underlined hyperlinks. Note that when line length forces you to break a Web address, always break it after a slash mark.

The *Modern Language Association Style Manual* acknowledges that all source tracking information may not be obtainable. Therefore, the MLA recommends that if you cannot find some of this information, cite what is available.

USAGE tip

The Modern Language Association of America website answers basic questions about MLA documentation style, particularly documentation of Web sources. From the home page, select "MLA Style."

Examples of Bibliography Cards

This site has no original or revised date:

> Parfit, Michael. "Lost at Sea: What's killing the great Atlantic salmon." April 2000. <u>Smithsonian Magazine Web</u>. Accessed 17 April 2003.
> <http://www.smithsonianmag.si.edu/smithsonian/issues02/apr02/salmon.html >.

This site has no name of the database or online source:

> Bryan, William Jennings. "Cross of Gold Speech." July 9, 1896. Accessed 17 April 2003.
> <http://www.tntech.edu:8080/www/acad/hist/crosgold.html>.

This site has no author:

> "Giant Hissing Cockroaches Invade Conservation World on Park District Conservation Day." August 2, 2001. <u>Illinois Association of Park Districts</u>. Accessed 17 April 2003.
> <http://www.ilparks.org/newsroom_pdconservation_roaches.htm>.

This is the citation for an e-mail message:

> Harkin, Tom (tom_harkin@harkin.senate.gov). "New Farm Policy." E-mail to Trent Lott (senatorlott@lott.senate.gov). 17 April 2003.

Try It Yourself

EXERCISE 7
Understanding Internet Documentation
Visit the following websites about Theodore Roosevelt and write a bibliography card for each site.

http://www.whitehouse.gov/history/presidents/tr26.html
http://www.theodoreroosevelt.org
http://memory.loc.gov/ammem/trfhtml

EXERCISE 8
Understanding Internet Documentation

You've just found an interesting Civil War website called The Valley of the Shadow at http://jefferson.village.virginia.edu/vshadow2/choosepart.html. Click on one of the links at this site, such as The Eve of War, The War Years, Aftermath, or one of your choice. Make a bibliography card for the link.

EXERCISE 9
Using Internet Documentation in Your Writing

Using the information you found on Mongolia in Exercise 6, create four bibliography cards for sites you would use in your report.

UNIT *18* REVIEW

TEST YOUR KNOWLEDGE

EXERCISE 1
Identifying Netiquette

Tell whether each of the following is a "Do" or "Don't" when communicating on the Internet. (10 points)

EXAMPLE
always fill in the subject line (Do)

1. use "back to all" to reply to the sender of an e-mail
2. write brief e-mails
3. use all lowercase letters
4. edit your writing
5. use e-mail as a formal thank-you note
6. write when angry
7. send newsy updates to friends
8. share personal information
9. schedule events
10. limit the use of acronyms

EXERCISE 2
Understanding Netiquette

Based on your own experience with Internet communication, which netiquette guideline do you most frequently see violated? Explain why you think that guideline is ignored so often. (10 points)

EXERCISE 3
Understanding Proper Netiquette
Rewrite the following e-mail, correcting any improper netiquette. (10 points)

From: Sid Neighbors <sneighbors@company.com>
To: Frank Foley <ffoley@company.com>
Date: Wednesday, April 3, 2002 11:29 P.M.
Subject: <<no subject>>

YO FRANK—FWIW I think we should do something about Gina. She is assigning too much work to each of us in payroll. I think we should meet F2F to discuss how to thwart her new operations plan. IMHO, she is totally incompetent and never should have been promoted. She has no leadership skills. I think we need to go over her head. HER INEPTITUDE IS WRECKING THE DEPARTMENT!!

BTW, nice presentation Monday afternoon. Keep practicing and someday you'll be as valuable to the company as I am. J/K

L8R dude,
The Sidmeister

EXERCISE 4
Understanding Internet Searches and Sources
Follow the directions for each item. (20 points)

1. Use the Internet to locate information about the economy of Luxembourg. Write down two URLs that you find.
2. You want to buy a new stereo system and are comparing two different brands. Where would you expect to get the most unbiased product information—from a .com, .edu, .gov, .org, or .net site? Why?
3. Choose two search engines and do a search on *British poets*. List two relevant hits you get from each search engine.
4. What is the URL of a site with photos of structures from ancient Rome?

5. What is the URL of a site that provides an online tour of an ancient Egyptian tomb or pyramid?
6. Use the Internet to find out who served as the first commissioner of Major League Baseball.
7. Your topic is Elizabeth Cady Stanton. You've found two sites:
   http://www.nps.gov/wori/ecs.htm
   http://www.libertynet.org/edcivic/stanton.html
   Write a brief evaluation, comparing and contrasting the two sites.
8. How would you cite the following e-mail message?

From: Julie Hanson <jhanson@mttu.edu>
To: Betty Schultz <bschultz2@warmmail.com>
Date: Thursday, May 4, 20__ 10:07 A.M.
Subject: Dissertation Copies

Ms. Schultz:

You may have permission to make eleven photocopies of Chapter 7 from my dissertation, "Forgotten Achievements: the Presidency of William Henry Harrison," for use in your research seminar.

Julie Hanson

9. Use the Internet to locate information about universities offering a major in Chinese. List five different universities.
10. What is the URL of a site that allows you to check the financial markets in Moscow, Russia?

Understanding Internet Searches

List two or three key terms you might use to narrow a search on each of the following topics. (10 points)

EXAMPLE
flower gardens
(Marigolds + planting + gardening)

1. jazz music
2. *Sputnik*
3. gravity
4. social security
5. Canadian hockey teams
6. Harriet Tubman
7. copy machines
8. sharks
9. eighteenth-century writers
10. employment in Olso, Norway

Using the Internet in Your Writing

Imagine you are preparing a report on the Battle of Shiloh for your history class. Conduct a search on this topic, narrowing your search to a specific aspect of the battle. Create an Internet Research Log to track your process. Include key words or phrases for searching, the search engines you use, and a list of promising sites you locate. A sample research log appears on page 402. (20 points)

Using Internet Documentation in Your Writing

Using the information you found on the Battle of Shiloh in Exercise 6, create four bibliography cards for sites you would use in your report. (20 points)

PART FOUR

UNIT *19* WRITER'S WORKSHOP
Building Effective Sentences

UNIT OVERVIEW

WRITER'S WORKSHOP: BUILDING EFFECTIVE SENTENCES

SENTENCE FRAGMENTS

A sentence contains a subject and a verb and should express a complete thought. A **sentence fragment** is a phrase or clause that does not express a complete thought but that has been punctuated as though it did.

Writing tip

When reading a sentence fragment, ask yourself, "What is missing?" A sentence fragment is usually missing either a subject, a verb, or both subject and verb.

EXAMPLES

complete sentence   The gray fox ran across the field.
sentence fragment   Ran across the field. (The subject is missing.)
sentence fragment   The gray fox. (The verb is missing.)
sentence fragment   Across the field. (The subject and verb are missing.)

Try It Yourself

EXERCISE 1
Identifying Sentence Fragments in Literature
As a rule, sentence fragments should be avoided. For stylistic reasons, however, authors sometimes include sentence fragments in their work. Identify each of the following items as either a sentence or a sentence fragment.

Literature
MODEL

1. For the first time, I shifted in the chair.
2. Everybody needed a coat.
3. Not coming back in here.
4. Ever again.
5. She came back and sat behind her desk.
6. We stood.
7. We walked the first five blocks.
8. Stayed out all hours.
9. Drank and drank some more.
10. Even our friends ran for cover.

excerpts from "Getting the Facts of Life"
Paulette Childress

Understanding Sentence Fragments
Tell what is missing in each of the following sentence
fragments—subject, verb, or subject and verb.

1. underneath the black chair
2. rammed the wooden ship
3. his large white dog
4. the winding river
5. slept for three hours in the cellar
6. over the whole city
7. in the jar underneath the sink
8. trimmed the hedges in the backyard
9. administrators, teachers and students
10. sold the family farm

Correcting Sentence Fragments
Correct each of the following sentence fragments. Make each
fragment into a complete sentence by supplying the missing
element(s).

1. drank orange juice and milk
2. on the coffee table
3. the old oak tree
4. ran for office
5. an angry otter
6. past the fencepost
7. at the second gas station
8. the peaceful lake
9. above the garage
10. talked directly to the audience

RUN-ON SENTENCES

A **run-on sentence** is made up of two or more sentences that
have been run together as if they were one complete thought.
A run-on sentence can confuse the reader about where a
thought starts or ends.

Take a look at the following examples of run-on sentences. In the first run-on, no punctuation mark is used between the run-on sentences. In the second run-on, a comma is used incorrectly.

> **EXAMPLES**
> The umpire watched the two teams warm up before the game his headache had gone away.
>
> At the start of the American Revolution, about three million people lived in the thirteen colonies, about one third of them supported the British government.

You can correct a run-on by dividing it into two separate sentences. Mark the end of each idea with a period, question mark, or exclamation point. Capitalize the first word of each new sentence.

> **EXAMPLE**
> The umpire watched the two teams warm up before the game. His headache had gone away.

You can also correct a run-on by using a semicolon. The second part of the sentence is not capitalized. Use a semicolon to join two sentences only if they are very closely related.

> **EXAMPLE**
> At the start of the American Revolution, three million people lived in the thirteen colonies; about one third of them supported the British government.

Try It Yourself

EXERCISE 4
Identifying Run-on Sentences
Identify which of the following sentences are run-ons.

1. The American Revolution began in 1775 the Declaration of Independence was written the next year.
2. George Washington commanded the Continental Army the Continental Congress gave him command of this force.

3. Few observers in Europe thought the colonists had much of a chance against the British.
4. The British government hired Hessians to help put down the uprising, they were professional soldiers.
5. In the early years of the war, Washington lost many battles to the British.
6. The Continental Army was vulnerable in 1776 and 1777, the British missed their chance to end the revolution.
7. France agreed to support the colonists, providing money, arms, and troops for the cause.
8. Benedict Arnold helped the Americans win the Battle of Saratoga he later switched sides.
9. British troops occupied Philadelphia, but the colonists did not give up.
10. Yorktown was a great victory for the Americans and the French in 1881, it was the last major battle of the war.

EXERCISE 5
Understanding Run-on Sentences
Correct each of the following run-on sentences. Decide whether the run-on sentence can be corrected by dividing it into two separate sentences or by using a semicolon and forming one sentence.

1. The bears wandered into the campsite Frank watched them from the trees.
2. Frank was simultaneously frightened and amused by the bears he did not make a sound.
3. Each bear stuck its head into a tent the boy wondered what they were looking for.
4. One bear started clawing at a bag he smelled food inside.
5. Frank calmly watched the spectacle, the bears did not notice him.
6. The bear ripped open the bag spilling the campers' food onto the ground the other bears shared in the prize.
7. Frank thought those bears must really be hungry he was amazed at how fast they devoured the food
8. The bears quickly finished eating they knocked over the three tents looking for more food.

9. After ransacking the campsite the bears wandered away they left a mess in their wake.
10. Frank walked among the remains of the campsite he wondered what his parents were going to say.

WORDY SENTENCES

A **wordy sentence** includes extra words and phrases that can be unnecessarily difficult, confusing, or repetitive to read. When you write, use only words necessary to make your meaning clear. Revise and edit your sentences so that they are not unnecessarily wordy or complicated. Review the following examples to learn about three different ways that you can correct wordy sentences.

Replace a group of words with one word.

EXAMPLES	
wordy	I quit my job **because of the fact that** the company wanted me to work overtime each week.
revised	I quit my job **because** the company wanted me to work overtime each week.

Replace a clause with a phrase.

EXAMPLES	
wordy	**When the batter hit the ball over the fence into the stands,** the crowd cheered wildly.
revised	**When the batter hit the ball over the fence,** the crowd cheered wildly.

Delete a group of unnecessary or repetitive words.

When revising, read your sentences aloud to check for wordiness. A wordy sentence will not only sound awkward, but it will feel like a mouthful of words to you, too!

EXAMPLES	
wordy	**What I think is** your book will appeal to children in grade school.
revised	**I think** your book will appeal to grade school children.

CONTINUED

| wordy | Joe suffers from insomnia, **and he doesn't sleep well at night.** |
| revised | Joe suffers from insomnia. |

Do not confuse a wordy sentence with a lengthy or necessarily complicated sentence. Writers vary their sentence lengths to create rhythm and add variety and liveliness to their work. Note the lengthy sentence underlined in the following excerpt. Even though the sentence is long, it does not contain "extra words." The precise word choices in the long sentence make its meaning clear and create a vivid picture.

Literature
M O D E L

The old man, I mentioned, was absent in the country. I took my visitors all over the house. I bade them search— search *well*. I led them, at length, to *his* chamber. I showed them his treasures, secure, undisturbed. <u>In the enthusiasm of my confidence, I brought chairs into the room, and desired them *here* to rest from their fatigues, while I myself, in the wild audacity of my perfect triumph, placed my own seat upon the very spot beneath which reposed the corpse of my victim.</u>

   The officers were satisfied. My *manner* had convinced them. I was singularly at ease. They sat, and while I answered cheerily, they chatted of familiar things.

from "The Tell-Tale Heart"
Edgar Allan Poe

Try It Yourself

EXERCISE 6
Identifying Wordy Sentences
Read the following sentences. Underline any unnecessary words and phrases in each of the sentences.

1. Father told me I needed to do more dishwashing and said I should wash the dishes more often.
2. The peasants were upset due to the fact that their village had been burned down.

3. Hannah called during dinner when we were eating.
4. We looked in the barrel full of apples, and there were many apples in the barrel.
5. The shiny new car glistened in the sun, and many of its parts shone brightly.
6. We saw a variety of animals, lions, tigers, zebras, bears, and monkeys, at the zoo.
7. After a short and brief speech, the mayor returned to her office.
8. Father set the watch in the sun so that it would dry out from the sun's rays.
9. Nathan talked about his book to the crowd and explained that in the book he wrote from many different perspectives.
10. Manny is part of a fast crew of rowers who can row a boat quickly through the water.

EXERCISE 7

Correcting Wordy Sentences

The following paragraph contains some wordy sentences. Revise the paragraph by eliminating unnecessary words and making the meaning clear.

I like to jog five miles after I wake up and get out of bed each morning. Many people believe that consistent exercise is important for good health. I usually run on a path in the forest that cuts through a wooded area. I see many animals while I am jogging, including for example squirrels, rabbits, and woodchucks. On the weekends, I see more people out jogging on Saturday and Sunday. I like to jog because of the fact that it makes me feel better about myself.

EXERCISE 8

Using Only Necessary Words in Your Writing

Write a paragraph for the school newspaper about one of your favorite ways to stay healthy and fit. When writing your paragraph, try to use only necessary words. After writing, read your paragraph aloud to yourself, or ask a classmate to read it aloud while you listen. Correct any sentences that sound wordy.

COMBINING AND EXPANDING SENTENCES

A series of short sentences in a paragraph can make your writing sound choppy and boring. The reader might have trouble understanding how your ideas are connected. By **combining and expanding sentences** you can connect related ideas, make sentences longer and smoother, and make a paragraph more interesting to read.

One way to combine sentences is to take a key word or phrase from one sentence and insert it into another sentence.

EXAMPLES	
short, choppy sentences	The girl rode a bicycle. It was pink.
combined sentence (with key word)	The girl rode a **pink** bicycle.
short, choppy sentences	We took a trip in the summer. We went to the Texas coast.
combined sentence (with key phrase)	We took a summer trip **to the Texas coast.**

Writing tip

When you insert a key word from one sentence into another, you might need to change the form of the word.

Sara mailed her application to the summer basketball camp. She was *eager to mail it.*

Sara *eagerly* mailed her application to the summer basketball camp.

Another way of combining sentences is to take two related sentences and combine them by using a coordinating conjunction—*and, but, or, so, for, yet,* or *nor.* By using a coordinating conjunction, you can form a compound subject, a compound verb, or a compound sentence.

EXAMPLES	
two related sentences	Stephen lived close to the ocean. He often sailed on his boat in the summer.
combined sentence	Stephen lived close to the ocean, **and** he often sailed on his boat in the summer. (compound sentence)

Writing tip

When combining two related sentences to form a compound sentence, you need to insert a comma before the coordinating conjunction.

CONTINUED

Writing tip

When you form a compound subject, make sure the compound subject agrees with the verb in number.

two related sentences	Dandelions sprang up in the backyard. There were also broadleaf weeds.
combined sentence	Dandelions **and** broadleaf weeds sprang up in the backyard. (compound subject)
two related sentences	Rain beat down upon the trail. It drenched the weary travelers.
combined sentence	Rain beat down upon the trail **and** drenched the weary travelers. (compound verb)

Try It Yourself

EXERCISE 9

Understanding How to Combine and Expand Sentences
Combine each of the following sentence pairs by taking the underlined word or phrase from the second sentence and inserting it into the first sentence. Remember: You might need to change the form of words when combining sentences.

1. The rain came down for four straight days. It was a driving rain.
2. Mandy's ship returned to Lisbon yesterday. It had sailed from London.
3. This girl found where you lost your watch. She is bright.
4. The pack animal we had for the trip was a mule. He was stubborn.
5. Sandi's ears detected the opening of the latch. Her ears were sharp.
6. The boss ordered us to quit talking. His tone was harsh.
7. When Fred went on vacation, we watered his plants. He went to Paris.
8. Jim packed the books. He packed them in cardboard boxes.
9. Three times the soldiers charged up the hill. Their efforts were valiant.
10. The cat and the dog napped. They slept on the rug.

EXERCISE 10

Using Coordinating Conjunctions to Combine Sentences
Combine each of the following sentence pairs by using one of
the following coordinating conjunctions—*and, but, or, so, for,
yet,* or *nor*. Remember to insert a comma if necessary.

1. Randy had a question about the assignment. He didn't
   raise his hand during class.
2. Randy wanted to earn good grades. He studied diligently
   for each test.
3. Candace practiced playing the piano each afternoon. She
   studied with Randy in the evenings.
4. While studying English, the pair listened to music. They
   studied Algebra, too.
5. The teacher delayed the English test another day. The
   students had more time to prepare.
6. Randy reviewed his English notes late into the evening.
   Candace decided to go to a movie.
7. Maybe she thought she was already prepared. Perhaps she
   didn't care about the test.
8. The students took the test. They discussed their answers
   afterward.
9. Randy was displeased that Candace didn't study with him.
   He did not talk to her.
10. Candace visited Randy after piano practice. She
    apologized for not studying with him.

MAKING PASSIVE SENTENCES ACTIVE

A verb is **active** when the subject of the verb performs the action.
It is **passive** when the subject of the verb receives the action.

EXAMPLES	
active	Lenny **bought** Rachel a scarf.
passive	A scarf **was bought** for Rachel by Lenny.

Writing tip

Overusing passive
verbs in sentences
makes your writing
dull and weak.
Active verbs engage
your reader's
attention and make
your sentences
sound more natural,
alive, and
interesting.

EXERCISE 11
Identifying Active and Passive Verbs in Sentences in Literature

Indicate whether the underlined verbs in the passage below are active or passive.

Literature
MODEL

> Lester <u>shut off</u> the space heater to avoid an explosion, <u>nailed</u> shut all doors and windows to keep out intruders, and <u>unplugged</u> every electrical appliance. Good weather <u>was predicted</u>, but just in case a freak storm came and <u>blew out</u> a window, shooting deadly glass shards in his direction, he <u>moved</u> a straight-backed chair into a far corner, making sure nothing was overhead to fall on him.
>
> from "The 11:59"
> Patricia McKissack

EXERCISE 12
Understanding Passive and Active Sentences

Identify each of the verbs in the following sentences as being either passive or active. Then make each of the passive verbs into an active verb.

1. My dog Nero was given a bath this morning.
2. Mother told me to keep him from playing in the mud.
3. I had been told many times before by Mother to not let Nero get so dirty.
4. I had received the same lecture from my father.
5. Upon going outside, I noticed that Nero was barking at a rabbit.
6. The bunny dined upon the flowers Mother planted yesterday.
7. The rabbit soon was being chased.
8. Most of the flowers were already devoured by the time Nero sprang into action.
9. I remembered my parents' instructions but wondered if this could be an exception.
10. Unfortunately the garden was destroyed by the rabbit, and Nero was needing a bath again.

Using Active Sentences in Your Writing
Write a paragraph describing for classmates a favorite memory
you have from last summer. Use at least five active verbs in
your paragraph. Underline the active verb(s) in each sentence.

ACHIEVING PARALLELISM

A sentence has **parallelism** when the same forms are used to
express ideas of equal—or parallel—importance. Parallelism
can add emphasis and rhythm to a sentence. Words, phrases,
and clauses that have the same form and function in a sentence
are called **parallel**.

EXAMPLES

not parallel The singers **took** the stage, **dazzled** the crowd,
and then **had returned** to their dressing rooms.
(The highlighted verbs are not in the same tense.)

parallel The singers **took** the stage, **dazzled** the crowd,
and **returned** to their dressing rooms.

not parallel The performers are **talented, lively,** and **dance.**
(The three highlighted words include two
adjectives and one verb.)

parallel The performers are **talented, lively,** and **energetic**
dancers.

 tip

> When revising for
> parallelism, read
> your sentences
> aloud. Any errors in
> parallelism will
> sound awkward.

Try It Yourself

Identifying Parallelism in Literature
Identify examples of parallelism in the following passage.

> It was the half-term holiday, so after breakfast Mark was
> able to take the empty packet away to the playroom and
> get on with the job of cutting out the stone walls, the row
> of little trees, the fountain, the yew arch, the two green
> lawns, and the tiny clumps of brilliant flowers. He knew
> better than to "stick tabs in slots and secure with paste,"

Literature
M O D E L

CONTINUED

as the directions suggested; he had made models from packets before and knew they always fell to pieces unless they were firmly bound together with transparent sticky tape. It was a long, fiddling, pleasurable job.

from "The Serial Garden"
Joan Aiken

EXERCISE 15
Correcting Errors in Parallelism
Rewrite each of the following sentences that contain errors in parallelism, making sentence parts parallel. If a sentence is already parallel, write *correct*.

1. Today I washed the car, mowed the lawn, trimmed the hedges, and was painting the shed.
2. Next weekend we will be attending a play, watching a baseball game, and shop for a new car.
3. Do you like cooking meals yourself or to eat out at a restaurant?
4. Our car needs to have the tires rotated and an oil change.
5. Jessica likes singing in musicals and acting in plays.
6. I found an assortment of round, square, and oval pieces in the box.
7. Ned concluded that the show was long, boring, and poorly written.
8. Ivan stood his ground boldly, courageously, and was filled with resolve.
9. We walked to the school, talked to the teacher, and had received the answer we wanted.
10. Your collie ran across the street, through the Smith's yard, and around their house.

EXERCISE 16
Using Parallelism in Your Writing
Write a paragraph to a foreign pen pal in which you explain what you like best about living in this country. Use five examples of parallelism in your paragraph.

ADDING COLORFUL LANGUAGE TO SENTENCES

When you write, use words that tell your readers exactly what you mean. **Colorful language**—such as precise and lively nouns, verbs, and modifiers—tells your readers exactly what you mean and makes your writing more interesting.

Precise nouns give your reader a clear picture of who or what is involved in the sentence.

EXAMPLES

original sentence	The **cat** walked into the **building**.
revised sentence	The **Siamese cat** walked into the **grocery store**.

Colorful, vivid verbs describe the specific action in the sentence.

EXAMPLES

original sentence	Her brother **ran** across the yard.
revised sentence	Her brother **darted** across the yard.

Modifiers—adjectives and adverbs—describe the meaning of other words and make them more precise. Colorful or surprising modifiers can make your writing come alive for your readers.

EXAMPLES

original sentence	The **tired** farmer planted the last row of corn.
revised sentence	The **exhausted** farmer **wearily** planted the last row of corn.

Writing tip

> Think of colorful language as a way to help your readers see, hear, smell, taste, and/or feel what you are describing.

Try It Yourself

EXERCISE 17
Identifying Colorful Language in Literature
Identify examples of colorful language in the following passage. Think about how each example makes the meaning of a sentence more precise and vivid.

What the snake did next was so fast that the whole movement couldn't have taken more than a hundredth of a second, like the flick of a camera shutter. There was a green flash as the snake darted forward at least ten feet and struck at the snake-man's leg. Nobody could have got out of the way of that one. I heard the snake's head strike against the thick cowhide boot with a sharp little crack, and then at once the head was back in that same deadly backward-curving position, ready to strike again.

from "The Green Mamba"
Roald Dahl

EXERCISE 18
Understanding Colorful Language
Revise each of the following sentences, using precise nouns, vivid verbs, and colorful modifiers.

1. The birds flew out of the tree.
2. He put on his coat.
3. Jill walked over to the window and looked out at the grass.
4. Several different dogs were in the park.
5. The rain came down for a long time.
6. Donovan smelled the pie on the windowsill.
7. A young doctor parked his car in the lot.
8. The people walked slowly across the desert.
9. A big snake appeared before them on the sidewalk.
10. A mouse ran under the table and went into its hole.

EXERCISE 19
Using Colorful Language in Your Writing
Write a description of an individual who faces great danger but narrowly escapes. Use precise nouns, vivid verbs, and colorful modifiers to make your description vivid to your readers.

VARYING SENTENCE BEGINNINGS

Just as you probably wouldn't like to eat the same thing for breakfast every morning, your readers don't enjoy reading the same sentence pattern in every paragraph. By **varying sentence beginnings** you can give your sentences rhythm, create variety, and keep your readers engaged.

Sentences often begin with a subject. To vary sentence beginnings, start some sentences with a one-word modifier, a prepositional phrase, a participial phrase, or a subordinate clause.

EXAMPLES	
subject	**She** usually finishes her test before the rest of the class.
one-word modifier	**Usually,** she finishes her test before the rest of the class.
prepositional phrase	**Before lunch** he plans the following day's activities.
participial phrase	**Humming a lively tune**, the warden reviewed the parole cases.
subordinate clause	**Since it rarely rains where he lives**, Jeff leaves the top down on his convertible.

Try It Yourself

EXERCISE 20
Identifying Varying Sentence Beginnings in Literature
Underline the varying sentence beginnings in the following passage. Read the passage aloud to hear the rhythm and interest that the variety creates.

The bird was a young one, no more than a year old. She was born in a northern land far, far across the seas, a land belonging to England. Flying to the south to escape the snow and ice and bitter cold, a great storm had seized her and whiled and buffeted her about. It was a truly terrible

Literature
M O D E L

CONTINUED

storm, stronger than her great wings, stronger than anything. For days and nights it held her in its grip and there was nothing she could do but fly before it. When finally it had blown itself out and her sure instincts took her south again, she was over a different land and surrounded by strange birds that she had never seen before. At last, exhausted by her ordeal, she had sunk to rest in a friendly green marsh, only to be met by the blast from a hunter's gun.

from *The Snow Goose*
Paul Gallico

EXERCISE 21
Understanding How to Vary Sentence Beginnings
Revise the following paragraph to vary sentence beginnings.

Walter Zane plays football at Southern Tech University. He is the quarterback of his team. Zane led the conference in passing yards last season. He hopes to lead his team to a bowl game as a senior. He will be joined by seven returning offensive starters this year. His coach is confident that the team will be ready for every opponent on the schedule. Zane and his teammates have been working hard during the off-season to stay in shape. He is looking forward to the first game of the season on September 4.

EXERCISE 22
Using Varying Sentence Beginnings in Your Writing
Write an alternative concluding paragraph to one of the short stories in your literature text. Vary sentence beginnings in the paragraph.

UNIT *19* REVIEW

TEST YOUR KNOWLEDGE

EXERCISE 1

Identifying Sentence Fragments and Run-on Sentences
Identify each of the following items as a complete sentence, a sentence fragment, or a run-on sentence. (10 points)

1. The whale swam swiftly.
2. Muddy water in the barrel.
3. He looked in the closet and found the bat.
4. A bird circled in the air above us it occasionally swooped down near our heads.
5. Without warning, a raccoon jumped on the picnic table.
6. Looking into the crystal ball.
7. A large growling black bear.
8. Before bedtime Dad reads us a story it is usually a fairy tale.
9. Riding in the back of the pickup truck.
10. The playful kitten batted at the mobile.

EXERCISE 2

Identifying Passive and Active Verbs
Identify each of the following sentences as having either a passive or active verb. (10 points)

1. A bake sale was organized by Edna.
2. The house was painted by Tom.
3. A hole was dug in the yard by an animal.
4. Rafael shoveled the snow off the driveway.
5. Slowly, the alligator crept closer to the camera operator.
6. The missing llama was spotted by Luther.
7. This display was set up by the fourth graders.
8. A police officer directed us to pull our car over.
9. Three orangutans escaped from the zoo last night.
10. Mounds of dirt were piled in your backyard.

EXERCISE 3

Understanding Fragments, Run-ons, and Wordy Sentences

Correct the following fragments, run-ons, and wordy sentences. (10 points)

1. The professor lectured for ninety minutes I took eight pages of notes.
2. Over the grassy hill.
3. Tripped over the toy in the middle of the room.
4. The old rusty car does not look very appealing because it is covered in rust.
5. A bird landed on the windowsill it looked at us curiously and flew away.
6. I cannot attend the reunion because of the fact that my car is in the shop.
7. Would you like to go to the game I have an extra ticket.
8. A large steaming vat of stew.
9. About fourteen miles from here.
10. Singing in the shower.

EXERCISE 4

Combining and Expanding Sentences

Combine the following sentence pairs. (10 points)

1. The snowstorm caused the schools to close. It also caused several businesses to close.
2. Bill studied all night for the test. He did not receive a passing score.
3. Betty won eight million dollars in the lottery. She decided to quit her job.
4. Thomas refurbished the house. The house was old and creaky.
5. James is a brilliant intellect. He is a poor public speaker.
6. We have to attend a departmental meeting today. It is at 10:00 A.M.
7. Grandma baby-sat the kids both nights last weekend. She was happy to baby-sit.

8. Edith swam across the river today. It was wide and choppy.
9. The dog watched the door for his owner to return. The dog was hopeful.
10. Place the trophy in the den. Place it on the shelf.

EXERCISE 5
Correcting Errors in Parallelism
Correct any errors in parallelism in the following sentences. If a sentence contains no errors in parallelism, write *correct*. (10 points)

1. I will spend my vacation reading novels, walking on the beach, and I might write some poetry.
2. The soldiers dug foxholes, built a barrier, and were keeping an eye on the ridge.
3. Larry bought a new motorcycle and riding it home.
4. His house is freshly painted, tastefully decorated, and neatly cleaned.
5. After school I will jog around the track and swim a couple laps in the pool.
6. Sheila likes singing country songs and to play the fiddle.
7. In history class, we talked about Roosevelt, discussed Taft, and debating Wilson.
8. A frisky puppy leapt upon the chair, wagged its tail, and was barking noisily.
9. The ball flew across the street, bounced down the alley, rolled into the bakery, and landed in a shoe.
10. This afternoon we were proofreading the reports, checking the facts, and suggested possible improvements.

EXERCISE 6
Using Active Sentences in Your Writing

Using active verbs, write ten sentences about the habits and actions of a pet or favorite animal. Underline the active verb(s) in each sentence. (10 points)

EXERCISE 7
Using Colorful Language in Your Writing
Write a paragraph for a friend describing a fictional character that you have created. In your paragraph, use precise nouns, vivid verbs, and colorful modifiers to describe the character. Try to make your word portrait of the character as clear as possible. (20 points)

EXERCISE 8
Using Varying Sentence Beginnings in Your Writing
To a person who opposes your views, write a paragraph describing a cause that you favor and your reasons for supporting it. Vary sentence beginnings in your paragraph. (20 points)

UNIT *20* WRITER'S WORKSHOP
Building Effective Paragraphs

WRITER'S WORKSHOP: BUILDING EFFECTIVE PARAGRAPHS

THE PARAGRAPH

In Unit 19 you learned how words are organized to create effective sentences. In this unit, you'll learn how sentences work together to create effective paragraphs.

A **paragraph** is a carefully organized group of related sentences that focus on or develop one main idea. As the sentences within a paragraph are connected—like links in a chain—so are a series of paragraphs connected to create a longer piece of writing, whether an essay, short story, or research paper.

Most effective paragraphs have a **main idea** or point that is developed with **supporting details**—such as examples, sensory details, facts, anecdotes, and quotations. Paragraphs can serve different purposes—to narrate, to describe, to persuade, or to inform—but all effective paragraphs share two key elements: unity and a logical method of organization.

Read the following paragraph from "Luke Baldwin's Vow." The paragraph is unified because every sentence in the paragraph contributes to the paragraph's main idea—a description of Uncle Henry.

Literature MODEL

Uncle Henry, who was the manager of the sawmill, was a big, burly man weighing more than two hundred and thirty pounds, and he had a rough-skinned, brick-colored face. He looked like a powerful man, but his health was not good. He had aches and pains in his back and shoulders which puzzled the doctor. The first thing Luke learned about Uncle Henry was that everybody had great respect for him. The four men he employed in the sawmill were always polite and attentive when he spoke to them. His wife, Luke's Aunt Helen, a kindly, plump,

CONTINUED

straightforward woman, never argued with him. "You should try and be like your Uncle Henry," she would say to Luke. "He's so wonderfully practical. He takes care of everything in a sensible, easy way."

from "Luke Baldwin's Vow"
Morley Callaghan

EXAMINING THE *Model*

Notice how the main idea of this paragraph is developed with specific sensory details that provide the reader with a clear picture of Uncle Henry's physical appearance.

Try It Yourself

EXERCISE 1
Identifying Main Ideas in Paragraphs in Literature
Read each of the following paragraphs, all of which are literary excerpts. Then identify the main idea of each paragraph.

1. It appears slowly out of the mist, like something from an Arthurian legend, a large, inflatable life raft, the depressing khaki and olive-drab of military camouflage. A man kneeling in front directs the raft with a paddle. He waves when he sees me, stands up and calls out in an urgent voice, but I can't make it out. As the raft drifts closer I can see that the lone occupant is tall and athletic-looking, dark-skinned, with a long jaw and flashing eyes.

from "Searching for January"
W. P. Kinsella

Literature
M O D E L S

2. My father on the other hand, along with most of the early aviators, was not impressed by the growing enthusiasm for parachute jumping as a sport. Young daredevils like my brother could call it "sky-diving" if they wanted to, but the aviation pioneers referred to it disgustingly as "jumping out of a perfectly good airplane." In their day, a pilot only jumped when he had to: if it was absolutely certain that the airplane was headed for a crash and the parachute was his only hope for survival.

from "Flying"
Reeve Lindbergh
CONTINUED

3. The wagon, without any direction from Pierre, would roll three blocks down St. Catherine Street, then turn right two blocks along Roslyn Avenue, then left, for that was Prince Edward Street. The horse would stop at the first house, allow Pierre perhaps thirty seconds to get down from his seat and put a bottle of milk at the front door, and would then go on, skipping two houses and stopping at the third. So down the length of the street. Then, Joseph, still without any direction from Pierre, would turn around and come back along the other side. Yes, Joseph was a smart horse.

from "A Secret for Two"
Quentin Reynolds

4. In many countries where students outperform their American counterparts academically, school dress codes are observed as a part of creating the proper learning environment. Their students tend to be neater, less disruptive in class and more disciplined, mainly because their minds are focused more on learning and less on materialism. It's time Americans realized that the benefits of safe and effective schools far outweigh any perceived curtailment of freedom of expression brought on by dress codes.

from "Appearances Are Destructive"
Mark Mathabane

5. Almost from her infancy Elizabeth was trained to stand in for ruling men, in case the need should arise. So she had to master whatever they were expected to know and do. Her tutors found the child to be an eager student. She learned history, geography, mathematics, and the elements of astronomy and architecture. She mastered four modern languages—French, Italian, Spanish, and Flemish—as well as classic Greek and Latin. She wrote in a beautiful script that was like a work of art. The earliest portrait of her—when she was thirteen—shows a girl with

CONTINUED

innocent eyes holding a book in her long and delicate hands, already confident and queenly in her bearing.

from "Elizabeth I"
Milton Meltzer in *Ten Queens: Portraits of Women in Power*

EXERCISE 2
Understanding Main Ideas and Supporting Details in a Paragraph

Write two to three supporting sentences for each of the following main ideas. Make sure that each supporting sentence develops the main idea and that all the sentences are related.

1. Staying up really late before an important test is not a good idea.
2. I will always remember the day a bear wandered into our cabin.
3. My friend Bob has no real basketball skills.
4. In tournament chess, players must keep an eye on the clock.
5. The school is making big cuts in its budget.

EXERCISE 3
Using Related Sentences to Develop a Main Idea in a Paragraph

Write a single paragraph to a pen pal in which you describe your favorite season of the year. Use five or six sentences to explain why you enjoy this particular season.

THE TOPIC SENTENCE

The main idea of a paragraph is often stated directly in a **topic sentence**. The topic sentence can be placed at the beginning, middle, or end of a paragraph. Usually the topic sentence appears at the beginning of a paragraph and is followed by one or more supporting sentences. In the following example, the topic sentence is the first sentence in the paragraph.

Literature
MODEL

I started to return serve differently. Usually, I would stand just behind the baseline and wait for the ball. Now I dropped back a yard and a half or so and charged the ball when my opponent served. I had never been comfortable charging the ball because of my clay-court background, but with my new aggressiveness, I developed new techniques to catch the ball on the rise. In the course of some weight-shifting drills suggested by Larry, I developed a topspin backhand, which worked very well for moving the ball cross-court as I charged forward.

from *Off the Court*
Arthur Ashe

In many paragraphs, however, the main idea is implied rather than stated in a topic sentence. This means that the sentences in the paragraph work together to suggest—rather than directly state—the main idea.

Literature
MODEL

She said nothing. She just walked on, churning away under a sun that clearly meant to melt us. From here to the tracks it was mostly gardens. It felt like the Dixie Peach I'd used to help water-wave my hair was sliding down with the sweat on my face, and my throat was tight with thirst. Boy, did I want a pop. I looked at the last little store before we crossed the tracks without bothering to ask.

from "Getting the Facts of Life"
Paulette Childress

Notice how, in the excerpt from "Getting the Facts of Life," the implied main idea is that the characters are walking on a very hot day. The author does not directly state the main idea; instead, she provides sensory details that lead readers to this conclusion.

When writing a topic sentence, consider the point you wish to make in your paragraph and the details that will support, explain, or describe your point. It might be helpful to think of your main idea as a problem or to ask it in the form of a question.

Writing tip

An effective topic sentence draws readers into a paragraph.

> EXAMPLE
> Motorists out on the road often face the problem of a flat tire. What do you do when a tire goes flat while you are driving?

The statement of the main idea as a problem or a question can lead you to refine the main idea into a specific topic sentence.

> EXAMPLE
> Every motorist should know how to change a flat tire.

Try It Yourself

EXERCISE 4
Identifying Stated and Unstated Topic Sentences in Paragraphs in Literature
Read each of the following paragraphs, all of which are excerpts from literature. If the paragraph has a stated topic sentence, identify it. If the paragraph has an implied topic sentence or main idea, tell what it is in your own words.

1. Life in the refugee camp was very difficult. Rice, fish vegetables, and water were delivered to the camp, but the ration for each family was never enough. Many times, the food my family received did not last until the next delivery. My parents went out to work in the fields to earn a little extra money to buy food. As a child, I did not understand why we had to work so hard and live so poorly.

from "An Unforgettable Journey"
Maijue Xiong

Literature
M O D E L S

CONTINUED

2. Time had always been on his side. Now it was his enemy. Where had the years gone? Lester reviewed the thirty years he'd spent riding the rails. How different would his life have been if he'd married Louise Henderson and had a gallon of children? What if he'd taken that job at the mill down in Opelika? What if he'd followed his brother to Philly? How different?

from "The 11:59"
Patricia McKissack

3. But when I turned fifteen, it was as if my body, which hadn't grown for so many years, suddenly made up for lost time. I grew five inches in seven months. My mother was amazed. Even I couldn't get used to it. I kept knocking into things, my cloths didn't fit right, I felt awkward and clumsy when I moved. Dumb things that I had gotten away with, like paying children's prices at the movies instead of junior admission, I couldn't do anymore. I wasn't a shrimp or a small fry any longer. I was suddenly normal.

from "Hollywood and the Pits"
Cherylene Lee

4. Donald Macfarlane, the snake-man, may have been old and small but he was an impressive-looking character. His eyes were pale blue, deep-set in a face round and dark and wrinkled as a walnut. Above the blue eyes, the eyebrows were thick and startlingly white, but the hair on his head was almost black. In spite of the thick leather boots, he moved like a leopard, with soft slow cat-like strides, and he came straight up to me and said, "Who are you?"

from "The Green Mamba"
Roald Dahl

Understanding Topic Sentences
Write a topic sentence for each group of sentences below.
Think about what the details have in common—what they are
describing or explaining.

EXAMPLE
Goldfish cost much less to own than a dog or cat does. Most
pet stores have a large supply of fish to choose from. Goldfish
make no noise and require little care. Feeding consists of
sprinkling a few flakes in a bowl each day. Moreover, goldfish
do not need to be walked once a day.
(Topic sentence: *Goldfish are inexpensive, low-maintenance pets.*)

1. The leaves are off all of the trees and the birds have flown
   south. The wind has grown chilly and bitter. Snow
   blankets the ground.
2. The teacher passed out the tests. Most of the students
   looked nervous. Many were thinking about their summer
   plans, which were only an hour away.
3. Rays from the sun cracked through the darkness,
   illuminating the horizon. A rooster crowed off in the
   distance. The chirping of birds filled the air.
4. The cat lay motionless on the top of the sofa. She
   watched the mouse walk along the woodwork, periodically
   stopping to sniff for food. Soon the mouse would be only
   a leap away. The cat remained still.
5. The stands are empty. Paper cups, scorecards, and other
   debris swirl about the stadium in the brisk breeze. The
   bases and home plate have been removed. The once-
   white chalk baselines are now barely visible.

Using Topic Sentences in Your Writing
Write down at least five ideas about your favorite holiday or
special occasion. Review your list and write five effective topic
sentences—one for each of five different paragraphs you might
develop about the holiday.

CREATING UNITY IN A PARAGRAPH

In the novel *The Three Musketeers*, Alexandre Dumas wrote, "All for one, one for all, that is our motto." The motto of the Three Musketeers—good friends and renowned swordsmen—could very well serve as the motto for a group of sentences within a paragraph. To create **unity** in a paragraph, all the sentences within the paragraph work to support the one main idea. You can create unity in a paragraph through the use of supporting details and transitions.

Supporting details include examples or illustrations, sensory details, anecdotes, facts, and quotations. By using supporting details that best develop or explain your main idea, you can help your reader understand what you are trying to say.

Writing tip

Sensory details that convey how things look, taste, smell, feel, and sound can make a description come alive for your readers.

Each of the different kinds of details listed below supports the following topic sentence: *Today is a typical Saturday in autumn.* Of course, depending on the purpose of your paragraph or longer piece of writing, one kind of supporting detail may be more appropriate or effective than another.

Writing tip

Remember to use quotation marks when directly quoting a statement.

EXAMPLES	
example/illustration	Leaves on the trees are changing colors.
sensory details	The air is cool and crisp, cheers echo from football stadiums, and paths in the park are crunchy with fallen leaves.
anecdote	My father always changed the oil in his lawnmower on the first Saturday of October.
fact	October is the first full month of autumn.
quotation	The poet Carl Sandburg wrote, "I spot the hills / With yellow balls in autumn."

A **transition** is a word or phrase that is used to connect ideas and to show relationships between them. Transitions can show time/chronological order, place/spatial order, cause and effect order, comparison and contrast order, and order of importance. The following examples include some of the more common transitions.

EXAMPLES	
time/chronological order	first, next, before, after, then, later, finally
place/spatial order	above, behind, next to, on top of, near, to the left
cause and effect	therefore, because, since, as a result, consequently
comparison and contrast	on the other hand, similarly, in contrast
order of importance	of least importance, more important, most importantly

Try It Yourself

EXERCISE 7
Identifying Supporting Details and Transitions in Literature
Identify the topic sentence in the following paragraph. Then identify one example of sensory detail, one example of illustration, and one example of transition.

After Laos became a Communist country in 1975, my family, along with many others, fled in fear of persecution. Because my father had served as a commanding officer for eleven years with the American Central Intelligence Agency in what is known to the American public as the "Secret War," my family had no choice but to leave immediately. My father's life was in danger, along with those of thousands of others. We were forced to leave loved ones behind, including my grandmother who was ill in bed the day we fled our village. For a month, my family walked through the dense

Literature
MODEL

CONTINUED

tropical jungles and rice fields, along rugged trails through many mountains, and battled the powerful Mekong River. We traveled in silence at night and slept in the daytime. Children were very hard to keep quiet. Many parents feared the Communist soldiers would hear the cries of their young children; therefore, they drugged the children with opium to keep them quiet. Some parents even left those children who would not stop crying behind. Fortunately, whenever my parents told my sisters and me to keep quiet, we listened and obeyed.

from "An Unforgettable Journey"
Maijue Xiong

EXERCISE 8
Understanding How to Create Unity in a Paragraph
Follow the directions to provide supporting details and/or transitions to each topic sentence.

EXAMPLE
Going to a park is a wonderful way to enjoy a weekend afternoon. (one example/illustration, one comparison and contrast transition)
Visiting a park is a wonderful way to spend a summer afternoon. A variety of activities can be enjoyed such as tossing a Frisbee, flying a kite, playing catch, or even reading under a tree. The open expanses of grass are inspiring, in contrast to the cramped offices where many people spend much of their week.

1. I will always remember my tenth birthday. (one sensory detail, one time/chronological order transition)
2. Negative actions produce negative consequences. (one example/illustration, one cause and effect transition)
3. We need to elect Sara Sanford mayor of this town. (two examples/illustrations)
4. Robert Frost was one of the most popular poets of the twentieth century. (one quotation, one cause and effect transition)
5. Your car should be retired to the junkyard. (one sensory detail, one place/spatial order transition)

Using Supporting Details and Transitions in Your Writing
Write a one-paragraph letter to an overseas pen pal describing
a typical day at school. You may choose to write about the
academic and/or social events of the day. Use at least two
different kinds of supporting details and at least two different
transitions in your letter. Use transitions that will make the
chronological order of the day's events clear to your pen pal.

TYPES OF PARAGRAPHS

Paragraphs can serve different purposes—to describe, to
narrate, to persuade, or to inform. If you wanted to introduce
a character, for example, you could write a descriptive
paragraph and create a picture in your readers' minds of the
character's physical features and personality. If you wanted to
tell about a series of events, you could write a narrative
paragraph to relate the events in the order in which they
happened.

Type of Paragraph	Purpose
descriptive	to describe, to set a scene, to create a mood, to appeal to the readers' senses
narrative	to tell a story, to relate a series of events, to tell about people's lives
informative	to inform, to present or explain an idea, to explain a process
persuasive	to persuade, to present an argument, to suggest a course of action

Try It Yourself

EXERCISE 10
Identifying Types of Paragraphs in Literature
Identify each of the following excerpts as either a descriptive,
narrative, informative, or persuasive paragraph.

1. The sun is only one among 200 billion stars that are bound together by gravity into a large cluster of stars called the galaxy. The stars of the galaxy revolve about its center as the planets revolve about the sun. The sun itself participates in this rotating motion, completing one circuit around the galaxy in 250 million years.

from "The Size of Things" in *Red Giants and White Dwarfs*
Robert Jastrow

2. Members of the fire department were starting to arrive at the front door, but Albert ignored them. He was white now, like death, and he made a low terrible sound. He didn't exactly pull his lips back from his teeth and growl, but the result was similar. It was like the sound a dog makes before he leaps for the throat. And what he said was *"You jest leave me be, woman!"*

from "Be-ers and Doers"
Budge Wilson

3. As public schools reopen for the new year, strategies to curb school violence will once again be hotly debated. Installing metal detectors and hiring security guards will help, but the experience of my two sisters makes a compelling case for greater use of dress codes as a way to protect students and promote learning.

from "Appearances Are Destructive"
Mark Mathabane

4. Across the street lived old Dikran, who was almost blind. He was past eighty and his wife was only a few years younger. They had a little house that was as neat inside as it was ordinary outside—except for old Dikran's garden, which was the best thing of its kind in the world. Plants, bushes, trees—all strong, in sweet black moist earth whose guardian was old Dikran. All things from the

CONTINUED

sky loved this spot in our poor neighborhood, and old
Dikran loved *them*.

from "The Hummingbird That Lived through Winter"
William Saroyan

EXERCISE 11
Understanding Different Types of Paragraphs
Choose an article from a newspaper or magazine that covers
an event or story of local interest. Identify in the article the
different kinds of paragraphs that the writer created and the
purpose of each paragraph. For each paragraph, identify one
supporting detail that develops, explains, or describes the main
idea.

EXERCISE 12
Using Different Types of Paragraphs in Your Writing
Select a photograph or painting that is printed in one of your
books or displayed at your school. Write a descriptive
paragraph about the image. Then use the same image as a
prompt to write either a narrative, informative, or persuasive
paragraph. After writing the two paragraphs, compare the
main ideas and supporting details you used in each. How do
they differ?

METHODS OF ORGANIZATION

As you've learned, supporting details and transitions develop
and explain the main idea or topic sentence in a paragraph.
Those same elements can be organized in different ways to
show the relationship or connection between ideas. These
different methods, or patterns, of organization include
time/chronological order, place/spatial order, order of
importance, comparison and contrast order, and cause and
effect order.

Chronological Order

Events are arranged in the time order in which they happened. This method of organization is used to tell a story, to present a series of events, or to describe the steps in a process. Transition words and phrases, such as *at the beginning, next, then,* and *finally,* are used to show the order of events.

> **EXAMPLE**
> Expecting the enemy to attack at dawn, we worked through the evening to prepare our defenses. First, we dug trenches in the side of the hill. Next, we strung barbed wire several yards in front of our trenches. Finally, we positioned artillery to cover the approaches to our position.

Spatial Order

Details are described in the order of their location in space, such as from back to front, left to right, or top to bottom. Transition words and phrases such as *next to, beside, above, below,* and *beyond* are used to connect the descriptions. This method of organization is used to set a scene, to establish a location, and to place the reader's mind in a specific setting.

> **EXAMPLE**
> The explorer carefully entered the cave. To his left, a small brook trickled along the floor and out through a crevice. Straight ahead, an unusually shaped table of rock occupied the center of the cavern. Sitting by the far back wall, a glowing object shimmered in the surrounding darkness.

Order of Importance

Ideas are organized from least important to most important or from most important to least important. Transition words and phrases such as *first, best, worst, more/most important, less/least important,* and *to a greater/lesser degree* are used to show the ranking among the ideas, people, places, objects, and events being discussed.

EXAMPLE
If you want to take up bowling, you need to have the right equipment. First, buy a ball that is the right weight for you and that is drilled to match your hand. Next, buy a pair of bowling shoes so you don't have to keep paying a rental fee. Of a lesser importance is a bowling glove, which may or may not be helpful to you when you bowl.

Comparison and Contrast Order

The similarities and differences between two subjects are organized in one of two ways. In the first method, the characteristics of one subject are presented, followed by the characteristics of the second subject. In the second method, both subjects are compared and contrasted characteristic by characteristic. Transition words and phrases such as *also*, *like*, *both*, *similarly*, and *in the same way* show similarities. Transition words and phrases such as *in contrast*, *however*, *but*, *yet*, and *on the other hand* show differences.

EXAMPLE
Korea and Vietnam were two countries that were divided because of the Cold War. Both countries had a northern government and a southern government. Both were the site of a bloody war fought between Communists and non-Communists. Korea, however, remained divided after its war, while Vietnam was united under a Communist government in 1975.

Cause and Effect Order

The causes and effects of events are organized in one of two ways to show the relationships between events and their results. In the first method, one or more causes are stated in the topic sentence, then details about the effects are presented. In the second method, one or more effects are presented followed by a discussion of the cause or causes of those effects. Transition words and phrases such as *one cause*, *another effect*, *as a result*, *consequently*, *therefore*, *since*, *because*, and *if . . . then* show cause and effect.

EXAMPLE
If our ace pitcher's arm is broken, then the team will fall out of the pennant race. Consequently, attendance will drop at the team's home games. Team owners are already worried about declining revenues. As a result, ownership may resort to raising ticket prices to try to generate more income.

Try It Yourself

EXERCISE 13

Identifying Methods of Organization in Literature

Identify the principal method of organization used in each of the following literature excerpts.

Literature
MODELS

1. The tiny electron, and two sister particles, are the building blocks out of which all matter in the world is constructed. The sister particles to the electron are the proton and the neutron. They were discovered even more recently than the electron; the proton was identified in 1920 and the neutron was first discovered in 1932. These two particles are massive in comparison with the electron—1840 times as heavy—but still inconceivably light by ordinary standards. The three particles combine in an amazingly simple way to form the objects we see and feel. . . .

from "The Size of Things" in *Red Giants and White Dwarfs*
Robert Jastrow

2. But when the snow goose returned to its summer home, it was as though some kind of bar was up between them, and she did not come to the lighthouse. One year the bird did not return and Rhayader was heartbroken. All things seemed to have ended for him. He painted furiously through the winter and the next summer and never once saw the child. But in the fall the familiar cry once more rang from the sky, and the huge white bird, now at its full growth, dropped from the skies as mysteriously as it had departed. Joyously, Rhayader sailed

CONTINUED

his boat into Chelmsbury and left his message with the
postmistress.

from *The Snow Goose*
Paul Gallico

3. The American comes to with a start. In India, milk in a
bowl means only one thing—bait for a snake. He realizes
there must be a cobra in the room. He looks up at the
rafters—the likeliest place—but they are bare. Three
corners of the room are empty, and in the fourth the
servants are waiting to serve the next course. There is
only one place left—under the table.

from "The Dinner Party"
Mona Gardner

4. So great was the queen's role, however, that her time
became known as the Age of Elizabeth. Not only did
many fine musicians flower, but writers too, such as
Christopher Marlowe and John Donne and Ben Jonson
and Edmund Spenser. And above all, the incomparable
William Shakespeare, whose plays were sometimes
performed at court. Astronomers, naturalists,
mathematicians, geographers, and architects pioneered in
their fields.

from "Elizabeth I" in
Ten Queens: Portraits of Women in Power
Milton Meltzer

5. I also learned on the court. During a tournament at
Barraud Park in Norfolk, I had won the first set against
another boy my age and was leading in the second when I
started feeling sorry for him. It happens all the time
among club players, but not on the prize-money tour
anymore. I decided to let my opponent win a few games
by making a few intentional errors. I lost the second set,
was down, 2-0, in the third, and then began to panic. I

CONTINUED

tried to come back, but the more I pressed, the more mistakes I made. I lost the third set—and the match. My opponent was elated; I was in tears, angry at myself. It was an important lesson. . . .

from *Off the Court*
Arthur Ashe

EXERCISE 14
Understanding Methods of Organization
Tell which method of organization you think would be best for each of the following writing purposes.

1. to list reasons why smoking is harmful to your health
2. to describe the placement of the military units at the Battle of Gettysburg
3. to explain how to tie a shoe
4. to discuss two books you recently read
5. to explain why the minimum wage should be raised.
6. to explain the contributions John Adams made to the American Revolution.
7. to describe the buildings in an old gold mine ghost town
8. to discuss the platforms of the Democratic and Republican parties
9. to explain what happened in the ninth inning of a baseball game
10. to explain the consequences of not preparing for a speech

EXERCISE 15
Using Different Methods of Organization in Your Writing
Select one of the topics from Exercise 14 and write a paragraph using the method of organization that you think will best present the subject matter.

UNIT 20 REVIEW

TEST YOUR KNOWLEDGE

Identifying the Main Idea in a Paragraph

Identify the stated or unstated main idea in each of the following paragraphs, all of which are literary excerpts. If the main idea is stated in a topic sentence, identify the topic sentence. If the main idea is unstated, write the main idea in your own words. (10 points)

Literature
M O D E L S

1. When I had made an end of these labors, it was four o'clock—still dark as midnight. As the bell sounded the hour, there came a knocking at the street door. I went down to open it with a light heart,—for what had I *now* to fear? There entered three men, who introduced themselves, with perfect suavity, as officers of the police. A shriek had been heard by a neighbor during the night; suspicion of foul play had been aroused; information had been lodged at the police office, and they (the officers) had been deputed to search the premises.

from "The Tell-Tale Heart"
Edgar Allan Poe

2. When I got national recognition as a tennis player in my senior year in high school, it was an important step in my personal campaign to overcome assumptions of inequality. But I also knew that no one in Richmond's white tennis establishment had done anything to help me to get where I was. My memories and experiences about Richmond remain firmly rooted in the 1960s. The support I got—from teachers, relatives, and people like Ron Charity and Dr. Johnson—prepared me for the life I would lead outside the South.

from *Off the Court*
Arthur Ashe

CONTINUED

3. I rose and made my way to the kitchen, the Great Beast padding along behind me. On the floor were three dishes. One had held canned dog food, a second dry dog food and the third water. They were all empty, licked shiny, and I took the sack of dry food down and filled one of the bowls.

from "Caesar the Giant"
Gary Paulsen in *My Life in Dog Years*

4. As it happens, some of the most disturbing images of environmental destruction can be found exactly halfway between the North and South poles—precisely at the equator in Brazil—where billowing clouds of smoke regularly blacken the sky above the immense but now threatened Amazon rain forest. Acre by acre, the rain forest is being burned to create fast pasture for fast-food beef; as I learned when I went there in early 1989, the fires are set earlier and earlier in the dry season now, with more than one Tennessee's worth of rain forest being slashed and burned each year. According to our guide, the biologist Tom Lovejoy, there are more different species of birds in each square mile of the Amazon than exist in all of North America—which means we are silencing thousands of songs we never have even heard.

from "Ships in the Desert"
Al Gore

5. When I was your age, I was flying. I wasn't flying all the time, of course, and I didn't fly by myself, but there I was, nonetheless, on Saturday afternoons in the 1950s, several thousand feet in the air over the state of Connecticut, which is where I grew up. I sat in the back cockpit of a small airplane and looked down at the forests and the fields and the houses and the roads below me from an intense, vibrating height and hoped that my father, in the front cockpit, would not notice that I had cotton balls stuffed in my ears.

from "Flying"
Reeve Lindbergh

EXERCISE 2
Understanding the Paragraph
Complete each of the following sentences. (10 points)

1. A paragraph is a carefully organized group of _____ related.
2. Sentences in a paragraph focus on or develop one _____.
3. Most effective paragraphs have a _____ that is developed with _____.
4. Paragraphs can serve different purposes—to describe, to narrate, to _____, or to inform.
5. All effective paragraphs share two key elements: _____ and a logical method of organization.

EXERCISE 3
Understanding Topic Sentences and Supporting Details
For items 1–5, write a topic sentence for each group of supporting details. For items 6–10 write two supporting details for each topic sentence. (20 points)

1. The wind suddenly picked up. A chill pervaded the night air. The horses galloped nervously out in the field.
2. A thick green jungle spread out in front of us. Behind us across the gorge, Prince Hoku's warriors cautiously eyed the fragile rope bridge. I put my torch to the cords on our side. There would be no turning back.
3. At the bottom of the stacks a book had been pushed back a couple of inches. I pried it out and blew off the dust. Its ancient cover was cracked, but the title was legible. The book-burning committee had not destroyed all of my great-grandfather's works.
4. Toe touches are exercises that can be helpful before playing softball. Calf raises and hamstring stretches also help loosen the leg muscles. A slow jog to the outfield fence and back is another good preparation.

5. Thousands of Japanese Americans were confined to interment camps during World War II. None of them were proved to be disloyal. In fact, many Japanese-American men served in the U.S. Army and fought bravely in Europe.
6. It is important to regularly water newly planted grass seed.
7. I like to read for a half-hour each night before I go to bed.
8. Harrison Park downtown should have better lighting at night.
9. The author was very productive last year.
10. Our dog and cat are not getting along.

E X E R C I S E 4
Understanding Different Kinds of Supporting Details
For each kind of supporting detail, write a sentence that supports the topic sentence: *Our town (or city) has many great attractions.* (10 points)

1. example/illustration
2. sensory details
3. anecdote
4. fact
5. quotation

E X E R C I S E 5
Using Different Types of Paragraphs and Methods of Organization in Your Writing
Write five different paragraphs, following the directions for each. Use at least one transition in each paragraph. (10 points each)

1. narrative paragraph organized in chronological order
2. informative paragraph organized in cause and effect order
3. informative paragraph organized in comparison and contrast order
4. persuasive paragraph organized in order of importance
5. descriptive paragraph organized in spatial order

UNIT *21* THE WRITING PROCESS

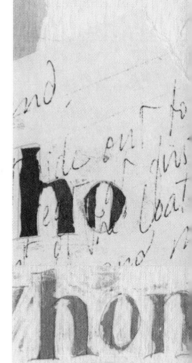

THE WRITING PROCESS

THE SIX STAGES IN THE WRITING PROCESS

How do you begin to tackle a new writing project? Do you bravely dive in with both hands on the keyboard? Do you grab pen and paper and start jotting down ideas? Or do you let an idea simmer for a few days? All writers—whether they are beginning writers, famous published writers, or somewhere in between—go through a process of writing that leads to a complete piece of writing. The specifics of each writer's process may be unique, but for every writer, writing is a series of steps or stages. In this unit you'll learn about the six stages in the writing process and about strategies and ideas for putting them into action.

Here is a brief overview of the six stages in the writing process.

 tip

Before reading this unit, you may want to review the sections "Types of Paragraphs" and "Methods of Organization" in Unit 20 on pages 449–456.

Quotables

"When you're young, you think you have all the time in the world. You don't. Don't wait to be inspired. Just write."
—Virginia Hamilton

SIX STAGES IN THE WRITING PROCESS	
Stage	**Tasks**
1. **Prewriting**	Plan your writing; choose a topic, audience, purpose, and form; gather ideas; and arrange them logically.
2. **Drafting**	Get your ideas down on paper.
3. **Self- and Peer Evaluation**	Evaluate, or judge, the writing piece and suggest ways to improve it. Judging your own writing is called self-evaluation. Judging a classmate's writing is called peer evaluation.
4. **Revising and Proofreading**	Work to improve the content, organization, and expression of your ideas. Check your writing for errors in spelling, grammar, capitalization, and punctuation. Correct these errors, make a final copy of your paper, and proofread it again.
5. **Publishing and Presenting**	Share your work with an audience.
6. **Reflecting**	Think through the writing process to determine what you learned as a writer, what you accomplished, and what you would like to strengthen the next time you write.

Writers move through these stages when creating a work, but writing is also a continuing cycle. For example, to strengthen your work, you may need to return to a previous stage before proceeding to the next one. Understanding the six stages of the writing process—from prewriting to reflecting—will help you to become a better writer.

/ PREWRITING

Think of prewriting—the first step in the writing process—as the stage that helps you answer the question, "Where do I begin?" During the prewriting stage, you identify your topic, purpose, audience, and form of writing.

Identifying and Focusing a Topic

In school, writing topics are often assigned to you, or you may be instructed to choose your own topic. When you're unsure of what to write about, here are some techniques you can use to find an interesting topic.

WAYS TO FIND A WRITING TOPIC	
Check your journal	Search through your journal for ideas that you jotted down in the past. Many professional writers get their ideas from their journals.
Think about your experiences	Think about people, places, or events that affected you strongly. Recall experiences that taught you important lessons or that you felt strongly about.
Look at reference works	Reference works include printed or computerized dictionaries, atlases, almanacs, and encyclopedias.
Browse in a library	Libraries are treasure houses of information and ideas. Simply looking around in the stacks of a library can suggest good writing ideas.

EXAMPLES

writing topic ideas
invention of the radio
tornadoes
Vietnam Veterans Memorial
the roaring twenties
pop artist Andy Warhol
dinosaurs in the Mesozoic era

Often a new writing topic is too general and broad or becomes too big to handle—especially if you're excited about the topic and gushing with ideas about what you'd like to say. Here are a few ways you can focus your writing topic.

Break the Topic into Parts. Break down your topic into a series of smaller parts or subtopics.

EXAMPLE

general topic   the roaring twenties
possible subtopics changes in women's lives, progress of technology, urban social problems, cultural achievements

Ask Questions about the Topic. Write down questions about your topic. Begin your questions with the words *who, what, where, when, why,* and *how.* Then ask yourself what stands out about the topic and what interests you most.

EXAMPLES

Who were some of the famous figures during the 1920s?

What were some of the cultural achievements of the decade?

Where were women testing their new personal freedoms?

When did women earn the right to vote?

Why did many social problems develop in urban areas?

How did certain inventions and new technologies in the period change American society?

Make a Cluster Chart. Write your general topic in the middle of a piece of paper. Draw a circle around this topic. Draw more circles branching out from your center circle, and fill them with subtopics related to your main topic.

Writing tip

Highlight the subtopics that interest you the most. Then break down those topics into smaller parts until you've identified and focused your writing topic.

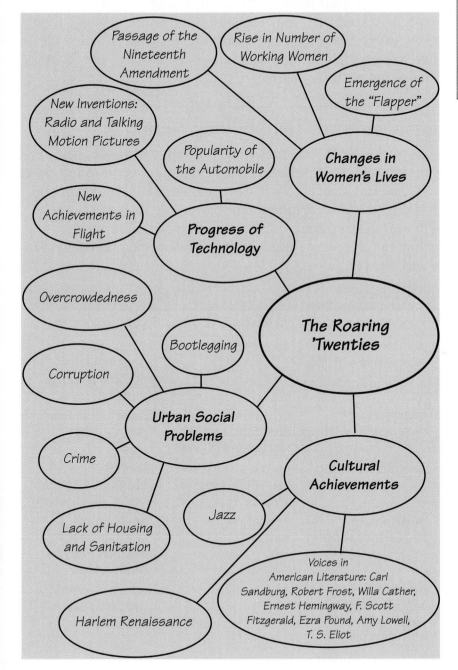

Passage of the Nineteenth Amendment

Rise in Number of Working Women

Emergence of the "Flapper"

New Inventions: Radio and Talking Motion Pictures

Popularity of the Automobile

Changes in Women's Lives

New Achievements in Flight

Progress of Technology

Overcrowdedness

Bootlegging

The Roaring 'Twenties

Corruption

Urban Social Problems

Cultural Achievements

Crime

Jazz

Lack of Housing and Sanitation

Voices in American Literature: Carl Sandburg, Robert Frost, Willa Cather, Ernest Hemingway, F. Scott Fitzgerald, Ezra Pound, Amy Lowell, T. S. Eliot

Harlem Renaissance

Writing tip

Ask yourself: *Why am I writing?* The answer to this question will help you identify your purpose.

EXERCISE 1

Understanding How to Identify and Focus a Topic

Flip through your journal, think about your personal experiences, and ask yourself questions beginning with *who, what, where, when, why,* and *how.* Then make a list of at least five writing topic ideas. Select one of these topics and focus it by making a cluster chart.

Quotables

"Writing comes more easily if you have something to say."
—Shalom Asch

Identifying Your Purpose for Writing

The goal of your writing is to accomplish a **purpose**, or aim. For example, your purpose for writing might be to reflect on a personal experience, to tell a story, to entertain, to inform, or to persuade. Your writing might have more than one purpose. For example, a piece of writing might inform your readers about an important event while persuading them to respond in a specific way.

MODES AND PURPOSES OF WRITING		
MODE	**PURPOSE**	**WRITING FORMS**
personal/ expressive writing	to reflect	diary entry, personal letter, autobiography, personal essay
imaginative/ descriptive writing	to entertain, to describe, to enrich, and to enlighten	poem, character sketch, play
narrative writing	to tell a story, to narrate a series of events	short story, biography, legend, myth, history
informative/ expository writing	to inform, to explain	news article, research report, expository essay, book review
persuasive/ argumentative writing	to persuade	editorial, petition, political speech, persuasive essay

EXERCISE 2
Understanding How to Identify Your Purpose for Writing
Review the list of five general topics you identified in Exercise
1. For each of the general topics and for your focused topic,
identify a suitable purpose and mode.

Identifying Your Audience

An **audience** is the person or group of people intended to read
what you write. For example, you might write for yourself, a
friend, a relative, or your classmates. The best writing usually is
intended for a specific audience. Choosing a specific audience
before writing will help you make important decisions about
your work. For an audience of young children, for example,
you would use simple words and ideas. For an audience of your
peers in an athletic group, you would use jargon and other
specialized words that your peers already know. For an adult
audience, you would use more formal language.

Use the following questions to help identify your audience.

- Who will be most interested in my topic? What are their
  values?
- How much do they already know about the topic?
- What background information do they need in order to
  understand my ideas and point of view?
- What words, phrases, or concepts will I need to define for
  my audience?
- How can I capture my audience's interest from the very
  start?

EXERCISE 3
Understanding How to Identify Your Audience
Keep your focused topic in mind. Then write down your
answers to each of the questions above. After answering the
questions, write a brief description of your audience.

Choosing a Form of Writing

Another important decision that a writer needs to make is what form his or her writing will take. A **form** is a kind of writing. Once you've identified your topic, your purpose for writing, and your audience, a particular form of writing may become immediately obvious as the perfect one to convey your ideas. But, sometimes, an unexpected choice of form may be even more effective in presenting your topic. The following chart lists some of the many different forms of writing.

FORMS OF WRITING		
Adventure	Experiment	Petition
Advertisement	Fable	Play
Advice column	Family history	Police/Accident
Agenda	Fantasy	report
Apology	Greeting card	Poster
Appeal	Headline	Proposal
Autobiography	History	Radio or TV spot
Biography	Human interest story	Rap
Book review	Instructions	Recipe
Brochure	Interview questions	Recommendation
Calendar	Invitation	Research report
Caption	Itinerary	Résumé
Cartoon	Joke	Schedule
Character sketch	Journal entry	Science fiction
Cheer	Letter	Short story
Children's story	Magazine article	Slide show
Comedy	Memorandum	Slogan
Consumer report	Menu	Song lyric
Debate	Minutes	Speech
Detective story	Movie review	Sports story
Dialogue	Mystery	Statement of belief
Directions	Myth	Summary
Dream report	Narrative	Tall tale
Editorial	Newspaper article	Thank-you note
Epitaph	Obituary	Tour guide
Essay	Parable	Want ad
Eulogy	Paraphrase	Wish list

EXERCISE 4

Understanding How to Choose a Form of Writing

Now that you've identified your topic, purpose and mode, and audience, select from the chart the two possible forms of writing that you think would work best. Select one form that seems obvious. For example, if your purpose is to tell a story, select the short story as a form. Then, for your second choice, select a form that is unexpected or surprising. Write a brief explanation of why you think both of the forms would work well.

EXERCISE 5

Understanding Different Forms of Writing

Sometimes what you know first about a piece of writing is its form. A specific form may be assigned to you by your teacher, or you just may want to experiment with a different writing form. Select one of the writing forms from the chart, perhaps one that you've never used before or one that especially interests and intrigues you. Then apply what you've learned so far about prewriting to identify a topic, purpose, and audience specifically for that form of writing.

Gathering Ideas

After you have identified your topic, purpose, audience, and form, the next step in the prewriting stage is to gather ideas. There are many ways to gather ideas for writing. This section will introduce you to some of the most useful strategies.

Brainstorming. When you **brainstorm**, you think of as many ideas as you can, as quickly as you can, without stopping to evaluate or criticize the ideas. Anything goes—no idea should be rejected in the brainstorming stage. Sometimes even silly-sounding ideas can lead to productive results.

Writing tip

When you brainstorm in a group, one person's idea will often help another person to build on that concept. Welcome all ideas with an encouraging response.

Learning from Professional Models. Professional models are works by published authors. They can be an excellent way to shape your own ideas. For example, if you are interested in topics related to the progress and impact of technology in the 1920s, you might be impressed by the way Gia Marie Garbinsky relates Charles Lindbergh's achievements in flight in "The Spirit of Charles Lindbergh." Notice how Garbinsky uses a firsthand account to conveys the drama and importance of Lindbergh's historic solo flight.

Literature
MODEL

> During the hours that Lindbergh traveled alone across the Atlantic, the world waited, desperately hoping. In his nationally syndicated newspaper column on the afternoon of May 20, 1927, Will Rogers wrote:
>
> > No attempt at jokes today. A . . . slim, tall, bashful, smiling American boy is somewhere over the middle of the Atlantic Ocean, where no lone human being has ever ventured before. He is being prayed for to every kind of Supreme Being that had a following. If he is lost it will be the most universally regretted loss we ever had (Berg 121).
>
> from "The Spirit of Charles Lindbergh"
> Gia Marie Garbinsky

Keeping a Journal. A **journal** is a record of your ideas, dreams, wishes, and experiences. Composition books, spiral notebooks, loose-leaf binders, and bound books with blank pages all make excellent journal books. You may want to use a journal to write thoughts, collect ideas for writing, organize tasks, or keep a learning log. A journal is very handy to be able to turn to when you're looking for writing ideas.

Quotables

"Freewriting is writing as fast as you can for ten minutes, without worrying about grammar, spelling, or punctuation."
—Patricia Cumming

Freewriting. Freewriting is simply taking a pencil and paper and writing whatever comes into your mind. Try to write for several minutes without stopping and without worrying about spelling, grammar, usage, or mechanics. If you get stuck, just repeat the last few words until something new pops into your mind.

EXAMPLE
The motion-picture industry boomed in the 1920s (talking pictures introduced later—1927? 1930?) with the silent, flickering images of such stars as Mary Pickford, Douglas Fairbanks, Gloria Swanson, Clara Bow, and Charlie Chaplin. What did the new technology of motion pictures promise these moviegoers? Perhaps a chance to escape from their own lives for a little while.

Clustering. Another good way to tap into what you already know is to make a **cluster chart**. To make a cluster chart, draw a circle in the center of your paper. In it write a topic you want to explore. Draw more circles branching out from your center circle, and fill them with subtopics related to your main topic. Review the example in "Identifying and Focusing a Topic" on page 465.

Questioning. Ask the **reporting questions** *who, what, where, when, why,* and *how* about your topic. This questioning strategy is especially useful for gathering information about an event or for planning a story.

Imagining. If you are doing imaginative or creative writing, ask questions that begin with the words *what if.* "What if" questions can spark your imagination and lead you down unexpected and interesting paths. They can also help you to see another side of events and issues.

EXAMPLES
What if the entertainment provided by motion pictures wasn't so easily available?

What if Americans needed to rely more on themselves to create their own amusements?

What if the technology for motion pictures and "talking pictures" hadn't been invented?

Completing Venn Diagrams. If you are writing a comparison and contrast essay, one of the best ways to gather ideas is by completing a Venn diagram. A **Venn diagram** shows two slightly overlapping circles. The outer part of each circle shows what aspects of two things are different from each other. The inner, or shared, part of each circle shows what aspects the two things share.

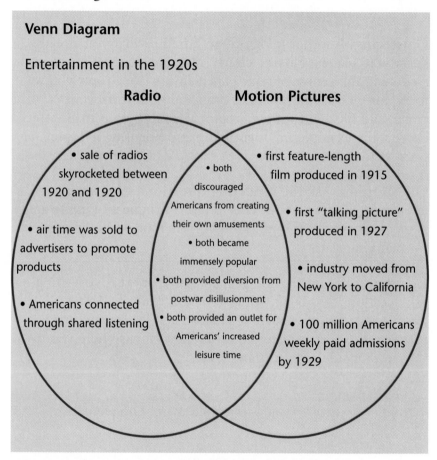

Venn Diagram

Entertainment in the 1920s

Radio

Motion Pictures

- sale of radios skyrocketed between 1920 and 1920

- air time was sold to advertisers to promote products

- Americans connected through shared listening

- both discouraged Americans from creating their own amusements
- both became immensely popular
- both provided diversion from postwar disillusionment
- both provided an outlet for Americans' increased leisure time

- first feature-length film produced in 1915

- first "talking picture" produced in 1927

- industry moved from New York to California

- 100 million Americans weekly paid admissions by 1929

Creating a Sensory Detail Chart. A **sensory detail chart** helps you to collect information about details that you can describe through the use of the five major senses: sight, sound, touch, taste, and smell.

Sensory Detail Chart for Description of 1920s Movie Experience				
SIGHT	SOUND	TOUCH	TASTE	SMELL
hundreds of people in line at ticket booths young women dressed in "flapper" fashions glass ticket booth with sign in window "5¢" darkness of the theater flicker of shadow and light flashlight of usher	tinny sound of the player piano audience's laughter, cries, etc. whispers candy being unwrapped	smooth surface of the small, printed ticket the bump of knees and stub of toes as people find their way to vacant seats	sugary flavor of penny candies	perspiration perfume slight burning scent from heat of projector

Creating a Time Line. A time line can be useful when you are planning to write a story or a historical account. A **time line** gives you an overview of the sequence of events during a particular time period. To make a time line, draw a line on a piece of paper and divide it into equal parts. Label each part with a date or a time. Then add key events at the right places along the time line.

Time Line

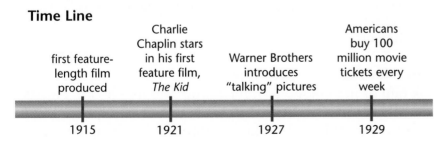

Creating a Story Map. A **story map** is a chart that shows the various parts of a fable, myth, tall tale, legend, short story, or other fictional work. Most story maps include the following elements:

ELEMENTS OF A STORY MAP	
Element	**Description**
setting	the time and place in which the story occurs
mood	the emotion created in the reader by the story
conflict	a struggle between two forces in the story
plot	the series of events taking place in the story
characters	the people (or sometimes animals) who play roles in the story
theme	the main idea of the story

Creating a Pro and Con Chart. A **pro and con** chart shows arguments for and against taking a particular position on some issue. To create a pro and con chart, begin by writing a statement, called a proposition, at the top of a piece of paper. Under the proposition, make two columns, one labeled *Pro* and the other, *Con*. In the *Pro* column, list arguments in favor of the proposition. In the *Con* column, list arguments against the proposition.

PRO AND CON CHART	
Proposition: Original film of early movies should be preserved.	
Pro	**Con**
—would provide rich, cultural archive of history of motion pictures —would provide education and research for film students	—might be expensive to fund —might be too late to preserve some of the more damaged film reels

Interviewing. In an **interview**, you meet with someone and ask him or her questions. Interviewing people who are experts or authorities on a particular topic is an excellent way to gain information. When planning an interview, list the questions you would like to ask, including some about the person's background as well as about your topic. Other questions might occur to you as the interview proceeds.

Researching for Ideas. No matter what your topic is, you can probably find information about it by doing research in **reference works**. Reference works include encyclopedias, dictionaries, almanacs, atlases, indexes, Internet sites, and others.

Try It Yourself

EXERCISE 6
Using Strategies to Gather Ideas
Select two of the strategies to gather ideas about your writing topic—one strategy for the more obvious form and another strategy for the more unexpected or surprising form of writing you selected in Exercise 4. Carry out both strategies to gather ideas for your topic.

Organizing Ideas

How will you present the information you've gathered? After you have gathered ideas for a piece of writing, the next step is to organize these ideas in a useful and reader-friendly way. The most basic organization of ideas occurs in forming paragraphs. As you learned in Unit 20, a good paragraph is a carefully organized unit of writing. Review Unit 20 for information on topic sentences, paragraph unity, main ideas and supporting details, and methods of organization.

Outlining. Outlines can also help you organize your ideas. An **outline** is often an excellent framework for highlighting main ideas and supporting details. Rough and formal outlines are the two main types of outlines writers commonly use. To create a **rough outline**, simply list your main ideas in some logical order. Under each main idea, list the supporting details set off by dashes. A **formal outline** has headings and subheadings identified by numbers and letters. One type of formal outline is the **topic outline**. Such an outline has entries

Writing tip

Many of the graphic organizers that you learned to use to gather information, such as the Venn diagram and story map, are also helpful in organizing information. They can help you to organize points to compare and contrast, to organize events in sequential order, and to record the steps in a process.

that are words or phrases rather than complete sentences. In the following topic outline, the writer has listed a progression of ideas she'd like to include in her informative essay about the early years of the film industry.

EXAMPLE
Movies: The Early Years
— Introduction: set scene for popularity of films (use Chaplin quote)
— Brief history of young motion-picture industry
  — first feature-length film
  — move from New York to southern California
  — introduction of "talking" pictures
— Reasons for popularity of films
  — more leisure time available to people
  — money for entertainment also available because of postwar prosperity
  — escape from postwar disillusionment provided
— Evaluation of impact of early years of film

Try It Yourself

EXERCISE 7
Understanding How to Organize Your Ideas
Use what you learned about paragraphs in Unit 20 and the information you gathered in Exercise 6 to create a rough outline or topic outline for the subject you've been exploring in this unit's exercises. List your main ideas, using an appropriate method of organization, such as time/chronological, place/spatial, order of importance, comparison and contrast, or cause and effect.

Writing tip

If you've selected a structured form of writing, such as a research paper or a problem-solution essay, you may want to create your draft from a plan, such as a formal outline.

2 DRAFTING

After you have gathered your information and organized it, the next step in writing is to produce a draft. A **draft** is simply an early attempt at writing—at getting your ideas down on paper. Different writers approach drafting in different ways. Some prefer to work slowly and carefully from a plan or to create a careful draft that is perfected, part by part. Others like to see where their ideas lead them by writing a discovery draft in which they get all their ideas down on paper in rough form and then go back over the ideas to shape and focus them.

Drafting an Introduction

The purpose of an introduction is to capture your reader's attention and establish what you want to say. Think about the kinds of things that capture your attention when you're reading and thereby hook you to keep on reading. Some effective introduction openers include a quote, question, anecdote, fact, or description. The following literature model is the opening paragraph from Gia Marie Garbinsky's "The Spirit of Charles Lindbergh." Notice how Garbinsky uses facts to establish the historic time and place of the dramatic event and to support her main idea.

Quotables

"Almost all good writing begins with terrible first efforts. You need to start somewhere. Start by getting something— anything—down on paper."
—Anne Lamott

Literature
M O D E L

Charles Lindbergh packed into one lifetime enough adventure, excitement, heartbreak, and conflict for ten lifetimes. On May 20, 1927, Lindbergh's famous plane, the *Spirit of St. Louis*, left the ground of Long Island, New York. Less than 34 hours later Lindbergh landed, becoming the first person to fly solo across the Atlantic Ocean from New York to Paris, France. The moment his plane touched down in Paris, he became one of the most famous and popular men of the twentieth century. Waiting for him were huge parades, parties, invitations to visit with kings and presidents, and offers to star in movies. Lindbergh, however, had made the flight for different reasons—a passion and respect for aviation (Lindbergh, *Autobiography* 13-14).

from "The Spirit of Charles Lindbergh"
Gia Marie Garbinsky

In the following draft of an introduction, the writer uses facts and descriptive details to set the scene and establish the main idea for her informative essay.

EXAMPLE

By the 1920s millions of people throughout America eagerly exchanged their nickels for movie tickets on Saturday afternoons. Even though the motion-picture camera had been invented in 1895, it wasn't until the 1910s and 1920s that silent films achieved greater length and complexity and featured the silent, flickering images of such stars as Mary Pickford, Douglas Fairbanks, Gloria Swanson, Clara Bow, and Charlie Chaplin. Although the novelty of motion pictures soon wore off, their popularity with the American public boomed. Among the causes behind the popularity of this new form of entertainment were an increase in leisure time, the return of prosperity after World War I, and a growing sense of disillusionment.

Try It Yourself

EXERCISE 8

Understanding How to Draft an Introduction
Draft an introduction for your topic, using a quotation, fact, question, anecdote, or description.

Drafting Body Paragraphs

When writing the body of an essay or another form of structured writing, refer to the outline you created in Exercise 7. Use each heading in your outline as the main idea of one of your paragraphs. To connect ideas for your reader and to move smoothly from one idea to the next, use transitions. Whether you are writing a persuasive essay or a narrative poem, include details—in the form of evidence, facts, sensory description, and so on—to support and develop your main idea.

Writing tip

> Transitions are words and phrases that help you connect and move smoothly from one idea to the next in your writing. Before writing Exercise 9, you may want to review transitions in Unit 20 on page 447.

In the following excerpt from "The Spirit of Charles Lindbergh," Gia Marie Garbinsky wrote this body paragraph to explain the series of events behind Lindbergh's flight across the Atlantic Ocean. Notice how she uses transitions that show time/chronological order.

At the age of 20, Lindbergh enrolled at a flying school in Nebraska. He enlisted in the U.S. Army in 1924, and the next year he became chief pilot on an airmail route between St. Louis, Missouri, and Chicago, Illinois. On one of these flights, he imagined crossing the Atlantic Ocean by air. A few years earlier, a New York hotel owner had offered $25,000 to the person who could complete the first transatlantic flight from New York to Paris. Other pilots had made shorter flights across the Atlantic Ocean. A few men even had tried the flight from New York to Paris—but none had made it (Muha 100). Lindbergh persuaded a group of St. Louis businessmen to invest in his venture. Working with an aircraft company, he designed the *Spirit of St. Louis*, the plane that would carry him across the Atlantic.

from "The Spirit of Charles Lindbergh"
Gia Marie Garbinsky

Try It Yourself

EXERCISE 9
Understanding How to Draft Body Paragraphs
Write two body paragraphs to follow your introduction. Use transitions to connect your ideas, and use a method of organization to present your ideas effectively.

Drafting a Conclusion

In the conclusion, bring together the main ideas you included in the body of your essay and create a sense of closure to the topic you presented. There is no single right way to conclude a piece of writing. Possibilities include the following:

- making a generalization
- restating the main idea and supporting ideas in different words
- summarizing the points made in the rest of the essay
- drawing a lesson or moral

- calling on the reader to adopt a point of view or take action
- expanding on your main idea by connecting it to the reader's own interests
- linking your topic to a larger issue or concern

In the closing paragraph of the essay "The Spirit of Charles Lindbergh," Garbinsky connects current events in Lindbergh's life with his historic transatlantic flight.

Literature
MODEL

In 1977, a half-century after Lindbergh's transatlantic flight, the Charles A. Lindbergh Fund was established. In 1994 the name of the organization became the Charles A. and Anne Morrow Lindbergh Foundation to recognize the "shared vision" and "devoted partnership they formed in pioneering aviation, exploration, conservation, writing, and philosophy." The foundation's mission is to encourage an equal relationship between technological advancement and environmental preservation.

from "The Spirit of Charles Lindbergh"
Gia Marie Garbinsky

USAGE tip

Remember to use quotation marks when directly quoting a statement.

Try It Yourself

EXERCISE 10
Understanding How to Draft a Conclusion
Draft a conclusion for your topic. Even though you haven't yet written all the body paragraphs, use your outline to guide you in writing your conclusion.

Writing tip

It's a good idea to set aside your writing for a day or two. Then read your work with a fresh pair of eyes.

3 SELF- AND PEER EVALUATION

When you evaluate something, you examine it carefully to find its strengths and weaknesses. Evaluating your own writing is called **self-evaluation**. A **peer evaluation** is an evaluation of a piece of writing done by a classmate, or peer. The following tips can help you become a helpful peer reader, learn to give and receive criticism, and improve your writing.

Tips for evaluating a piece of writing:

- **Check for content.** Is the content, including the main idea, clear? Have any important details been left out? Do unimportant or unrelated details confuse the main point? Are the main idea and supporting details clearly connected to one another?
- **Check for organization.** Are the ideas in the written work presented in a logical order?
- **Check the style and language.** Is the language appropriately formal or informal? Is the tone appropriate for the audience and purpose? Have any key or unfamiliar terms been defined?

Tips for delivering helpful criticism:

- **Be focused.** Concentrate on content, organization, and style. At this point, do not focus on proofreading matters such as spelling and punctuation; they can be corrected during the proofreading stage.
- **Be positive.** Respect the writer's feelings and genuine writing efforts. Tell the writer what you like about his or her work. Answer the writer's questions in a positive manner. In a tactful and positive manner, present any changes you are suggesting.
- **Be specific.** Give the writer concrete ideas for improving his or her work.

Tips for benefiting from helpful criticism:

- **Tell your peer evaluator your specific concerns and questions.** If you are unsure whether you've clearly presented an idea, ask the evaluator how he or she might restate the idea.
- **Ask questions to clarify comments that your evaluator makes.** When you clarify, make sure you understand your evaluator's comments.
- **Accept your evaluator's comments graciously.** Criticism can often be helpful, but you don't have to use any or all of the suggestions.

Writing tip

Ask a peer to summarize briefly the main idea(s) of your piece of writing. This is a good test to find out if you've expressed your ideas clearly.

Quotables

"No passion in the world is equal to the passion to alter someone else's draft."
—H. G. Wells

EXERCISE 11

Understanding How to Evaluate Writing

Select a completed work or your current draft-in-progress to exchange with another student for evaluation. Provide your peer evaluator with a clean copy of your writing, and give your evaluator enough time to read and respond to your work. While the peer evaluator is reviewing your work, self-evaluate the same piece of writing. Compare your own comments with those of the peer evaluator. What strengths did each of you recognize? What weaknesses did each of you identify?

---

4 REVISING AND PROOFREADING

After identifying weaknesses in a draft through self-evaluation and peer evaluation, the next step in the process is to **revise** and **proofread** the draft. Here are four basic ways to revise your writing to improve meaning and content.

Adding or Expanding. Sometimes writing can be improved by adding details, examples, or transitions to connect ideas. Often a single detail will provide the necessary support for an idea or an adjective can make a piece of writer clearer or more vivid.

Quotables

"Master the tools of writing. I know that spelling, punctuation, and grammar are boring, but they are necessary."
—Beverly Cleary

EXAMPLE
draft
There are a number of great films from the silent film era.

revision
The numerous great films from the silent era include such classics as *The Cabinet of Dr. Caligari, Nanook of the North,* and *The Gold Rush.*

Cutting or Condensing. Often writing can be improved by cutting unnecessary or unrelated material. For example, too many adjectives or adverbs may be included in a draft.

EXAMPLE
draft
Early directors that directed the silent films included D. W. Griffith, Sergei Eisenstein, Fritz Lange, and Charlie Chaplin.

revision
Directors of silent films included D. W. Griffith, Sergei Eisenstein, Fritz Lange, and Charlie Chaplin.

Replacing. Replace weak writing with words and phrases that are active, more concrete, more vivid, and more precise.

EXAMPLE
draft
The Russian film director Sergei Eisenstein made many contributions to the development of cinema.

revision
The Russian film director Sergei Eisenstein is noted for his innovative use of editing and film montage, particularly in the film *Potemkin*.

Moving. Often you can improve the organization of your writing by moving part of it so that related ideas appear near one another.

EXAMPLE
draft
One of the most memorable characters from the silent film era is Charlie Chaplin's sentimental and melodramatic Tramp. Even when the silent film era ended, Chaplin refused to appear in sound films and continued to play the role of the Tramp in the later silent films *City Lights* and *Modern Times*. Moviegoers immediately recognized and identified with the Tramp, who represented the underdog in his ill-fitting suit, floppy shoes, bowler hat, and cane.

revision
One of the most memorable characters from the silent film era is Charlie Chaplin's sentimental and melodramatic Tramp.

CONTINUED

> Moviegoers immediately recognized and identified with the Tramp, who represented the underdog in his ill-fitting suit, floppy shoes, bowler hat, and cane. Even when the silent film era ended, Chaplin refused to appear in sound films and continued to play the role of the Tramp in the later silent films *City Lights* and *Modern Times*.

After you've revised the draft, ask yourself a series of questions. Think of these questions as your "revision checklist."

REVISION CHECKLIST

Content
- Does the writing achieve its purpose?
- Are the main ideas clearly stated and supported by details?

Organization
- Are the ideas arranged in a sensible order?
- Are the ideas connected to one another within paragraphs and between paragraphs?

Style
- Is the language appropriate to the audience and purpose?
- Is the mood appropriate to the purpose of the writing?

When you proofread your writing, you read it through to look for errors and mark corrections. When you mark corrections to your writing, use the standard proofreading symbols as shown in the following chart.

PROOFREADER'S SYMBOLS

Symbol and Example	Meaning of Symbol
The very first time	Delete (cut) this material.
cat cradle	Insert (add) something that is missing.
George	Replace this letter or word.
All the horses king's	Move this word to where the arrow points.
french toast	Capitalize this letter.
the vice-President	Lowercase this letter.
housse	Take out this letter and close up space.
book keeper	Close up space.

CONTINUED

ge**b**ril	Change the order of these letters.
end⸠"Watch out," she yelled.	Begin a new paragraph.
Love conquers all⸠	Put a period here.
Welcome⸠friends.	Put a comma here.
Ge⎮the stopwatch	Put a space here.
Dear Madam⸠	Put a colon here.
She walked⸠he rode.	Put a semicolon here.
name⸗brand products	Put a hyphen here.
cat⸠s meow	Put an apostrophe here.
cat's cradle (s+e+t)	Let it stand. (Leave as it is.)

After you have revised your draft, make a clean copy of it and proofread it for errors in spelling, grammar, and punctuation. Use the following proofreading checklist.

PROOFREADING CHECKLIST	
Spelling	• Are all words, including names, spelled correctly?
Grammar	• Does each verb agree with its subject? • Are verb tenses consistent and correct? • Are irregular verbs formed correctly? • Are there any sentence fragments or run-ons? • Have double negatives been avoided? • Have frequently confused words, such as *affect* and *effect*, been used correctly?
Punctuation	• Does every sentence end with an end mark? • Are commas used correctly? • Do all proper nouns and proper adjectives begin with capital letters?

After proofreading your draft, you will want to prepare your final manuscript. Follow the guidelines given by your teacher or the guidelines provided here. After preparing a final manuscript according to these guidelines, proofread it one last time for errors.

- Keyboard your manuscript using a typewriter or word processor, or write it neatly using blue or black ink.
- Double-space your paper.
- Use one side of the paper.
- Leave one-inch margins on all sides of the text.
- Indent the first line of each paragraph.
- Make a cover sheet listing the title of the work, your name, the date, and the class.
- In the upper right-hand corner of the first page, put your name, class, and date, On every page after the first, include the page number in the heading, as follows:

EXAMPLE
Melissa McKay
English 7
April 1, 2003
p. 2

Try It Yourself

EXERCISE 12
Understanding How to Revise a Draft
Use one or more of the four basic ways discussed above to revise your draft. After revising, take your draft through the revision checklist.

EXERCISE 13
Using Proofreading Marks
Proofread your revision for errors in spelling, grammar, punctuation, and capitalization. If you are unsure about a word's spelling, check it in a dictionary or use the spell-check on your computer. After proofreading your revision, prepare your final manuscript. Then proofread your manuscript one last time for errors.

5 PUBLISHING AND PRESENTING

In the **publishing and presenting** stage, you share your work with an audience. Some writing is done just for oneself—journal writing, for example. Most writing, however, is meant to be shared with others. There are many ways to share your work, among which are the following:

Keep a collection of all the pieces that you write in a writing portfolio. From time to time, examine the pieces in your portfolio and identify the improvements you have made in your writing.

- Submit the work to a local publication, such as a school literary magazine, school newspaper, or community newspaper.
- Submit the work to a regional or national publication.
- Enter the work in a contest.
- Read your work aloud to classmates, friends, or family members.
- Work with other students to prepare a publication—a brochure, online literary magazine, anthology, or newspaper.
- Prepare a poster or bulletin board, perhaps in collaboration with other students, to display your writing.
- Make your own book by typing or word processing the pages and binding them together.
- Hold an oral reading of student writing as a class or schoolwide project.
- Share your writing with other students in a small writers' group.

Try It Yourself

EXERCISE 14
Publishing and Presenting Your Work
After you've prepared your final manuscript, decide how you will share your work with others. Select one of the ways listed above in which to publish your work or present it to others.

6 REFLECTING

In the **reflecting** stage, you think through the writing process to determine what you learned as a writer, what you learned about your topic, how the writing process worked or didn't work for you, and what skills you would like to strengthen. Reflection can be done on a self-evaluation form, in small-group discussion, or simply in your own thoughts. By keeping a journal, however, you'll be able to keep track of your writing experience and pinpoint ways to make the writing process work better for you.

Here are some questions to ask as you reflect on the writing process and yourself as a writer:

"I cannot expect even my own art to provide all of the answers—only to hope it keeps asking the right questions."
—Grace Hartigan

- Which part of the writing process did I enjoy most and least? Why? Which part of the writing process was most difficult? least difficult? Why?
- What would I change about my approach to the writing process next time?
- What have I learned in writing about this topic?
- What have I learned by using this form?
- How have I developed as a writer while writing this piece?
- What strengths have I discovered in my work?
- What aspects of my writing do I want to strengthen? How can I strengthen them?

Try It Yourself

EXERCISE 15
Reflecting on Your Writing
Take yourself back through your experience with the writing process as you identified, focused, wrote, revised, and published and presented your manuscript. Did you remain interested in your topic throughout the process? Why, or why not? Is there another aspect of the topic you wish you had explored? Write the answers to these questions and those listed above as you reflect on the manuscript you wrote for this unit.

UNIT 21 REVIEW

TEST YOUR KNOWLEDGE

EXERCISE 1

Identifying the Stages in the Writing Process
Match each stage in the writing process with a description of
the tasks involved. (10 points)

__1. Prewriting

__2. Drafting

__3. Self- and Peer
Evaluation

__4. Revising and
Proofreading

__5. Publishing and
Presenting

__6. Reflecting

A. Work to improve the content
and organization. Check for
errors in spelling, grammar, and
capitalization.

B. Get your ideas down on paper.

C. Think through the writing
process.

D. Identify your topic, purpose,
form, audience; gather ideas;
organize your ideas.

E. Review your own work or a
classmate's and suggest ways to
improve it.

F. Share your work with an
audience.

EXERCISE 2

Understanding Modes and Purposes of Writing
Write a brief description of the purpose(s) for each of the
following modes of writing. (10 points)

1. personal/expressive writing
2. imaginative/descriptive writing
3. narrative writing
4. informative/expository writing
5. persuasive/argumentative writing

EXERCISE 3
Understanding Different Forms of Writing
For each of the following modes of writing, list five examples of different forms of that writing. (20 points)

1. personal/expressive writing
2. imaginative/descriptive writing
3. narrative writing
4. informative/expository writing
5. persuasive/argumentative writing

EXERCISE 4
Understanding How to Gather Ideas
Use each of the following strategies to gather ideas about the assigned topic. (20 points; 5 points each)

1. strategy: brainstorming; topic: your favorite movies
2. strategy: clustering; topic: causes of pollution
3. strategy: sensory detail chart; topic: riding a rollercoaster
4. strategy: time line; topic: important cultural events of the 1920s

EXERCISE 5
Understanding How to Draft an Introduction
Select one of the topics in Exercise 4. Use the ideas that you gathered to write an introduction. Identify your purpose, mode, form, and audience. (20 points)

EXERCISE 6
Using Revising Methods in Your Writing
Select a piece of writing from your writing portfolio. Revise to improve the meaning and content of the work by using at least two of the following methods: adding or expanding, cutting or condensing, replacing, or moving. (20 points)

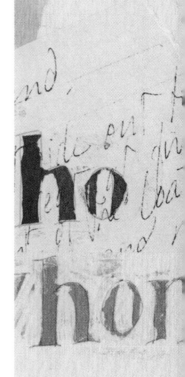

UNIT 22 MODES AND PURPOSES OF WRITING

MODES AND PURPOSES OF WRITING

IDENTIFYING YOUR PURPOSE

A **purpose,** or **aim**, is the goal that you want your writing to accomplish. As explained in Unit 21, The Writing Process, you need to determine your purpose in order to choose the correct mode and style for your writing. You might write to reflect (personal/expressive writing), to entertain (imaginative/descriptive writing), to tell a story (narrative writing), to inform (informative/expository writing), or to persuade (persuasive/argumentative writing.) Your writing might have more than one purpose. For example, a piece of writing might inform about an important event while persuading the audience to respond in a specific way.

Writing tip

Before reading this unit, you may want to review the Modes and Purposes of Writing chart in Unit 21 on page 466.

PERSONAL/EXPRESSIVE WRITING

The purpose of **personal/expressive writing** is to reflect on your thoughts and feelings. Sometimes personal writing may be writing that you do for yourself, perhaps in a journal or a diary, that you do not want others to read. If you want to share your thoughts and feelings with others, you might write a letter, a personal narrative, or a personal essay.

Writing about an autobiographical incident is one way people can express their observations, thoughts, and feelings. An **autobiographical memoir** is a form of personal writing about events that happened in your own life. The following literature model is an excerpt from an autobiographical story written by writer Gary Paulsen about his experiences with his Great Dane.

Quotables

"The next thing most like living one's life over again seems to be a recollection of that life, and to make that recollection as durable as possible by putting it down in writing."
—Benjamin Franklin

I had gone about forty yards, saying hello to people and picking up a can of soda, when I met an old friend and stopped to chat. I had my back to the parking area and I suppose heard some of the commotion that was starting but it didn't enter my mind until the man I was speaking to looked over my shoulder and said, "Isn't that Caesar?"

I turned and my heart froze. Caesar was standing next to a small girl—she couldn't have been four—and he towered over her. That wasn't so frightening as what the little girl was doing. She had taken a bite off a hot dog and was holding the remainder out to Caesar.

Images of destruction roared through my mind. He had truly enormous jaws (I could fit my head inside his mouth) and he snapped at his food violently, especially hot dogs. It was too far for me to run in time and I yelled but it was too late by ages and I wanted to close my eyes but didn't dare and as I watched, Caesar incredibly, with the gentleness of a baby lamb, reached delicately forward and took the hot dog from the girl. He swallowed it in one bite, then licked her face and moved on—though I was calling for him—looking for the next child.

from "Caesar the Giant" in *My Life in Dog Years*
Gary Paulsen

EXAMINING
THE *Model*

In this autobiographical excerpt, Paulsen shares the thoughts and feelings he had during an incident involving his dog at a picnic.

Try It Yourself

Writing about an Autobiographical Incident

In this assignment, you will write about an **autobiographical incident,** an event in your own life. The purpose of your writing is to clarify your thoughts about an event or incident that happened to you. You may be writing just for yourself, or you may choose to share your writing with someone else. If you want to share your writing, keep that particular person in mind as you write.

Writing
A S S I G N M E N T

Writing tip

Voice is the way a writer uses language to reflect his or her personality and attitude toward a topic, form, and audience. Since you are writing to explore your thoughts and feelings, your voice should be personal and sincere.

1. Prewriting

To get ideas for what you will write about, think about an event or an experience that happened to you recently or when you were younger. *What* happened? *When* did it happen? *Where* did it happen? *Why* did it happen? *How* did the event affect you? Has your perspective about the event or experience changed over time?

To get your ideas flowing, try freewriting on a piece of your own paper. Copy a sentence starter such as "I remember . . . I feel . . . I think . . ." Then, just write whatever comes to mind for several minutes. As you freewrite, decide on a topic for your expressive writing.

The next step is to recall specific ideas about your topic. A good way to begin this process is to make a **graphic organizer.** Copy the following graphic organizer on a piece of paper. List specific feelings, memories, and details about the topic. Then fill in how your perspective has changed over time, and think about what you learned from the event or experience.

Graphic Organizer

Writing tip

Try to include a simile in your writing. A **simile** is a comparison of unlike things using *like* or *as*. You can help clarify your own thoughts by thinking about how one thing is similar to something else and expressing your idea in a simile.

2. Drafting

Use the information from your freewriting and your graphic organizer to guide you as you write your rough draft. Concentrate on capturing your experience. Put in details that will help you bring this incident back to life. Tell how you reacted at the time.

Be sure in your last paragraph to write about your perspective on the incident as you look back on it. What did you learn from it? How did it help you? What do you do or think differently as a result of this experience? All of this goes in your conclusion.

Language, Grammar, and Style

WRITING COMPLETE SENTENCES

Identifying Complete Sentences. A **sentence** is a group of words that expresses a complete thought. Simple sentences can be divided into two parts: the subject and the predicate. In most common English sentences, the first part of the sentence tells what or whom the sentence is about. This it the **complete subject**. Then it gives information about the subject; this second part of the sentence is called the **complete predicate**. In the following examples, the complete subject is underlined once. The complete predicate is underlined twice.

EXAMPLES
The large dog was in the truck.
No one saw the dog climb out of the vehicle.
It had been parked in the lot.

A sentence **fragment** is a phrase or clause that does not express a complete thought but has been punctuated as though it does. A fragment means a "part." A sentence fragment is only part of a sentence and is either missing a subject, verb, or both subject and verb. It does not make sense by itself.

EXAMPLES
Following the large dog.
Not mine.
No way.

Identifying Complete Subjects and Complete Predicates. Identify the complete subject and the complete predicate in each of the sentences below.

1. Caesar jumped out of the truck and approached the little girl.
2. The narrator in the story tried to explain the situation.
3. The girl fed a hot dog to the large dog.

CONTINUED

Correcting Sentence Fragments. Look at the following section from a first draft and revise any sentence fragments so they are complete sentences.

My hair was flying behind me. I felt the wind rush. Against my face. I was six and I was riding on my bike that my sister handed down to me. It was pink and white (now an off white). I loved it. It wasn't too big. Or too small. It fit just right!

Using Complete Sentences in Your Writing. Look at your own writing and examine each of your sentences. Does each sentence contain a complete subject and a complete predicate? If you have any sentence fragments, rewrite them as complete sentences.

3. Self- and Peer Evaluation

After you finish your first draft, complete a self-evaluation of your writing. If time allows, you may want to get one or two peer evaluations. As you evaluate your draft or a classmate's draft, ask these questions:

- What feelings or thoughts are expressed in the writing? What words communicate these feelings or thoughts? Which words are the strongest? Which words are the weakest?
- What perspective is expressed about the event or experience? Has the perspective changed over time?
- Check each sentence. Are there any fragments that could be written as complete sentences?

4. Revising and Proofreading

As you consider your writing, self-evaluation, and peer reviews, think about the changes that would help clarify your thoughts and express your ideas. Try to include a simile that compares two unlike ideas. Which parts do you need to clarify? Which details do you need to add? Which words do you need to delete or change?

Next, proofread your narrative for errors in spelling, grammar, usage, punctuation, and capitalization. If you are unsure about a word's spelling, check it in a dictionary or use the spell-check on your computer. Also, check each sentence. Rewrite any sentence fragments as complete sentences.

 tip

When you proofread your writing, mark your corrections using the standard proofreading symbols. (See the Proofreader's Symbols chart in Unit 21 on pages 484–485.) With just a little practice, you'll find them easy and convenient to use.

5. Publishing and Presenting

Sharing your expressive writing is a way you can let others—parents, grandparents, siblings, friends—know and understand you better. Choose an individual with whom you would like to share your memoir, then prepare a final copy that can be mailed or presented in person to the individual.

6. Reflecting on Your Writing

As you reflect on your expressive writing, ask yourself these questions:

- What have I learned in writing this essay?
- What kind of voice does my writing have?
- What strengths have I discovered in my work and myself? in myself?

IMAGINATIVE/DESCRIPTIVE WRITING

The purpose of **imaginative/descriptive writing** is to entertain, enrich, and enlighten by using a form such as fiction or poetry to share a perspective. Poems, short stories, and plays are examples of imaginative or creative writing. **Imaginative writing** is created from the writer's imagination. **Descriptive writing** uses visual and other sensual details, emotional response, and imagery. Descriptive writing is used to describe something, to set a scene, to create a mood, and to appeal to the readers' senses.

Poetry uses language in special ways so that its sound reflects its meaning more powerfully than in ordinary speech and writing. A poem can tell a story or capture a moment in time in a way no other form of writing can. Composing a poem is a way to describe experiences in your life when words barely seem able to convey what you saw or felt. Poetry is about looking with your whole body—paying attention to an object, an event, a feeling. Poetry lets you play with language, with the rich sounds and meanings of words, and in the process express the almost inexpressible.

In the following poem, Carl Sandburg describes the abstract concepts of death and love.

Quotables

"Poetry is the language in which man explores his own amazement."
—Christopher Fry

Literature
MODEL

EXAMINING
THE *Model*

In this poem, the author uses **figurative language** to represent abstract concepts that cannot be perceived by the senses.

CONTINUED

Under the harvest moon,
When the soft silver
Drips shimmering
Over the garden nights,
Death, the gray mocker,
Comes and whispers to you
As a beautiful friend
Who remembers.

Under the summer roses
When the flagrant crimson
Lurks in the dusk
Of the wild red leaves,

CONTINUED

Love, with little hands,
Comes and touches you
With a thousand memories,
And asks you
Beautiful, unanswerable questions.

"Under the Harvest Moon"
Carl Sandburg

> For example, he uses *personification* to describe love, giving it the human characteristic of having "little hands." He also creates a simile when he describes death as "a beautiful friend."

Try It Yourself

Composing a Poem

Are there any moments in your life that seem to be made for poetry? For this assignment, you will compose a **poem.** You will be writing for yourself and other classmates who would enjoy your subject.

1. Prewriting

In this writing assignment, you will want to be playful and free to express new ideas that come to you. This is the attitude inside you that enjoys living. Let that come out in your voice in this poem.

The power of poetry is in its concentrated language. That means ideas and descriptions are condensed into a few words or phrases. You condense language every day when you make comparisons between one thing and another. Comparisons are a quick way to condense language. When you say, "Hank is as shy as a hedgehog," you are transferring one quality of a hedgehog—shyness—to Hank. This type of comparison that uses *like* or *as* is called a **simile.** When you leave out the part about being shy and say, "Hank is a hedgehog," you create a metaphor. A **metaphor** is a figure of speech in which one thing is spoken or written about as if it were another.

> ### *Writing* tip
>
> Poets often use techniques of sound in their poems. **Alliteration** is the repetition of initial consonant sounds: *"And whitely, whirls away."* **Onomatopoeia** is the use of words that sound like what they mean: *bang* or *beep.* **Rhyme** is another way to add emphasize important ideas and add a strong, musical element to your writing: *"Or luck or fame / When trouble came."*

For your poem, you will create images, similes, and metaphors around a color.

Choose a color. Write down the ideas that come to mind when you consider your color in relation to the six senses. Use a graphic organizer like the one below to organize the ideas about your color.

Graphic Organizer

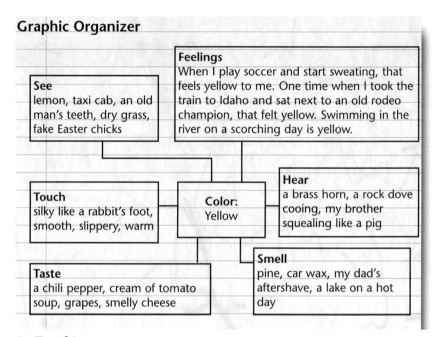

Writing tip

While writing the rough draft, don't focus yet on line breaks or techniques of sound like alliteration and rhyme. Also, do not worry about whether or not your poem makes sense. The surprising and delightful language of poetry often comes from letting your inner ear play with words.

2. Drafting

Use your graphic organizer and the descriptions you wrote about your color as you begin your rough draft. Try to tell about experiences from your life by comparing them to your color. You will find many descriptive words and comparisons from your prewriting that you can use in your poem. You will also think of others as you write the first draft.

Use strong images that appeal to the senses of sight, smell, taste, sound, or feel. Use at least one image from each sense in your poem. Expand on some of your metaphors. Instead of saying "Scarlet is a cold drink," you could say "Scarlet is cold berry juice after running hard up a hill."

Language, Grammar, and Style

USING FIGURATIVE LANGUAGE

Identifying Figurative Language. Language that suggests a meaning beyond or different from the literal meanings of the words is called **figurative language**. Many writers, especially poets, use figures of speech to create vivid, memorable images and to help readers see and understand things in new ways. Think about the difference in meaning in the following two examples.

EXAMPLES
literal meaning   Leslie danced across the stage.
figurative meaning   Leslie's eyes danced with laughter.

Two common figures of speech are simile and metaphor.

A **simile** compares one thing with another using the words *like* or *as*.

EXAMPLES
The runners were sweating **like** ice sculptures melting at a summer party.
He wore an expression **as** neutral as a white plaster wall.

A **metaphor** compares one thing to another without using the words *like* or *as*. In a metaphor, one thing is spoken or written about as if it were another. Metaphors can be especially helpful when describing difficult or abstract ideas, such as love, joy, sorrow, truth, and so forth.

EXAMPLES
Their love was a prairie wind, large, fast, and all-encompassing.
The mountains were dark-skinned fists against the yellow sky.

Understanding Figurative Language. To help you understand how to compare dissimilar objects and ideas, write three characteristics for each item on the list below. Then think about what else shares these characteristics and make a comparison.

EXAMPLE
brain   can process information quickly
               has an extensive memory
               has ability to classify information

Comparison: human brain = computer

CONTINUED

1. dog
2. speech
3. audience
4. happiness
5. rain
6. yell
7. bookstore
8. music
9. passenger jet
10. bird

Using Figurative Language in Your Writing. Look at each sentence in your poem. Underline five examples of figurative language and identify whether each example is a simile or metaphor. Try to use original and striking figurative language in your work.

3. Self- and Peer Evaluation

Once you have a rough draft of your poem, read it aloud several times. This helps you hear the music of the lines. If time allows, you may want to do peer evaluations. After you and your peer editor discuss the following questions, you should have a good idea about how to revise your piece.

- What feelings or thoughts are expressed in the poem, and what words communicate these feelings or thoughts?
- Images refer to things we can see, hear, smell, touch, and taste. Which images in the poem are specific and strong? Which are general and weak?
- Which similes and metaphors make unusual and fresh comparisons? Which ones could be more interesting?
- Which lines or phrases sound musical? Where could techniques of sound emphasize meaning?
- Do any of the lines sound awkward? Are there places where obvious rhymes or too much alliteration have been used? How could those lines be improved?
- Are there any places where breaking the line would help the rhythm or meaning?
- Which verbs are active and strong? Which verbs could be changed from state of being verbs to action verbs?

4. Revising and Proofreading

Based on your self- and peer edit, make changes to your draft. Add action verbs, delete extra words, and play with the sound of your poem. Trust your ear to tell you when you need a shorter or a longer line. Some forms of poetry require certain rhyme patterns or a specific number of syllables in a line. But since you are writing in free verse form, you get to decide the length of your lines and whether to use rhyme.

5. Publishing and Presenting

Poetry is best when shared either out loud or as a printed piece of art. To share your poetry out loud, consider reading to a small group of students. You may wish to publish your poem as a work of art by printing the poem in a way that suggests its color and content. Adding art or designs will further draw out the ideas of the poem. You may want to publish your poem in the school newspaper or literary supplement.

6. Reflecting on Your Writing

Do you see how poetry suggests new meanings and ways of understanding? What happened when you started comparing your sense observations to color? Which sense surprised you or gave you the most unusual images and comparisons? Consider how writing a poem offers a way to express ourselves, play with words, and entertain and enlighten others. Which of these would you say your poem strives for? In addition to color, what other topics might you explore in poetry?

Writing tip

After you have made changes to your poem, read over your draft for errors in spelling and punctuation. In poetry you are often dealing with lines instead of sentences, so capitalization and punctuation are a matter of choice. However, you should stick to a consistent pattern of capitalization and punctuation within the poem so that your format is clear to the reader.

NARRATIVE WRITING

Quotables

"When stories nestle in the body, soul comes forth."
—Deena Metzger

Narrative writing tells a story or relates a series of events. Narrative writing can be used to entertain, to make a point, or to introduce a topic. Describing an event, or narrating, involves the dimension of action over time. Narrative writing uses time, or *chronological order*, as a way of organization. It requires you to observe carefully, or recall vividly a series of moments. Narrative writing answers these questions:

> *Who* was involved?
> *What* happened?
> *When* did it occur?
> *Where* did it take place?
> *Why* and *how* did the events unfold the way they did?

Using the **5 *W*s and an *H*** questioning strategy is especially helpful for gathering information about an event or for planning a story. Narrative writing is much like telling stories out loud. It requires you to give your readers enough information to understand what is happening—but not so much that they cannot follow the story. You decide which details to include based on your purpose and your audience.

Narratives are often used in essays, reports, and other nonfiction forms because stories are entertaining and fun to read. Just as important, they are a good way to make a point. Biographies, autobiographies, and family histories are also examples of narrative writing.

Sometimes narrative writing is based on the spoken word. **Recording an oral history** is narrative writing based on a story told to you by another person. The following excerpt from Christina Kolb is taken from an ancient story that originally had been passed along orally.

Utnapishtim took Gilgamesh to Urshanabit, the boatman, to lead him back to his own land. Just as Gilgamesh was leaving, Utnapishtim called out, "You have toiled and worn yourself out, so I will give you a gift to carry back to your own country. I shall reveal to you a great secret. Under the water there grows a plant with deep roots. It will prick your hand like a thorn, but hold on to it. If you succeed in getting that plant, you will have eternal life."

Gilgamesh dove under the waters for the plant and wrested it from the bottom of the sea. Gilgamesh called the plant "The-Old-Man-Will-Be-Made-Young," and he planned to give it to the elders of Uruk and then eat it himself. Once on land, Gilgamesh journeyed for several leagues, making his way toward Uruk. He saw a pool of cool water, and he went down to the water to bathe. A snake smelled the plant and rose out of the water and carried the plant away to eat it. As the snake turned to go back to the water, it shed its skin. Ever since that time, snakes have been able to cast off their skin and become young again, but death has remained the lot of humans.

Gilgamesh cried, "For whom have I labored? For whom has my heart's blood dried? I have not brought a blessing on myself. I did the lowly snake a good service."

Gilgamesh sat down and wept bitter tears.

from "The Epic of Gilgamesh"
retold by Christina Kolb

Literature
MODEL

EXAMINING THE *Model*

The author creates a narrative based on stories that were told long before they were ever written down. First written around 2000 BC, the stories were eventually combined into an epic poem.

Try It Yourself

Recording an Oral History

Interview a person you know to uncover a true story and then record it. The story may be about an event, a memory, or an object that holds special meaning for that person. The person may be a grandparent, great-grandparent, or another acquaintance two or more generations older than yourself.

Writing
ASSIGNMENT

1. Prewriting

Your first task is to select a person to interview. Before you select whom to interview for your narrative, consider a pre-interview with several people to determine the types of experiences each person has had. Decide whose experiences and background are of greatest interest to you and then make your selection. Arrange with that person a specific time and place for the interview to occur. When you make the contact, be sure to explain your mission—to record oral history. Also explore with your interview subject what event, memory, or object he or she would like to tell about.

Before the interview, prepare a list of questions to draw from the person everything he or she can possibly recall about the event or object you plan to discuss. A good selection of who, what, where, when, why, and how questions will help you gather pertinent details and explanations. Use a graphic organizer like the one on page 507 to help you prepare for the interview. Be open to the possibility that the focus of your interview may change. After the interview you can narrow what you actually write about.

- Begin the interview by double-checking that you have the person's permission to take notes or tape-record and to print or otherwise share what is said.
- Ask about newspaper clippings, photographs, or other mementos that will spark more details about the event or time period.
- If possible, record the interview. Write down main ideas, key words, your observations, and direct quotations on paper or with a laptop computer.
- Observe the subject's facial expressions and mannerisms for possible inclusion in the narrative.
- As the interview concludes, thank your subject, give a date when you expect to have the writing completed, and offer to share the finished project.

Writing tip

Voice. Even though the narrative you write will be told to you by another person, your voice will uniquely express that story through your word choice, sentence structure, and tone. Carefully choosing the subject of your interview, conveying interest in the interview itself, and committing yourself to the writing that follows will help you develop a voice that is honest, effective, and engaging.

Oral History Interview Organizer

Interview with: *my grandfather, Thomas Murphy*

Date: *September 21*

Time: *2 PM*

Place: *Grandpa's home at 106 S. Sanborn St. See if we can meet in his study, where he keeps all his old photos and souvenirs*

Permission to take notes, tape-record, and print: *Yes*

My goal for the interview: *learn about his cross-country trip by train*

The event, memory, or object: *cross-country trip in 1937 with his parents and five siblings*

Questions for the interview:

Who?
1. Who went on the trip?
2. Whom did you meet or see on the trip?

What?
1. What did you do on the trip?
2. What did your parents and siblings do?
3. What did you see that you would never forget?

Where?
1. Where did you start?
2. Where did the trip end?
3. Where was your favorite place on the trip? Where was your least favorite?

When?
1. When, or what time of year, did you go on the trip?
2. When during the day did you travel?

Why?
1. Why did you go on the trip?
2. Why especially do you remember the trip?
3. Why was it such an important trip for your family to take?

How?
1. How did the trip affect you at the time?
2. How did the trip change the way you saw things?
3. How did the trip affect the people in your family?

Mementos: *(newspaper clippings, photographs, scrapbooks, clothing, jewelry)*

Direct quotations:

Main ideas, key words, and observations:

Gestures and expressions worth noting:

Reflecting. Before you begin to write your narrative, think about the stories that you have heard told and retold. Which stories are most interesting to you? What experiences and memories did the writer capture? How did the writer convey those experiences and memories? How did you benefit from hearing those stories?

2. Drafting

Review your notes and, if you used a tape recorder, listen to the taped interview several times until the story is clear and complete in your mind. You may also want to transcribe—type out—the interview or parts of it. If necessary, mark your notes to identify the correct time order for the events. Put a question mark in your notes beside anything that is unclear to you and, if possible, check back with the person you interviewed to clarify those questions. Work to include sensory details that will make your writing memorable.

If you haven't already done so, determine the focus. Once you have the main idea for your narrative, begin telling the events of the story in chronological order. Telling the story in time order will help your reader understand and experience just what your subject has shared with you.

The first paragraph should introduce and identify the subject, specify the time period, and indicate the focus of the story. Continue to tell the story in several more paragraphs, drawing from your notes and the recorded interview. Use your observations to develop your subject's character. Use direct quotations and interesting details. This is also the time to incorporate what you observed of your subject when you interviewed him or her.

After the story is told, wrap it up with a short conclusion. You might wish to summarize the years that followed in the life of the subject or explain the situation at the present time. The conclusion is the place for you to editorialize a bit, too. How did you benefit from talking with this person? What has been captured for others' benefit or enjoyment?

Language, Grammar, and Style

USING SENTENCE VARIETY

Identifying Different Types of Sentences. Even the most exciting story might sound dull if the writer does not use a variety of sentence structures. There are four types of sentences that you can use to keep your writing interesting: simple, compound, complex, and compound-complex.

A **simple sentence** is made up of one independent clause. A simple sentence has a complete subject and a complete predicate.

EXAMPLE
The sky turned grayish green.

Combining two or more simple sentences makes a **compound sentence**. The independent clauses are usually combined with a **coordinating conjunction** such as *and*, *but*, *for*, *nor*, *or*, or *yet*. A semicolon can also be used to combine independent clauses.

EXAMPLES
The sky turned grayish green, and then the tornado hit.
Trees were split in two; a foot of water filled the street.

Combining an independent clause with at least one dependent clause makes a **complex sentence**.

EXAMPLE
When the sky turned grayish green, we ran into the basement.

You can create a **compound-complex sentence** by combining a dependent clause with two or more independent clauses.

EXAMPLE
As the wind began to blow, the lawn chairs flew off the front porch, and we ran into the basement.

Correcting Incorrect Compound and Complex Sentences. Identify and correct the error in each compound sentence below.

CONTINUED

Grandpa Tom's father, Patrick Murphy, had been suffering from heart problems; and it was difficult for him to farm his land just north of Reliance, South Dakota.

They rented out the farm and then the family of eight packed up their belongings and boarded the passenger train to Oregon.

Identify and correct the error in each complex sentence below.

When it rained they closed the windows to keep the rain out and the family dry and comfortable.

The family got quite a scare, when a black crow flew into an open window of the train.

Using a Variety of Sentences in Your Writing. Examine the kinds of sentences that you have used in your writing. You will want to vary the length and type of your sentences. Try to combine two simple sentences into a compound sentence. Next, combine other sentences to create a complex sentence. Try putting the dependent clause at the beginning of the complex sentence. Then create another complex sentence with the dependent clause at the end of the sentence.

3. Self- and Peer Evaluation

After you finish your first draft, complete a self-evaluation of your writing. If time allows, you may want to get one or two peer evaluations. As you evaluate your draft or a classmate's draft, ask these questions.

- What is your overall impression of the narrative? Is it inviting to read, interesting, and purposeful?
- Does the narrative present a complete story with a beginning, middle, and end?
- What information is presented to create a sense of time and place for the narrative?
- What techniques in the narrative give the reader a sense of the subject's character?
- What details could be added to help the reader get to know the subject better?
- How well do the sensory details create a vivid picture of the story's events and characters?

Writing tip

While answering the questions on the checklist, be sure to provide concrete suggestions for improvement or specific evidence of why the writing works or does not work.

- Does the narrative contain information that could be eliminated?
- How do word choice and tone contribute to an honest, effective, and engaging voice?
- Where would the narrative benefit from a greater variety of sentence structures?
- How significant is the story to the storyteller? the author? the reader? What might make the story more significant to the reader?

4. Revising and Proofreading

If possible, let your draft and evaluation comments rest a day before you begin editing. Reading the draft aloud is an excellent technique for hearing as well as seeing where you need to make changes or corrections. Think about the strengths and weaknesses identified in the evaluation comments. Using these comments, decide how to revise your draft so that the final narrative is interesting, lively, and significant.

Proofread your narrative for errors in spelling, grammar, punctuation, and capitalization. If you are unsure about a word's spelling, check it in a dictionary. Correct any punctuation errors in the narrative.

5. Publishing and Presenting

Your narrative could become a piece of your family's or your community's history. How can you best present it and preserve it? You might create a booklet that includes your story, a short biographical entry about the person whose story you have told, photographs, and photocopies of any newspaper clippings or mementos associated with the story. You might work with several classmates or your entire class to create a book that includes all of your classmates' narratives. Be sure to make your narrative available to the person that you interviewed.

 Writing tip

Do a search at your library using the key words "oral history" to find books written by authors who interviewed their subjects.

6. Reflecting on Your Writing

In the process of interviewing your subject and writing your narrative, you probably gained some insights that you did not have before starting this assignment. What was the most significant insight you learned about the person you interviewed? What do you know about the environment or time period in which your subject lived that you did not know before? What insights did you gain from your classmates' writing?

INFORMATIVE/EXPOSITORY WRITING

The purpose of **informative** or **expository writing** is to inform, to present or explain an idea, or to explain a process. News articles and research reports are examples of informative or expository writing.

One function of expository writing is to define, since a definition explains what something is. Another function of expository writing is to explain how something is done. A **scientific essay** is writing that explains a scientific concept or analysis in a concise, straightforward manner. It might also tell how an object, such as a lawnmower, functions according to a scientific principle. Other types of scientific writing might explain the scientific facts of our universe. In the following literature model, Robert Jastrow describes the size of the Milky Way galaxy.

Quotables

"Writing is an exploration. You start from nothing and learn as you go."
—E. L. Doctorow

Literature
MODEL

The stars within the galaxy are separated from one another by an average distance of about 36 trillion miles. In order to avoid the frequent repetition of such awkwardly large numbers, astronomical distances are usually expressed in units of the light year. A light year is defined as the distance covered in one year by a ray of light, which travels as 186,000 miles per second. The distance turns out to be six trillion miles; hence in these units the average distance between stars in the galaxy is five light years, and the diameter of the galaxy is 100,000 light years.

In spite of the enormous size of our galaxy, its boundaries do not mark the edge of the observable universe. The 200-inch telescope on Palomar Mountain has within its range no less than 100 billion others galaxies, each comparable to our own in size and containing a similar number of stars. The average distance between these galaxies is one million light years. The extent of the visible universe, as it can be seen in the 200-inch telescope, is 15 billion light years.

from "The Size of Things" in *Red Giants and White Dwarfs*
Robert Jastrow

EXAMINING
THE *Model*

Although the author is explaining a complicated subject, he avoids using language beyond the grasp of the average reader. The information Jastrow presents is logical, clear, and easy for the audience to understand.

Writing
ASSIGNMENT

Writing a Scientific Essay

Your assignment is to write a **scientific essay** that describes and explains how a household appliance, one based on a scientific principle, works. You can use any scientific process you already understand—the production of sound waves, photosynthesis, and volcanic eruptions are examples. You can create an appliance or write about one that already exists, such as an iron, a microwave oven, or a toaster.

1. Prewriting

You will be explaining both the appliance and the underlying concept it demonstrates. Don't attempt to show off your technical knowledge, but instead try to teach your readers so they will come to understand what you know. Since you are not writing for scientific experts, present the information in everyday language.

Your job is to explain step-by-step how an appliance works. To do this, you will need to observe the appliance in action and explain the scientific principle that the appliance uses. You will need to decide whether your essay will describe an appliance that you created, perhaps in a science lab experience or a shop class, or an appliance that already exists.

If you are writing about an existing appliance, check to make sure the appliance demonstrates a scientific principle. Then begin your observation and notes for your essay. Watch how the appliance works. List the appliance's actions or reactions in the order that they occur.

Identify the scientific principle that the appliance demonstrates. List the steps involved in the scientific process (see chart on next page). Coordinate the appliance's actions with the steps involved. List the terms with definitions that you will need to explain. Describe the appliance's purpose. Draw a diagram demonstrating how the appliance works.

Writing tip

Technical writing is usually enhanced by visuals. As you think through each step, consider what will be the best method to give your audience a visual picture: posters, overheads, a slide show, a PowerPoint or HyperCard presentation. See what technologies are available.

The Scientific Process
Step 1. Ask a question. What is the purpose of your scientific research? Choose one area or subject that you are most interested in and ask a question to which you do not know the answer.
Step 2. Read and research. Go to your school library or the public library and check out books about the subject you chose. Read all you can. Conduct research on the Internet.
Step 3. Form a hypothesis. Now that you have done some reading about your subject, try to answer the question in Step 1. What do you think will happen?
Step 4. Experiment or observe. Keep accurate records of what you observe. Tell what happens to answer your questions or prove or disprove your hypothesis.
Step 5. Reach a conclusion. What did happen? Did you find out the answer to your question? Was your hypothesis correct?

The following graphic organizer outlines the development, research, and observation steps involved using the scientific process to explain how a coffee maker works. Copy the graphic organizer on your own paper and go through this process for the appliance that you chose. Gather any additional classroom notes, assignments, or drawings that might contain helpful information.

Lab Notes Appliance Demonstrating a Scientific Principle
Step 1. How can I describe a household appliance that demonstrates a scientific principle? Brainstorm ideas, create several drawings, and think of things in real life that work.

Step 2. Research sites for my topic:
Internet:
   http://www.howstuffworks.com/index.htm
   http://dmoz.org/Home/Consumer_Information/Appliances/
Books:
   How Things Work: The Physics of Everyday Life by Louis
     Bloomfield
   Things Around the House by Herbert Spencer Zim

Step 3. How does a coffee maker work? What scientific principal does it demonstrate? When the coffee maker is plugged in, electricity heats the water. The hot water runs through the filter and makes coffee. <div align="right">*CONTINUED*</div>

Step 4. Observations / collect data and record data / take notes:

When I took the top off of the coffee maker, I found three things:

1. a little bucket that holds the water when you pour it into the pot at the start of the coffee-making cycle with a hole in the bottom
2. a black tube that carries the hot water to the drip area
3. a drip area that water arrives into from the black hot-water tube and falls through the holes into the coffee grounds

Step 5. Conclusion:

Electricity heats the resistive heating element (a coiled wire, similar to the filament of a light bulb, which gets hot when you run electricity through it). The heating element has two jobs:

1. When you first put the water in the coffee maker, the heating element boils it.
2. Once the coffee is made, the heating element keeps the coffee warm.

tip

Here is a useful pattern for writing a scientific essay:

1. Introduce the subject.
2. Present the explanation of the process in a logical order.
3. Use transition words.
4. End with a strong conclusion.

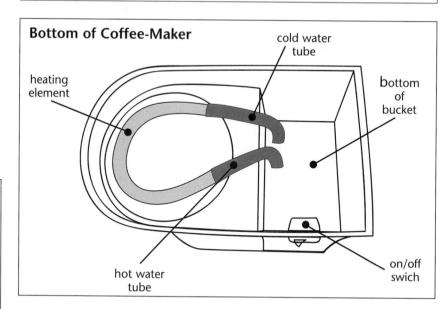

Bottom of Coffee-Maker

cold water tube

heating element

bottom of bucket

hot water tube

on/off swich

Develop an outline that will give your paper structure and order. You might introduce the appliance and its purpose first, then describe how the appliance actually works, and finally explain the scientific principle.

2. Drafting

Begin writing your paper in sections according to your outline. Stop at appropriate sections and begin new paragraphs. Use key words on your outline to help remind you about finer details in your paper. Remember to define technical words your audience might not understand.

Language, Grammar, and Style

CORRECTING WORDY SENTENCES

Identifying Wordy Sentences. You should only use words necessary to make your meaning clear to your reader.

EXAMPLES

wordy	I am certainly appreciative of your thoughtful gesture of bringing chicken soup for me to eat when I was ill and didn't feel like getting out of bed.
clear and direct	Thank you for bringing chicken soup when I was sick.

Fixing Wordy Sentences. Each sentence below is too wordy. Revise them so that they are more concise.

1. The one part that is not at all visible in this coffee maker is something that is a valve that is one-way.
2. The heating element is the thing that presses directly against the underside of the warming plate.
3. There is a device that is attached directly to the coil and it is called the primary temperature sensor.
4. What the thermal fuses do is that if they start to sense that the temperature is too high they very simply cut the power.

Using Editing Skills. Read through your paper again and stop after each sentence. Look to see that they do not contain too many words to state the idea. If you find general words, replace them with specific ones. If one sentence seems too complicated, see if any words could be replaced or left out.

3. Self- and Peer Evaluation

When you have finished with the rough draft of your paper, ask one or two students to evaluate your work before you hand in your paper. Have them consider the following questions and give you feedback.

Writing tip

If something does not sound right, you may have to revise the outline and the written piece. Make sure key information is clear, written in short sentences, and direct. Create visuals if needed.

- Which sentences explain how the appliance operates?
- Which sentences explain how the scientific process works?
- What technical terms are defined?
- What, if anything, about the visuals captures the reader's attention?
- What simple or specific words could be used in the place of general or complicated words?
- How clear, concise, and direct is the writing? Where could wordiness be eliminated?
- Where, if anywhere, is the process unclear?

4. Revising and Proofreading

Review the comments of your peer evaluators. Also listen for indications that your explanations clarified ideas for them. For example, someone might say, "So that is how it works!" or "The word you use there makes it so clear." Check to see if your visuals work well together. Then proofread your writing for errors in spelling, grammar, usage, punctuation, capitalization, and paragraph form.

5. Publishing and Presenting

Writing tip

Consider delivering your essay to other audiences. Who else might be interested in this information? If the topic is appropriate, perhaps you could give a presentation to an elementary class.

Print or copy the final draft of your report. Check your visuals. Are the diagrams clear? Is the writing legible? When your final draft and visuals are prepared, you are ready to present your essay. Present the essay to your classmates showing that the appliance demonstrates a scientific principle.

6. Reflecting on Your Writing

Explaining how something works is difficult. Not everyone can visualize the "workings" of something through words. How important was thinking about your audience when writing your paper? How could you use this experience in other areas? How can knowing how something works help you in your life?

PERSUASIVE/ARGUMENTATIVE WRITING

The purpose of **persuasive/argumentative writing** is to persuade readers or listeners to respond in some way, such as to agree with a position, change a view or an issue, reach an agreement, or perform an action. Examples of persuasive writing are editorials, petitions, political speeches, and essays.

A **persuasive essay** is a short nonfiction work written to influence the opinion or actions of the reader. In the following literature model, author Mark Mathabane expresses his opinion about establishing dress codes in the schools.

Quotables

"By persuading others, we convince ourselves."
—Junius

Literature
M O D E L

The fiercest competition among students is often not over academic achievements, but over who dresses most expensively. And many students now measure parental love by how willing their mothers and fathers are to pamper them with money for the latest fads in clothes, sneakers and jewelry.

Those parents without the money to waste on such meretricious extravagances are considered uncaring and cruel. They often watch in dismay and helplessness as their children become involved with gangs and peddle drugs to raise the money.

When students are asked why they attach so much importance to clothing, they frequently reply that it's the cool thing to do, that it gives them status and earns them respect. And clothes are also used to send sexual messages, with girls thinking that the only things that make them attractive to boys are skimpy dresses and gaudy looks, rather than intelligence and academic excellence.

The argument by civil libertarians that dress codes infringe on freedom of expression is misleading. We observe dress codes in nearly every aspect of our lives without any diminution of our freedoms—as

CONTINUED

In his speech,
Mathabane seeks to
change the minds
of people who do
not agree with him.
What reasons does
he use to support
his argument? What
effect do you think
his words would
have on his
audience?

demonstrated by flight attendants, bus drivers, postal employees, high school bands, military personnel, sports teams, Girl and Boy Scouts, employees of fast-food chains, restaurants, hotels.

In many countries where students outperform their American counterparts academically, school dress codes are observed as part of creating the proper learning environment. Their students tend to be neater, less disruptive in class and more disciplined, mainly because their minds are focused more on learning and less on materialism. It's time Americans realized that the benefits of safe and effective schools far outweigh any perceived curtailment of freedom of expression brought on by dress codes.

from "Appearances Are Destructive"
Mark Mathabane

Try It Yourself

Writing
ASSIGNMENT

Writing a Persuasive Essay

Writing a **persuasive essay** offers you the opportunity to express an informed opinion about a topic that interests you. Persuasive words have power. You can use your awakened emotions, your analytical mind, and your writing ability to bring about change in society, the lives of others, and yourself.

1. Prewriting

To write a persuasive essay, you first need to choose a topic. To help you decide, you might ask yourself these questions:

- What concerns me?
- What conditions, locally, nationally, or internationally, disturb me?
- Where does school, government, or society need to make changes?

Writing tip

To be persuasive,
you must identify
your audience.
Whose mind do you
need to change to
take action on this
matter? Consider
what your readers
already know about
the subject, what
arguments they've
probably heard
before, and what
objections they may
have.

After you have selected a topic, begin by **freewriting** for ten to fifteen minutes. Put down everything you know, feel, or think about this issue. Include points for both sides of the argument. Don't be concerned yet about organization or writing mechanics.

Use a graphic organizer like the following to state your topic, set up a pro and con chart, and record a thesis statement. You will fill in the lower boxes after the evaluation stage.

Prewriting

Topic:	Should schools enforce stricter dress codes?

Pro	Con
· Reduces competition over who dresses most expensively · Creates the proper learning environment · Students will be more focused on learning than on materialism	· Infringes on freedom of expression · Gives some students more status and respect · Reduces individuality

Thesis:	School dress codes should be observed to create the proper learning environment.

After Self- and Peer Evaluation

Objections to My Stand	My Answers to Those Objections
· What if students don't want to conform? · What about encouraging individuality? · Dress codes infringe on freedom of expression.	· Dress code will create equality among students. · Students can still be individuals in their behavior—not just their dress. · Students can express themselves in more constructive ways.

2. Drafting

Write a rough draft of your piece. Don't worry at this point about the details of spelling, grammar, usage, and mechanics. Instead, simply concentrate on getting your ideas down on paper. Get your reader's attention in the first paragraph. You can give startling statistics or a frightening example of the problem. You want to engage the reader's interest or curiosity right away. State your thesis clearly at the end of the first paragraph.

Writing tip

If you argue a position on an issue that you care about, your natural voice, personality, and attitude will come through in your writing. For the persuasive essay, strive to use your most reasonable voice to convince readers your position is logical.

In the body of your essay, include three reasons that support your opinion. Give examples or facts as evidence that your thinking is logical. Discuss concerns or counterarguments your readers may have. Show you have thought through those questions.

In persuasive writing the conclusion is critical, so consider putting your strongest argument last. After all, you are trying to persuade your audience to agree with you. The last things you say in your essay will stick with your reader, so it is important to make that concluding paragraph especially strong. This is your call-to-action time. What do you want your audience to do as a result of reading your words?

Language, Grammar, and Style

USING VERB TENSES CORRECTLY

Identifying Consistent Verb Tense. Verbs carry a concept of time called **tense**. Two kinds of tenses are the **simple tenses**—these express simple past, present, and future—and the **perfect tenses** that give information about actions taking place over time. One error that students make is to shift tense in the middle of a piece of writing. Each piece needs to maintain a consistent tense.

Reread the "Verb Tenses" section in Unit 6. Read the following passage from Mark Methabane's persuasive essay "Appearances are Destructive." Identify the verb tenses for the verbs or verb forms that are underlined. How does the author use verb tense consistently and to convey action happening over time?

CONTINUED

Shortly after my sisters <u>arrived</u> here from South Africa I <u>enrolled</u> them at the local public school. I <u>had</u> great expectations for their educational experience. . . .

But despite these benefits, which students in many parts of the world only dream about, my sisters' efforts at learning <u>were</u> almost derailed. They <u>were</u> constantly <u>taunted</u> for their homely outfits. A couple of times they <u>came</u> home in tears. In South Africa students <u>were required</u> to wear uniforms, so my sisters <u>had never been preoccupied</u> with clothes and jewelry.

Correcting Inconsistent Verb Tense. Look at the following sentences. Explain why each shows inconsistent verb tense. Then explain how you would correct each sentence.

Joe sees the cat up in the tree yesterday and tomorrow planned to find out who owns it.

We build a fence in our backyard to keep the dog from getting away.

When Dad returns home, do you think Mom decided where she wants to go for dinner?

Using Consistent Verb Tense in Your Writing. Look at each sentence in your persuasive speech. Correct any inconsistent verb tense. Make sure your verbs accurately depict the passage of time.

3. Self- and Peer Evaluation

For this essay you want your evaluator to determine if the argument is strong, if the reasoning is sound, and if you have acknowledged the other side of the argument. As you evaluate your draft or that of a classmate, ask the questions below. After receiving the evaluations of your work, complete your graphic organizer to show you what you need to keep and what you might want to add to your final copy.

- What is the single focused point of view of the essay?
- What reasons are given for this point of view?
- Which point is the most important? Where is it located in the sequence of points?

- What details, examples, and personal observations have been made to support the argument?
- Which point is the weakest logically? Why?
- Where does the opposing view appear?
- What transitions provide coherence in the essay?
- How does the essay engage the reader in the introduction?
- How does the conclusion invite the reader to act/react?
- How well does the conclusion succeed in calling the reader to action?
- What lingering doubts, if any, still exist for the reader?
- What, if anything, links the conclusion to the introduction?

Writing tip

A good way to finish a paper is to read it aloud and listen for problems. You are more apt to spot inconsistent verb tense and other technical glitches when you read aloud.

4. Revising and Proofreading

Use your self- and peer evaluations to decide what changes you want to make in your paper. Note especially where your arguments are clear and where they are weak. Pay attention to how your peers respond to your arguments. If your readers need more convincing, determine how to strengthen your paper. If you need more information, find it now. If you need to adjust your word choice, the argument structure, or the tone of the piece, do that now.

5. Publishing and Presenting

Write or print a final copy of your informed opinion essay. Read it to your classmates, and then send it to a person who could make some changes in the conditions related to the issue. If the person is local, invite him or her to come to your class and discuss the issue with you and your classmates. Other final formats may include an editorial or letter to the editor sent to your local newspaper, an e-mail, or a report. You could also develop your informal opinion essay into a persuasive speech.

6. Reflecting on Your Writing

Writing an opinion piece forces you to think more deeply than you might normally do about a particular issue. How do you feel about the issue you addressed in your paper? Did you learn anything about the topic that helps you understand another viewpoint? How did examining pros and cons benefit you? What discoveries did you make through freewriting? How did peer comments about your topic support or affect your thinking? If your writing was acknowledged by an audience, how did they, and you, respond? If your writing was not acknowledged by an audience, what could you try next to have better success?

THE RESEARCH PAPER

A **research paper** is a large writing project that requires an organized approach. Although a research paper is similar to an essay, there are key differences. An essay tends to be shorter than a research paper. An essay usually contains one or more opinions supported by some facts, whereas a research paper may present many facts, from a variety of sources, as evidence in support of one major opinion. The main idea of a work of nonfiction such as an essay or a research paper is called the **thesis.**

You will need to do a considerable amount of research to support your thesis. To research your topic, you need to know where to look and how to focus your search. Documenting your sources is critical because you thereby give proper credit, as well as leading other researchers to sources you found useful.

A research paper may be informational, persuasive, or narrative writing. A **narrative research paper** informs by telling a factual story in chronological order about something significant that happened. Read the model narrative research paper on pages 536–538.

Quotables

"Story is far older than the art of science and psychology, and will always be the elder in the equation no matter how much time passes."
—Clarissa Pinkola Estes

Try It Yourself

Writing
ASSIGNMENT

Writing a Narrative Research Paper
By preparing a **narrative research paper** you will narrate a story in chronological order and cite factual information about the events. You will not include personal views or unneeded information, but will instead focus on the events of your topic. Finally, you will document the sources that you used to write your paper.

1. Prewriting
Finding a suitable topic is critical. If you do not already have a topic in mind, carry a notebook with you for a few days. Brainstorm several questions about what you are learning in each of your classes. Write a question about an idea that you want to investigate, and write it so that it will help you tell a story.

Before you begin your research and writing, do a quick check to see if you have enough resources available at the library. Also look on the Internet for reliable websites that can provide both primary and secondary sources of information. A primary source is a firsthand account of what happened. For example, Neil Armstrong's account of the moon landing is a primary source of information. Try to use at least one primary source. If you do not have at least three or four good sources of information including at least one primary source, you may need to think of a different question.

After you have selected your topic, use a graphic organizer like the one below with several *who, what, where, when, why,* and *how* questions to help you start your research.

Research Paper Topic:

Elizabeth I and the Spanish Armada

WHO
was Elizabeth I?
did Queen Elizabeth govern?
were her adversaries?

WHAT
were Elizabeth's goals as Queen?
were the obstacles she faced?
was the outcome of the Spanish invasion?

WHERE
did the battle of the Spanish Armada take place?
were England's soldiers stationed?

WHEN
was Elizabeth's reign?
was the invasion of England launched?

WHY
did Spain invade England?
was Elizabeth such a powerful ruler?

HOW
was the invasion attempted?
did Elizabeth react to the invasion?
many battles were there?

Keeping Track of Your Sources. Take your graphic organizer to the library, and collect your source material. In a research journal like the one below, write down the title, the authors, the publishing company, the place and date of publication, the location, and the call number for each book.

CONTINUED

Write down the addresses of any reliable Internet websites you plan to use. Record the names of articles in magazines, along with the magazine titles, dates, and volume numbers.

Writing tip

For more information on conducting Internet research see Unit 18 Electronic Communications, pages 400–405.

RESEARCH JOURNAL

1. Author _____

    Title _____

    Place, Publisher, Date _____

    Location, Call Number, or URL _____

2. Author _____

    Title _____

    Place, Publisher, Date _____

    Location, Call Number, or URL _____

3. Author _____

    Title _____

    Place, Publisher, Date _____

    Location, Call Number, or URL _____

4. Author _____

    Title _____

    Place, Publisher, Date _____

    Location, Call Number, or URL _____

5. Author _____

    Title _____

    Place, Publisher, Date _____

    Location, Call Number, or URL _____

Taking Notes. Keep formal notes for a research paper on 4 x 6-inch index cards. Give each source you list a number. Write that number next to the source and circle it. This number will enable you to identify the source of the note later on when you write your bibliography.

Read the questions on your graphic organizer again. Look through each source for answers to your questions. When you find an answer, paraphrase, summarize, or quote the information on a piece of paper or on a note card. Do not copy the author's exact words unless you are quoting the author. For each note, include the question you are answering, the number of the source you are using, and the page number where you found the information. You may find that you need to add more *who, what, where, when, why,* and *how* questions to your graphic organizer.

Preparing Note Cards
- Identify the source at the top right corner of the card. (Use the source numbers from your Research Journal or bibliography cards.)
- Identify the subject or topic of the note on the top line of the card.
- Use a separate card for each fact or quotation.
- Write the pertinent source page number or numbers after the note.

Arranging Note Cards. After finishing your research, think about what happened at the beginning, middle, and end of your story. Arrange your note cards in chronological order. Number your cards so you can use them later to write your draft.

SAMPLE NOTE CARD

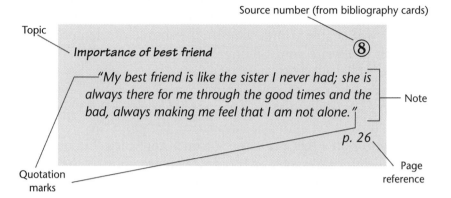

As you do research, your notes will include **quotations, paraphrases**, and **summaries**.

Type of Note	When to Use	What to Watch For
Quotation	When the exact wording of a primary source is important to your topic	Copy spelling, capitalization, punctuation, and numbers exactly as in the source.
	When you are providing a definition	Place quotation marks around all direct quotations.
Paraphrase	When the idea of a secondary source is particularly memorable or insightful, but you want to say it in your own words	Record, when appropriate, explanatory background information about the speaker or the context of a quotation.
	Most of the time	Focus on your main purpose, and note only points related to your topic.
Summary	When the point you are making does not require the detail of a paraphrase	Place quotation marks around any quoted words or phrases. Reread the source after writing your summary to be sure that you have not altered the meaning.

2. Drafting

Thesis Statement and Introduction. One way to organize your writing is to identify the main idea of what you want to say. Present this idea in the form of a sentence or two called a thesis statement. A **thesis statement** is simply a sentence that presents the main idea of your paper. Begin your draft with an introductory paragraph that clearly identifies your topic and contains a thesis statement.

Body. Use your ordered note cards or your outline to write the body of the paper. As you draft, include evidence from documented sources to support the ideas you present. This evidence can be paraphrased, summarized, or quoted directly. Write your ideas in chronological order using smooth transitions between ideas. Use active verbs and precise language. Give specific examples that will make the story interesting to readers.

Conclusion. Your paper will need to have a conclusion. Use the conclusion to summarize the main points and to consider the results of your research. Your conclusion could encourage readers to discover more about the topic or related topics. Include in the conclusion a summary statement about your thesis and the results of your research.

You should have at least six well-written paragraphs in your paper. At the end of the paper you will need to include a bibliography telling where you got your information. A **bibliography** is a list of sources used for the writing. (For more information on preparing your bibliography, see "Documenting Sources" in the following Language, Grammar, and Style section.)

Language, Grammar, and Style

DOCUMENTING SOURCES

Identifying Proper Documentation. As you research your writing, you must document your sources of information. Remember to

- Credit the sources of all ideas and facts that you use.
- Credit original ideas or facts that you express in text, tables, charts, and other graphic information.
- Credit all artistic property, including works of literature, song lyrics, and ideas.

As you work on your paper, write down on note cards the information for each source that you use. Include all of the information shown on the sample bibliography card. Be sure to punctuate correctly and to capitalize proper nouns and the titles of print and online resources.

SAMPLE BIBLIOGRAPHY CARD

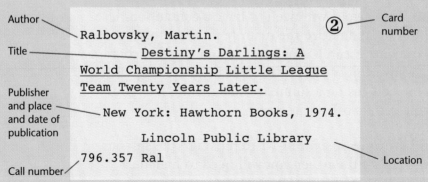

Forms for Bibliographic Entries
- **A book**

  Ralbovsky, Martin. *Destiny's Darlings: A World Championship Little League Team Twenty Years Later.* New York: Hawthorn Books, 1974

- **A magazine article**

  Ferling, John. "Jefferson's War." *American History.* February 2001: 36–44.

- **An encyclopedia entry**

  "Henry V." *The Harper Encyclopedia of Military Biography.* Dupuy, Trevor N. 1995 ed.

CONTINUED

- **An interview**

  Aieta, Nicholas J. Personal interview. 29 January 1998.

- **An Internet page**

  Will, George F. "Texas Democrat Seeks Senate Seat." *The Sacramento Bee.*
  May 5, 2002. <http://www.sacbee.com/content/opinion/national/will>

Understanding Parenthetical Documentation. Parenthetical documentation is currently the most widely used form of documentation. To use this method to document the source of a quotation or an idea, place a brief note identifying the source in parentheses immediately after the borrowed material. This type of note is called a **parenthetical citation,** and the act of placing such a note is called **citing a source.** The first part of a parenthetical citation refers the reader to a source in your bibliography. The second part of the citation refers the reader to a specific page or place within the source. If the source is clearly identified in the text, omit it from the citation and give only the page number.

- **For works listed by author or editor, use the author's or editor's last name.**

  Sample bibliographic entry
  McGuinn, Taro. East Timor: Island in Turmoil. Minneapolis: Lerner, 1988.

  Sample citation
  "It's unlikely that the problem in East Timor will be solved militarily" (Brown 364).

- **For works listed by title, use the title (abbreviate if necessary).**

  Sample bibliographic entry
  "East Timor." Encyclopedia Britannica. 2000 ed.

  Sample citation
  Indonesia's rule over East Timor is disputed by the United Nations
  ("East Timor" 632).

- **When the author's name is used in the text, cite only the page number.**
  McGuinn believes that military forces cannot end the problems in East Timor (80).

Using Proper Documentation in Your Writing. Read your narrative research paper again. Are there places where you paraphrased an author's ideas that you need to reference? Are there exact quotations that you need to reference? Fix any documentation in the body of your paper. Then look at your bibliography. Be sure each source is documented correctly. Be sure to punctuate and capitalize correctly.

3. Self- and Peer Evaluation

After finishing your rough draft, you can do a self-evaluation of your work. If time allows, you may also want to do peer evaluations. As you evaluate your research paper draft or that of a classmate, ask the following questions:

- What true story does the research paper narrate? What is the significance of this story?
- How does the introduction capture the reader's attention? What is its thesis statement?
- Does the body of the research paper use chronological order? How do you know?
- Does the body of the research paper provide enough information about the topic? What information might be added or deleted?
- What transitions help the reader move between ideas? How could transitions be improved?
- Which words are examples of precise language? Which sentences are examples of active voice? Which words and sentences could be improved?
- Does each sentence in the body of the paper support the thesis statement? Which ones need improvement?
- Is there adequate and accurate documentation in the paper? Does the research paper contain a bibliography? How do the sources support the paper? Are the sources documented correctly?
- Does the paper use standard grammar and correct punctuation, capitalization, and proper manuscript format?

4. Revising and Proofreading

Review your self- and peer evaluations, consider these comments, and then revise your writing where revision will strengthen it. Think about the story line that you have developed. Take out information that distracts from that story. If there are gaps in the story, go back and fill them in. Check that each paragraph has a stated or inferred topic sentence that is related to your thesis statement. Also check that the details in each paragraph support the topic sentence.

Proofread your revised draft for errors in spelling and grammar. Be sure each source in your paper and in your bibliography is referenced correctly. Finally, give your teacher a double-spaced paper as your final product.

5. Publishing and Presenting

Write your final copy neatly in ink or print it from the computer. Prepare a bibliography on a separate sheet of paper and attach it to the end of your paper. Add a title page to the front of the paper that includes the title, your name, and the date. If possible, include a graph, chart, or illustration with your report. Put a copy of your research paper in a folder and display it in the classroom for other students to read. Plan to read several of your classmates' papers. Tell your classmates the part of the research paper you enjoyed most.

6. Reflecting on Your Writing

After you complete your final product, think about the process you used to prepare your paper. Which part of the process did you enjoy most? least? Which part was easiest for you? most difficult? What does this reveal about you as a learner? as a writer? What would you do differently for your next research paper?

A model narrative research paper appears on pages 536–538.

RESEARCH PAPER MODEL

Elizabeth I and the Spanish Armada

by Matt Cross
English 7
April 1, 2003
p. 1

Elizabeth I became the Queen of England in 1558. During her years on the throne, the country grew into a thriving world power. Elizabeth, however, faced many difficult challenges during her reign. The country experienced severe religious turmoil in the 1500s. Elizabeth was a Protestant but did not want religion to divide her subjects. Catholic leaders in Europe opposed the Protestant queen. Philip II of Spain, a Catholic, wanted to overthrow Elizabeth. In 1588, he launched a major invasion of England that would change the course of history for both countries.

Philip believed he had many advantages in his fight with Elizabeth. About half of the English population was Catholic at the time. For many years, he and Pope Pius V had encouraged English Catholics to overthrow the queen. They wanted to put Elizabeth's Catholic cousin Mary on the throne and establish Catholicism as the national faith of England. Catholics living in England, however, did not join together in rebellion against the queen. Only a handful of missionary priests conspired against Elizabeth. Most of the plotters, such as Edmund Champion, were caught and executed (Meltzer).

Despite his failure to incite England's Catholics to rebellion, Philip believed they would welcome him as their leader when he invaded the island. In 1588, he possessed the most powerful military in the world. An armada of 130 ships with 17,000 soldiers and 2,400 guns sailed from Spain to England. At the time, it was the largest naval force ever assembled. Philip and many observers in Europe believed that Elizabeth could do little to stop his Spanish Armada (Meltzer, Garraty).

Upon receiving news of the invasion from her spies in Spain, Elizabeth did not panic. She personally supervised the establishment of England's defenses. She stationed soldiers along the coast to oppose any landings and sent Charles Howard out to attack the Spanish Armada with a fleet of English ships. At home, the queen rallied her subjects to defend the island against the foreign aggressors. She inspired the English with her determined words (Meltzer).

Let tyrants fear; I have always so behaved myself that, under God, I have placed my chiefest strength and safeguard in the loyal hearts and good will of my subjects. And therefore I am come amongst you at this time, not as for my recreation or sport, but being resolved, in the midst and heat of the battle, to live or die amongst you all; to lay down, for my God, and for my kingdom, and for my people, my honor and my blood, even the dust (Sourcebook).

A great battle raged out at sea. When the English set several small ships on fire and sailed them into the midst of the Spanish formation, Philip's armada went into disarray. Howard's fleet defeated the Spanish in three separate battles, with Vice-Admiral Sir Francis Drake distinguishing himself in battle for the English. After the battles, the defeated Spanish Armada sought to return home but on its way back to Spain, the fleet was devastated by sea storms. More of Philip's military power was thereby destroyed. The English were overjoyed at their monumental victory, while Elizabeth became an even greater national hero *(Dictionary of American History)*.

The defeat of the Spanish Armada in 1588 was a major event in the reign of Queen Elizabeth. The queen had defended her throne against Europe's most powerful nation. Although she later faced an occasional assassination plot, Elizabeth's reign would never again face such a serious challenge. Spain's military power went into decline after the defeat of the Armada, with Spain eventually falling from the ranks of a top world power. In contrast, England's military power and prestige increased following the battle. The strong leadership of Elizabeth I laid the foundation for England to become the most powerful nation in the world by the 1700s.

Bibliography

Queen Elizabeth I. "Against the Spanish Armada." Modern History Sourcebook. 1997. <http://www.fordham.edu/halsall/mod/1588elizabeth.html>

Garraty, John A. *A Short History of the American Nation.* New York: Longman, 1997.

Meltzer, Milton. "Elizabeth I" in *Ten Queens: Portraits of Women in Power.* New York: Dutton Children's Books, 1998.

"Spanish Armada." *The Dictionary of American History.* New York: Oceana Publications, 1963.

UNIT 22 REVIEW

Identifying Writing Modes in Literature
Identify the following excerpt as *personal/expressive*, *narrative*, *imaginative/descriptive*, *informative/expository*, or *persuasive/ argumentative* writing. (10 points)

> Cannon to right of them,
> Cannon to left of them,
> Cannon behind them
>   Volley'd and thunder'd;
> Storm'd at with shot and shell,
> While horse and hero fell,
> They that had fought so well
> Came thro' the jaws of Death
> Back from the mouth of Hell,
> All that was left of them,
>   Left of six hundred.
>
>   —from "The Charge of the Light Brigade"
>   Alfred, Lord Tennyson

Literature
M O D E L

EXERCISE 2
Identifying Writing Modes
Identify the following writing forms as *personal/expressive*, *narrative*, *imaginative/descriptive*, *informative/expository*, or *persuasive/argumentative* writing. (10 points)

1. diary entry
2. editorial
3. family history
4. personal letter
5. petition
6. poem

7. essay
8. biography
9. report
10. short story

EXERCISE 3

Understanding the Purposes of Writing

Complete the following sentences by writing the correct mode of writing. (10 points)

1. Writing that allows the writer to reflect is called
   _____ writing.
2. The purpose of _____ writing is to share a
   story about an event.
3. Writing that persuades readers or listeners to respond in
   some way is called _____ writing.
4. The purpose of _____ writing is to entertain,
   enrich, and enlighten.
5. Writing that informs is called _____ writing.

EXERCISE 4

Understanding Proper Documentation

Using the facts below, write a bibliography card for each reference. Be sure to include a call number and library location where appropriate. Check your cards for correct punctuation and capitalization. (20 points)

Author	Title	Publication Facts
Books		
Harry Stein	*Hoopla*	Dell Publishing, New York, 1983
Oliver Zunz	*Making America Corporate 1870–1920*	University of Chicago Press, Chicago, 1990
Magazines		
Tim Kurkjian	"He's Not Standing Pat"	*Sports Illustrated,* 8 January 1996, pp. 50–57
Patrick B. Miller	"The Manly, the Moral, and the Proficient: College Sport in the New South"	*Journal of Sport History* 24, No. 3 (Fall 1997): 285–316

CONTINUED

Encyclopedias		
Not given	"Nervous System"	*The American Medical Association Encyclopedia of Medicine,* 1989 ed.
David L. Bongard	"Arnold, Benedict"	*The Harper Encyclopedia of Military History,* 1995 ed.
Internet		
Molly Ivins	"The Scoop on George Dubya"	The Progressive, <http://www.progressive.org/ivins9906.htm> 1999
Tom R. Johnson	"The Lizards of Missouri"	Conservation Commission of Missiouri, <http://www.conservation.state.mo.us/nathis/herpetol/molizard/> 17 August 2002

EXERCISE 5

Correcting Documentation

Prepare a bibliography card for each of the following sources. Be sure to check your cards for correct punctuation and capitalization. (10 points)

1. "Rafting" by unknown author in *World Book Encyclopedia,* pp. 553–555, 1999 edition

2. David Hackett Fischer, *Paul Revere's Ride,* 1994, Oxford University Press, New York

3. "Modern Muckrakers," Kenneth Klee, *Book,* September/October 2001, 46-51

EXERCISE 6

Using Writing Modes in Your Writing

Choose one of the following short writing prompts and write a brief example demonstrating this writing mode. (20 points)

1. a summary of a magazine or newspaper article (informative)
2. a story about a scary incident (narrative)
3. a poem about a wild animal (imaginative)
4. a persuasive letter to the editor of your local paper (persuasive)
5. a journal entry (personal expressive)

EXERCISE 7

Using Proper Documentation in Your Writing
Choose a topic that has always interested you. Use library and Internet resources to do preliminary research about it. Find at least one book, one encyclopedia article, one magazine or newspaper article, and one Internet site that you might use for your report. Prepare a bibliography card for each reference. Be sure to punctuate and capitalize correctly. (20 points)

INDEX OF TOPICS

H

Had, perfect tense and, 116
Had ought, hadn't ought, 300
Hardly, scarcely, 301
Has, perfect tense and, 116
Have
    as helping verb, 110
    perfect tense and, 116
He, she, they, 301
Helping verb, 110–112
    common, 110
    definition of, 51, 110
    as part of contraction, 111
    passive voice, 118
Hisself, theirselves, 301
Homophones
    definition of, 384
    spelling errors and, 384
How come, 301
Hyphen, 336–337
    compound noun, 68–70
    review for, 345–346

I

Ideas for writing, 469–475
    brainstorming, 469
    clustering, 471
    freewriting, 470
    imagining, 471
    interviewing, 474–475
    keeping a journal, 470
    learning from professional models, 470
    organizing, 475–476
    pro and con chart, 474
    questioning, 471
    researching ideas, 475
    sensory detail chart, 472–473
    story map, 474
    time line, 473
    Venn diagram, 472
Idiom, 10
Ie/ei spelling rule, 378
Imaginative/descriptive writing, 497–503
    definition of, 497
    drafting, 500
    figurative language and, 500–501
    poetry, 497–503
    prewriting, 498–499
    publishing and presenting, 502
    purpose, 466
    reflecting on your writing, 503
    revising and proofreading, 502
    self- and peer evaluation, 501–502
Imagining, in prewriting, 471

Imperative sentence, 31–33
    definition of, 31
    diagrammed, 267
    end mark, 318
    review for, 41–42, 44
In, into, 301
Indefinite pronoun, 90–92
    agreement with antecedent, 90
    definition of, 50, 80, 90
    plural, 90, 147–148, 286
    singular, 90, 147–148, 285–286
    subject-verb agreement, 90, 147–149, 285–286
Independent clause, 245–246, 253, 257
Indirect object, 132–135
    definition of, 132
    diagrammed, 269–270
    distinguished from object of preposition, 133
    object pronoun and, 133
    review for, 139
    tests for, 133
Infinitive, 184–185
    definition of, 184
    diagrammed, 276–277
    distinguished from prepositional phrase, 184
    split, 240, 295–296
Infinitive phrase, 240–242
    definition of, 240
    diagrammed, 276–277
    review for, 256
Informal English, 8–11
    colloquialism, 10
    definition of, 8
    dialects, 8–9
    idiom, 10
    review for, 21, 22
    slang, 9
Informative/expository writing, 513–518
    correcting wordy sentences, 517
    definition of, 513
    drafting, 517
    prewriting, 514–516
    publishing and presenting, 518
    purpose, 466
    reflecting on your writing, 518
    revising and proofreading, 518
    self- and peer evaluation, 518
Informative paragraphs, 449–451
Intensive pronoun, 92–94
    definition of, 50, 81, 92
    plural, 93
    singular, 93
Interjection, 216–218
    definition of, 47, 216
    as part of speech, 47–49
    review for, 225–226

INDEX OF LITERATURE MODELS

ACKNOWLEDGMENTS

Literary Acknowledgments

Diana Rivera. "Under the Apple Tree" by Diana Rivera. Copyright © 1996 by Diana Rivera. Reprinted by permission of the author.

Harcourt, Inc. "Under the Harvest Moon" from CHICAGO POEMS by Carl Sandburg, © 1916 by Holt, Rinehart and Winston and renewed 1944 by Carl Sandburg, reprinted by permission of Harcourt, Inc.

Photo Acknowledgments

24 © Nicole Katano/Brand X Pictures/PictureQuest; **44** Library of Congress; **56** Library of Congress; **72** © Joe Sohm, Chromosohm/Stock Connection/PictureQuest; **78** © AP/Worldwide Photos; **124** © AP/Worldwide Photos; **154** © PhotoDisc/Getty Images; **158** © PhotoDisc/Getty Images; **212** © CORBIS/Jerry Cooke; **230** Unit 11 © William McKellar/Brand X Pictures/ PictureQuest; **339** © PhotoDisc/Getty Images; **394** © Eyewire/Getty Images; **436** © Greg Smith; **542** © Eyewire/Getty Images.